ERADICATING F
GENITAL MUTI1

CW01064117

Not since Efua Dorkenoo's *Cutting the Rose* (1994) has a monograph on female genital mutilation outshone Hilary Burrage's. Outraged at ineffective child protection, Burrage provides a comprehensive, scholarly yet accessible guide – among the best ever to deal with FGM – to professionals and all people of conscience.

Tobe Levin von Gleichen, Harvard University, USA and
University of Oxford, UK

Eradicating Female Genital Mutilation

A UK Perspective

HILARY BURRAGE

ASHGATE

Published by
Ashgate Publishing Limited
Wey Court East
Union Road
Farnham
Surrey GU9 7PT
England

Ashgate Publishing Company
110 Cherry Street
Suite 3-1
Burlington, VT 05401-3818
USA

www.ashgate.com

British Library Cataloguing in Publication Data
A catalogue record for this book is available from the British Library.

The Library of Congress has cataloged the printed edition as follows:
Burrage, Hilary.
    Eradicating female genital mutilation : a UK perspective / by Hilary Burrage
Ashgate.
        pages cm
    Includes bibliographical references and index.
    ISBN 978-1-4724-1997-2 (hardback : alk. paper) – ISBN 978-1-4724-1994-1 (pbk. : alk. paper) – ISBN 978-1-4724-1995-8 (ebook) – ISBN 978-1-4724-1996-5 (epub)
    1. Female circumcision – Great Britain. 2. Women – Crimes against – Great Britain. I. Title.

    GN484.B87 2015
    392.1–dc23

                                                                                          2015014508

ISBN 9781472419972 (hbk)
ISBN 9781472419941 (pbk)
ISBN 9781472419958 (ebk – PDF)
ISBN 9781472419965 (ebk – ePUB)

MIX
Paper from
responsible sources
FSC
www.fsc.org   FSC® C013985

Printed in the United Kingdom by Henry Ling Limited, at the Dorset Press, Dorchester, DT1 1HD

Contents

List of Figures

About the Author

This book is not about me, but it may be helpful to explain my background and how I came to write it.

I am a sociologist who has worked in settings across the public service sector, including stints as a Senior Lecturer in Health and Social Care, as a Medical School Research Associate investigating teenage pregnancy and as an advisor to Sure Start (early years provision) Centres, focusing largely on health and engagement.

I have always had a keen interest in social and political policy and, with an MSc in the Sociology of Science, have been a member of the UK Department for Food, Environment and Rural Affairs (DEFRA) Science Advisory Committee as well as an honorary Election Agent for a Member of Parliament.

A qualified school teacher, I was founding national secretary in the 1980s of the Forum for Academic and Teaching Associations in the Social Sciences (FACTASS[1]), which fought successfully to retain personal, social and health education (PSHE) in the mainstream curriculum.

Throughout my career I have been involved in analysis and commentary concerning gender and other aspects of equality – issues also informed on a personal level by my experience as a ('working') wife, mother and grandmother.

My concern about FGM first arose in the late 1980s from comments by my mother, Peggy Bartlett, who heard about it at Quaker meetings. We asked some questions and were assured legislation had just been passed[2, 3] which would secure the abolition of FGM in Britain soon.

It was therefore a very unpleasant shock to learn years later, via news of one of the early annual 6 February global days against FGM,[4, 5] that this was far from the case, with millions of girls still being harmed every year. At that point I began to make further enquiries, using the quite new facility of the internet, which revealed the (growing) extent of FGM in the UK.

So, after being made aware by my mother back in the 1980s that what-was-then-called 'female circumcision' existed at all, two things took me to an active concern about FGM – the inspired creation by African women of an annual global day of defiance of the practice, and the growing capacity of the World Wide Web,[6] which made it possible to discover more concerning both the act itself, and the contexts in which it occurs.

And once I had grasped what FGM really comprises, and how ubiquitous it is, I began to blog and lobby to support campaigns to bring it to a halt – which in turn has taken me to the company of many incredibly dedicated people across the world who have given their knowledge, skills and much of their working lives to eradicating this cruel traditional practice.

My book brings together whatever I can offer, drawing on professional experience I have accrued over the years, and the information and contacts I have acquired to date. I hope it will help others to think through some of the complexities, both of FGM itself and of the political, moral and policy demands which that terrifying practice places on us all.

Moving Forward

This book has evolved along with the events which it reports. The years since the Millennium have in some ways seen tremendous progress in tackling FGM, both globally and in the UK.

There is, however, as yet no cause for celebration. Girls and women around the globe continue to be victims of this cruel traditional practice, their lives and that of their families blighted by the harm it inflicts. The battle is a long way still from being won.

I have tried to reflect the situation as it is. On the one hand, we in Britain have learned a great deal in the past few years, and our responses to FGM are, in parallel with the increasing numbers of citizens known to be affected, now more forthcoming and focused.

But on the other hand, I see little evidence that the reality of the challenge is to date fully recognised and understood. The UK Government, and many of those who provide services to address FGM, continue to see it as 'the other', as something shocking which happens, regretfully, to people not quite like 'us'.

The serious intent to stop FGM is genuine; but there is scant acknowledgement that Britain too is a place where, historically and to the present, women and people from various minorities are vulnerable and some citizens are far less equal than others – a place for instance where, despite claimed good intentions, some women and children remain at significant socially determined risk.

All these factors have influenced the way I, as a sociologist committed to the prevention of FGM and all traditional harmful practices, currently perceive and have analysed the situation in regard to FGM in Britain (and probably also in most other Western states).

Things are, however, changing rapidly, and largely positively. What I have described and discussed as of March 2015 may very rapidly become history.

By the time the book is published there will be a new government in the UK, more demographic data and almost certainly also new legislation. The factual information offered here will very likely have been supplanted by new statistics and contexts.

I hope nonetheless that what I have to say will remain pertinent as a way of seeing FGM and the circumstances in which it occurs, or has perhaps ceased to do so.

My intention has been to start a wider conversation about FGM and the challenges it produces. To that end I have explored a variety of wider contexts, and have offered a few perspectives which not everyone will consider self-evident. My motive has not been to provoke, but rather to invite the reader, with me, to probe, to attempt to find new ways forward.

I am acutely conscious that this book contains many half-told stories, inevitably some errors and doubtless also misinterpretations. There is much still to relate and to explore.

With this in mind, I have created a website (http://nofgmukbook.com/) via which you, the reader, are invited to correct factual inaccuracies, discuss further the issues my book considers, and offer alternative ways to see the task in hand. I hope what I have written here is helpful. Your further engagement and contributions will be much appreciated.

Endnotes

All weblinks accessed on 1 March 2015.

1   See see http://hilaryburrage.com/pshe-factass.
2   Prohibition of Female Circumcision Act 1985, http://www.legislation.gov.uk/ukpga/1985/38.
3   http://en.wikipedia.org/wiki/Prohibition_of_Female_Circumcision_Act_1985.
4   http://www.prb.org/Publications/Articles/2013/fgm-zero-tolerance-2013.aspx.
5   http://www.un.org/en/events/femalegenitalmutilationday/.
6   http://www.internetworldstats.com/emarketing.htm.

Preface and Acknowledgements

This book has been four long and complicated years in the making. In that time a great deal has happened and many people have given generously of their time, knowledge and expertise to help bring everything together.

Far too many people are owed sincere thanks for them all to be mentioned here – if you or your organisation are referred to in what follows, I am genuinely grateful for your efforts and contribution to the debate – but there are a few who must be acknowledged by name.

Firstly, I am enormously grateful to Jonathan Norman and Claire Jarvis of the Gower and Ashgate publishing houses. It was Jonathan way back in 2009 who encouraged me to think about writing a book, and Claire who has steered me through the convolutions of producing a text on female genital mutilation. I value very much their belief that I could produce something positive about such a challenging subject.

I must also thank Emily Ruskell, my production editor, for her generous support and help in bringing everything together, and acknowledge too Rebecca Cardone and Ramona Garland for their assistance at various points on formal referencing.

There are also all those lovely, good people who have helped and advised me as I found my way forward with this difficult topic. Amongst those truly remarkable activists and thinkers who have been so generous with their time, support and deep knowledge are, especially, Tobe Levin and Linda Weil-Curiel, along with Phoebe Abe, Hazel Barrett, Dexter Dias, the late much-missed Efua Dorkenoo, Louise Ellman, Paula Ferrari, Felicity Gerry, Leyla Hussein, Lucy Mashua, Sarah McCulloch, Comfort Momoh, Naana Oto-Oyortey, Becky Rowland, Hawa Sesay, Keir Starmer, Ron Stewart, Karl Turner, Diane Walsh, Hibo Wardere and a number of other heroically resolute survivors. All of whom have contributed variously to my awareness and understanding, and who I hope I may think of as colleagues and friends – and many others whose names crop up at various points throughout the book. If you are mentioned by name or inference, you are sincerely appreciated; I would like to think that overall everyone will feel some justice has been done to the information and ideas so kindly shared.

I must also acknowledge Maggie O'Kane, Multimedia Investigations Editor of the *Guardian*, whose inspired global media campaign to End FGM has probably had wider impact than any other single programme before, and who asked me to become their consultant when that newspaper decided to campaign to stop FGM, and through whom I have encountered so many significant players around the world. It's been an incredible experience, and it has brought a lot of us, including most of those above, together in new and exciting ways.

It is, however, inevitable, in a field moving as fast as current efforts to eradicate female genital mutilation, that there are matters to which less than full and fair recognition has been served. I have tried to combine many threads and thoughts, but without a doubt there are points where the narrative is less than complete, and even inaccurate. All such errors or omissions are mine alone and I hope that we can together – you as the reader and I as the author seeking accuracy – remedy them via the interactive website which I have set up alongside this publication.

And, to complete my thank yous ... writers always say, without my family whatever I've managed to achieve wouldn't have happened. That is so true. It was my mother Peggy who first alerted me to the shocking reality of FGM, and who has check-read much of what I have written. Penny and Ian McKee, my sister and brother-in-law, both medical doctors, have advised me on many clinical issues. My daughter Anna has applied her forensic scientific eye to every chapter of the book, as, for the final proofs, has my brother, John Bartlett. And my husband, Tony (Martin Anthony Burrage to those who know him as a professional violinist), has supported me unstintingly, keeping me fed and afloat both practically and in spirit, throughout the long gestation of this text. His unerring – indeed, touching – conviction that I would complete the task has meant more than I can say.

So, finally, to the whole point of this publication.

I wish for every child what I wish for my own very precious and beautiful grandchildren: a healthy, happy and nurturing childhood and, as adults, the chance to blossom and contribute to the common good. If my book helps to achieve this desire, via some small contribution to the eradication of female genital mutilation and the horrors which that cruel scourge brings, it will have been time well spent.

Introduction

This book is not a comfortable read, nor has it been an easy book to write.

The subject is of itself both exceedingly unpleasant and very distressing to contemplate, even at a safely cerebral distance. Close up or at first hand female genital mutilation (FGM) is traumatising: harrowing to observe and painful beyond endurance to experience directly. It is sometimes lethal and often permanently damaging, both physically and psychologically. Its consequences[1] carry on through generations, as women who have undergone FGM encounter obstetric problems, and their children – boys and girls, both – in turn are more likely than others to die, or to live lives marred by their difficult entry into the world.

Every eleven seconds a girl baby, child or young woman somewhere in the world undergoes genital mutilation, often by force and without pain relief or asepsis. FGM is a global epidemic of immense proportions; 3 million mutilations are estimated to be carried out every year.[2]

The World Health Organization[3] defines female genital mutilation as comprising:

> all procedures that involve partial or total removal of the external female genitalia, or other injury to the female genital organs for non-medical reasons.

The WHO states that:

- Female genital mutilation (FGM) includes procedures that intentionally alter or cause injury to the female genital organs for non-medical reasons.
- The procedure has no health benefits for girls and women.
- Procedures can cause severe bleeding and problems urinating, and later cysts, infections, infertility as well as complications in childbirth and increased risk of newborn deaths.
- More than 125 million girls and women alive today have been cut in the 29 countries in Africa and the Middle East where FGM is concentrated (there are also other places).
- FGM is mostly carried out on young girls sometime between infancy and age 15.
- FGM is a violation of the human rights of girls and women.

1

A recent document which gives very substantial information and statistical data about FGM as a global phenomenon is the 2013 UNICEF *Joint Evaluation of the UNFPA-UNICEF Joint Programme on Female Genital Mutilation/Cutting: Accelerating Change 2008–2012.*[4]

The fundamental premise of these publications is that FGM must be eradicated as a matter of utmost urgency, wherever it occurs.

There are, however, as yet few clear answers to the question of how to make female genital mutilation a matter simply of historic interest, a subject only for anthropologists and archivists. That is not as yet, despite the committed efforts over decades of many serious campaigners and strategists, how things are.

And the uncertainty about clear answers is also why the present text comprises in effect a series of observations (chapters) on topics currently regarded as central to the eradication of FGM. This book raises more questions than it provides verified prescriptions for action.

Female genital mutilation (FGM) is practised daily in communities both in many parts of Africa, the Middle East and Asia, and also in the United Kingdom, in other parts of Western Europe and in countries such as the United States, Canada and Australia. That is the truth which must be confronted, achieving a balance in reportage and discussion of the fact that FGM persists and is probably on the increase in a number of modern Western democratic societies.

For some the first response to FGM is disbelief; for others, bewilderment, horror or disgust. Any or all of these reactions is understandable, but gut feelings alone are not always helpful as the quest to eradicate the practice continues.

What is required is to gain as much insight into FGM as a 'harmful traditional practice' as possible, and then to think carefully and strategically about how to tackle the task of ensuring it is eradicated. That is the task this book sets out to achieve.

We cannot here address all the contexts in which FGM arises. It would be presumptuous even to try; proposals about how to halt FGM in the areas of the globe where it has traditionally occurred – Africa, parts of Asia in particular – are beyond the experience and competence of the present author. But those in first-world countries can learn much from established programmes to halt harmful practices in their traditional locations, as they consider how to achieve the same goal in modern, Western nations.

Likewise, although the major focus of this book is the United Kingdom, it seeks also to address, and learn from, the experience of other Western states. It is an alarming fact that in most such countries FGM has only recently become a publicly acknowledged (and growing) problem. This is in part because so little was generally known about the practice, and in part because, until the past few decades, African and other diaspora had only a small impact on Western nations.

The intended readership of *Eradicating Female Genital Mutilation: A UK Perspective* is wide. Those with any form of professional safe-guarding responsibilities (medical and legal personnel, teachers and trainers, social and youth workers and other front-line public servants and personal service providers) may find it helpful, as may anti-FGM activists and lobbyists; but beyond that there are also other potential readers with a serious interest in the issues, such as school governors, journalists, politicians and policy-makers, community and faith leaders, directly concerned parents and guardians and perhaps even potentially young women who may themselves be at risk of FGM, as well as their concerned brothers and boyfriends.

In general until recently, we in the West were unaware of FGM as a phenomenon anywhere, nor was it a pressing issue (in the minds of the general public) in Western societies anyway. That has changed dramatically in the second decade of the twenty-first century, as people in Britain, Europe, America and, for instance, Australia realise that tens, even perhaps hundreds, of thousands of women and children living in our midst have been subject to (or may be at serious risk of) this terrifying damage. It is for all these people that this book is written.

Value-oriented, not Culturally Relativist

From whatever initial experience or vantage point, no one reading this book is likely to approach FGM with a completely open mind; and nor does this text.

The facts and ideas which follow are located squarely within a value framework of outright opposition to female genital mutilation of any sort. In this we stand firm alongside the leading humanitarian global organisations of our time: both the United Nations and the World Health Organization are expressly and overtly against this life-changing, sometimes fatal, traditional practice. Our task is to eradicate FGM – and all similar traditional harmful practices – as rapidly as we possibly can.

That said, however, there are nuances of understanding, sometimes expected and sometimes perhaps even counterintuitive, which must become the consciously adopted tools in trade of our imperative to stop FGM.

The current text attempts to meet this challenge via a coldly clinical combination of tested evidence and data, and of historical and anthropological analysis, mixed with a conviction, shared surely with all readers, that female genital mutilation is a singularly cruel form of oppression and criminal child abuse.

Certainly, evidence and context are both crucial; but neither excuses anything less than total commitment to the eradication of the practice in all its forms. That is the starting point for everything which now follows in this book.

The Vocabulary of Female Genital Mutilation

Any serious review of a social or cultural practice must begin from an understanding of the meanings which selected words to refer to it convey.

This is especially true of analyses such as this book attempts to develop. Frequently in conversations about FGM between different parties, confusion arises because there are variations in perceptions of the meanings that various terms are intended to convey.

Examples of these varying perceptions include the vocabularies employed to refer to the experience and cessation of FGM and to the words used to describe those who do it. What, one might ask, do words such as 'survivor', 'victim', 'mutilation', 'cutting', 'eradication' and 'abolition' mean to different actors and observers in this context?

Circumcision, cutting or mutilation?

A glossary of some names for FGM used in practising communities[5] has been developed by FORWARD (The Foundation for Women's Health, Research and Development), a UK-based charity which is an African diaspora women's campaign and support charity to advance sexual and reproductive health and rights (FGM, vesico-vagina and recto-vagina fistulae[6] and child, early and forced marriage[7] and similar abuses) as central to the well-being of African women and girls.

These terms for FGM are used variously by practising community members and by others who work to stop the practice. Here, however, our focus is on modern Western world English words which refer to FGM.

There is general informed consensus that the proper term for cutting or other clinically unnecessary intentional physical intervention which harms the female genital area must be 'mutilation', regardless of the age or other status of the person on whom it is inflicted.

This broad consensus is both hard-won and relatively new. The term 'female genital mutilation' was adopted in 1990 by the Inter-African Committee (IAC) on Traditional Practices Affecting the Health of Women and Children, and in 1991 the World Health Organization (WHO) recommended that the United Nations adopt it as well. It has now been confirmed by the United Nations and the World Health Organization.[8]

The turning point in this debate was the Bamako Declaration of 6 April 2005,[9] issued by the sixth General Assembly of the IAC, in Mali. It is important to acknowledge the Bamako message in detail:[10]

> … An issue of concern at the 6th General Assembly … [has] been attempts to dilute the terminology Female Genital Mutilation (FGM) and replace it with the

following: 'Female Circumcision', 'Female Genital Alteration', 'Female Genital Excision', 'Female Genital Surgery', and more recently 'Female Genital Cutting' (FGC). ...

Female Genital Cutting (FGC) does not reflect the accurate extent of harm and mutilation caused by all types of FGM. This terminology has been adopted by some UN specialized agencies and bi-lateral donors ... influenced by specific lobby groups largely based in western countries.

... These changes trivialize the nature of female genital mutilation and the suffering of African women and girls ... [and] ... made without consultation, [they] override the consensus reached by African women in the front line of the campaign as well as the ... millions of African girls and women who suffer in silence.

We want the world to know that in 1990 African women [activists] adopted the term FGM at the IAC General Assembly in Addis Ababa, Ethiopia. They took this brave step to confront the issue head on with their practicing communities.

[Why? To avoid confusion, to emphasize] the nature and gravity of the practice; to recognize that [only] a [continuing and painful] struggle [can alter] the mentality and behaviours of African people, [yet to insist] that this pain [is] integral to [empower] girls and women ... to address FGM [and to take] control of their sexuality and reproductive rights. ...

Experience indicates that long-term change occurs [only] when change agents help communities to go through this painful process. Not to confront the issue is to [promote] denial of the gravity of FGM, thus resulting in mere transient change ... .

We recognize that while it may be less threatening for non-Africans to adopt other less confrontational terminology in order to enter into dialogue with communities, it is imperative that the term FGM [be] retained.

The term FGM is not judgmental. It is instead a medical term that reflects what is done to the genitalia of girls and women. It is a cultural reality. Mutilation is the removal of healthy tissue. The fact that the term makes some people uneasy is no justification for its abandonment.

We would highlight that ... FGM was adopted [by] consultation and consensus [among ...] African experts [at] the first technical working group meeting held in Geneva in 1995 and gained ... world-wide currency and acceptance. The Beijing conference also adopted and used ... female genital mutilation. ...

FGM has been adopted and endorsed by the European Union [and] the African Union; [it] is currently utilized in all their documentation including the most recent Additional Protocol to the African Charter on Human and Peoples' Rights, on the Rights of Women [Maputo].

While we appreciate the efforts made in response to FGM on the continent and the Diaspora, it is patronizing and belittling to African women and girls to have outsiders define their oppression. Indeed what gives anyone but Africans the right to change a term agreed upon by the largest group of African activists on this issue in the world? This is at best paternalism and is a sad reflection of how, after many years of African women working against FGM ... when FGM was a taboo, the campaign has been hijacked by others ... not involved at the beginning and who do not appreciate the nature of the struggle.

1. We, the participants at the 6th IAC General Assembly, demand a halt to this drift towards trivializing the traditional practice by adopting a subtle terminology.
2. We demand that all organizations and international bodies revert to the terminology adopted by the IAC in 1990, and reinforced in 2002.
3. We demand that international agencies recognize the right of NGOs in the field to continue to use FGM and not to be denied funding because of this.
4. We demand that the voices of African women be heard and that their call to action against FGM [be] heeded.

The word 'mutilation' is, therefore, employed in formal contexts, as the World Health Organization *Interagency Statement*[11] explains, because by definition (as above) it emphasises the gravity of the act.[12] (In French FGM is called female 'sexual' mutilation, to make this point even more strongly.)

Inevitably, however, given the uncompromising directness of the word 'mutilation', this consensus is sometimes fragile, and some organisations nonetheless refuse to adopt the terminology of the WHO, IAC and Bamako Declaration. This is particularly true of various foundations,[13] activists and anthropologists[14] in the United States of America[15] and also, for example, in Australia,[16, 17] and of some UK[18] and USA organisations which may share financial connectivity.[19, 20, 21]

Significantly, the continuing practice of FGM (renamed by these organisations 'FGC') in America and Australia is still also often denied or seriously understated. Observation suggests a strong relationship between organisations and/or nations which underplay the seriousness of FGM, or excuse it, and the insistence on using words such as 'circumcision' or 'cutting'. Those who seek to circumvent discomfort, or to avoid embarrassment, use euphemisms, drawing on a whole range of rationales for their choice of terms; but there is little hard evidence to demonstrate that such diplomacy equates to sparing more children from FGM, at least in the long run.

Various such campaigners on the ground have, however, asserted that the word 'mutilation', with its connotation of intended violence, fails to show 'respect' for people and communities who engage in FGM. This was the position of Halima Embarek Warzazi, the Special Rapporteur on Traditional Practices (ECOSOC, Commission on Human Rights) in her 1999 report,[22] in which she questioned both the expectation in Germany that all acts of 'excision' should be reported (because then mothers may 'refuse to take their daughters to the doctor'), and the practice in France of penal sanctions for perpetrators (because 'punishments and sentences based on value judgements could sometimes be counter-productive and encourage communities to close ranks and cling to practices … expressing their cultural identity').

Mrs Warzazi also stressed the need for tact and patience, with understanding of the role of FGM in some traditional communities, claiming that, 'More and more anthropologists and other experts support the education and training approach. Traditional practices such as female genital mutilation, which are deeply entrenched across generations, cannot be treated as intentional forms of child abuse.'

For many, however, the requested patience has now been exhausted. Whilst some reduction in rates of FGM has been made in various communities, FGM continues every year to blight the lives of millions of women and girls. There is now greater global recognition[23] that tact and superficial modification of traditional ways of doing things, as the writers of the Bamako Declaration so clearly told us back in 2005, will not alone achieve eradication.

But the delay in addressing FGM robustly may also, however, be in part attributable to another euphemism which, like 'cutting', draws attention away from the extent of the harm which it can do. Until the past few years FGM was generally known in English-speaking countries as 'female circumcision' – a term which puts it on a par with the centuries-old tradition of male genital cutting practised (and in some cases mandated or otherwise enforced, even for adults[24]) by some communities almost everywhere around the globe.

Male and female 'circumcision'

Campaigners against male circumcision (especially of minors) are, with reason, vehement that this too is a fundamental violation of human rights, regardless of the claimed[25] (and contested[26]) public health advantage of male circumcision in some contexts where HIV is prevalent or where hygiene may be an issue. They may also be correct that historically one of the many rationales for male circumcision, also applicable to FGM, is another breach of human rights, the reduction of adolescent and adult sexual pleasure;[27] but whether this is so or not, the circumcision of boys is not undertaken specifically in order to add future market value at marriage to the sale of male children – though financial benefit to those who undertake the male and female 'procedures' is a factor often in common.

The epidemiology, some rationales and often the physical extent of male and female circumcision are moreover demonstrably different. Like girls, boys too are harmed or die[28] needlessly because of genital 'cutting', especially but not only in traditional practising countries,[29] and every avoidable child death, male or female, is a double tragedy of misfortune or happenstance and of what might with other conscious choices have been. The mortality rate[30, 31] amongst affected populations is overall significantly less for boys than for girls, but those who want to see the end of male circumcision[i] point out that its distribution is different because of the very significant numbers of male children who undergo it in modern America, as well as in Africa and other emerging nations[32] (where procedural lack of hygiene and other factors make 'surgery' more dangerous anyway).

The life-long blight of FGM on large numbers of girl children, vulnerable women, and then in turn their children (of both sexes, when their safe delivery is obstructed) – all underpinned by patriarchy – adds, however, yet another gender-oppressive dimension to female genital injury, for which there has never been any (rational) claim to benefit of any sort for the health of the person concerned.

Further, the word 'circumcision' has in some places delayed recognition of the serious harm resulting from FGM for decades throughout the latter part of the twentieth century. Indeed, the use of the term circumcision may explain why many people in positions of trust and child safeguarding have not hitherto taken action following indications or suggestions that girls may be at risk; they believed it was, as male circumcision/genital mutilation is mistakenly claimed to be, another relatively innocuous or even medically desirable routine.

Issues around male circumcision are self-evidently a matter of serious concern,[33] but it is probable nonetheless that using the term 'female circumcision' has cost girls and young women much suffering and many lives.

In this text we therefore employ the term used also in formal dialogue by the Inter-African Committee on Harmful Traditional Practices, the World Health Organization and the United Nations.

All intended medically unnecessary injury to female genitalia is mutilation.

Survivor, victim or 'just' another person?

As with other terms in the FGM lexicon, there is no universally accepted way to refer to or name women and girls who have experienced FGM.

Some of the people who have been subject to FGM describe themselves as 'survivors' – a term often also adopted by, especially, 'victims' of domestic violence in the conventional sense.

For professionals and others concerned with FGM, because they wish to emphasise that it is a crime, and to stop it, the term 'victim' is helpful – it draws attention to the illicit and harmful nature of genital mutilation. Children cannot 'choose' to have FGM; there is no scope in law for volition. They are minors and as such victims of a serious crime.

---

i   This writer, for the removal of any doubt, is against circumcision.

Likewise, where such vocabulary is deliberately adopted by those with direct experience of FGM, victimhood terminology is appropriate; but not everyone with FGM chooses to be referred to as a victim;[34] nor does everyone want to think of themselves as 'living with the consequences' of FGM.

For some, such terms imply a status where they continue to have little or no control over their lives, whereas they might themselves assert emphatically that they remain empowered to view FGM as an act which did and does not frame their identity thereafter.

Difficulties about the choice of word to describe a woman or girl who has been genitally mutilated are further compounded by the fact that the act may, at least at the point of delivery (whether as a child or as an adult), have been with the explicit consent, informed or otherwise, of that person.

Stories abound of little girls in some communities who (usually innocent of the consequences and/or of what is involved) are eager to undergo the process,[35, 36, 37] which they believe will confer adult status on them. For such individuals there may subsequently be at least two senses in which they feel betrayed.

Firstly, perhaps even whilst others celebrate nearby, they are subjected, powerless and by family members or their agents, to an excruciating betrayal and perhaps thereafter to a relentlessly painful and life-changing nightmare.

Secondly, those who undergo FGM may discover at some later point that very few adult women in society as a whole have experienced FGM, and there is in the wider population a growing articulation of revulsion about the act.

There can be few words which capture adequately how someone who has been genitally mutilated might feel in this situation. Reactions are surely individual, changing as perceptions develop over a lifetime. 'Sufferer'? 'Victim'? 'Survivor'? At any point, who, other than the person concerned, can say?

Except, therefore, when considering the consciously articulated perspectives of particular parties, for most purposes in this book we will usually refer to 'people with, or who have experienced, FGM'. The term is clumsy, but it does not imply that individuals with personal knowledge of undergoing FGM have chosen to adopt any particular shared understanding or image of what it means to them.

Criminal, perpetrator, procurer (or even also victim)?

Time and context are highly relevant to the appropriate naming of those who cause children to undergo FGM.

Tensions are inherent between activists' wish to 'understand' the cultural beliefs and socio-economic pressures which give rise to the mutilation of girl children, and their resolve to prevent this ever happening again.

There may on one hand be a genuine desire on the part of parent/s or grandparent/s to ensure, however mistakenly and brutally, that a girl is prepared for womanhood. That after all was what happened to them (her mother and other female relations). So when they inflict FGM on their daughters they become themselves both procurers or actual 'perpetrators', and by dint of previous history are 'victims' as well.

On the other hand, however, there are operators and others who benefit directly from the procedure. Those who perform FGM are usually women of status in the community, the *grandes dames* or matriarchs, themselves also mutilated, who gain economically[38] but in so doing also confer status on the child as she approaches adulthood – assuming she survives at all.

And then there are the men, who usually stay at arm's length from the procedure itself but may pay up to a year's harvest to have FGM performed on their daughters,[39] so the girl-brides can be married off as virgins for considerable sums of money.[40] These fathers will have themselves previously purchased (possibly several) brides on the basis of guaranteed 'purity'.

FGM is not 'only' a so-called cultural practice. It is also in many instances an economic transaction,[41] the rationales for which necessarily influence perceptions of the actors concerned.

These complex interactions between belief and action, some of them self-serving on the part of the perpetrator, and some intended to serve the interests of the girl undergoing FGM, make for difficulties when it comes to deciphering the roles and culpability of the adults who cause mutilation to occur.

For these reasons it is important to distinguish between on one hand the criminality of the actual act itself (motives and sanctions are a matter for the court, not the police and prosecutors, whose role is to uphold the law), and on the other the understandings in practising communities which must be tackled if FGM is to be prevented (largely a matter for community workers, teachers and clinicians).

In UK law, even knowingly arranging transport for a child to be mutilated is a criminal act and may, on being found guilty of such an act of procurement, result in serious legal sanctions. All who are involved in perpetrating FGM are in UK law criminals.

Nonetheless, some perpetrators of this abuse have also themselves experienced it and sincerely (but without exception erroneously) believe it to be in the best interests of the child. It is therefore important in seeking to stop FGM that account is taken of such beliefs, even as they are vigorously contested.

Further, and adding another layer of complication to an already complex field, we must acknowledge that people who were abused as children may be themselves more likely to abuse their own offspring in the same way. In a large-scale study of child abuse in the United States, for instance, it was found that about 30 per cent of abused and neglected children will later abuse their own children.[42] Cause and culpability are complex matters.

Nonetheless, the law in Britain on FGM as a crime, whilst currently untested, is clear. What is more contested is how actually to stop the crime, and how to determine judicial and social outcomes for those who, with many different agendas, commit it.

For the purposes of this book, therefore, we may at some points find ourselves referring to 'victims' (of violence) who are also (following this circumstance) perpetrators or otherwise criminally responsible for the damage which is inflicted by FGM on girls and young women.

Barbaric, cultural, religious?

The revulsion and disbelief of those who encounter FGM for the first time is predictable; how can any otherwise apparently caring and responsible parent allow it to happen? FGM is by any measure cruel and brutal. It is, in the view of many, therefore 'barbaric'.

Such a judgement is both unsurprising and in a limited sense accurate. Barbaric acts are by general consensus brutal.

In another sense, however, the word 'barbaric' becomes a source of confusion. The societies where FGM occurs are often, whilst certainly foreign to Western ways, far from crude or unsophisticated. Social hierarchies will often have been developed over centuries and the understandings underpinning FGM, accepted in these communities as irrefutable, are frequently elaborate and complex.

FGM practising communities may be very primitive (barbaric) in their rational understandings of, say, human physiology, but their social structures and belief systems have been established over thousands of years and are aspects of a world view.

Given this context, FGM is commonly regarded as a 'cultural' or even a 'religious' issue. To a degree that may be so, but this view is useful only in the sense that it may pinpoint some of those in a practising community whose influence can be brought to bear in stopping FGM. FGM is at base about tradition rather than about culture; its rationales can change quite rapidly whilst the practice as such endures.

FGM has occurred in widely different societies for millennia; it cannot be attributed meaningfully to any specific source or belief system. Those who promote FGM within their own culture or religion are responding to perceptions of the human condition – and specifically the social status of women – which are much more deeply embedded than any single culture or specific religious belief.

In other words, overt, named cultures and faiths are shaped by fundamental perceptions of the world which lie very largely unexamined underpinning them. We may observe that people with particular cultural assumptions or religious beliefs practise FGM, but this does not explain the practice as such, since these overt belief systems vary enormously between different places and different times.

Just as the word 'barbaric' has only limited meaning or usefulness in the study of FGM, so too there is only limited value to be derived from referring to FGM as 'religious' or 'cultural' in the commonly understood sense. These terms may help only in identifying specific underpinning beliefs and influential actors – thought leaders – within the community.

In another sense, however, the term 'cultural' is indeed helpful: in its deeper, anthropological or sociological sense, it encourages a look beneath the surface to find out what the fundamental understandings and rules of any given society or community might be.

Developing insights into socio-cultural influences concerning FGM in the context of these more profound values is one aim of this book.

'Purity'

One of the most profound values relating to FGM is 'purity'. The basic rationale for FGM in many practising communities is that it makes the girl child 'pure', so she can emerge into adulthood ready for the economic transaction which will result in her early marriage, and cleansed of the genital organs which are regarded as unclean, perhaps taboo.

To most Westerners this emphasis on purity is strange; but it is not as alien to Western thinking as may be imagined. As various observers have demonstrated,[43] there remain many taboos around women and sexuality even in the most modern societies – the position of the American extreme right on, for example, abortion or even family planning makes this point well.[44] Indeed, it is replicated to varying degrees by people of a variety of religious faiths in many Western states.

Further, whilst FGM is now extremely rare amongst modern white women, there are other practices such as labiaplasty and breast enlargement which could be seen as similar (debate continues[45]), and there are confirmed reports of FGM occurring in the USA[46] and in Britain up to and beyond the 1950s.[47] The reasons for these procedures may have been presented differently, but the concern around women's imperfect bodies and aspects of female sexuality are common threads.

Nor can it be said that the cruelties comparable to FGM are alien to Western society. Cases of other forms of horrific child abuse continue to arise and the history of cruelty to women in Britain and other Western nations abound with gruesome stories of witches being burned, women being ducked, chastity belts, the sexual exploitation of children and much else.

It is therefore important to remember that history reveals direct experience of appalling and oppressive acts against women and girls in all societies, and indeed against children of both sexes.

FGM is in many ways the ultimate in sickening patriarchal oppression, it is indeed patriarchy incarnate, but it is and has not been the only form of cruelty in modern societies. Nor is it the only practice underpinned by a deep and often unspoken, incoherent fear of female sexuality.

Modern Western societies too have their grimly dark side; all child cruelty and abuse is wrong, whoever inflicts it. But our search for ways to stop FGM also offers wider hope: if this shocking practice can be arrested, then so might other forms of abuse against women and girls specifically, and vulnerable people in general.

Patriarchy and Feminism

It must be said that not all who strive ceaselessly to eradicate FGM do so under the banner of 'feminism'. Their work is critically important whether or not they subscribe to the feminist agenda, but for this writer it is an essential analytical concept.

In some contexts or circumstances feminism is understood to constitute a rejection of men, or to suggest that women are in some way 'better' than men. That is not, however, the sense in which the notion is employed in this book.

Rather, the ideas of 'feminism', and in contrast 'patriarchy', here are intended to demonstrate the inequalities of resources, influence and sheer power, which patriarchy implies, whereas feminism refers to the idea that all men and women are (or should be) equal, having the same human rights and status as human beings in common.

In this sense of feminism men may be (and quite frequently are) as 'feminist', or if they prefer 'pro-feminist', as women may be.

On the other hand, women may through their preferences and actions promote patriarchy – a theme we shall return to on many occasions. Rarely, however, do women promote the power of men from a totally level playing field; more often their choice may be influenced by the advantage (overtly perceived or not) which comes from 'supporting' men.

A great deal of analysis of feminism, and of patriarchy, has been developed and debated over the past half century and more, but this is not the place to delve deeply into the subject, tempting though that might be. Rather, perhaps, it is helpful to perceive feminism in this instance as being about equality – as Dale Spender asks in her much-cited commentary *Feminism has Fought no Wars*,[48] why should it be a problem to support a stance which has fought for education, the vote, better working conditions, safety on the streets, women's refuges, reforms in the law and much else?

'Honour', FGM and Child, Early and Forced Marriage (CEFM)

This book is about female genital mutilation, but it is impossible wholly to distinguish completely between the question of 'honour' and issues of FGM and child, early and forced marriage (CEFM).[49] This complication is increased, in respect of the UK, by the fact that the Department for International Development (DfID) and other government departments now allocate funding globally to be shared between FGM and CEFM,[50, 51] on the basis that they are two powerful examples of harmful practices, driven by social norms, which stop girls and women fulfilling their potential.[52]

Whilst there is good reason to connect the notion of 'honour' to the concepts which underlie FGM, CEFM and, indeed, so-called 'honour' killing[53] itself, there are also complexities in this linkage which lie beyond the scope of the current publication. For instance (to give a few examples from amongst the multitude which might be cited):

- whilst FGM may be followed by CEFM, it is sometimes done many years before even child marriage is likely to occur; and conversely it may be carried out well after a woman is married, perhaps at the time of her giving birth;
- 'honour' killings do not usually occur (intentionally, as opposed to as a consequence of FGM) in many communities where FGM is the norm;
- (as in the case of male genital mutilation or circumcision) early and forced marriage can be imposed on young men as well as on young women, and the consequences of this being the case for both women and men, when it comes to the delivery of overall prohibition programmes, remain largely yet to be addressed; and
- issues around the ideal age at which marriage should be permitted (often suggested to be 18) will not easily be resolved, when even in countries such as the UK that age is 16.[ii]

---

ii   The minimum age for marriage in the UK is 16. In England, Wales and Northern Ireland anyone under 18 requires parental consent, but in Scotland such consent is not required at any permitted age.

One resolution of the ages of consent and marriage dilemma is obvious, especially in an era when contraception and other sexual advice could with the right determination be made available to all. This, if possible universally, would be to make the age of consent 16 (thereby not criminalising perhaps the majority of teenagers), and the age for marriage 18 (with easy legal registration of the birth of any children born when one or both the parents are under 18).

How to face up to these challenges, with all the legal, social, political, cultural and economic nuances they bring, is too multidimensional a question to be addressed here. Suffice to say, in the context of England and Wales, it must be noted that FGM and CEFM have been brought together by the DfID and are therefore elements conjoined in the politics of the UK, albeit they relate primarily to the mainstream social norms of other societies.

Further discussion of the agendas required to stop the abuses of CEFM is offered in a paper on the matter by CARE International,[54] following the 2014 Girl Summit.

For the purposes of the present discussion, however, it is important to note also that both FGM and CEFM are illegal under UK law. This is the case whatever the age of the girl or woman (or boy or man) involved. And if the offence occurs in respect of someone under 18, it, like all other harmful traditional practices (HTPs),[55] is recognised across much of the globe – and definitively in the UK – as an illegal act of child abuse.

The importance of that legal fact in ensuring the safety of young women (and young men) must not be put aside; the law is clear and must be enforced when an offence has occurred, albeit appropriate sanction of the offender/s will be at the discretion thereafter of the court.

But that does not mean that there is only one way, that is, via the law, to prevent the crimes of FGM, CEFM and other HTPs. There is a risk when dealing with different crimes which (correctly) have the same general designation – child abuse – that necessary distinctions in programmes of prevention will be lost (or, inadvertently, that inappropriate differences in legal perspectives will arise).

For this reason too our focus here will be clearly on FGM. FGM is child abuse and even it alone requires a wide variety of approaches if it is to cease.

Abolish? Eliminate? Eradicate?

The objective of all campaigners against FGM is the same: to stop it happening. How to achieve that objective is not, however, something on which everyone agrees.

One of the main stumbling blocks to a united approach between activists is in fact how to describe what they are trying to do. Are they seeking to 'abolish' FGM? Or to 'eliminate' it? Or to 'eradicate' it?

There is a self-evident overlap between these words; we understand that they all mean 'remove completely'. The choice of one rather than another, though, is sometimes an indication of the angle from which we approach the task, as use of the nouns rather than the verbs may indicate.

'Abolition' suggests a crusade. It is the way that pioneers against the slave trade described their objective and may be the term of choice of, for example, those who lobby decision-makers to persuade them that FGM must stop.

'Elimination' suggests an austere approach, linear and unswerving. It is probably applicable to, say, techniques for formal action, police enforcement and similar approaches and may focus mostly on procurers and perpetrators.

'Eradication' might refer to a comprehensive programme to achieve the halting of FGM. It is a term often to be found in the lexicon of public health praxis. In this light, FGM is an issue which impacts on those who experience it. The focus is on both victims and perpetrators, but it also encompasses the wider contexts (cultures) in which the act of FGM occurs.

This public health framework will be adopted frequently in the present text. There is a strong case – argued in more detail in what follows – that, especially in modern Western nations, such a framework best serves articulation of the challenges of making FGM history.

'Eradication' is therefore generally the term of choice in this book. But that is not to exclude or diminish the relevance and significance also of the other terms.

Cultural Relativity

It is evidently difficult to see a way through the moral maze presented by the complexities of practices such as FGM. Sometimes we feel the need to name things and describe them in ways which others say are objectionable; sometimes we ourselves perceive how others name and describe the facts of FGM as plainly wrong.

The ideas behind cultural and ethical relativism can help here.

In essence (and simplifying hugely exchanges between numerous anthropologists and other scholars over many decades), cultural relativists historically have claimed that there are no fundamental rights or wrongs – every society has its own beliefs and ways of life, and in each of them those ways are the 'best' for that community.

This position has, however, become increasingly challenged.[56, 57] There are, to most of us, things which are unacceptable in any circumstance – FGM, for readers of this book, probably being one of them.

Nonetheless, having an unshakable conviction that something is wrong does not excuse us from trying to find out why others in different places, or at different times, have thought otherwise. The concept of cultural relativity can be used to examine a situation or event, whilst also saying the phenomenon itself is wrong.

In this case we are practising cultural relativity whilst also rejecting ethical relativity.[58] We are trying to understand why something happens, but with the intention of stopping it from occurring any more. This is the position now frequently adopted by many activists, as well as bodies such as the World Health Organization, as they face up to FGM and other harmful traditional practices (HTPs).

But not everyone takes this approach. There are still those – some of whom might be called 'Anthr/Apologists[59] – who assert it is no business of white people in the West to 'interfere' with the practices of people of colour in other places.

As noted above, most of the small minority of writers on the subject who maintain this position are anthropologists with a focus on 'race', 'culture' or ethnicity – radical feminists who insist that women may do as they wish with their bodies, or perhaps populist/nationalist politicians from traditionally practising countries.[60]

This view can, and will in this text, be rejected out of hand, by no means least because it denies fundamental human rights and accepts that needless suffering of children.

There is no loss of analytical rigour in acknowledging the human rights must trump anthropological 'even-handedness'.

Such a position is also illogical as well as morally downright wrong. Increasing numbers of the children who are harmed are citizens of Western countries (as are their parents and sometimes their mutilators); and in direct contradiction of the 'Anthr/Apologist' position, there are growing numbers of activists against FGM[61, 62] who maintain vehemently that if the children being mutilated were white, the abuse would not continue for even another day, but because they are mostly darker skinned, no-one cares enough to take effective action.

That observation or belief is one this book hopes to help prove hereonafter mistaken. We must and will protect every child.

Multi-agency or Inter-disciplinary?

The question of how the eradication of FGM should be structured and led in a country such as Britain will arise many times in the course of this volume. It is important from the onset to understand the value which will be placed on the open sharing of ideas, if significant progress towards making FGM history is to be achieved.

Much of the work done to date in the UK has been under the umbrella of (hypothecated, if not always real) multi-agency approaches.

Even those with the very best of intentions who work in the relevant agencies, however, have an obligation to their organisation as well as to their clientele, patients or customers, albeit these may be highly vulnerable people.

Organisations require funding and are perforce natural competitors for resources. The multi-agency approach is not, therefore, without drawbacks.

For this reason it is suggested that serious thought be given also to the development of a more open interface for ideas and information, drawing on the (idealised) academic mode of exchange. The debate is for later, but it is difficult to see how a multi-agency approach can operate effectively, in the absence of either a transparently open discussion and agreement, or a fully articulated top-down political direction with clear accountability at that level.

Articulated consensus between all parties, about the fundamental issues, and conscious agreement about who will do what with what resources, is surely essential if genuine progress is to be made.

There is a currently unexplored role for the academy in combatting FGM, for more research and for the putting forward and analysis, by people with the skills and experience to do that dispassionately, of models and ideas about how progress may be made.

To date there is no fully articulated paradigm, or even transparent shared framework, for the eradication of FGM; but pulling together the threads of what is being done and proposed such a template will be required. The analyses currently available are (necessarily) short on data and incomplete as a basis for action.

In one sense, making the case for such a paradigm, analysis or template is centrally what this book is about. It is difficult to see how substantive progress towards the eradication of FGM can be made without establishing the topic also as a substantive and coherent field of study with a core of generally accepted concepts, frameworks and protocols as a basis from which to proceed.

What we have here is not, however, such a fully articulated account of the issues – that would be impossible – nor is it a fully formed framework for action.

Rather, this is a best effort to represent some of the major challenges which must be faced if FGM is to become history in the UK, together with an attempt to propose some ways forward for consideration, towards that end.

It took many of us – regretfully, this writer included[63] – years to discover the grim reality and vast impacts of FGM, to perceive clearly the nature of the fundamental abuse of human rights which FGM comprises, and to find and join meaningfully with long-committed agitators against it. Now at last, however, moves at national and global levels to stop FGM are becoming evident.

2015 is a fascinating time to be identifying some of the threads in the convoluted journey towards the eradication of female genital mutilation, but it is not a point at which those threads can be pulled together with ease. A lot is happening, but the shape of things to come is not yet entirely clear.

I welcome warmly contributions, corrections and additions to what is written here, and I hope very much indeed that readers will find my book helpful in thinking through the issues and deciding for themselves what must now be done.

Thank you for your concern about the babies, girls and women who, with their families and our shared communities, are the focus of everything I have written in the pages that follow.

Hilary Burrage
March 2015
www.hilaryburrage.com

Discuss this chapter at http://nofgmukbook.com/2015/01/29/introduction/.

Endnotes

All weblinks accessed on 1 March 2015.

1   Amnesty International (2010) *Ending Female Genital Mutilation to Promote the Achievement of the Millennium Development Goals*. Available at: http://www.endfgm.eu/content/assets/Ending_Female_Genital_Mutilation_to_Promote_the_Achievement_of_the_Millennium_Development_Goals.pdf.

2   Forward UK (2014) *Female Genital Mutilation*. Available at: http://www.forwarduk.org.uk/key-issues/fgm.

3   World Health Organization. (2014) *Fact sheet No 241: Female Genital Mutilation*. Available at: http://www.who.int/mediacentre/factsheets/fs241/en/.

4   UNFPA Evaluation Office, UNICEF Evaluation Office (2013) *UNFPA/UNICEF Joint Programme on Female Genital Mutilation/Cutting: Accelerating Change 2008–12*. Available at: http://www.unicef.org/evaldatabase/files/ENG_FGM_executive_summary_FINAL.pdf.

5   Forward UK (2006) *Definitions and Terms for Female Genital Mutilation*. Available at: http://www.forwarduk.org.uk/key-issues/fgm/definitions.

6   Forward UK (2014) *Fistula*. Available at: http://www.forwarduk.org.uk/key-issues/fistula.

7   Forward UK (2014) *Child Marriage*. Available at: http://www.forwarduk.org.uk/key-issues/child-marriage.

8   World Health Organization (2014) *Fact sheet No 241: Female Genital Mutilation*. Available at: http://www.who.int/mediacentre/factsheets/fs241/en.

9   Inter-African Committee (2005) *DECLARATION: on the Terminology FGM; 6th IAC General Assembly, 4–7 April, 2005, Bamako/Mali*. Available at: http://umarfeminismos.org/images/stories/mgf/Bamako%20Declaration%20on%20the%20Terminology%20FGM_%206th%20IAC%20General%20Assembly_4%20-%207%207%20April%202005.pdf (precis by Dr Tobe Levin).

10 NoFGM (UK) (2014) *The Bamako Declaration: Female Genital Mutilation Terminology* (Mali, 2005). Available at: http://nofgm.org/2014/11/12/the-bamako-declaration-female-genital-mutilation-terminology-mali-2005/.

11 World Health Organization (2008) *Eliminating Female Genital Mutilation: An Interagency Statement UNAIDS, UNDP, UNECA, UNESCO, UNFPA, UNHCHR, UNHCR, UNICEF, UNIFEM, WHO*. Geneva: WHO Press. Available at: http://www.un.org/womenwatch/daw/csw/csw52/statements_missions/Interagency_Statement_on_Eliminating_FGM.pdf.

12 Inter-African Committee on Traditional Practices (2009) *Female Genital Mutilation*. Available at: http://www.iac-ciaf.net/index.php?view=article&id=18%3Afemale-genital-mutilation-&format=pdf&option=com_content&Itemid=9.

13 Tostan (2013) *New UNICEF Report Provides Statistical Overview of Female Genital Cutting*. 22 July. Available at: http://tostan.org/news/new-unicef-report-provides-statistical-overview-female-genital-cutting.

14 Anthropologi.Info (2010) *Yes to Female Circumcision?* 15 February. Available at: http://www.antropologi.info/blog/anthropology/2010/female-circumcision.

15 See for instance this report's reference to genital 'surgeries', which the present writer does not endorse: The Public Policy Advisory Network on Female Genital Surgeries in Africa (2012) Seven Things to Know about Female Genital Surgeries in Africa. *The Hastings Center Report* 42(6): 19–27. DOI: 10.1002/hast.81. Available at: http://onlinelibrary.wiley.com/doi/10.1002/hast.81/abstract.

16 Aftab, A., Bedar, A. and El Matrah, J. (2014) Respectful Dialogue: A Guide for Responsible Reporting on Female Genital Cutting. *Australian Muslim Women's Centre for Human Rights*. Available at: http://ausmuslimwomenscentre.org.au/2014/a-guide-for-responsible-reporting-on-female-genital-cutting.

17 Bich, H., Ibrahim, M., Keogh, L., Tobin, J., Vaughan, C., White, N., et al. (2014) *Listening to North Yarra Communities about Female Genital Cutting*. Melbourne: The University of Melbourne. Available at: http://newsroom.melbourne.edu/sites/newsroom.melbourne.edu/files/Listening%20to%20North%20Yarra%20Communities%20-%20Final%5B1%5D.pdf.

18 Orchid Project (2014) *Home*. Available at: http://orchidproject.org/.
19 Tostan (2014) *Annual Report 2013*. Senegal: Tostan. Available at: http://www. tostan.org/sites/default/files/reports/annual_report_2013_0.pdf.
20 Orchid Project (2014) *What We Do*. Available at: http://orchidproject.org/ category/what-we-do/about-orchid-project/.
21 Orchid Project (2014) *Orchid Project's Annual Reports*. Available at: http:// orchidproject.org/wp-content/uploads/2014/09/Orchid-Project-Trustee-Report-2013-2014.pdf.
22 Warzazi, H. (1999) Third Report on the Situation Regarding the Elimination of Traditional Practices Affecting the Health of Women and the Girl Child. *United Nations Commission on Human Rights, Sub-Commission on Prevention of Discrimination and Protection of Minorities* (51): 1–20. Available at: http:// ap.ohchr.org/documents/alldocs.aspx?doc_id=7079.
23 United Nations Children's Fund (2013) *Female Genital Mutilation/Cutting: A statistical overview and exploration of the dynamics of chance*. New York: UNICEF, July. Available at: http://www.unicef.org/media/files/FGCM_Lo_res.pdf.
24 Rush, J. (2014) A Dozen Men are Ambushed, Stripped Naked and Forced to Undergo Circumcisions in Kenya after Their Wives Complained That They Were Not as Good in Bed as Circumcised Men. *Daily Mail*, 5 August. Available at: http://www.dailymail.co.uk/news/article-2715741/A-dozen-men-ambushed-stripped-naked-forced-undergo-circumcisions-Kenya-wives-complained-not-good-bed-circumcised-men.html.
25 World Health Organization (2014) *Male Circumcision for HIV Prevention*. Available at: http://www.who.int/hiv/topics/malecircumcision/en/.
26 Doctors Opposing Circumcision (2008) *The Use of Male Circumcision to Prevent HIV Infection*. Available at: http://www.doctorsopposingcircumcision.org/info/ HIVStatement.html.
27 Larue, G. (1991) Religious Traditions and Circumcisions. San Francisco: *The Second International Symposium on Circumcision*, May. Available at: http://www. nocirc.org/symposia/second/larue.html.
28 Men's Health Forum (2014) *Circumcision FAQs*, 14 April. Available at: http://www.menshealthforum.org.uk/circumcision-faqs.
29 Fogg, A. (2014) The Death and Deformity Caused by Male Circumcision in Africa Can't Be Ignored. *Guardian*, 25 August. Available at: http://www. theguardian.com/commentisfree/2014/aug/25/male-circumcision-ceremonies-death-deformity-africa.
30 Circumcision Information Australia (2014) *100+ Circumcision Deaths Each Year in the United States*. Available at: http://www.circinfo.org/USA_deaths.html (USA).
31 Meel, B.L. (2010) Traditional Male Circumcision-related Fatalities in the Mthatha Area of South Africa. *Med Sci Law* 50(4): 189–91. Available at: http:// www.ncbi.nlm.nih.gov/pubmed/21539284 (Africa).
32 Joint United Nations Programme on HIV/AIDS, World Health Organization (2007) *Male Circumcision: Global Trends and Determinants of Prevalence, Safety and*

Acceptability. Switzerland: WHO Press. Available at: http://whqlibdoc.who.int/publications/2007/9789241596169_eng.pdf.

33 Levin, T. (2014) 'Fearful Symmetries' Essays and Testimony on Female Genital Mutilation and (Male) Circumcision. *Wissenschaftliches Symposium: 'Genitale Autonomie: Körperliche Unversehrtheit, Religionsfreiheit und sexuelle Selbstbestimmung – von der Theorie zur Praxis'.* Universität zu Köln, 6 May. Available at: http://genitale-autonomie.de/videos-der-vortraege/levin/.

34 Womankind Worldwide (2013) *FGM Advertising in Womankind's Name.* Available at: http://www.womankind.org.uk/what-we-do/frequently-asked-questions/fgm-advertising-in-womankinds-name/.

35 Taylor, D. (2013) Female Genital Mutilation: 'I want to help other girls'. *Guardian,* 21 January. Available at: http://www.theguardian.com/society/2013/jan/22/female-genital-mutilation-help-girls.

36 BBC News (2006) Kenya Shock at Mutilation Death. *BBC News,* 23 June. Available at: http://news.bbc.co.uk/1/hi/5109094.stm.

37 Torome, J. (2008) The Secret World of Female Circumcision. Kenya: *Project Syndicate,* 27 October. Available at: http://www.project-syndicate.org/print/the-secret-world-of-female-circumcision.

38 Gray, A. (2009) Another Way Microfinance is Changing the World. *Kiva Fellows Blog,* 31 March. Available at: http://www.kiva.org/updates/fellows/2009/03/31/another-way-microfinance-is-changing-the-world.

39 Weber, K., ed. by Jensen, L. (2013) Ugandan Communities Scrutinize a Violent – Sometimes Deadly – Rite of Passage. *UNFPA,* 1 February. Available at: http://unfpa.org/public/home/news/pid/12673.

40 African Women Organization (2009) *Myths and Justifications for the Perpetuation of FGM.* Available at: http://www.african-women.org/FGM/myths.php.

41 Burrage, H. (2014) The Real Economics of FGM: It's (Much) More than 'Wages'. *Hilary Burrage,* 11 April. Available at: http://hilaryburrage.com/2014/04/11/the-real-economics-of-fgm-its-much-more-than-wages/.

42 Child Welfare Information Gateway (2013) *Long-Term Consequences of Child Abuse and Neglect.* Washington, D.C.: U.S. Department of Health and Human Services, July. Available at: https://www.childwelfare.gov/pubs/factsheets/long_term_consequences.cfm.

43 Valenti, J. (2010) *The Purity Myth: How America's Obsession with Virginity is Hurting Young Women.* United States: Seal Press. Available at: http://sealpress.com/books/the-purity-myth/.

44 Politicus USA (2012) *Proof of the GOP War on Women.* Available at: http://www.politicususa.com/proof-war-women-2.

45 Zakaria, R. (2010) Female Genital Mutilation vs. Female Breast Mutilation. *Ms. Magazine Blog,* 19 May. Available at: http://msmagazine.com/blog/2010/05/19/female-genital-mutilation-vs-female-breast-mutilation/ (the AAP has subsequently withdrawn the 'just a nick' proposal – see comment by Taina Bien-Aime).

46 Involuntary Foreskinectomy Awareness. (2014) *America's Forgotten History of Female Circumcision*. Available at: https://sites.google.com/site/completebaby/female.

47 Darby, R. (2014) Circumcision of Females: Cultural and medical rationales. *History of Circumcision*. Available at: http://www.historyofcircumcision.net/index. php?option=com_content&task=category&sectionid=13&id=76&Itemid=6.

48 Spender, D. (1998) *Man Made Language*. London: Pandora.

49 Plan UK (2014) *Help Us End Early and Forced Marriage Now*. Available at: http:// www.plan-uk.org/because-i-am-a-girl/about-because-i-am-a-girl/violence-against-girls/early-and-forced-marriage.

50 Department for International Development, Cabinet Office, Home Office (2014) *Girl Summit 2014*. Available at: https://www.gov.uk/government/topical-events/ girl-summit-2014.

51 Department for Communities and Local Government and Government Equalities Office (2014) *Community Projects to Tackle Female Genital Mutilation and Forced Marriage. GOV.UK*, 31 October. Available at: https://www.gov.uk/ government/publications/community-projects-to-tackle-female-genital-mutilation-and-forced-marriage.

52 Department for International Development (2014) *A Future Free from FGM and Child and Forced Marriage*. See: https://www.gov.uk/government/news/pm-hosts-girl-summit-2014-a-future-free-from-fgm-and-child-and-forced-marriage.

53 Chesler, P. (2010) Worldwide Trends in Honor Killings. *Middle Eastern Quarterly* 17(2): 3–11. Available at: http://www.meforum.org/2646/worldwide-trends-in-honor-killings.

54 Care International (2014) *CARE International Position on Child, Early and Forced Marriage (CEFM) and the Girl Summit, July 2014*. Available at: http://www.care. org/sites/default/files/documents/CI%20position%20on%20the%20Girl%20 Summit_final%20170714.pdf.

55 OHCHR (1979) *Fact Sheet No. 23, Harmful Traditional Practices Affecting the Health of Women and Children*. Available at: http://www.ohchr.org/documents/ publications/factsheet23en.pdf.

56 Dorkenoo, E. (2006) Female Genital Mutilation (FGM). In: *The Bayan Tree Paradox: Culture and human rights activism*. Washington, D.C.: International Human Rights Internship Program, Institute of International Education, 112–15. Available at: http://www.forwarduk.org.uk/key-issues/fgm/human-rights.

57 Moges, A. (nd) What is Behind the Tradition of FGM? *African Women Documents*. Available at: http://www.african-women.org/documents/behind-FGM-tradition.pdf.

58 Rosaldo, R. (2000) Of Headhunters and Soldiers: Separating Cultural and Ethical Relativism. *Ethics*, Markkula Center for Applied Ethics 11(1). Available at: http://www.scu.edu/ethics/publications/iie/v11n1/relativism.html.

59 Levin, T. (2010) Female Genital Mutilation, 'Highly Valued by Both Sexes'? Anthr/apologists versus Activists. *Feminist Europa. Review of Books*. 10(1): 11–21. Available at: http://www.ddv-verlag.de/issn_1570_0038_FE%2009_2010.pdf.

60 Dorkenoo, E. (2006) Female Genital Mutilation (FGM). In: *The Bayan Tree Paradox: Culture and human rights activism*. Washington, D.C.: International

Human Rights Internship Program, Institute of International Education, 112–15. Available at: http://www.forwarduk.org.uk/key-issues/fgm/human-rights.

61 Saner, E. (2013) Waris Dirie: 'Female genital mutilation is pure violence against girls'. *Guardian*, 14 October. Available at: http://www.theguardian.com/ lifeandstyle/2013/oct/14/waris-dirie-female-genital-mutilation-fgm.

62 O'Casey, E. (2013) The 'Cutting Season' and FGM in the UK: A national disgrace, a national shame. *National Secular Society*, 2 July. Available at: http:// www.secularism.org.uk/blog/2013/07/the-cutting-season-and-fgm-in-the-uk--a-national-disgrace-a-national-shame1.

63 Burrage, H. (2014) Sing and Shout Against FGM: Where the Arts, Human Rights, The 'Old Days' and a Big UN Announcement All Came Together. *Hilary Burrage*, 30 October. Available at: http://hilaryburrage.com/2014/10/30/sing-and-shout-against-fgm-where-the-arts-human-rights-the-old-days-and-a-big-un-announcement-all-came-together/.

1 Demography and Epidemiology of FGM

The Global Picture

Female genital mutilation is recognised internationally as a violation of the human rights of girls and women.[1] As discussed in the Introduction, it is a criminal and potentially lethal, almost always harmful, assault, both on a person's body and on her mind.

Whilst however there is no dispute about the status of this abuse, ascertaining with any precision the incidence of female genital mutilation in any location (including the UK) is difficult, given both its general illegality and the intimate nature of the practice itself. Estimations of how frequently FGM occurs, and of the likelihood of risk for given populations, inevitably require informed guesswork and a considerable degree of sensitivity to the issues as they are interrogated.

The damage caused by FGM is intensely personal and private, and even more so because the subjects are (most usually) minors who cannot give meaningful consent either to the procedure itself, or to any subsequent proposed medical examination.

Difficulties in regard to disclosure of FGM also arise because of its likely context. The ancient custom of FGM is not based on understandings open to rational-scientific debate, but often rather on deeply held cultural mores which brook no challenge and which are in effect invisible or secret. FGM may not be mentioned, let alone questioned, in most traditionally practising communities.

Further, FGM is already in many (but not all) countries against the law, whether observed or not. This too is self-evidently a powerful incentive to secrecy.

Embedded almost inextricably in a set of beliefs about sexually appropriate behaviours and gendered power hierarchies which no amount of disclosure is likely to dislodge, FGM is what Gerry Mackie labels a 'belief trap',[2] that is, a set of convictions or understandings which it is too dangerous or scary to test.

25

If for instance the belief is that the clitoris will grow into a 'third leg', or kill men and babies on contact, precautionary measures to ensure its removal are obviously required. It would be irrational and dangerous for anyone to test these understandings in real situations.

Many perpetrators (sometimes grandmothers), procurers (often mothers) and victims may therefore believe that FGM is necessary, proper and, by its very nature, private.

FGM is of interest, in this view, only on a need-to-know basis, usually in regard to future marriage prospects, within the relevant family or social grouping. There is no need within practising communities to question it; in fact the possibility or prospect inside such groups of interrogating the custom is unlikely ever to arise.

What Do We Need to Know?

Infinite resources cannot be available even to tackle FGM; it is therefore important that working approximations of incidence and probable location are made, to ensure the best use of personnel and funding to eradicate the practice. Estimates of where and to what extent FGM occurs in the UK are required at a level of precision which enables the effective local operationalisation of safeguarding, enforcement and, where necessary, remediation.

The requirement that there be data adequate to identify comparative risk of exposure to FGM is also complicated by another factor: for some professionals and policy-makers, there are fears that the identification of groups or communities where FGM may occur will be seen as 'racist', or as a failure to 'understand' a given culture.

Given these concerns, it is critical that female genital mutilation be seen for what in the legal statutes of many nations it is: a gross, brutal, violation of physical integrity which often inflicts enduring pain and serious long-term harm on its victims – and in turn later also during childbirth on their own babies.[3, 4] FGM is a 'procedure' which carries significant risk of fatality (estimated in one study as up to one third of those experiencing it in places such as the Sudan, if no antibiotics are available[5]) and at whatever age or stage in life it is done. And it also directly crosses generations, affecting, for instance, the life chances of children born to women with FGM – the risk of infants (boys and girls) dying rises dramatically if the mother dies[6] and even, in some cases, where the previous child did not survive.[7] The burden of maternal death often also affects older girls, who are required to take on their mothers' roles.[8]

In short, FGM is an unremittingly damaging tradition, defined by World Health Organization and United Nations resolution, and in the UK by law, as an act of bodily harm. At its worst it is an act of homicide. It also causes long-term physical, psychological and socio-economic damage.

Once this is perceived, everyone with safeguarding and other relevant responsibilities can start from the same place. There is widespread agreement amongst observers and activists, both statutory and voluntary, that the prevalence (epidemiology) of FGM must be properly established in order that the practice can be prevented and perpetrators sanctioned, and so that services can be focused to ensure that girls and women who are already victims are offered support and whatever remediation is possible.

Put in such a context, it becomes clear both that research to identify at-risk communities is essential and that anyone who suspects this crime has been, or will be, committed must be obliged to report their suspicions to the appropriate authorities.

Types of FGM

'Female genital mutilation' is a generic term encompassing a number of different actions. All involve permanent physical damage to a girl or woman's external genitalia and all are illegal in the UK, but some are more likely to cause severe and long-lasting physical harm than others. The more extensive forms also put babies born to women with FGM at serious risk during labour and delivery. Psycho-social issues also often arise for victims of FGM.

The United Nations[9] and the World Health Organization,[10] both of which condemn the practice of FGM, are amongst the bodies which have together developed a typology of female genital mutilation. This is now almost universally accepted by medical and other observers and professionals.

Types of female genital mutilation (FGM I–IV)[11]

I: *Clitoridectomy*: partial or total removal of the clitoris (an elongated, sensitive and erectile part of the female genitals) and, in very rare cases, only the prepuce (the fold of skin surrounding the clitoris). See Figure 1.2.

II: *Excision*: partial or total removal of the clitoris and the labia minora, with or without excision of the labia majora (the labia are the 'lips' that surround the vagina). See Figure 1.3.

III: *Infibulation*: narrowing of the vaginal opening through the creation of a covering seal. The seal is formed by cutting and repositioning the inner, or outer, labia, with or without removal of the clitoris. See Figure 1.4.

IV: *Other*: all other harmful procedures to the female genitalia for non-medical purposes, for example pricking, piercing, incising, scraping and cauterising the genital area, or labial stretching etc. See Figure 1.5.

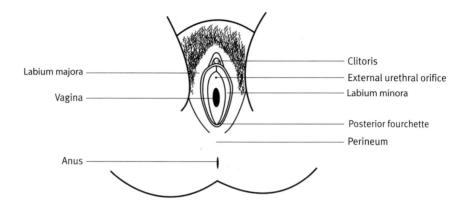

Figure 1.1   Normal external female genitalia

Source: Royal College of Nursing (2015) *Female Genital Mutilation. An RCN Resource for Nursing and Midwifery Practice,* 2nd edition, London: RCN. Available at: www.rcn.org.uk.

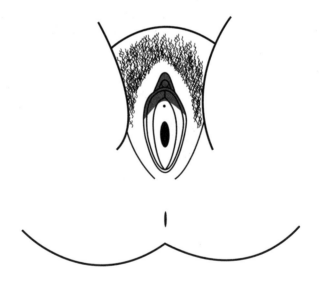

Figure 1.2   Clitoridectomy – Type I FGM

Source: Royal College of Nursing (2015) *Female Genital Mutilation. An RCN Resource for Nursing and Midwifery Practice,* 2nd edition, London: RCN. Available at: www.rcn.org.uk.

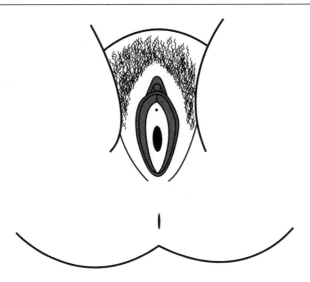

Figure 1.3   Excision – Type II FGM

Source: Royal College of Nursing (2015) *Female Genital Mutilation. An RCN Resource for Nursing and Midwifery Practice* 2nd edition, London: RCN. Available at: www.rcn.org.uk.

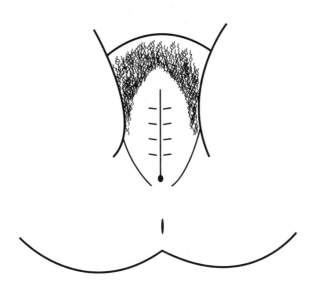

Figure 1.4   Infibulation – Type III FGM

Source: Royal College of Nursing (2015) *Female Genital Mutilation. An RCN Resource for Nursing and Midwifery Practice,* 2nd edition, London: RCN. Available at: www.rcn.org.uk.

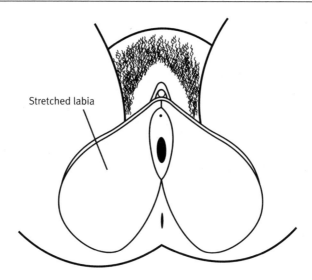

Stretched labia

Figure 1.5   Other (for example stretched labia) – Type IV FGM

Source: Royal College of Nursing (2015) *Female Genital Mutilation. An RCN Resource for Nursing and Midwifery Practice,* 2nd edition, London: RCN. Available at: www.rcn.org.uk.

Where Does FGM Occur?

Female genital mutilation has occurred at many times and in many places. The incidence of FGM between nations in the same part of the world, and even between different areas or regions of a country, can vary significantly in response to different sets of beliefs and customs. It may be found in one community or location but not in the next one, even if the geographical separation is small.[12]

Until recently the focus in considering FGM occurrence has been almost entirely on Africa, and more specifically the sub-Saharan area. Increasingly, however, it is being recognised that the areas of the world which host FGM-practising communities are far more widespread than that; even between the years 2009 and 2011 the information to hand changed, and more data became available.[13, 14]

Nations where FGM is prevalent include Egypt, Eritrea, Ethiopia, Gambia, Sierra Leone, Somalia and Sudan. It also occurs in the Middle East,[15] as well as in a few other places such as limited parts of Pakistan and India, and in certain ethnic groups in South America.[16] In half of the countries for which the 2013 UNFPA study obtained data, the majority of girls undergo FGM before the age of 5. In the Central African Republic, Chad,

Egypt and Somalia, at least 80 per cent of girls are mutilated between the ages of 5 and 14.[17]

The variation of incidence and type of FGM between different places is now better charted than previously, but there is still much to be done in terms of securing a sound knowledge of incidence around the globe.

Further, it is possible, even likely, that in most countries the incidence of FGM has been under- rather than over-stated. Whilst there are reports of girls claiming to have had FGM although they have not – and thereby, they hope, escaping it[18] – FGM is a secret tradition and has probably become even less liable to be reported[19, 20] since many countries have now adopted laws against it.

Age at which FGM Occurs

FGM can occur at any age between just a few days after birth until puberty. It also sometimes occurs just prior to marriage or even before the birth of a baby. Women may also undergo reinfibulation after the birth of a baby, or if their husbands plan to be away for any length of time.

The most common ages for mutilation are between infancy and 15,[21] with the larger number happening after the age of about 6. There is, however, growing concern that the incidence of FGM on very young children and infants is increasing[22, 23] as awareness of legislation against it increases. Very young children cannot remember or report what is being done, they will not seek to avoid the procedure, and they do not attend school so scheduling is easier if the intention is to ensure the matter remains secret. Some parents also regard early mutilation as 'kinder'.

The age may also vary with the type of mutilation being done.[24]

Why Does FGM Occur?

Female genital mutilation is an age-old phenomenon. It precedes all the major world religions and has been known, like other harmful traditional practices (HTPs),[25] from the earliest times.[26]

The claim is regularly made that FGM is a 'Muslim' practice, but in fact it occurs amongst animists and in both Muslim and Judeo-Christian countries. A large majority of spiritual leaders of global faiths – though certainly not all leaders in, especially, the Islamic tradition[27] – reject it as an inhumane transgression of basic rights to physical integrity and freedom from fear and oppression.[28, 29]

Nonetheless there is a widespread belief that Islam and FGM are linked, because it is most often encountered in countries where that religion is in the ascendant. The reality is that it is perceived in large numbers of traditional communities to be required. The association of FGM and Islam is, however weak the evidence that the relevant scriptures deem it necessary, a significant aspect of the way that FGM is perceived by many, and must therefore be acknowledged in order that it can be challenged (not least by the large non-practising majority of adherents of that faith).[30]

The reality is that over millennia female genital mutilation has occurred principally as a way to ensure the ascendancy of patriarchy.[31] FGM therefore presents itself variously in different places and at different times:

- In some instances, FGM occurs very early in a girl child's life, in others later, even perhaps in adulthood.[32, 33, 34]
- Sometimes the preferred 'procedure' is relatively minor/non-invasive (though never risk-free); in others it is routinely life-threatening.[35]
- Some communities link FGM to large-scale festivities, with much ritual and celebration. In others, especially since the introduction in many places of laws forbidding the practice, it is carried out without ceremony and in secret.[36]

Similarly, the rationales of FGM are diverse:[37, 38]

- FGM may be an early marker of belonging to a particular group, perhaps carried out when the child is only a few days or weeks old. (Similarly, migrant groups may adopt it as a way of indicating difference from their host community.)[39]
- In some communities FGM is seen as a rite of passage, an initiation to adulthood during which pain must be endured, which occurs as the girl approaches puberty and thus 'becomes a woman' (Chad).[40] FGM also often has religious and social significance. The shedding of blood may be seen as a symbolic stream connecting the woman to the rest of her close-knit community.[41]
- FGM is sometimes required to 'preserve' family 'honour'.[42]
- It may be done in order to 'cleanse' a girl, in the belief that it is more hygienic and will stop unpleasant genital secretions and odours as the child develops to maturity.[43, 44]
- Another rationale is that the girl must be made 'pure' and chaste, and virginity must be assured before she can be made available at a good bride price for marriage.[45] She may be sewn up almost completely as she approaches puberty, when she reaches marriageable age, or even after each birth, so that sexual intimacy is almost impossible unless the infibulation is reversed, on her husband's say-so.[46]

- A corollary of bride price is that a girl for whom a good price can be secured (that is, whose 'purity' is assured) is also a safety net for her parents in old age; pensions are not part of the experience of elders in traditional communities, but a good (that is, economically sound) marriage offers a degree of assurance for parents as they become more frail.
- FGM may be deemed a beautifying procedure, or to remove 'masculine' aspects of a girl's or woman's body[47] to reinforce gender 'differences'. The clitoris may be seen as 'male' and removed to ensure the girl doesn't develop perceived 'male' traits, such as aggression or promiscuity.
- Excision of the clitoris may be believed to ensure women will not be like men in regard to sexual appetite or aggression, and that it will control the rampant sexual desires which adolescent girls are believed to harbour.[48]
- Fear of the clitoris may be a factor, with the belief that it must be excised because otherwise it will grow into a 'third leg' (like a penis, only perhaps longer), and/or will cause the girl discomfort when she becomes a woman.[49]
- Fear of the clitoris, and its consequent excision, is also a rationale in communities which believe a man – or baby – will die if they come into contact with it during intercourse or labour[50] (in a few communities such as the Samburu in Kenya a baby born to an uncircumcised woman is deemed impure, and may even be killed[51]).
- Excision of the clitoris is believed to reduce a woman's sexual pleasure or desire, thus reducing the likelihood that she will become sexually active with anyone other than her husband.[52]
- FGM may be undertaken in part to protect a girl or woman caught in a conflict zone, as it is thought, like early 'marriage', to be a way to preserve virginity and prevent rape, which is sometimes used by combatants as a 'weapon' against communities.[53]
- Some communities believe men's sexual pleasure will be enhanced by FGM.[54]
- There may be a belief that bearing the pain of FGM is proof of strength, and thereby a 'good' preparation for childbirth.[55] Other physical hurt, such as cutting (male circumcision, body scars, and so on) and piercing, may also be done to boys and girls from an early age, as a way for them to demonstrate bravery en route to adulthood.

Underlying all these rationales, however, is another factor, essential to understanding FGM. It is a ritual, much more than just a mere customary action, which has continued unquestioned for millennia. Those in traditional communities who perpetrate FGM have known no other. For large numbers of such people there is in a very real sense no alternative. As the anthropologist Gerry McKee points out, the risks of neglecting to inflict FGM may be too high to take. The practice is bound to a belief trap.[56] Who knows what horrors might befall an individual or community where it ceased?

FGM in Britain

FGM in the main countries of origin for British residents and their families

Research by a range of organisations shows that FGM is highly prevalent in some (especially African and Middle Eastern) countries from which people migrate to Britain, but that it is almost unknown in other countries of origin of current British residents.

It is reasonably likely that women in the UK from high incidence countries (for example in sub-Saharan Africa) will have undergone FGM, and that the incidence of FGM in these women's daughters will also to an extent reflect the degree of risk which exists in the country of origin. The main traditional-cultural influences on diaspora communities in Britain may or may not, however, be the same as those in the country of origin.

Quantifying FGM Incidence in the UK

A research programme was carried out in England and Wales by FORWARD in 2007.[57] This programme made an estimation of the incidence and likely future risk of FGM in England and Wales.

The study estimated in this way that some 24,000 British (English and Welsh) girls and babies were, on the basis of the 2001 census, at significant risk of FGM annually, which, averaged over the year, suggested some 50 girls and female babies are at significant risk of, or undergo, the procedure every day.

The numbers of women and girls from each of the places where FGM is known to be practised were estimated using 2001 census material. Then for each location and number an approximation of how many women and girls were at risk or had already been subjected to FGM was calculated on the basis of information about what percentage of people from that area were known or suspected to be subject to FGM. Finally, these individual locations of origin and incidence figures were added together to give an indication of overall incidence of FGM in England and Wales.

This report was considered again as part of an FGM Research Methodology Workshop[58] and that general estimate reconfirmed.

The incidence of FGM in Scotland and Northern Ireland was not included in the FORWARD study.

British FGM statistics for the early 2000s show, however, that the trend appears to be upwards.[59] The figure of 24,000 per annum may have risen since 2007, as more children in relevant communities reach the at-risk age/s and perhaps also as more people from countries where FGM is practised enter the UK.

Since 2007 two other estimates of the incidence of FGM in the UK or England and Wales have been produced.

In 2014 Julie Bindel published her study, commissioned by the New Culture Forum and entitled *An Unpunished Crime: The lack of prosecutions for female genital mutilation in the UK*,[60] in which she estimated that the number of women and girls living with FGM in the UK is more likely to be around 170,000 – almost three times the existing official figures – and that 65,000 girls aged 13 and under are at risk of mutilation.

Later, in July of the same year (2014), Alison Macfarlane and Efua Dorkenoo from City University London and Equality Now produced a second report for Trust for London[61] in which they estimated that in 2011 about 137,000 women and girls with FGM, and born in countries where FGM is practised, were permanently resident in England and Wales.[62]

Macfarlane and Dorkenoo therefore believed that the numbers of women and girls with, or at risk of, FGM in the UK has increased, but not by as much as Bindel suggests. (A more detailed analysis of the differences in estimations is presented in their report.[63])

Further information (aggregated data sets) on prevalence in areas of England is now becoming available from the Health and Social Care Information Centre,[64] as the data accrued from hospitals making monthly reports since September 2014 about numbers of patients newly observed with FGM begins to indicate trends and cluster points.

Figures for Wales have been estimated for the Welsh Government on the basis of census and other data as above. They suggest that in 2011 there may have been 140 cases of FGM (0.4 per cent of births in Wales).[65] Further research is planned to see whether this desktop calculation is valid.

In Scotland, the Dignity Alert and Research Forum (DARF) in Edinburgh and the Police estimate that, in 2009, there were 3,000 women living there who have experienced FGM.[66, 67] They believe the figures may have increased since that time. Since then more research on prevalence and distribution has been undertaken by the Scottish Refuge Council and others, resulting in an overview report published in December 2014.[68] This work will be taken forward in 2015, to produce data at a greater level of certainty.

As of later 2014 there has been no systematic estimate of the prevalence of FGM in Northern Ireland,[69] but the expectation is that incidence may be less than in some parts of England.

Whilst the incoming diaspora is a central factor in the expectation that numbers of women and girls with FGM, whether numbers have increased or decreased for other reasons is unclear.

Evidence from global studies suggests that there may be a reduced risk of FGM amongst younger, more educated girls (such as those in the UK, as opposed to those remaining in traditional communities elsewhere),[70, 71] although it has also been noted[72] that differences of education and generation may be less, in more homogenous diaspora communities, than in Western state populations as a whole. Further, in some places (such as Egypt, and even though FGM is illegal) increased education and greater access to clinical skills has simply resulted in the medicalisation of the mutilation, rather than its abandonment.[73]

It is also possible that in other, more closed migrant British communities FGM serves as a 'marker' which distinguishes members of that community from outsiders,[74] and thus increases the risk that it will occur.

Chain migration (where people from the same area or community follow others to a new location) and subsequent high-density local groupings may also bring about large percentages of women and girls with FGM in places.[75]

Similarly, it may be that members of some groups within FGM-practising countries migrate to the UK (or other Western nations) more frequently than people from other groups with a greater or lesser propensity to FGM; and even when overall figures for migration from given nations is known, the proportion of men to women (and also that of different age groups) amongst migrants may not be clear. It is therefore difficult with any accuracy to calculate from available data the numbers of women and girls at risk of, or with, FGM.

It is also likely that some women in FGM-practising groups will be undocumented in official statistics because they opt for invisibility from their host authorities. Such 'invisible' women may include informal immigrants, asylum seekers and/or refugees.

It might be thought that the best way to achieve clarity on the incidence of FGM in the UK would be a survey of the general population, or perhaps to include questions in the next census. Such an approach has been put aside on every occasion when it was considered, not least because of cost and the probability that many relevant potential respondents would not be identified and surveyed. Further, the likelihood is that answers to questions, if they were forthcoming at all, would be unreliable.

To date, however, estimates of the prevalence of FGM have been based on information about the countries of birth of women who have subsequently migrated to the United Kingdom. Not only does this exclude women who have moved to another country, not their place of birth, before they migrate to the UK, but these estimates are inevitably also hampered by only partial knowledge of the actual prevalence at given times of FGM in mothers' locations of origin.

Another obvious source of information on the extent of FGM in UK communities would be obstetric records. Until September 2014, however, there has been no nationally standardised, commonly agreed or shared method of recording even routine obstetric information. When pregnant women presented themselves for care – as, although not all women with FGM ever become pregnant, nearly every expectant mother does – their clinical records were not standardised and, more specifically, were rarely complete in regard to the presence and type, or (inferred) absence, of FGM, even if these medical records could actually be accessed.

Nonetheless, the 2012 Research Methodology Workshop findings suggest that using primary data collected in the course of clinical care during pregnancy and childbirth offers the best, most cost-effective way of identifying the incidence of FGM in the UK. Subsequent wider discussions at the level of policy formation are expected to confirm that this is the preferred way forward.[76]

Information on numbers of people from different minority ethnic communities, plus information, where recorded, on incidence of FGM amongst women attending hospitals for obstetric care, were all until recently that was available as proxies for more precise and accurate data on prevalence.

In October 2013, however, the UK Government's Public Health Minister Jane Ellison MP announced that, after examining options,[77] more precise methods for the assessment of FGM would be put in place for England and Wales. These data began to be reported in September 2014, and almost 600 new cases of FGM in England and Wales are now being diagnosed in acute hospital settings every month – a figure which suggests a very high actual incidence overall. Separate data are now also being collected for Scotland.[78]

An outline of what was required for a greater understanding of where FGM mostly occurs in the UK was indicated in a submission in June 2013 by Efua Dorkenoo, who was before her death Advocacy Director of Equality Now,[79] to the House of Commons International Development (DfID) Committee.[80] It was, however, noted that, although proposals based on established peer-reviewed methodologies already used in Europe were presented to the Department of Health in 2012, delayed responses by the Home Office meant that detailed new national and regional data cannot be fully available until later 2015.

An annexe to the submission prepared by Professor Alison Macfarlane, Professor of Perinatal Health at the City University London in February 2013, gave details of the data already routinely recorded at birth and during maternity care in England.[81]

Details until 2013 required only parents' dates and countries of birth and the baby's ethnicity as reported by parents or clinicians. If the birth occurred in an NHS hospital (and also in a small minority of home births), details of the delivery are also routinely noted for the Maternity Hospital Episode Statistics (HES). Where complications were observed during delivery, these are recorded using the International Classification of Diseases (ICD).

The information available was therefore limited because no ICD or other code for FGM existed, nor did the HES data themselves include the mother's country of birth. This could, however, be conjectured by linking HES information with birth registration records. Collating these various data would be one basis for estimating prevalence of FGM by mothers' own countries of birth.

Professor Macfarlane proposed that a one-off audit for a given time period of FGM in women giving birth in the UK was the best immediate option to determine which methodological instruments will best give sound data on incidence overall in the UK, including women migrating from other parts of the world as well as second-generation women born in Britain.

Professor Macfarlane also urged that the World Health Organization be lobbied to ensure that the revision of the ICD now under way includes FGM, including subdivisions for different types of the practice. She further advised that funding should be made available so that previous estimates of FGM prevalence (based on 2001 census data) are updated in the light of the 2011 census data now to hand.

Another complication is that by no means all clinical obstetric staff are trained in protocols for the assessment or recording of FGM. (Even post-September 2014 there is a category code for recording uncertain diagnoses resulting from genuine uncertainty or from inexperienced clinicians being unsure.) Nor, in addition to issues around agreeing ethical protocols for this research, was there until September 2014 any government directive requiring that FGM in patients be recorded.

The new data relate only to the incidence of FGM for women who have been previously identified and are currently being treated (for FGM-related or non-FGM-related conditions as at the end of the month) and newly identified women within the reporting period. Reporting has been mandatory[82] since 1 September 2014 by acute hospitals in England. As above, the data is then aggregated on a monthly basis by the Health and Social Care Information Centre (HSCIC).[83, 84]

The HSCIC return for September 2014 (with 125 of the 160 mandated acute trusts in England having submitted signed off data) was 1,279 active cases and 467 newly identified cases of FGM reported nationally. In October 2014, 109 of 157 eligible trusts reported in total 1,468 active cases, with 455 new ones; and in November 2014, 124 of 157 trusts reported in all 1,803 active cases, with 466 newly identified patients. The first three months of reporting, with around 80 per cent reporting compliance, therefore identified nearly 1,400 observed new cases of FGM in England alone.[85]

For the period September 2014 to March 2015 inclusive the same source indicates a cumulative total of 3,963 newly identified cases of FGM reported nationally, of which 60 were under the age of 18.

Other potential sources of information on FGM which arise are cervical screening services, family planning clinics and abortion services. These have yet to be put fully to use; their records may be submitted, at the discretion (and cost) of the organisations concerned.[86] Such services are, however, aspects of UK health care provision with which women in traditional communities are sometimes unfamiliar. Even if the facilities are in fact known about and valued by the women themselves, these services may be viewed hostilely by older, and especially male, members of the community (for example husbands) who have a controlling say in what 'their' womenfolk may or may not do.

Women with FGM are likely to be less frequent users of these services than other women; and, as with the first two, the third service, abortion, is a highly sensitive and confidential matter which, even if a woman does choose to use it, does not facilitate documentation of FGM.

These omissions in service use and in user documentation are important because they make it difficult to derive general figures for the incidence of FGM in the UK.

Sound information on the incidence of FGM at both national and local level is nonetheless critical to effective policy development. Certain local areas are thought to have high concentrations of women with FGM; provision of specialist FGM-related medical care in these areas is both necessary and dependent on information to identify locations as it becomes available.

UK Locations with a High Incidence of FGM

Data on which UK locations have the greatest incidence of women and girls with, or at risk of, FGM remains incomplete, but some estimates and formal records are already available. These suggest, in line with general demographic expectations, that FGM is a particular issue in (though not exclusive to) Britain's larger cities.

In the summer of 2014 the Home Secretary, Theresa May, announced a poster campaign[87] to advise women from the Somali, Kenyan and Nigerian[88] communities on how to ensure FGM does not happen (although, oddly, at the same time a Nigerian women was refused asylum on the grounds that her small daughters were not at risk of FGM).[89] The posters were displayed in 17 London boroughs and in Birmingham, Manchester, Leicester, Bristol, Sheffield, Liverpool and Cardiff[90] – presumably therefore the cities in England and Wales currently deemed to have the highest probability that FGM will occur.

In December 2014, however, further funding for community initiatives to prevent FGM was allocated largely to organisations based in the London area, on the basis that current figures justified such a distribution of monies.[91] It was not clear which hospitals had, as at the end of 2014, failed to report aggregated data, or where, therefore, prevalence is not yet known.

We may expect, with data now becoming more reliably available, that a more accurate picture in regard to the incidence of FGM in the UK will emerge in 2015.

Discuss this chapter at http://nofgmukbook.com/2015/01/29/chapter-1-demography-and-epidemiology-of-fgm/.

Endnotes

All weblinks accessed on 1 March 2015.

1   World Health Organization (2014) *Fact sheet No 241: Female Genital Mutilation.* Available at: http://www.who.int/mediacentre/factsheets/fs241/en/.
2   Mackie, G. (1996) Ending Footbinding and Infibulation: A Convention Account. *American Sociological Review* 61(6) (Dec., 1996): 996–1017. Available at: http://polisci2.ucsd.edu/gmackie/documents/MackieASR.pdf.
3   World Health Organization (2006) New Study Shows Female Genital Mutilation Exposes Women and Babies to Significant Risk at Childbirth. *The Lancet*, 2 June. Available at: http://www.who.int/mediacentre/news/releases/2006/pr30/en/.
4   Dirie, W. (2010) FGM Major Factor in High Maternal Mortality Rates in Africa. *Desert Flower – The Blog*, 2 August. Available at: http://warisdirie.wordpress.com/2010/08/02/fgm-major-factor-in-high-maternal-mortality-rates-in-africa-fgm-verantwortlich-fur-hohe-muttersterblichkeit-in-afrika/.
5   Women's Policy, Inc. (July 12, 1996). 'Female Genital Mutilation'. Women's Health Equity Act of 1996: Legislative Summary and Overview. *Women's Policy, Inc.* p. 48.
6   Broström, G. (1987) The Influence of Mother's Death on Infant Mortality: A Case Study in Matched Data Survival Analysis. *Scandinavian Journal of Statistics* 14(2): 113–23. Available at: http://www.jstor.org/discover/10.2307/4616055?uid=3738032&uid=2134&uid=2&uid=70&uid=4&sid=21102839085077.
7   Gughaju, B.B. (1985) The Effect of Previous Child Death on Infant and Child Mortality in Rural Nepal. *Stud Fam Plann* July–August, 16(4): 231–6. Available at: http://www.ncbi.nlm.nih.gov/pubmed/4035724.
8   Women Deliver (2013) *Invest in Maternal and Newborn Health.* Available at: http://www.womendeliver.org/knowledge-center/facts-figures/maternal-health/.

9   World Health Organization (2008) *Eliminating Female Genital Mutilation: An interagency statement UNAIDS, UNDP, UNECA, UNESCO, UNFPA, UNHCHR, UNHCR, UNICEF, UNIFEM, WHO*. Geneva: WHO Press. Available at: http://www.un.org/womenwatch/daw/csw/csw52/statements_missions/Interagency_Statement_on_Eliminating_FGM.pdf.

10   World Health Organization (2014) *Fact sheet No 241: Female Genital Mutilation*. Available at: http://www.who.int/mediacentre/factsheets/fs241/en/.

11   World Health Organization (2014) *Fact sheet No 241: Female Genital Mutilation*. Available at: http://www.who.int/mediacentre/factsheets/fs241/en/.

12   Von der Osten-Sacken, T., Uwer, T. (2007) Is Female Genital Mutilation an Islamic Problem? *Middle East Quarterly* 14(1): 29–36. Available at: http://www.meforum.org/1629/is-female-genital-mutilation-an-islamic-problem.

13   Dirie, W. (2010) Global Map Showing Prevalence of FGM. Available at: http://warisdirie.files.wordpress.com/2010/09/map_prevalence-of-fgm.jpg.

14   The Woman Stats Project (2011) Prevalence of Female Genital Cutting. Available at: http://womanstats.org/substatics/Prevalence%20of%20Female%20Genital%20Cutting_2011tif_wmlogo3.png.

15   UNICEF (2013) *Female Genital Mutilation/Cutting: A statistical overview and exploration of the dynamics of change*, UNICEF, New York, 2013. Available at: http://www.unicef.org/publications/files/FGM_Report_Summary_English__23Aug2013.pdf.

16   Amnesty International (2012) *Fight against Female Genital Mutilation Wins UN Backing*. Amnesty International, 26 November. Available at: http://www.amnesty.org/en/news/fight-against-female-genital-mutilation-wins-un-backing-2012-11-26.

17   UNICEF (2013) *Female Genital Mutilation/Cutting: A statistical overview and exploration of the dynamics of change*, UNICEF, New York. Available at: http://www.unicef.org/publications/index_69875.html.

18   Ahmed, N., Amin, S., Farrelly, P., Kinnane, S., Montminy, J., O'Kane, M., et al. (2013) FGM: The film that changed the law in Kurdistan – video. *Guardian*, 24 October. Available at: http://www.theguardian.com/society/video/2013/oct/24/fgm-film-changed-the-law-kurdistan-video.

19   Masinde, A. (2013) Into the Land of the Sabiny to Witness Female Circumcision. *New Vision: Uganda's Leading Daily*, 7 January. Available at: http://www.newvision.co.ug/mobile/Detail.aspx?NewsID=638695&CatID=396.

20   Brady, B., Cahalan, P. (2013) Special Report: Female genital mutilation – unreported, ignored and unpunished. *The Independent*, 6 January. Available at: http://www.independent.co.uk/news/uk/crime/special-report-female-genital-mutilation--unreported-ignored-and-unpunished-8439824.html.

21   World Health Organization (2014) *Fact sheet No 241: Female Genital Mutilation*. Available at: www.who.int/mediacentre/factsheets/fs241/.

22   World Health Organization (2008) *Eliminating Female Genital Mutilation: An interagency statement UNAIDS, UNDP, UNECA, UNESCO, UNFPA, UNHCHR,*

UNHCR, UNICEF, UNIFEM, WHO. Geneva: WHO Press. Available at: http://www.un.org/womenwatch/daw/csw/csw52/statements_missions/Interagency_Statement_on_Eliminating_FGM.pdf.

23 Batha, E. (2013) Baby Girls Cut in Secret as Burkina Faso Cracks Down on FGM. *Thomas Reuters Foundation*, 25 February. Available at: http://www.trust.org/item/20130225174500-wh24c/?source=shtw.

24 Ismail, E.A. (2012) Female Genital Mutilation Survey in Somaliland. *Edna Adan University Hospital, Somaliland, East Africa*. Available at: www.ednahospital.org/hospital-mission/female-genital-mutilation.

25 French, H.W. (1997) Africa's Culture War: Old Customs, New Values. *New York Times*, 2 February. Available at: http://www.nytimes.com/1997/02/02/weekinreview/africa-s-culture-war-old-customs-new-values.html.

26 FGM National Clinical Group (2013) *Historical & Cultural*. Available at: http://www.fgmnationalgroup.org/historical_and_cultural.htm.

27 Von der Osten-Sacken, T., Uwer, T. (2007) Is Female Genital Mutilation an Islamic Problem? *Middle East Quarterly* 14(1): 29–36. Available at: http://www.meforum.org/1629/is-female-genital-mutilation-an-islamic-problem.

28 Daily News Egypt (2013) FGM is not a Religious Duty Says Dar Al-Ifta Representative. *Daily News Egypt*, 23 June. Available at: http://www.dailynewsegypt.com/2013/06/23/fgm-is-not-a-religious-duty-says-dar-al-ifta-representative/.

29 *The Economist* (2007) A Little Less Purity Goes a Long Way. *The Economist*, 7 July. Available at: http://www.economist.com/node/9444160/.

30 FORWARD UK and The Islamic Cultural Centre and The London Central Mosque (2014) *FGM and Islam*. Available at: http://www.forwarduk.org.uk/key-issues/fgm/fgm-islam.

31 The Coexist Initiative (2012) *FGM*. Available at: http://www.coexistkenya.com/wp-content/uploads/2012/12/FGM-community-study.pdf.

32 Bartha, E. (2013) Baby Girls Cut in Secret as Burkina Faso Cracks Down on FGM. *Thomson Reuters Foundation*, 25 February. Available at: http://www.trust.org/item/20130225174500-wh24c/.

33 Feldman-Jacobs, C., Clifton, D. (2010) Female Genital Mutilation/Cutting: Data and trends update 2010. *Population Reference Bureau*. Available at: http://www.prb.org/Publications/Datasheets/2010/fgm2010.aspx.

34 World Health Organization (2014) *Female Genital Mutilation and Other Harmful Practices*. Available at: http://www.who.int/reproductivehealth/topics/fgm/fgm_trends/en/index.html.

35 World Health Organization (2014) *Fact sheet No 241: Female Genital Mutilation*. Available at: http://www.who.int/mediacentre/factsheets/fs241/en/.

36 Afya Bora (2013) *Female Genital Mutilation: Community based FGM-Project in Simanjiro-District/Manyara-Region*. Available at: http://www.afya-bora.com/fgm.htm.

37 World Health Organization (2014) *Fact sheet No 241: Female Genital Mutilation*. Available at: http://www.who.int/mediacentre/factsheets/fs241/en/.

38 FGM New Zealand (2011) *Beliefs and Issues*. Available at: http://www.fgm.co.nz/
    beliefs-and-issues.
39 Whitehorn, J. et al. (2002) Female Genital Mutilation: Cultural and
    psychological implications. *Sexual and Relationship Therapy*, 17:2. Available
    at: http://www.tandfonline.com/doi/abs/10.1080/14681990220121275#.
    VN1kzun30uU.
40 Barrett, H., Brown, K., Otoo-Oyortey, N., Naleie, Z., and West Midlands
    European Centre (2011) *Pilot Toolkit for Replacing Approaches to Ending FGM in
    the EU: Implementing Behaviour Change with Practising Communities*. Belgium:
    Coventry University (REPLACE). Available at: http://replacefgm.eu/sites/
    default/files/pressroom/REPLACE%20Toolkit.pdf.
41 BBC (2005) *Ethics Guide: Female circumcision/genital cutting*. Available at: http://
    www.bbc.co.uk/ethics/femalecircumcision/femalecirc_1.shtml.
42 FGM New Zealand (2011) *Beliefs and Issues*. Available at: http://www.fgm.co.nz/
    beliefs-and-issues.
43 Crossley, P. (2010) *Female Genital Mutilation*. Available at: http://www.
    patriciacrossley.com/FGM.htm.
44 Crossley, P. (2004) Africa/Vignettes/2004–5/Oct 104.htm. *Patricia Crossley*,
    1 October. Available at: http://www.patriciacrossley.com/Africa/
    Vignettes/2004-5/Oct%20104.htm.
45 Islam Ali, N. (9 September 2014) *Islam 21C.com*. Violence Against Women:
    Female Genital Mutilation. Available at: http://www.islam21c.com/politics/
    violence-against-women-female-genital-mutilation/.
46 World Health Organization (2004) *Female Genital Mutilation and Other Harmful
    Practices*. Available at: http://www.who.int/reproductivehealth/topics/fgm/
    fgm_reinfibulation_sudan/en/index.html.
47 African Women Organization (2009) *Myths and Justifications for the Perpetuation
    of FGM*.
48 IRIN (2005) Kenya: FGM among the Maasai Community of Kenya. Nairobi:
    IRIN, 1 March. Available at: http://www.irinnews.org/indepthmain.aspx?InDep
    thId=15&ReportId=62470.
49 Bahemuka, A. (2009) *Patriarchy Fuels Genital Mutilation*. Uganda: New Vision
    Online, 9 March. Available at: http://www.newvision.co.ug/D/8/459/674071.
50 Nordqvist, C. (15 February 2012) *Medical News Today*. What is Female Genital
    Mutilation? Knowledge Center (re Amnesty International advice). Available
    at: http://www.medicalnewstoday.com/articles/241726.php.
51 KTN Prime (2013) *A Story of Samburus who Kill Infants Born to Uncircumcised
    Mothers*. Kenya: The Standard Group, 27 October. Available at: http://www.
    standardmedia.co.ke/ktn/video/watch/2000071089/-a-cursed-culture-samburu-
    kill-unclean-infants.
52 Sheikh Abdi, M., Askew, I. (2009) *A Religious Oriented Approach to Addressing Female
    Genital Mutilation/Cutting among the Somali Community of Wajir, Kenya*. Available at:
    http://www.popcouncil.org/pdfs/frontiers/reports/Kenya_Somali_FGC.pdf.

53 Frazier, C. (2009) Women and Violence – A Briefing Book Complied for the Xenia Institute. Available at: http://www.wfok.org/files/5213/5731/4857/ Women_and_Violence_Briefing_Book.pdf.

54 Ali, N., Mohamud, A., Reymond, L. (1997) Female Genital Mutilation – The Facts. *PATH*. Available at: http://www.path.org/files/FGM-The-Facts.htm.

55 Countries and Their Cultures (2015) *Maasai*. Available from: http://www. everyculture.com/wc/Tajikistan-to-Zimbabwe/Maasai.html.

56 Mackie, G. (December 1996) Ending Footbinding and Infibulation: A Convention Account. *American Sociological Review* 61(6): 999–1017. Available at: http:// www.jstor.org/discover/10.2307/2096305?uid=3738032&uid=2&uid=4&s id=21105174417523.

57 FORWARD (2007) *A Statistical Study to Estimate the Prevalence of Female Genital Mutilation in England and Wales.*

58 Equality Now (2012) *Female Genital Mutilation: Report of a Research Methodological Workshop on Estimating the Prevalence of FGM in England and Wales*, London, March 22–23 2012. Available at: http://www.equalitynow.org/sites/default/files/ UK_FGM_Workshop_Report.pdf.

59 BBC News (2004) Female Circumcision 'on the Rise'. *BBC News*, 24 March. Available at: http://news.bbc.co.uk/1/hi/3564203.stm.

60 Bindel, J. (2014) *An Unpunished Crime: The Lack of Prosecutions for Female Genital Mutilation in the UK*. Available at: http://www.justiceforfgmvictims.co.uk/the-report/.

61 Macfarlane, A., Dorkenoo, E. (2014) *Female Genital Mutilation in England and Wales: Updated statistical estimates of the numbers of affected women living in England and Wales and girls at risk Interim report on provisional estimates*. Available at: http://www.trustforlondon.org.uk/research/publication/female-genital-mutilation-in-england-and-wales-updated-statistical-estimates-of-the-numbers-of-affected-women-living-in-england-and-wales-and-girls-at-risk-interim-report-on-provisional-estimates/.

62 Macfarlane, A., Dorkenoo, E. (2014) *Female Genital Mutilation in England and Wales: Updated statistical estimates of the numbers of affected women living in England and Wales and girls at risk Interim report on provisional estimates.*

63 Macfarlane, A., Dorkenoo, E. (2014) *Female Genital Mutilation in England and Wales: Updated statistical estimates of the numbers of affected women living in England and Wales and girls at risk Interim report on provisional estimates.*

64 Health & Social Care Information Centre (2014) *Female Genital Mutilation Datasets*. Available at: http://www.hscic.gov.uk/fgm.

65 Berry, V., Stanley, N., Radford, L., McCarry, M., Larkins, C. (2014) *Building Effective Responses: An independent review of violence against women, domestic abuse and sexual violence services in Wales*. pp. 35–6. Available at: http://wales.gov. uk/statistics-and-research/building-effective-responses-independent-review-violence-against-women/?lang=en.

66 Mhoja, M., Azong, J., Lawson, A. (2010) *DARF Baseline Survey in Glasgow and Edinburgh on the Beliefs, Views and Experiences of FGM*. Available at: http://www.darf.org.uk/page12.htm#141455.

67 Adams, L. (2013) *Female Genital Mutilation 'Rising in Soft-touch Scotland'*. BBC Scotland. Available at: http://www.bbc.co.uk/news/uk-scotland-24915967.

68 Baillot, H., Murray, N., Connelly, E., Howard, N. (2014) Tackling Female Genital Mutilation in Scotland – A Scottish Model of Intervention. Available at: http://www.scottishrefugeecouncil.org.uk/news_and_events/latest_news/2545_scottish_national_action_plan_needed_on_fgm.

69 Northern Ireland Department of Health, Social Services and Public Safety (2014) *Multi-Agency Practice Guidelines: Female Genital Mutilation*. Available at: http://www.dhsspsni.gov.uk/fmg.pdf.

70 Gulland, A. (2013) Fewer Younger Women are Undergoing Female Genital Mutilation, Study Finds. BMJ 2013;347:f4754. Available at: http://www.bmj.com/content/347/bmj.f4754#alternate.

71 Better Health Channel (2011) *Female Genital Mutilation*. Available at: http://www.betterhealth.vic.gov.au/bhcv2/bhcarticles.nsf/pages/Female_genital_mutilation.

72 Farina, P., Ortensi, L. (2012) *Migration Effect on the Future of Female Genital Mutilation: The case of African women in Italy*. Available at: http://epc2012.princeton.edu/papers/120790.

73 UNFPA Egypt (2008) *Who Performs It and When*. Available at: http://egypt.unfpa.org/english/fgmStaticpages/8b9eaf39-33d5-4ff5-924b-7e0b76d1091d/Who_performs_it_and_when.aspx.

74 UNICEF (2007) *Technical Note Coordinated Strategy to Abandon Female Genital Mutilation/Cutting in One Generation: A human rights-based approach to programming leveraging social dynamics for collective change* (p.33). Available at: http://www.childinfo.org/files/fgmc_Coordinated_Strategy_to_Abandon_FGMC__in_One_Generation_eng.pdf View shared post.

75 Equality Now (2012) *Female Genital Mutilation: Report of a Research Methodological Workshop on Estimating the Prevalence of FGM in England and Wales*, London, March 22–23 2012. Available at: http://www.equalitynow.org/sites/default/files/UK_FGM_Workshop_Report.pdf.

76 Macfarlane, A. (2013) Supplementary Written Evidence submitted by Alison Macfarlane, Professor of Perinatal Health, City University London. *International Development Committee*, 19 February. Available at: http://www.publications.parliament.uk/pa/cm201314/cmselect/cmintdev/107/107we05.htm.

77 Bentham, M. (2013) My Blueprint for Preventing FGM, by New Health Minister Jane Ellison. *London Evening Standard*, 25 October. Available at: http://www.standard.co.uk/news/uk/my-blueprint-for-preventing-fgm-by-new-health-minister-jane-ellison-8904147.html.

78 Keel, A., Moore, R. (2014) *Re: Female Genital Mutilation (letter to Scottish Health Professionals)*. Available at: http://www.sehd.scot.nhs.uk/cmo/CMO(2014)19.pdf.

79 Equality Now (2014) *Remembering Efua*. Available at: http://www.equalitynow.org/remembering_efua.

80 International Development Committee (2013) *Supplementary written evidence submitted by Efua Dorkenoo, OBE, Advocacy Director, Equality Now*. Available at: http://www.publications.parliament.uk/pa/cm201314/cmselect/cmintdev/107/107we04.htm.

81 International Development Committee (2013) *Supplementary written evidence submitted by Efua Dorkenoo, OBE, Advocacy Director, Equality Now*. Available at: http://www.publications.parliament.uk/pa/cm201314/cmselect/cmintdev/107/107we05.htm.

82 NHS England (2014) *Female Genital Mutilation Prevention Programme: Requirements for NHS staff*. Available at: http://www.england.nhs.uk/2014/12/08/fgm-prevention/.

83 Knighton, P., Audit Support Unit (2014) Female Genital Mutilation (FGM): September 2014, experimental statistics. *Health and Social Care Information Centre*, 16 October. Available at: http://www.hscic.gov.uk/catalogue/PUB15711.

84 Health & Social Care Information Centre (2014) *Female Genital Mutilation Dataset – Frequently Asked Questions*. Available at: http://www.hscic.gov.uk/media/15350/Frequently-Asked-Questions/pdf/FGM_Frequently_Asked_Questions.pdf.

85 Health & Social Care Information Centre (2015) *Find Data*. Available at: http://www.hscic.gov.uk/searchcatalogue?q=%22female+genital+mutilation%22&sort=Relevance&size=10&page=1#top.

86 Health and Social Care Information Centre (September 2014) *Female Genital Mutilation Prevalence Dataset: Frequently Asked Questions* (Point 5). Available at: http://www.hscic.gov.uk/media/16204/FGM-Frequently-Asked-Questions/pdf/FGM_Frequently_Asked_Questions.pdf.

87 Home Office (2014) *New Campaign Calls on Mothers and Carers to end Female Genital Mutilation*. GOV.UK, 2 June. Available at: https://www.gov.uk/government/news/new-campaign-calls-on-mothers-and-carers-to-end-female-genital-mutilation.

88 Burrage, H. (2014) *The UK Home Office (Says It) Has No Data On FGM Asylum Claims*. Available at: http://hilaryburrage.com/2014/05/19/uk-home-office-has-no-data-on-fgm-asylum-claims/.

89 Laville, S. (24 April 2014) Nigerian Mother Loses Battle to Stay in UK and Avoid FGM Risk to Daughters. *Guardian*. Available at: http://www.theguardian.com/uk-news/2014/apr/24/nigerian-mother-afusat-saliu-fight-asylum-fgm-daughters.

90 Davies, C. (2014) Female Genital Mutilation Poster Campaign Targets Mothers and Carers. *Guardian*, 2 June. Available at: http://www.theguardian.com/society/2014/jun/02/female-genital-mutilation-fgm-poster-campaign-mothers.

91 Department for Communities and Local Government, Home Office, Government Equalities Office and Williams, S. (2014) *Funding for Frontline Projects in Fight to End Female Genital Mutilation*. GOV.UK, 5 December. Available at: https://www.gov.uk/government/news/funding-for-frontline-projects-in-fight-to-end-female-genital-mutilation.

2　Socio-economic Analysis

Any serious look at the realities of female genital mutilation in modern Britain cannot be complete without an attempt at sociological analysis in parallel with empirical description and policy discussion.

FGM is a social and economic force as well as a fundamental issue around human rights and the imperative on us all to keep the most vulnerable and smallest members of our society safe.

It is important to consider how sociological and economic analysis can contribute to understandings of what FGM means in a modern, historically fully established Western society such as, but not exclusively, the nations of Europe, North America and Australia.

Sociology throws light on how FGM sits in the social order, and what its impacts for that order might be, overall and directly for those who experience it (whether at first hand or in other ways). Economics helps in considering the implications of FGM for the economies of communities and societies in which it is found.

The Sociology of FGM

There is a strong case for the contention that FGM creates a gendered 'underclass' wherever it occurs. Further, whilst in any community or society FGM is a marker for disempowerment and subordination to patriarchy, it may also be that in modern Western societies it is doubly disempowering because it puts women and girls even more firmly outside the mainstream.

So what is an 'underclass'? Generally it can be said to constitute a group of people with negligible power, influence or money, and extremely limited prospects. Usually individuals clustered in an 'underclass' also have little in the way of social capital – the know-how and contacts to make their way successfully and independently in the wider world.

Such a description is apposite to the position of many – though certainly not all – girls and women who have undergone FGM. To whatever degree, traditional expectations and prospects are ascribed (attributed to by others,

47

passively) rather than to be achieved (gained or earned, actively); their status might be akin to that of a low-status caste.

It is, however, important to be clear that 'underclass' is a term sometimes misunderstood. It has on occasion been appropriated by commentators (usually to the political right[1]) who use it loosely to suggest that those to whom it might apply are morally lacking – 'no moral compass' – or otherwise in some way to 'blame' for their misfortune. In this usage there are intimations that those who inhabit the underclass are 'feral', deviant by choice, perhaps drug users, or fecklessly unemployed. In that meaning of the term, the behaviour of the undeserving 'underclass' was claimed by some commentators, for instance, to be a significant factor in the 2011 riots[2] in the United Kingdom, mostly in London.

Others, however, contest this interpretation, which they claim with considerable justification to be a knowingly politically constructed notion, placing responsibility for worklessness and other characteristics onto individuals who experience it, rather than onto society and the way that the national economy operates.[3, 4]

Nor is this blame-laden interpretation the sense in which the term 'underclass' is utilised in this commentary. Rather, the suggestion is that society at large has placed some children in conditions of such disadvantage that they may be ill-equipped for normal social life: they have not been given any meaningful opportunity to gain a good education, or to acquire the social capital (know-how and contacts) which facilitate adult success.

In the sense of the word 'underclass' used in the analysis now offered here, ultimate responsibility for the situation in which affected children – in this case, girls with FGM – find themselves lies with society as a whole. We, members of the wider mainstream society, have not prevented the abuse which FGM constitutes, nor have we adequately resolved or repaired the damage which FGM inflicts on vulnerable children.

The term as used in this more formal sense carries no connotation of blame for those who are perceived as in an underclass or anomic (see below) situation. Instead, the idea of inequality as 'deserved' is challenged; there is no way in which the genital mutilation of a child can be her own responsibility. It is an act commissioned by adults within her specific community, but also permitted by default, if it comes about, by society as whole.

Children who are placed in an anomic or underclass situation because of FGM are children who have been grievously betrayed by those whose duty it is to protect them. These children are disempowered, perhaps even stigmatised, by what has been done to them, not by what they have themselves chosen to do.

FGM correlates closely with patriarchal oppression. One of the main rationales for FGM in traditional societies is that it prepares girls for marriage in communities where women who do not marry risk social ostracism and sometimes become literal outcasts.

In the worst case their physical survival may hinge upon their FGM status: no FGM, no adult status, access to support, not even perhaps to a roof over their heads, not permitted to handle food and other fundamental essentials, let alone engage in normal social interaction. Without FGM women may remain forever 'girls', perhaps barred from family and community occasions, or even funerals and similar events, with no standing or say in their communities[5] – a situation which may be made even worse if, potentially, it is linked to non-ownership of land,[6] perhaps, because a woman is denied adult status.

The cruel irony is that, whilst in modern societies FGM is in theory totally irrelevant to the normal status of women, the very act of inflicting it in a more open modern context may result in the anomic status – 'anomie' – which in traditional societies FGM is intended to avoid.

Anomie and social frameworks

'Anomie' is a term used to describe situations or social frameworks in which certain people have 'no place' – or in literal translation from the French, 'no name'.

The concept was first used by the French sociologist Emile Durkheim (1858–1917),[7] whose book *Suicide*[8] explored the isolating situations which lead individuals to attempt to end their lives. In his book, Durkheim demonstrates that suicide results principally from a lack of integration of the individual into society. He offers an understanding of the contexts (or lack thereof) which lead to suicide, and examines its psychological impact on the victim, family and society.

It can be argued that in some traditional societies anomie is the situation also confronting girls and women who resist FGM, defying the expectation or demand that they undergo mutilation. They risk being left to fend for themselves in communities where marriage is essential if a woman is to survive. She must be either the property of her father or of her husband, and there comes a time – often immediately, or even before, she reaches the menarche – when that transition needs to have been effected.[9]

If this transfer of 'ownership' does not occur, a girl or woman may find herself without support, alone and alienated, discarded by her family and peers. In some communities her physical existence may even be endangered. (It is important to stress that such jeopardy applies only in certain, not all, contexts. There are few imperatives in FGM which are universally applicable.)

This lack of a supporting social and even physical framework – outcast with no status or influence – is archetypically anomic.

But unlike some forms of, for example, depressive and other psychological illness which may lead to conventional forms of anomie, avoiding exclusion in the contexts of FGM-practising communities is externally negotiable: girls in practising communities with FGM will be 'safe'.

In some cases the girl will be compelled by adult group members, perhaps by brute force, to undergo the ritual and she will then be a full member of her community; she may even elect to undergo it of her own volition. But it has also been suggested that girls judged to be headstrong may be required to undergo FGM as a method of control.

Further, a child's immediate elevation via FGM to adult status may not serve her well. Adult status may confer additional rank and autonomy in her community, but it does not confer additional wisdom or judgement, thereby leaving her, as some informal commentaries have pointed out, at greater risk of ill-advised decisions made on the basis of her new 'adult' standing.

FGM is often perceived as an insurance against misfortune, a way to gain proper status for female adults; hence the social, economic and basic life imperatives to enforce the mutilation. It is in that economic sense that FGM may be seen as a 'kindness', a way in some cases for parents and others to ensure (they hope) that their daughters' futures are secured, that they do not end up outside the framework of the group in which they live.

Secret societies

In parts of Western Africa such as Sierra Leone, Liberia and Guinea, the major moving force behind FGM is a secret organisation[10] – important, in countries with fragile formal cohesion – such as that dedicated to the spirit Sande. The Sande Society, like similar women's organisations in the region such as the Bondo, is a powerful organisation which evolved centuries ago,[11] if not even longer into the past. It is a vehicle for tight control by a coterie of senior women – often from large and wealthy families, the *grandes dames* of these African societies – whose word, in conjunction with the powerful men in the group, is law.

The Sande Society acts as a corporate organisation[12] which dictates what will happen across a significant range of activities and behaviours. Along with male members of any local parallel secret societies (for instance, the Poro[13]), Sande members have huge influence in the distribution of wealth and power.[14]

Girl initiates to Sande undergo training in 'how to be a woman' and are then subjected to FGM before they are declared to have achieved adulthood. Once initiated their secret society provides these women with life-long benefits such as the right to meet amongst themselves without permission from anyone – a privilege not given in other spheres of adult life, where permission from husbands must be sought for many activities and tasks.

Marriage normally follows rapidly after initiation into adulthood for women in the Sande, Bondo (Bundu) and other similar secret societies.[15] The initiation programme itself, including FGM, is often a very expensive process in which families invest hard-earned savings in order to gain prestige and future financial security for both themselves and their daughters. Girls are married, usually very young (often as part of an economic exchange, and sometimes as an additional wife), to men deemed suitable by the potential brides' families. These men may then select their wives quite literally from a parade of initiated and just-circumcised 'women' (many of them in fact still young girls).

The criticality of this transaction in economic terms is illustrated by the fact that subsistence farming families may pay the cost of an entire harvest to initiate their daughters into Bondo. This huge investment – sometimes exploited further by excisors who stand to gain economically and in terms of status from the transaction – indicates to the wider community that the farmers are economically viable; and it ensures too that the daughter is not stigmatised, nor her adult existence jeopardised because she has not been accepted by the Sande.[16]

The supposed (and in some specific respects genuine) 'benefits' of initiation are not, however, always appreciated in the present day by intended recipients, who opt for Western ideas of education rather than their traditionally assigned status as traded wives.[17] There are numerous reports of girls seeking to escape the initiation process and various modern charitable bodies have set up 'safe houses' for unwilling intended victims.[18]

Reports[19] also show that rebellion by potential initiates is not well tolerated. In previous times there was a custom of 'arranged' kidnapping to initiate girls whose families could not afford the ceremony.[20] Impoverished parents knew on which day to ensure their daughters were alone outside the house, to be ostensibly abducted for 'cutting'; or, even more brutally, a man who cannot afford a wife may simply kidnap a girl, have her mutilated, rape her, and thereby trap her in a 'marriage' with him.[21] There are also now cases of girls and women who have been kidnapped (in the literal sense) and forced to undergo FGM; some of those responsible have been found guilty in courts of law and sent to prison.[22]

Further, the *grandes dames* of the Sande (known as 'Sowei') and other similar communities or societies have much to lose if they stop practising FGM. Their status and income depends on the continuation of the practice, and it is difficult in traditional communities to identify and establish alternatives which substitute this trade for a more benign professional service.

Such arrangements are about neither 'faith' nor harmless 'custom'. FGM is in this context about wealth and influence; many communities continue therefore to regard it as essential; in some cases it is now carried out earlier in childhood so the authorities will not become alerted,[23] or inflicted on children unexpectedly without warning,[24] or in babyhood.[25] That way, there is no opportunity to escape the mutilation or to stymie the economic exchange which follows it.

A society such as the Sande, which rests on the authority of 'spirits', is usually one in which hidden or secret practices are beyond question – an issue recognised as fundamental in the modern context to finding ways to eradicate FGM.

Thus, what began as a traditional practice may over time emerge as a religious diktat, at least at the level of local communities. It is these cultural considerations of chastity and purity which have resulted in FGM becoming enmeshed, long after it began, in some places with matters of religion, especially some versions of Islam, Judaism and Coptic Christianity.

The practice began even before these faiths took shape, but in some communities FGM and local religious beliefs have coalesced over time to the extent that it is almost impossible for community members to disengage one from the other.

This religious element is acknowledged by, for example, law enforcement strategies in Africa as well as elsewhere. For instance, the Office of the Director of Public Prosecutions in Kenya has recently published a report on FGM and CEFM, together with guidance on sensitisation to the issues, which includes recognition of the linkage with 'sunna' in Islam, in preparation for energetic policing to stop the practices.[26, 27]

But FGM is nonetheless an overtly socio-economic and a covertly practised activity. It is an element of deeply embedded traditional belief which has emerged with different rationales and modes of delivery over many centuries.

Group think

Not all FGM-practising communities have secret societies (these are a particularly sub-Sahara African phenomenon), and there are also other considerations. In many traditional societies the group or community has an importance beyond that of any, or at least most, of its members. And those who do have significance and influence as individuals need to have ways of exerting their will which do not break the sense of collectiveness.

FGM provides a powerful tool in this respect.

One of the major unspoken rationales for FGM is that women who have undergone it are deprived both physically and psychologically of much (some) of their sexuality. Girls and young women in traditionally practising communities are believed to be by nature sexually rampant; without FGM it is thought they will be promiscuous[28] and that lineage and 'purity' – very important aspects of the local economy and family finances – will be compromised.

Girls are therefore intentionally ritually harmed, usually before puberty, so they will procure a high bride price and be submissive to their husbands, who command full authority to support and take care of their wives, or not, as they wish.

Likewise, for those societies where Sande[29, 30] or similar organisations hold sway, the most powerful are those who are closely associated with the mutilation itself. In Sande society 'cutters' and their male counterparts, the Poro,[31] generally have the greatest influence and the most entitlement (and vested interest) to maintain the established order of things.

And excisors also stand to benefit the most directly from what Gerry Mackie calls the 'belief trap'.[32] Given the dire outcomes which may come to pass – for the girl, her future husband, her babies and her community – if mutilation does not occur, no one is prepared to risk abandoning the practice. There is therefore considerable reason in some communities for those who conduct the procedures to ensure that these feared outcomes are taken very seriously.[33]

There are nonetheless risks also attached to the genital mutilation of girls – not least, that the children will die or become permanently disabled. It is important for the group that these risks are managed in a way which does not reduce the authority of fathers and husbands, or of the mutilators themselves.

Considerable emphasis may therefore be placed on the role of spirits and similar beings. If a girl becomes ill or dies after the ritual, it may be made clear that bad spirits, perhaps already possessing the child, are responsible for the outcome.

Indeed, in some communities, girls who die following FGM are simply cast aside from their village and their bodies, believed to be a curse on the community, are left in the forest to be devoured by wild animals.[34] There can be no greater anomie than that.

Control of the wilful?

Beyond this there is also evidence from some accounts that FGM may be performed on girls who are perceived to be particularly wilful. One (male African) commentator reports[35] that women are disciplined for 'perceived crimes they have never committed'. Others have claimed similarly.

It may be that in some communities FGM is perceived as a mode of control of, or punishment for, general behaviour as well as sexual activity.

Such perceptions lie parallel to traditional notions of family honour. In both cases, stepping out of line can result not just in social rejection (anomie) but in the ultimate sanction, death. And this applies whether the alleged miscreant is in a traditional society or a community arising in a first-world country from the diaspora.

Honour killings – to which we shall return in Chapter 3 – continue to occur in Britain, along with grooming and what amounts to child 'marriage' (community-sanctioned paedophilia) and other atrocities. All are indicators of deep-rooted fear of or disrespect for girls and women as individuals in their own right, and of the fundamental expectation by the men involved that they may of right treat women as owned objects.

Thus, the more a girl or woman baulks at these assumptions and attempts to assert herself, the more vigorously these sanctions may be applied. Those with the greatest influence in such communities (usually men) cannot afford the group as an entity to be challenged by its less powerful members.

Prospects in the new world

And here we find the perilous bridge which links the experience of girls and women in the old world with their lives in the new.

In some respects it may be doubly dangerous for young women isolated in traditional communities in the modern world to rebel against their ascribed 'owned' status. Not only is this a direct threat to the previously unchallenged social order and status of their elders and betters, but the traditional sanctions may not be enforceable.

By rebelling, young women are in effect challenging the foundations of everything which holds together their seniors' communities.

It was one thing to demur when the only alternative prospect was exclusion from any means of survival. It is another thing, far more destabilising of communities attempting to maintain the traditions and hierarchies of centuries, when young women rebel because they have a realistic prospect of autonomous adulthood, totally away from that stultifying social order.

Instead of being outcast without FGM, as would be expected in the time-established way, a girl who wants to escape mutilation and the pre-ordained traditional social frameworks may find that she is not, as everyone has threatened, anomic, lost without any support or alternatives.

With good fortune, the big wide world of the modern order may offer young women who eschew tradition new opportunities and a freedom beyond any thus far imagined or previously available; but an ill-wind could see those who reject the old ways abandoned by their families and communities, with no support anywhere else. In some traditionally practising locations this situation has led to women selling the sole commodity they have – their own bodies. (Similar fate may become women who are abandoned by their husbands because, for example, they have obstetric fistula.[36, 37])

Small wonder then that recalcitrant daughters in traditional communities set within a modern context may even find themselves in great personal danger. Their own community may perceive them as jeopardising everything which has meaning in that group, a threat which may well be met with whatever sanction or force is required to prevent it.

One only has to observe the grim determination of those traditionalists who oppose girls' education in some parts of Nigeria,[38] Pakistan,[39] and so on, to see that women who resist the old ways, whatever the form of their resistance, are sometimes in deadly peril.

Fundamental tensions

For young women who refuse FGM, then, fate may or may not be kind. With enough encouragement and help they may become autonomous members of mainstream society, educated, employed and self-sufficient.[40] But at the other extreme they could instead become another victim of kidnap, forced marriage, brutally delivered mutilation, honour killing or trafficking.

Personal outcomes are therefore uncertain if dissenters seek a life in modern Western society, whilst still their traditional community steadfastly values unquestioned group cohesion more than notions of individual well-being, let alone any individual's human rights.

Even FGM apart, these deep-rooted and fundamental tensions between the old and new social orders have many repercussions, especially for young people.

At schools in Western society children learn not only the tools of a technological society, but also the ethos of democracy – that ideally each of us as an adult is autonomous, responsible for ourselves and entitled to the means to reach whatever 'potential' we may have.

Sometimes these massive contradictions between the expectations for young people with roots both in deeply traditional societies and in modern ones prove too much. For women, with so little autonomy, the conflicting demands may be almost irreconcilable, as is illustrated for instance in one study of married women in Iran.[41]

Research indicates that for some of the girls the teenage years may be blighted by withdrawal and perhaps psychological illness: the incidence of psychiatric conditions is significantly above the general norm[42, 43] for some young (and older) women facing ethnic cultural discrepancies.

It is also possible that some young men in their teens and twenties attempt to resolve these contradictions by adopting overtly active roles in extreme religious or political-military organisations, or in other groups or gangs: there are young men, for instance, who may even go abroad to join the jihad or, more probably (as with some girls[44, 45]), become involved in damaging gang behaviour nearer home.[46, 47]

In all these cases the contradictions and difficulties which young people from traditional communities may face when they seek also to accommodate modern Western societies are manifold.

For girls and young women from FGM traditional practising communities, the road towards adulthood in a first-world society may be strewn with hazards potentially leading to exclusion from the mainstream, perhaps anomie. The dilemmas may be almost irreconcilable. Do they or don't they accede to FGM? Do they buy into the modern narratives about education and personal autonomy? Is marriage, especially early, forced or arranged marriage, inevitable? Could it be dangerous to resist? Will it be possible to withstand the conflicting pressures in such formative years, or is withdrawing into oneself an increasingly likely outcome?

Whilst the perils of FGM anywhere are massive, the socio-economic (as opposed to health) complexities for young women from traditional practising communities of the issues in modern societies are of an even greater dimension. As in other 'traditional-to-modern' transition contexts, the major objective – to move away from individually damaging collective behaviours and towards greater personal autonomy – may be clear, but the social and other costs are not. Anomie or autonomy? It could be a close call.

From anomie to underclass

People who may be in an 'underclass' are by definition often invisible to those in the mainstream.

The concept of underclass is generally perceived as comprising those who are 'underprivileged' to the extent that they are excluded from mainstream society, having little money, few other resources and the least power.

From the perspective of the powerful, these people are of little interest. They are unlikely to express any public opinion or to vote, they are often ill-prepared for employment and they are usually isolated and unconnected with each other. They are often also subject to ill-health and have little energy left to tackle any challenge except the daily grind.

In other words, the underclass (or classes) comprises people who are anomic, alienated from society as most of us experience it.

Likewise, people in the underclass often present little risk to the mainstream; they have few or no resources to create a viable threat. This social class is rarely 'social' in the normal sense of the word. It is a non-collective assembled only in the sense that it comprises individual people who have no place in 'normal' society. United action will only occur if the majority of individuals in the assemblage perceive group oppression, and that is unlikely to happen.

Nonetheless, some of those who, for whatever reason, find themselves in the underclass, the anomic and the lost or alienated may present a threat to property or the social order because, in common with everyone else, they need food, shelter and other human comforts; and if these requirements are not available via the prescribed route, they may be obtained in less socially acceptable or legal ways. (Prostitution is a known outcome for women in traditionally practising societies who have not been 'cut'; their bodies are the only resource they can sell.[48])

The higher social orders may not hear the concerns of the anomic, but these elevated orders are frequently very keen to maintain law, uphold their status and protect their interests – with the result that people in the underclass may be subject to very active levels of policing and criminal justice.

Power

One telling way to represent the active constraints placed upon those with least influence anyway is to consider pathologies of power, a notion examined particularly by Paul Farmer,[49] a professor of medical anthropology, in the context of structural violence – which he defines as any offence against human dignity.

In Farmer's analysis the focus is often on infectious diseases, which can be seen as intimately related to the incidence also of injustice, poverty and malnutrition. Pathologies of power, Farmer tells us, are connected very directly with the social conditions (set by the powerful) determining who will suffer and who will not.

And just as infectious diseases fit the model for eradication, so too does FGM. Both could be mitigated, if not stopped, by appropriate socio-economic measures, and both arise because of human interaction.

In traditional FGM-practising societies, mutilation confirms the powerlessness of those on whom it is done – at least unless they also become 'professional' excisors and are thereby beneficiaries of the patriarchy which their actions uphold, reluctant of course to relinquish their income and influence.[50]

Even then, however, the power relationship between the men and women tends to be unequal, because of inequalities in other factors such as ownership of resources and access to additional forms of control.

First-world contexts

In modern Western societies, however, it is the act of FGM which itself creates the scenario which that actively commissioned harm is intended to mitigate.

Whilst the evidence continues to be partial, it is likely that some girls in the UK who undergo FGM disengage from school in much the same way as girls who experience it in traditional contexts. The reasons for this are physical, psychological and social: their bodies are damaged and so may be their confidence and outlook on the future.

Further, it is likely that in some cases the act of FGM, as in traditional societies, will be followed by *de facto*, if not overt, forced marriage or confirmation of betrothal. The girl child may have become a promised bride (or experience actual 'marital' rape) and her fate will be as the possession of her intended husband; investment in her education is now at an end; and so too, therefore, are curtailed the prospects of adult autonomy for this girl or young woman.

With perhaps few or no formal qualifications, and in any case with little social capital beyond her narrowing circle, some girls – but certainly not all; there are dramatic exceptions – are unlikely to find employment which offers independence.

In addition some of these young women may migrate on marriage from the household of their own fathers to those of their husband's parents.[51] Whilst current research does not reveal their FGM status, it is clear that for numbers of young brides this is a claustrophobic or even overtly oppressive regime, which reports of gendered violence suggest still exist in some families in the UK and other Western nations, as well as in more traditional societies.

The links (or not) between FGM and other forms of gendered violence and containment, such as issues around family 'honour', are yet to be clarified, but in some instances mothers-in-law may act as keepers, sometimes exploiters, of their sons' wives. The senior woman, most probably the head of a multi-generational household or domain, exerts her influence via the unquestioned authority of the men in her family.

Patriarchy

Patriarchy is maintained through this established social order – as with the act of FGM itself, at arm's length – but it is real. Its agents may themselves often be female, but they are agents of the oppression of women nonetheless through the mechanism, in the perception of some observers at least, of false consciousness (being unable to see things such as unequal relationships as they probably are). In this case their belief may be that the women have power; but that conviction is ultimately belied by the socio-economic evidence that real influence lies with a hierarchy of powerful people, the most influential of all being certain males.

And thus do the agents of the traditional way of things seek to perpetuate the control of women, in the modern societies as in the developing world. Patriarchy is at its most powerful when it is 'invisible', when the social order cannot be conceived by those who experience it in any other way.

First, access to education, financial independence and personal autonomy are curtailed through a life-threatening physical assault; men may refuse to accept as brides, or pay a bride price for, young women whose virginity is not (supposedly) assured by FGM. Second, early marriage becomes containment and control. Then, lastly, a new generation of girls who may experience the same fate is born and the process must be repeated.

One fundamental aspect of FGM is, or has historically by tradition and custom been – perhaps now perpetrated without knowing reference to origins – to perpetuate patriarchy. When FGM occurs, that objective is accomplished by the creation of an anomic, gendered underclass of people who have no power or influence of their own.

Racism

It might be said that there is an additional factor at play when FGM creates anomie in the historically developed nations – most of these nations place people with brown or black skin at a disadvantage; racism by white people against black ones is an element in social stratification which increases hardship for many.

There is at present, however, little information to determine whether racism and FGM interact to shape anomic, underclass experience independently of, or additionally to, the act of mutilation alone. One factor to be considered is, however, that FGM is almost always, except perhaps when 'medicalised', inflicted on girls by women of similar cultural or tribal affiliations.

In general, people in the Western tradition oppose FGM even though it has been tolerated, even promoted, by people from various parts of the developing world. Historically at least, questioning FGM was sometimes dangerous for those from other, Western cultures who attempted to stop it, as is evidenced by the 'Clitoridectomy Controversy' in Kenya in the late 1920s.[52]

On the other hand, however, the reluctance in historically Western countries actually to stop mutilation might be construed as a form of racism. There is a widely held view that this non-interference arises from a sense that FGM is a cultural observance which must be left unchallenged.

From this perspective 'political correctness' is at the root of the failure to stop FGM.

Insofar as this belief is well placed – a matter itself of debate – there may be substance to the notion that white girls must be protected from 'barbarism', whilst black girls should not be accorded that protection because their 'culture' demands it. If the anxiety about 'interfering' with customs harmful to black children is greater than it is for similar hypothetical action to protect white children, this anxiety could be thought to add substance to the underclass disadvantages accrued by girls who experience FGM.

As before, however, any additional weighting towards the creation of a gendered underclass which accrues from racist or cultural assumptions may be different depending on context. The significance of this factor is perhaps different, depending on whether the discussion relates to traditionally practising countries or to those of the diaspora, the diaspora being increasingly scattered populations of people with a common origin in (from) a smaller geographic area – that is, in this case, people from FGM traditionally practising communities who have left for Europe, North America, Australia, and so on.

Survivors and survival mechanisms

Nonetheless, it is critical to recognise that this dislocation via FGM of girls and women from resources and influence is real, but absolutely not, in Western or other societies, inevitable.

There are many striking examples of women who have not only survived FGM, but also defied it. Of those who become publicly visible, most rail against it and demonstrate by their fulminations the victory of personal determination over millennia of oppression. To these women is owed boundless gratitude and respect.

But still there is little to help us understand how some girls who undergo FGM emerge inveighing against it, or simply focused on a positive future for themselves and their daughters, whilst many others, perhaps the majority, find the challenge to survive is itself enough. As we saw in Chapter 1, FGM can make a person physically ill for her whole life, and without excellent obstetric care, it can also damage or kill her babies.

And FGM can and often does also – like other forms of child abuse which may not be so physically harming (some are) – trigger lifelong psychological unease, distress, or overt mental ill-health. Against these steep disadvantages, it is unsurprising that adult responses to the childhood hurt and (sometimes perceived) betrayal of FGM may vary.

So what differentiates the women who have undergone FGM and still emerge strong and autonomous from those who may or cannot do so? Personality perhaps excepted, very largely we do not know.

Nor do we know much about which sociological factors internal to communities enable mothers and daughters to resist FGM, whilst others do not.

Some external interventions have been shown to be of more value than others, but the socio-economic factors within practising communities which influence responses are a complex business, in first-world diaspora-receiving countries[i] as well as in traditional contexts.

As the example of Egypt demonstrates, however, even high educational attainment is not enough to protect girls and women from FGM in all circumstances.[53]

On a broader basis these questions are at present very hard to answer; but deeper insights into the economics of FGM could help to show how modern social structures might dis-enable the mechanisms which reinforce this blight on the lives of girls and women. It is to this theme that we now turn.

The Economics of FGM

If social class is based in large part on power and influence, that power in turn is based on access to resources.

Economics is therefore a critical aspect of FGM, and in many more ways than is sometimes assumed. The costs are multiple, and to a degree invisible to those involved; they are enmeshed in the basic social constructions of the group, entrenched within a 'belief trap' – a self-enforcing belief which cannot be reviewed because to do so might itself have devastating costs. (To give one behaviour-influencing example of belief traps, if a man believes that sexual contact with a clitoris will kill him, he is unlikely to want to put that belief to the test himself. A more directly economics-related example might be unwillingness to risk loss of bride price or dowry by refusing to have one's daughters undergo FGM.)

Also, beyond the direct costs of harmful but apparently immutable beliefs, there are also the costs of campaigners against FGM not always knowing which socio-economic drivers are optimal for behaviour change. Why, for instance, do alternative rites of passage work more effectively in some contexts than others, even amongst communities which have traditionally maintained that practice?

And, perhaps most critically of all, how much in the way of funding and resources currently consumed by FGM and by efforts to erase it could be directed more effectively at the well-being and health of people across the world, if FGM were no more?

---

i   These variations between European countries in readiness for change are the subject of research by REPLACE2. See: http://www.replacefgm2.eu/.

Local economics

Most immediately, as we have already seen, there is the economic market which FGM provides, in girls and women as chattels, services provided by mutilators, people who arrange associated celebrations, those who are part of the initiation preparations and bush schools (where such are elements of the practice), and in the marriage-related activities which follow the mutilation.

Alongside these services and provisions or offers is the necessity traditionally to raise the wherewithal to pay for the celebrations and/ or ceremonies (now less likely than previously, or perhaps conducted in private to evade the law,[54] but usually a responsibility of the girl's father) and to pay the bride price, that is, to buy the bride (the responsibility of the girl's husband-to-be and his family).

The ceremonies associated with FGM itself may involve as much as the proceeds of an entire year's harvest; whilst in some communities (perhaps more often Middle Eastern ones – though in, for example, Indonesia, mass ceremonies have begun to be introduced[55, 56]) there is little overt communal engagement, in others (traditional African communities in some cases) the 'festivities' may be prolonged and require considerable outlay.

Similarly, in some communities bride price may be nominal, but in others it is closely negotiated – cash, or perhaps livestock, or other valuables or services – and refunds[57] may be demanded if the bride falls short in some way, particularly is she has not undergone FGM or is deemed impure or inadequate. (This potential difficulty is another pressing reason for the bride's father to ensure she is mutilated.)

In communities where resources are scarce, it may be that these economic transactions – the actions required to ensure the satisfactory sale of a female child or young woman to her new keeper – can comprise a significant part of a local economy.[58]

It may be difficult to see how this complex interplay of different local economic interests can be broken. And to add to this complexity, there are now suggestions that in some cases cutters are being paid even more if they pretend to mutilate severely, but actually inflict slighter damage. How this will play out over a longer period in the struggle to eliminate FGM remains to be seen.

In the meantime, much has already been reported about the dependency of operators on the income from their business. It may be possible to exchange their tools for a goat or other type of employment, but the rewards can be less and the prestige accrued to a perpetrator will often be lost if she changes occupations. The mutilator's role is steeped in history and mystique; the goat farmer's role generally is not.

There is therefore a cost beyond the immediately economic in requiring mutilators to change their jobs; little discussion is, however, available concerning the economic value of the prestige which comes with the influence accorded lead members of organisations such as the Sande Society – or of the male equivalent societies such as Poro.

But that is not all. Other economic players have an interest which also needs to be recalibrated if FGM stops. There may for instance need to be alternative reasons for the 'leisure industry' retailers in the community to lay on elaborate celebrations, and there are the interests of those who initiate the girls and negotiate the ensuing marriages to consider.

Further, the market in agricultural goods – if such have traditionally been the source of income for initiation activities – may have become distorted through the reliance on conspicuous consumption during FGM ceremonies. Again, recalibration in different respects may be required if these ceremonies come to an end.

And then there is the whole matter of the negotiation of who marries whom. How does a potential husband acquire a(nother) suitable wife if the traditional markers of a good purchase have been removed? How is a fair price to be determined?

All these are serious questions. The critical point is that they are not 'moral' or 'social' matters. They are to do with the fundamentals of the distribution of hard-gained resources in situations where scarcity is often in any case a pressing concern.

It may be that the relatively low positive impact of some alternative rites of passage is at least in part because the substitute activities do not adequately recognise these economic challenges.

Addressing directly beliefs held for hundreds of years remains critically fundamental to efforts to eradicate FGM; but it also must be recognised that some people in practising societies may (in the absence of persuasive alternative incentives) have economic reasons to ensure that these beliefs and practices continue as they are and always have been.

There is serious incentive for some to encourage perceptions and belief systems (perhaps concerning mystery, witchcraft, and so on) which bolster ideas about why FGM remains a requirement of any cohesive traditional society.

Human and health costs

FGM is a life-threatening practice. Estimates vary, but between 10 per cent and 30 per cent of girls and women who undergo genital mutilation are thought to die from causes directly related to it. Some deaths are in the immediate aftermath (haemorrhage and shock are amongst the major factors here) and some are in the years that follow, perhaps after extended periods of pain and ill-health. The hazards of FGM, often also associated with early marriage and childbirth, are multiple and serious, lasting through generations.[59]

One study of FGM obstetric costs in six African countries (a 2006 WHO study of 28,393 women)[60] suggests that, with a potential relevant population of 2,800,000 15-year-old girls undergoing FGM in a year, obstetric haemorrhage alone will cost 130,000 life years – the equivalent of losing half a month from each individual's life span.

Whilst obstetric haemorrhage is but one of many hazards associated with FGM, the conclusion of the authors of this WHO study is that relatively very modest investment in preventing FGM Types II and III (see p. 29) could be offset by the savings from preventing obstetric complications.

Similar considerations may apply to ill-health related to FGM in other ways. One instance of this may be the avoidance of HIV and AIDS, which is prevalent in some FGM-practising communities, and which is more easily contracted by those who have had FGM. The direct economic health costs of AIDS in some communities, and the loss of economic return or capacity in those who are ill, are likely to be highly significant.

It may follow therefore that, were other health damage from FGM also to be included, investment in prevention would show a positive indirect economic return as well as (most crucially of all) in human terms.

FGM harm, as has many times been demonstrated, includes death and disability of many kinds, at the point of mutilation and throughout a woman's life. Even if she survives, she may be seriously and permanently incapacitated, immediately and/or after future childbirth; and her children may be at risk as well. Tellingly, there is a tradition which says women must face 'three sorrows' in their lives: when they are first mutilated, on their wedding night (and sometimes for months beyond…) as they endure attempts at penetration, and when they give birth, with a raised risk of infant mortality or morbidity or, for themselves, obstetric fistula.[61]

It is not 'only' FGM itself which causes pain and destroys well-being. Obstetric fistula,[62] for instance, renders many of its victims unable to engage in community activities long term, thereby reducing women to abject poverty, and even their well children to extreme vulnerability.

Infant harm

It is known that infants whose mothers die in these sorts of circumstances are twice as likely not to survive as others whose mothers live.[63] Risks are also therefore likely to attach to infants and children whose mothers are seriously incapacitated, even if they somehow continue to live. And for every infant who dies, more general statistics on infant mortality and morbidity suggest that ten children will experience some degree of incapacity although they survive.[64]

And there are also other sources of FGM-induced incapacity, amongst them the long-term psychological impacts of the original assault and trauma,[65] and of the ensuing states of dependency. The degree of permanent impact may vary, depending on the context and extent of the damage, but it is always damaging.

That FGM has negative health and well-being impacts is not open to question. The aggregate costs of this impact remain, however, to be explored.

The costs of medical treatment, or of its absence, for girls and women with FGM are almost certainly significant at the level of local and national expenditure.

The absence of medical care may be even more expensive to economies than its provision: the authors of the above obstetric costs calculated costs using a discounting model which accords greater (negative) value to early death than to later damage, on the basis that more economically productive years are lost.

Medicalisation

The World Health Organization (WHO) has identified the medicalisation of FGM[66, 67] as one of the most substantive blocks to its eradication. Estimates vary, but in some countries such as Egypt[68] most mutilation is now carried out, or at least supervised, by modern, formally trained clinicians, despite legislation to ban it.[69] (It is also thought girls in the UK are sent abroad, for example to Dubai and Singapore, for medicalised FGM.[70])

At low levels of intervention, girls may be sent for tetanus injections and local anaesthesia beforehand, but in significant numbers of cases they actually attend clinics set up for FGM. Sometimes hospitals even offer 'packages' whereby maternal delivery, post-delivery care and infant FGM are all provided for a set fee.

Usually, the clinicians involved see their fee as a useful addition to low salaries, for providing a 'safe' way for girls to undergo FGM.

This perception is likely to be challenged in the next few years, as doctors, dentists, nurses and health care assistants accused of doing FGM in locations as wide apart as, for example, Egypt, Australia and the UK find themselves facing their professional conduct bodies and the law courts.[71]

How these encounters with the legal system affect clinicians' behaviour may depend on the status of their occupation in the country in question. Where health workers' wages are very low, occasional risks of sanction alone may not be adequate deterrence, especially if the operator is able to rationalise the action in terms of exposing the subject ('patient') to less hazard than if FGM were done the traditional way.

Employment and enterprise

It is widely acknowledged that FGM correlates for those who experience it with reduced educational prospects. It becomes a mechanism whereby many girls who undergo mutilation become the members of the adult workforce least equipped to engage in modern economies – their adult status is bestowed before their experience can support that level of responsibility, they will usually then leave formal education (if any) early, they will probably have children before their bodies (let alone their social development) have matured, and they may be in effect the servants, if not the slaves, of their husbands (and perhaps their older co-wives or mothers-in-law).

In such circumstances it would be surprising to find that women with FGM attain their full economic potential. Even in otherwise favourable circumstances, neither their health nor their education may be good enough to achieve optimal personal economic performance, whether as an employee or as a private entrepreneur. In the unfavourable (for the women) overall contexts such as most places where FGM is traditionally practised, the negative economic outcomes may be even greater.

It is also probable that the general ethos of communities and societies in which FGM is practised is challenging for those who experience it. Women are sometimes the chattels of their husbands, a position from which it is difficult, even for those who may wish otherwise, to speak or act independently and with confidence as an adult.

Nonetheless, the decision to refuse FGM can be very difficult. In traditional communities women who are not 'cut' are likely to be rejected as brides,[72] and may end up with nothing at all.

These constraints prevent maximal economic impact in any circumstance, but may be especially significant in the context also of one's own family intentionally inflicting poor physical and/or psychological health.

Land and other non-monetary resources

Access to financial, basic day-to-day sustenance, social capital and well-being is not, however, alone in being influenced by FGM.

A connected resource is land. One way in which women in traditional communities may have a degree of independence is through land and farming.

Reports, however, suggest that, for instance, of the Maasai, women who refuse to undergo FGM may have been threatened with the removal of their right to land.

Similarly, there has traditionally been agreement between leaders of the Poro (male) and Sande (female) societies that women of high status may hold land for the purposes of bush school (preparation for womanhood and then the ceremony of FGM). In Sierra Leone in 2012 ownership of that land therefore reverted to the Poro as the Sande leaders agreed not to conduct more bush schools and FGM (illegal anyway, but a hugely embedded practice) for a duration.

Resource problems are further complicated in some societies by polygamy; multiple wives will not have the same access to means of support which coupledom might provide – but perhaps also leaving even less for any woman unable to procure a husband at all.

Over time land and other resource issues may, in the more modern context of civil litigation, be contested; already disputed evictions and land sales have been subject to overt challenge by some women who stand to lose their livelihoods.[73]

But whatever the outcome, such re-appropriations lay bare the as yet largely unexplored wider economic perils to which girls and women in traditional communities, not least those who resist FGM, may be exposed.

The 'shanty town' effect

Whether in traditionally practising locations or in communities excluded from the mainstream in places quite newly reached by the diaspora, it is evident that rejection of FGM can bring about economic disadvantage. Whilst avoiding FGM is always positive in terms of health prospects, this same avoidance could, as women reach their majority, make for significant loss of influence and even basic resources, if it results in non-adult status in the community and there are few other routes to self-realisation.

There is therefore a danger that both FGM itself, and its avoidance in certain contexts, will precipitate socio-economic situations from which it will be difficult, if not impossible, for survivors to escape. These more general difficulties have been examined by economic analysts from *The Economist*[74] and other institutions and authorities such as Richard Wilkinson and Kate Pickett, co-authors of *The Spirit Level: Why more equal societies almost always do better,*[75] in part a study of the impacts of inequality on health.

For those who have experienced FGM, one perennial difficulty may be illness. Those who are for whatever reason dispossessed in any case frequently find it difficult to disentangle themselves from the disadvantages they face; and one of the main reasons for the challenges they face is ill-health. This disadvantage is obviously amplified by FGM, and even more so if the original harm has been multiplied by problems later on with childbirth, fistula – surely the ultimate in debilitating damage – and infection, both chronic and also, at particular junctures, very acute and potentially lethal.

Likewise, there is some evidence to suggest that those who are excluded, particularly if in 'slums', fare even worse than people who live in the country. Income may drop over the years, and levels of health drop even more, as poverty becomes more grinding. Such a situation may be especially relevant to any women who have undergone FGM and now find themselves abandoned with children to care for and little social support. Prospects for all members of the remaining family may not be good in such circumstances.

Similar considerations may also apply to young women in Western countries who are disenfranchised, whether through subjection to FGM, or even because they lose their community anchor by refusing it.

Some shanty towns in the developing world are vast expanses of unregulated public health peril; some outcomes of FGM in the Western world may have comparable effects. Ill-health, physical and mental, is not only a personal disaster, but also a major economic hazard.

The combination of social, direct economic and health factors which FGM sometimes produces may be permanently toxic for those who experience them, and for their dependants.

Medical and other service provision costs

Whether modern clinical care is available or not, the costs to the wider community of FGM may be substantial.

If proper clinical provision is available, extra demands will be made on it, for instance, at the point of mutilation, in the aftermath of that practice, during subsequent pregnancies and deliveries, and in the care of children born to mothers with FGM.

Such infants and children may require additional attention because of difficult deliveries, because their mothers cannot care for them properly, and if their mothers die (motherless infants have much worse prospects and survival rates, perhaps twice the expected infant mortality rate, than children with continuing maternal care).

Similarly, little focused attention is currently paid to the health of adolescent girls in FGM-practising (or other) communities; yet the evidence suggests that anaemia may be a significant factor in their lives.[76] This condition, easily treated if those who experience it can be reached,[77] must surely be even more of a threat to the health and well-being of girls with FGM. Anaemia constitutes a form of 'vertical transmission of malnutrition' through generations – yet another drain on the quality of life of those who endure it, and also another disadvantage placed upon prospects for their communities' economic development.

If good clinical provision for girls and women with FGM is not available locally, the burden of care, such as it might be, falls on the wider society. In either case valuable resources, which could have been directed more positively, must be utilised to attend to the health care needs of those who have been mutilated. Whilst the human cost of suffering and need is unmeasurable, the economic cost of these consequences of FGM could in theory be quantified.

The same may be true also of other service provision. Police, the law courts, governance, social services and other civic and community services, media campaigns and much else as well, may be called into play to prevent or to punish the act of FGM, and there are also the requirements of FGM collateral – perhaps dependants such as children and elderly parents – to consider.

In nations and in isolated communities where resources are already scarce, the costs of government and other intervention because of the reality or threat of FGM must surely be large, whether this cost is met in monetary terms or via other resource allocation. Without FGM there would be more money and similar resources for other positive infrastructure, services and humanitarian developments.

Communities in the diaspora

Economic concerns for traditional FGM-practising communities may also be relevant to the economics of the FGM-created gendered underclass in established Western countries.

Where FGM creates an underclass in diaspora communities, the costs both to those communities themselves and to their host nation may be considerable.

The financial burdens FGM imposes on individuals, families and public services in any context may be only part of the total costs.

Already, it is known that considerable sums of money are spent in some communities on transporting children from, for example, the UK to countries where FGM is traditionally practised. Alternatively, tickets may be bought to bring traditional mutilators to Britain or Europe, for girls to undergo FGM in their local communities, sometimes in what is known as 'cutting parties'.

But what is not known, for instance, is how much money (if any) is sent from the UK to pay for FGM to be done to girls and young women in extended families 'back home'.

Whatever the sums involved, they are a loss to the economic wealth of people from traditional practising communities who have now settled in the first world.

Beyond this, however, are the costs of communities with poorly educated young women who are ill-equipped for employment and under-prepared to take their place as adult individuals in modern society. Along with those who have undergone forced marriage and other gendered human rights abuses, these women require, and must receive, considerable wider social and/or state support.

Such support is, however, particularly difficult to deliver to people in groups which are alienated from the mainstream; they belong to the category which was previously (and inaccurately) called 'hard to reach'[78] – a euphemism for being so distanced from conventional facilities that these services find it challenging, and are poorly equipped, to provide support.

Yet deliver appropriate services they must, for many reasons – the women are vulnerable and may need protection and support, their children may require particular care, without social connection there may be further costs (for example resulting from the activities of disengaged, perhaps hostile young people) to the wider society, and so forth.

Further, these detached communities are generally in the most impoverished and least privileged parts of their towns and cities. The local public services are likely already to be over-stretched and under-financed. FGM adds another layer of complicated and difficult to resolve need to that part of public service provision already under duress.

International programmes

Much larger than the costs to individual local government or even national government bodies must be the economic demands made on international bodies which seek to eradicate FGM. The 'FGM industry' has a growing and global reach. Conferences are held, travel for site visits is frequent, surveys and other research have been conducted for decades, publications come out almost daily. The UK Government alone in 2013 committed (potentially) around £35 million to global FGM eradication programmes.[79]

All this work is necessary whilst FGM still occurs. Relatively little, however, has been known until fairly recently about which parts of these activities have most positive impact; although there are now numbers of large (and needed) evaluations underway.

And even then other considerations must come into play, beyond the basic costs and expenditure. There are necessary international protocols, diplomatic issues and other unavoidable financial commitments to be met alongside the basic research and development.

But FGM is an artifactual, manfactured phenomenon. This human rights abuse would not exist if people didn't choose to expend resources on making it happen.

Those whose skills and energies are directed at eradicating FGM might otherwise be working on the eradication of public health hazards less directly amenable to human reason and debate, such as infectious diseases or malnutrition, or perhaps on governance or development.

Opportunity cost, the loss of these alternative prospects of improving the human condition – because people still elect, however unaware of the alternatives, to inflict FGM on members of their own communities – is a significant liability to be set against the alternative potential enhancement of the well-being of many whose interests are put aside whilst FGM continues to damage communities and economies.

Half the workforce, half the leadership

There is a dawning realisation globally that women are an essential element – potentially half – of the economic dynamic of any community or nation. Such a concern is acknowledged, for instance, in contemporary discussion of the Japanese economy,[80] where it is recognised that outdated systems and mores continue to emphasise women's low status at the expense of economic advantage.

What is true for Japan, where women are highly educated, must surely be true, much more so, for communities where women may not be able to achieve the status of adult, let alone act autonomously, unless they have been genitally mutilated.

Given the urgent need in many parts of the developing world to engage the skills and energy of all parties, it is time to recognise the enormous constraints which FGM places on national and local ambitions.

And indeed these matters have been recognised on various occasions over the years, sometimes at the highest level. Yet, as Navi Pillay, the United Nations High Commissioner for Human Rights,[81] and many others have pointed out, economic factors play a significant role in the persistence of FGM. This is true in regard to who does it, why it is done and the impacts it has on the wider economy.

Of course not everyone in FGM-practising communities seeks, or is even aware of, the potential benefits which a healthy and well-educated workforce can bring; but those at the higher levels of authority surely know, and have a duty to deliver.

The case for girls to complete their schooling, increase their independent incomes and contribute more effectively to their national economies has already been made on numerous occasions, including by the UK Prime Minister, David Cameron, in general terms during his 2012 Speech on Family Planning,[82] when he pointed out that providing girls in Africa with just one extra year of education can increase their wages by as much as 20 per cent; and, critically, that studies show Africa's economies would have doubled in size over the last 30 years were they not hampered by the limited educational and employment opportunities for women.

Such a view is reiterated with a specific focus on FGM and child marriage by *The Economist*.[83] Unless the pace of abolition picks up, the number of victims will grow from 3.6 million a year now to 4.1 million in 2035 (and, to cite Navi Pilay again, based on the current 1 per cent decrease per annum, the target of reducing FGM prevalence by half will not be achieved until 2074).

Babatunde Osotimehin, head of the United Nations Population Fund, also insists that the most important aspect of development, along with the eradication of FGM itself, is to ensure girls finish their studies.[84] According to 2014 estimates, if girls finished school and got employment at the same rate as boys, they would add $27 billion annually to the economy of Kenya, and $17 billion to the economy of Nigeria. Describing girls as 'the world's least exploited resource', Dr Osotimehin and the First Ladies of Africa have asked that the age for marriage be raised to 18; education will, he emphasised, empower women to adopt positive health behaviour.

Add to this the issues of child stunting, and the issues become both more complex and more transparent. At a roundtable of African heads of state, ministers, CEOs and civil society leaders on the eve of President Obama's 2014 US–Africa Leaders, the World Bank Group President Jim Yong Kim stated that up to 16 per cent of GNP in Africa is lost each year because malnourished children grow up to be less productive youths and adults.[85]

Not all stunted children will have mothers who experienced FGM (which puts their babies at risk during and after birth), but the numbers are probably significant; we already know that these children are at particular risk of failing to thrive.

One writer at least, Adam Burtle,[86] has ascribed this failure of babies, and in particular black babies, to thrive as 'structural violence', a term arising from the work of Paul Farmer.[87]

In Farmer's words:

> Structural violence is one way of describing social arrangements that put individuals and populations in harm's way. ... The arrangements are structural because they are embedded in the political and economic organization of our social world; they are violent because they cause injury to people ... neither culture nor pure individual will is at fault; rather, historically given (and often economically driven) processes and forces conspire to constrain individual agency. Structural violence is visited upon all those whose social status denies them access to the fruits of scientific and social progress.[88]

Such a description brings together the sociological and economic constraints which comprise the circumstances of women and girls (and their babies) across the generations experiencing FGM.

Legal sanctions, educational programmes and medical support are all part of the necessary package to address this fundamental attack on human rights. But ultimately FGM must be tackled at a deeper level even than the provision of particular services.

Opportunity costs

On one hand, the issue is about hearts and minds in the practising communities; and on the other it is about self-evidently avoidable lost socio-economic (as well as human development) opportunities. For those working to prevent FGM on the ground, there may be concerns about the risks to children born to women with FGM; and for those at the much wider strategic level there may be anxieties about the gratuitous forfeiture which FGM imposes of advantage to the economic well-being of nations.

It is enough that FGM must be eradicated because it is cruel and a grim abnegation of human rights; but a corollary of the eradication would be healthier economies as well as healthier girls, women and babies.

It's time these additional benefits – themselves also enhancers of human well-being – were quantified, both internationally and in communities in the UK and other Western nations.

Money speaks, and in the case of bringing economic costs of FGM into the spotlight, that money can also shore up, for any who continue to doubt, the criticality of eradicating FGM as soon as we possibly can.

Discuss this chapter at http://nofgmukbook.com/2015/01/29/chapter-2-socio-economic-analysis/.

Endnotes

All weblinks accessed on 1 March 2015.

1   Hastings, M. (2011) Years of Liberal Dogma Have Spawned a Generation of Amoral, Uneducated, Welfare Dependent, Brutalised Youngsters. *Daily Mail Online*. Available at: http://www.dailymail.co.uk/debate/article-2024284/UK-riots-2011-Liberal-dogma-spawned-generation-brutalised-youths.html.

2   Thelwell, E. (2011) FactCheck: Were the Rioters a 'Feral Underclass'? *Channel 4 FactCheck*, 6 September. Available at: http://blogs.channel4.com/factcheck/factcheck-were-the-rioters-a-feral-underclass/7732.

3   Cooper, N. (2011) Chavs, Scum or Feral Underclass: Who is your favourite scapegoat? *Church Action on Poverty*. Available at: http://www.church-poverty.org.uk/news/fabvouritescapegoat.

4   Tyler, I. (2013) The Riots of the Underclass? Stigmatisation, mediation and the government of poverty and disadvantage in neoliberal Britain. *Sociological Research Online* 18(4). Available at: http://www.socresonline.org.uk/18/4/6.html.

5   IRIN Humanitarian News and Analysis (2005) *Africa: When culture harms the girls – the globalisation of female genital mutilation*. Nairobi, 1 March. Available at: http://www.irinnews.org/in-depth/62462/15/razor-s-edge-the-controversy-of-female-genital-mutilation.

6   AGILE International *Factsheet*. Available at: http://agile-international.org/fact-sheet/.

7   Riley, A. (2011) Émile Durkheim. *Oxford Bibliographies Online: Sociology*. Available at: http://www.oxfordbibliographies.com/view/document/obo-9780199756384/obo-9780199756384–0014.xml.

8   Durkheim, É. (1997) *Suicide: A study in sociology*. USA: The Free Press.
9   Magu, J. (2014) Kuria Girls Resist Female Cut as Prevalence Falls. Kenya: *The Star*, 24 March. Available at: http://www.the-star.co.ke/news/ article-160002/kuria-girls-resist-female-cut-prevalence-falls.
10   Azango, M. (30 March 2012) The Costs for Girls: 'Why I Welcome Leaders' Decisions'. *Pulitzer Center of Crisis Reporting.* Available at: http://pulitzercenter. org/reporting/liberia-sande-secret-society-government-shutdown-female-circumcision-mae-azango.
11   Wikipedia (2014) *Sande society.* Available at: http://en.wikipedia.org/wiki/ Sande_society.
12   Lupick, T. (2012) 'This Needs to Stop': Tempers Flare over the Practice of Female Genital Mutilation in Liberia. Liberia: *Think Africa Press*, 30 March. Available at: http://www.tlupic.com/2020/this-needs-to-stop-tempers-flare-over-the-practice-of-female-circumcision-in-liberia/.
13   Fahey, R. (1971) The Poro as a System of Judicial Administration in Northwestern Liberia. *Journal of Legal Pluralism and Unoffical Law.* 4: 1–25. Available at: www.jlp.bham.ac.uk/volumes/04/fahey-art.pdf.
14   Vogel, H. (2012) *Societies within Society – The Secret Societies of Liberia.* Available at: http://bloggingwithoutmaps.blogspot.co.uk/2012/06/societies-within-society-secret.html.
15   Cultural Survival (2004) FGM: Maasai Women Speak Out, *Cultural Survival Quarterly*, Winter 2004. Women of the World Must Hear. Available at: http:// www.culturalsurvival.org/publications/cultural-survival-quarterly/kenya/ fgm-maasai-women-speak-out.
16   Mgbako, C., Saxena, M., Cave, A., Farjad, N., Shin, H. (2010) Penetrating the Silence in Sierra Leone: A blueprint for the eradication of female genital mutilation. *Harvard Human Rights Journal.* 23: 111–40. Available at: http:// harvardhrj.com/wp-content/uploads/2010/10/111–140.pdf.
17   Documentary film by Equality Now (2009) *Africa Rising.*
18   Equality Now (2013) *Kenya: Protect girls by enforcing FGM and child marriage laws.* Available at: http://www.equalitynow.org/take_action/fgm_action521.
19   Fanthorpe, R. (2007) *Sierra Leone: The influence of the secret societies, with special reference to female genital mutilation,* United Nations High Commissioner for Refugees, Status Determination and Protection Information Section. Available at: http://www.refworld.org/pdfid/46cee3152.pdf.
20   Vogel, H. (16 June 2012) *Societies within Society – The secret societies of Liberia.* Blogging without Maps Available at: http://bloggingwithoutmaps.blogspot. co.uk/2012/06/societies-within-society-secret.html.
21   Lackovich Van-Gorp, A. (2014) Abducting Brides and Stealing Girlhood, *Girls Globe.* Available at: http://girlsglobe.org/2014/09/17/abducting-brides-and-stealing-girlhood/.
22   Batha, E. (2013) Kidnappers Jailed for Forcing Liberian Woman to Undergo FGM, *Thomson Reuters Foundation,* 12 March. Available at: http://www.trust.org/

item/?map=kidnappers-jailed-for-forcing-liberian-woman-to-undergo-fgm/.

23 Cultural Survival (2004) FGM: Maasai Women Speak Out, *Cultural Survival Quarterly*, Winter 2004. Women of the World Must Hear. Available at: http://www.culturalsurvival.org/publications/cultural-survival-quarterly/kenya/fgm-maasai-women-speak-out.

24 La Rose, T. (2014) *In Guinea, one girl's story of violence reveals a commonplace nightmare*, UNICEF. Available at: http://www.unicef.org/infobycountry/guinea_71072.html.

25 IRIN News (2009) *Burkina Faso: Cutters turn razors on babies to evade FGM/C law*. Available at: http://www.irinnews.org/report/82600/burkina-faso-cutters-turn-razors-on-babies-to-evade-fgm-c-law.

26 Wanyee, D. (2013) *Standard Operating Procedure for FGM and Child Early and Forced Marriage*, Kenyan Office of the Director of Public Prosecutions. Available at: https://www.scribd.com/doc/246976429/SoP-FGM.

27 The Anti-FGM Prosecutions Unit (2014) *Draft Report on the Sensitization of Prohibition of FGM Act 2011*, Office of the Director of Public Prosecutions. Available at: https://www.scribd.com/doc/246975950/Final-FGM-Report.

28 FGM New Zealand (2011) *Beliefs and Issues*. Available at: http://fgm.co.nz/beliefs-and-issues.

29 Lupick, T. (2012) 'This Needs to Stop': Tempers Flare over the Practice of Female Genital Mutilation in Liberia. Liberia: *Think Africa Press*, 30 March. Available at: http://thinkafricapress.com/liberia/stop-female-circumcision-sande-press-freedom.

30 Hoffer, C.P. (1975) *Bundu: Political Implications of Female Solidarity in a Secret Society*. In: Raphael, D. (ed.) *Reproduction, Power, and Change*. Netherlands: Walter de Gruyter, pp. 155–63.

31 Fanthorpe, R. (2007) *Sierra Leone: The Influence of the Secret Societies, With Special Reference to Female Genital Mutilation*, United Nations High Commissioner for Refugees, Status Determination and Protection Information Section. Available at: http://www.refworld.org/pdfid/46cee3152.pdf.

32 Mackie, G. (1996) Ending Footbinding and Infibulation: A Convention Account. *American Sociological Review*. 61(6): 996–1017. Available at: http://polisci2.ucsd.edu/gmackie/documents/MackieASR.pdf.

33 Dorkenoo, E. (2006) Female Genital Mutilation (FGM). In: *The Bayan Tree Paradox: Culture and human rights activism*. Washington, D.C.: International Human Rights Internship Program, Institute of International Education, 112–15. Available at: http://www.forwarduk.org.uk/key-issues/fgm/human-rights.

34 Tanzania Media Women's Association (2013) *Gender Based Violence* Research Report, p15. Available at: http://www.tamwa.org/download/Investigative%20survey%20report.pdf.

35 Kamunyu, R.M. (2014) *Prostitution on Womanhood by Parents – The Butchers of Womanhood*. 13 March. Comment on: Burrage, H. (2014) The Global Economics

of Female Genital Mutilation. *Hilary Burrage*, 6 February. Available at: http://
hilaryburrage.com/2014/02/06/the-global-economics-of-female-genital-
mutilation-fgm/.

36 Maloney, C. (2013) *Obstetric Fistula*. Available at: http://maloney.house.gov/
issues/womens-issues/obstetric-fistula.

37 Inbaraj, S. (2004) *Married as Children, Women with Obstetric Fistulas
Have No Future*, Population Reference Bureau. Available at:
http://www.prb.org/Publications/Articles/2004/MarriedasChildren
WomenWithObstetricFistulasHaveNoFuture.aspx.

38 Filipovic, J. (2014) The Kidnapped Nigerian Girls Show that Religious
Conservatives Hate Education. *Guardian*, 2 May. Available at: http://www.
theguardian.com/commentisfree/2014/may/02/kidnapped-nigeria-school-girls-
boko-haram-education.

39 Gregory, M. and Nauman, Q. (2011) Pakistan Girls Defy Taliban School
Bombings. Pakistan: *Reuters*, 16 November. Available at: http://www.reuters.
com/article/2011/11/16/us-pakistan-taliban-schools-idUSTRE7AF0GP20111116.

40 Makoye, K. (2013) In Tanzania, Maasai Women Who Reject FGM Are Refused
As Brides. *Thomas Reuters Foundation*, 16 December. Available at: http://www.
trust.org/item/20131216094140-k5c2x/.

41 Burrage, H. (2014) Rational-Emotional 'Divorce' in Iran. *Hilary Burrage Blog*, 8 March.
Available at: http://hilaryburrage.com/2014/03/08/rational-emotional-divorce-in-
iran/.

42 NAMI (2011) Asian American Teenage Girls Have Highest Rates of Depression;
NAMI Releases Report. *NAMI Newsroom*, February. Available at: http://www.
nami.org/Template.cfm?Section=press_room&template=/ContentManagement/
ContentDisplay.cfm&ContentID=115681.

43 Mental Health Foundation (2014) *Black and Minority Ethnic Communities*.
Available at: http://www.mentalhealth.org.uk/help-information/mental-health-
a-z/B/BME-communities/.

44 Matthews, S., Smith, C. (2009) The Sustainability Of Gender Specific Provision
In The Youth Justice System, *The Griffins Society*, 2009/04. Available at: http://
thegriffinssociety.org/Research_paper_2009_4.pdf.

45 The Centre for Social Justice, XLP (2013) *Girls and Gangs*. Available at: http://
www.centreforsocialjustice.org.uk/UserStorage/pdf/Pdf%20reports/Girls-and-
Gangs-FINAL-VERSION.pdf.

46 London Street Gangs (2013) *London Street Gangs Home*. Available at: http://
londonstreetgangs.blogspot.co.uk/.

47 HM Government (2011) *Ending Gang and Youth Violence: A Cross-Government
Report*. London: The Stationery Office. Available at: https://www.gov.uk/
government/uploads/system/uploads/attachment_data/file/97861/gang-
violence-summary.pdf.

48 Children's Dignity Forum and FORWARD UK (2010) *Voices of Child Brides and
Child Mothers in Tanzania: A PEER report on child marriage*. Available at: http://

www.forwarduk.org.uk/wp-content/uploads/2014/12/Voices-of-Child-Brides-in-Tanzania.pdf.

49 Farmer, P. (2003) *Pathologies of Power: Health, human rights and the new war on the poor*. Berkeley: University of California Press.

50 Equality Now (2011) *Protecting Girls from Undergoing Female Genital Mutilation*. Available at: http://www.equalitynow.org/sites/default/files/Protecting%20 Girls_FGM_Kenya_Tanzania.pdf.

51 Burrage, H., Barzoki, M.H., Tavakoll, M. (2014) Rational-Emotional 'Divorce' In Iran. *Applied Research in Quality of Life*, 2 March. Available at: http://hilaryburrage.com/2014/03/08/rational-emotional-divorce-in-iran/.

52 Luongo, K.A. (2000) The Clitoridectomy Controversy in Kenya: The 'Woman's Affair' that Wasn't. *Ufahamu: A Journal of African Studies*. 28(2–3): 105–36. Available at: http://escholarship.org/uc/item/2hr9g5hd.

53 UNICEF (2005) *Egypt FGM/C Country Profile*. Available at: http://www.childinfo.org/files/Egypt_FGC_profile_English.pdf.

54 28 Too Many (2013) *Country Profile: FGM in Kenya*, p. 23. Available at: http://28toomany.org/media/uploads/final_kenya_country_profile_may_2013.pdf.

55 Stop FGM in the Middle East (2013) *Indonesia*. Available at: http://www.stopfgmmideast.org/countries/indonesia/.

56 Haworth, A. (2012) The Day I Saw 248 Girls Suffering Genital Mutilation. *Guardian*, 17 November. Available at: http://www.theguardian.com/society/2012/nov/18/female-genital-mutilation-circumcision-indonesia.

57 Equality Now (2011) *Protecting Girls From Undergoing Female Genital Mutilation*. Available at: http://www.equalitynow.org/sites/default/files/Protecting%20 Girls_FGM_Kenya_Tanzania.pdf.

58 African Women Organization (2009) *Myths and Justifications for the Perpetuation of FGM*. Available at: http://www.african-women.org/FGM/myths.php.

59 The Partnership for Maternal, Newborn and Child Health (2006) *Opportunities for Africa's newborns: Practical data, policy and programmatic support for newborn care in Africa*, Chapter 1, WHO on behalf of The Partnership for Maternal Newborn and Child Health. Available at: http://www.who.int/pmnch/media/publications/aonsectionIII_1.pdf.

60 Bishai, D., Bonnenfant, Y.T., Darwish, M., Adam, T., Bathija, H., Johansen, E., et al. (2010) Estimating the Obstetric Costs of Female Genital Mutilation in Six African Countries. *Bulletin of the World Health Organization*. 88(4): 241–320. Available at: http://www.who.int/reproductivehealth/publications/fgm/obstetric_costs/en/.

61 Muse, D.A. (2012) A Poem for Women Who've Suffered Female Genital Mutilation. *Sister Somalia*, 30 November. Available at: http://www.sistersomalia.org/a-poem-for-women-who%E2%80%99ve-suffered-female-genital-mutilation/.

62 Fistula Care Plus (2014) Module 6: Obstetric Fistula – Definition, Causes and Contributing Factors, and Impact on Affected Women. In: *Prevention and Recognition of Obstetric Fistula Training Package for Health Workers*. Fistula Care, 07.

Available at: http://www.fistulacare.org/pages/pdf/Training/Module_6_
Obstetric_fistula_causes_and_factors_Fistula_Care.pdf.

63   WHO Study Group on Female Genital Mutilation and Obstetric Outcome
(2006) Female Genital Mutilation and Obstetric Outcome: WHO collaborative
prospective study in six African countries, *Lancet*, 367(9525): 1835–41. Available
at: http://www.who.int/reproductivehealth/publications/fgm/fgm-obstetric-
study-en.pdf.

64   WHO Study Group on Female Genital Mutilation and Obstetric Outcome
(2006) Female Genital Mutilation and Obstetric Outcome: WHO collaborative
prospective study in six African countries, *Lancet*, 367(9525): 1835–41. Available
at: http://www.who.int/reproductivehealth/publications/fgm/fgm-obstetric-
study-en.pdf.

65   FGM National Clinical Group (2013) *Psychological Aspects*. Available at: http://
www.fgmnationalgroup.org/psychological_aspects.htm.

66   Njue, C., Askew, I. (2004) Medicalization of Female Genital Cutting among
the Abagusii in Nyanza Province, Kenya. *Frontiers in Reproductive Health
Program*. Population Council, December. Available at: http://www.who.int/
reproductivehealth/topics/fgm/medicalization_fgm_kenya/en/.

67   Desert Flower Foundation (2009) 'Medicalisation' of FGM is a Dangerous
Trend. *Daily Nation Kenya*. Available at: http://www.desertflowerfoundation.
org/en/2009/08/03/medicalisation-of-fgm-is-a-dangerous-trend-2/.

68   UNFPA Egypt (2008) *Who Performs it and When*. Available at: http://egypt.unfpa.
org/english/fgmStaticpages/8b9eaf39–33d5–4ff5–924b-7e0b76d1091d/Who_
performs_it_and_when.aspx.

69   UNFPA Egypt (2008) *Who Performs it and When*. Available at: http://egypt.unfpa.
org/english/fgmStaticpages/8b9eaf39–33d5–4ff5–924b-7e0b76d1091d/Who_
performs_it_and_when.aspx.

70   Kern (2014) UK: Uphill Battle in Fight against Female Genital Mutilation. *Gatestone
Institute*, 1 July. Available at: http://www.gatestoneinstitute.org/4381/uk-fgm.

71   Murdock, H. (2014) Female Genital Mutilation Trial Sheds Light on Egyptian
Practice. *Voice of America News*, 12 September. Available at: http://www.
voanews.com/content/inspector-refutes-doctors-claim-in-egypt-first-female-
genital-mutilation-trial/2447545.html.

72   Makoye, K. (2013) In Tanzania, Maasai Women Who Reject FGM Are Refused
As Brides. *Thomas Reuters Foundation*, 16 December. Available at: http://www.
trust.org/item/20131216094140-k5c2x/.

73   Kemei, K., Tanui, N. (2013) Maasai Women Want Say in Land Boards, *Standard
Digital News*, 9 May. Available at: http://www.standardmedia.co.ke/thecounties/
article/2000083254/maasai-women-want-say-in-land-boards.

74   *The Economist* (2014) Slums and Social Mobility: Down and Out. 8 February.
Available at: http://www.economist.com/node/21595939.

75   Wilkinson, R., Pickett, K. (2009) *The Spirit Level: Why more equal societies almost
always do better*. United Kingdom: Allen Lane.

76 Spicer, J. (2014) Anaemia Epidemic: We are neglecting adolescent girls'
    nutrition. *Guardian*, 10 November. Available at: http://www.theguardian.com/
    global-development-professionals-network/2014/nov/10/anaemia-epidemic-we-
    are-neglecting-adolescent-girls-nutrition.

77 World Health Organization (2014) *Micronutrient Deficiencies: Iron deficiency
    anaemia*. Available at: http://www.who.int/nutrition/topics/ida/en/.

78 Brackertz, N. (2007) *Who is Hard to Reach and Why?* Swinburne University of
    Technology. Available at: http://www.sisr.net/publications/0701brackertz.pdf.

79 Department for International Development, Featherstone, L. (2013) UK to Help
    End Female Genital Mutilation. *GOV.UK*, 6 March. Available at: https://www.
    gov.uk/government/news/uk-to-help-end-female-genital-mutilation.

80 *The Economist* (2014) *Japanese Women and Work: Holding back half the nation*,
    29 March. Available at: http://www.economist.com/node/21599763.

81 UN New Centre (2014) *Ending Female Genital Mutilation Vital for Healthy
    Communities, Stresses UN Official*, 4 June. Available at: http://www.un.org/apps/
    news/story.asp?NewsID=48057&hootPostID=9e1a0f20a6774416b93256d67caf5
    8d7#.VOKwQ-n30uV.

82 Cameron, D. (2012) *Prime Minister's Speech on Family Planning*. Family Planning
    Summit, 11 July. Available at: https://www.gov.uk/government/speeches/
    prime-ministers-speech-on-family-planning.

83 *The Economist* (2014) *Female Genital Mutilation and Child Marriage: Progress, but
    too slow*, 26 July. Available at: http://www.economist.com/node/21608769/print.

84 Adan, J. (2014) *Africa: Raise Marriage Age to 18 Years, First Ladies Ask
    African Governments*. Nairobi: All Africa. Available at: http://allafrica.com/
    stories/201409231514.html.

85 Shekar, M. (2014) Stunted Children, Stunted Economies: African Leaders
    Pledge Action on Nutrition. *Investing in Health*, 4 August. Available at: http://
    blogs.worldbank.org/health/health/stunted-children-stunted-economies-
    african-leaders-pledge-action-nutrition.

86 Burtle, A. (2013) Structural Violence. *What is Structural Violence?* Available
    at: http://www.structuralviolence.org/structural-violence/.

87 Farmer, P. (1999) Pathologies of Power: Rethinking Health and Human Rights.
    American Journal of Public Health. 89(10): 1486. Available at: http://www.ncbi.
    nlm.nih.gov/pmc/articles/PMC1508789/pdf/amjph00010–0028.pdf.

88 Partners in Health (2011) *How Structural Violence Impacts Maternal Mortality*,
    18 May. Available at: http://www.pih.org/blog/how-structural-violence-
    impacts-maternal-mortality.

3 Perceptions and Beliefs Over Time

One of the most puzzling questions around genital mutilation is how it arose, such a long time ago and spontaneously, in totally unconnected parts of the world. To date, just as there is no commonality in how genital mutilation is practised, there is also no universal answer. Nonetheless, one of the most interesting responses to the puzzle has been, as medical historian David Gollaher suggests, to examine the meanings assigned to it, to ask what people believe they are doing when they perform genital 'cutting'.[1]

There is a widespread – but erroneous – belief that female genital mutilation is required by adherents to Islam (Muslims). The general perception of a direct connection between female genital mutilation and Islam arises largely because it is most often found in Muslim countries such as those of the sub-Sahara region. The reality, however, is that FGM is practised by various denominations and sects of Islam, just as it has been adopted by some denominations and sects within Christianity and Judaism in that part of the world. But in every case FGM was in place before the various religious groups adopted it.

In fact, female genital mutilation actually precedes all the major world faiths and is also found in communities with animist or pantheistic beliefs. Despite claims to the contrary, FGM is fundamental to no global religion, even though at various times and in various places various faiths have adopted the practice.

Female genital mutilation is, however, profoundly and critically embedded in notions of purity and cleanliness; and it has over the centuries been especially evident in contexts where girls and women are seen as property owned and traded by men. FGM is a marker of chastity and sole ownership (by a husband; the wife may be one of several spouses he has or owns).

FGM is therefore an aspect of tradition, rather than a basic tenet of any particular religion. Given the great variation in the degree (and extent) to which FGM is practised even within small geographical areas, it is most usefully to be understood, in the formal, anthropological sense of that term, as a 'tribal' practice relating to family dynasties, identities, wealth, influence and power.

Historical Roots of FGM

The first records of female genital mutilation date back some thousands of years. It is found in communities as far apart as the Australian aboriginal tribes[2] and numerous African and other societies. Some of these communities were (and some still are) animist, and some later developed formal religions.

Some traditions give meaning to FGM as a public rite of passage; some inflict it, even in various communities very early in babyhood, to ensure 'purity' and 'cleanliness'; some view it as a private matter to be done around the time that girls reach puberty and are about to be married, in order to impose chastity; and some perform genital cutting on boys and girls to formally ascribe gender, believing that the 'male' or 'female' parts of children of the opposite sex must be removed before adulthood.

The question, however, remains: how can we explain that male and female 'circumcision' arose independently in so many disparate locations, and over an extended period of time when it would have been impossible for those concerned to have been in contact with each other?

The answer is patriarchy. FGM has emerged in societies where women are chattels, objects of (some) economic value, to be passed from father to husband, and for whom a life independent of male 'ownership' is generally unthinkable.

It is known that female slaves in Egypt sometimes had their labia pinned together with fibulae (brooches) to prevent them getting pregnant.[3] This has led in the present day to the name 'pharanoic circumcision' for the most invasive form of FGM, 'infibulation' – despite the fact that also scraping away most of the vulva has not been proven beyond doubt to have been practised by the Egyptians.[4]

Whilst there is evidence of male circumcision in earlier Old Kingdom Egypt (third millennium BC), there is none in that era for actual genital mutilation in females. There is nothing to suggest FGM in either the mummies or the art and literature of that time. Despite its name, infibulation as we currently understand it may not have occurred in ancient Egypt, alongside the generally undisputed use of fibulae.[5]

There is also evidence that fibulae were used on the wives of important noblemen, probably also to ensure the chastity of these women, who were the vehicles for the generational transmission of wealth; and because this procedure indicated social position, it may have become fashionable in other parts of the social hierarchy as well.

The first direct references to FGM alongside male circumcision are found in writings of a few centuries before the birth of Christ.[6] There is also a Greek papyrus of 163 BC which says the procedure was performed in Memphis (Egypt).[7] The Greek geographer Strabo similarly reported, following a visit he made to Egypt around 25 BC, that Egyptians 'zealously' raised every child, circumcising the males and excising the females.[8]

The papyrus report associates FGM with the stage in life when girls received their dowries, which suggests it was a rite of passage or an initiation. Later, however, another Greek, the physician Aetios, reports that Egyptians in the sixth century AD used FGM to remove what were regarded as the deformity of 'overly large' clitorises, to stop irritation and anticipated resulting sexual appetite – phenomena which were (and in some places still are[9]) generally seen as undesirable and a threat to the male social order.

FGM as Chastity, Purity and Cleanliness

Important aspects of FGM historically have included an emphasis on cleanliness or hygiene. This element of perceptions around FGM has arisen partly as a result of ritual meanings associated with bodily functions and secretions, and perhaps also partly because in many areas of the world where FGM has occurred there may historically have been genuine issues around hygiene: in a world of heat and sand, without running water, that problem has certainly been amongst the matters which in the past male circumcision has been claimed to address.

Nonetheless, there is absolutely no health benefit ever to be gained from FGM and other ways of accounting for it must therefore be found. One important factor here is the idea of 'purity'.[10]

'Purity' is associated with, though not exactly the same as, virginity and cleanliness. It is reflected in the practice of infibulation, which is seen as ensuring a girl or young woman is untouched until she is taken as a bride.[11] (This preoccupation with virginity, particularly in the conservative communities, has continued in one form or another in modern societies as well as traditional ones,[12, 13] as well of course as in much of Islamic society.[14])

Purity is also associated with ideas concerning menstruation, sexuality and sometimes masturbation. Clitoridectomy was and often still is believed to be a way of reducing sexual feelings and satisfaction; more extensive removal of the labia ensures that secretions (in fact, a completely normal and healthy aspect of female genital function) are not harboured in the genitalia; and infibulation goes even further, ensuring that illicit penetration is unlikely to occur, not least because of the pain involved, and usually demonstrably evidenced if nonetheless it does happen.

Likewise, re-infibulation after giving birth offered the husband a level of assurance (important in respect of the fear that women are innately sexually driven) that his wife was faithful. It took much the same role as the centuries-old tradition – also rooted in ancient times – of 'churching' women after childbirth[15] in some Eastern and Western Christian faiths. Both churching and FGM are billed as a celebration of womanhood: churching 'purifies' the woman in preparation for her returning to normal society after her (40-day) 'confinement' rather as in an infinitely more perilous way re-infibulation returns her to 'purity' after pregnancy and labour.[16]

There is also, as we saw in Chapter 2, a belief in some societies that once girls reach the menarche they will have voracious sexual appetites which must be restrained by force. FGM in this instance is, in addition to its other functions, a 'surgical' chastity belt, employed as a social sanction against the serious fear that once they begin to menstruate they will otherwise become promiscuous – a very dangerous thing to do in a community where one's adult survival may depend in the literal sense on attracting a husband with resources to provide food and shelter.

'Circumcision' in the Nineteenth and Twentieth Centuries

The early Egyptian and Greek surgeons who performed clitoridectomy would have found themselves in agreement with the thinking of surgeons in Victorian England and America, who also undertook the procedure in accordance with the theory of 'reflex neurosis', to 'treat' depression, masturbation and 'nymphomania'.[17]

Masturbation was seen as a dysfunction which required medical (surgical) intervention. The English doctor Isaac Baker Brown (1812–73) was amongst those who built a thriving – though eventually disastrous – career and reputation via the (in his view) 'harmless operative procedure' which he promulgated and which was believed by many to cure all kinds of medical ills. These 'ills' included a range of 'conditions' which would now under no circumstances be regarded as requiring medical intervention.[18]

Thus, concerns about purity and 'hygiene' were replaced in more rational societies by a focus on 'hysteria'; and these concerns, just as in traditional societies even today, afforded a decent living for those who could offer a service to remediate the worries of people with the money to pay.

Nonetheless, Baker Brown did meet with some professional medical resistance to his mode of operation even at the time, as an editorial on 'Clitoridectomy and Medical Ethics' in the *Medical Times and Gazette* of 1867 shows.[19] But at least in part this resistance by other doctors is thought to have been triggered by professional jealousies rather than fundamental disagreements about medical facts and practice. Clitoridectomy was a very lucrative business and, in good personal standing or not, Baker Brown managed to introduce the procedure to mainstream society in the United States before he died.[20]

The practice then continued from time to time until well into the twentieth century: Duffy[21] suggests that clitoridectomy in the USA ceased in the late nineteenth century – he cites, for example, an article by Dr A.J. Bloch of New Orleans, *Sexual Perversion in the Female* (1894) – but others have more recently found evidence that it continued until the 1950s and 1960s.[22] Thus, in 1958 Dr C.F. McDonald proposes clitoridectomy as a remedy for what he sees as the medical conditions of 'irritation, scratching, irritability, masturbation, frequency and urgency'.[23]

Clitoridectomy (FGM) was not therefore only a historic practice, even in the West. The last known medically unrequired excision of the clitoris was carried out in the United States in the mid-twentieth century (1960s). There was a gradual change of rationale over time from hygiene or hysteria to more 'aesthetic' considerations such as the shortening of the clitoris or labia, where parents (or husbands – or perhaps even the women themselves?) considered these too large or too long.[24]

From this aesthetic perspective has arisen the more recent emergence or acceptance of (adult) female genital cosmetic surgery – another issue in contention by some, especially as it may well be illegal under strict interpretations of some nations' legislations about FGM.[25]

Parallels with Male Circumcision

It is in these gradually changing rationales in Western countries that the connection between female genital circumcision and male circumcision becomes very clear – both have been held to reduce masturbation, thereby also being considered essential to upholding proper behaviour; both are also perceived to be issues of hygiene and aesthetics; and both are markers of cultural identity.

Male circumcision, as we saw earlier in the Introduction, continues to be the norm in the United States – where over half the male population has been circumcised[26] – though not in Britain: in the UK fewer than 10 per cent of boy babies now undergo non-therapeutic circumcision,[27] not least because since 1948 most medical care in the UK has been provided by the National Health Service rather than private practitioners: most British people do not pay directly for curative medical care, so clinicians have not generally expected to receive direct additional fees for non-medically-essential services such as the circumcision of baby boys,[28] even if their local service agrees to provide it.[29, 30]

But whilst in the UK only a very small percentage of younger men have undergone circumcision,[31] it remains an almost universal norm in larger Jewish and Muslim communities across the globe. There is occasional dissent – in Israel in 2013 a mother was fined by a religious court for refusing to permit her son's circumcision; a secular court may decide the issue[32] – but only a small, albeit growing, minority of members in these faith groups anywhere dispute infant male circumcision,[33] usually on safety and/ or human rights grounds.

In the past few years, however, the male circumcision debate has also incorporated a different line, with an increasing emphasis in particular parts of the world on serious health challenges such as HIV, which is epidemic in, for example, some African countries.[34]

More recently the World Health Organization and bodies such as the Bill & Melinda Gates Foundation have encouraged the medical circumcision of men,[35] in an effort to prevent the spread of AIDS. This strategy is the outcome of three studies in the field which are claimed to demonstrate its efficacy. Nonetheless, the funders also emphasise that alternative public health measures such as education and a focus on hygiene must be adopted as prevention programmes move forward. Others[36] continue to assert that circumcision is not an appropriate way to address the AIDS epidemic.[37]

Contemporary Islamic Beliefs and Customs

The issues around female genital mutilation are, however, becoming increasingly contentious (and politicised) as traditional practices and understandings are dislodged by more contemporary rationales. This is at the present time especially so in respect of Islamic practice. Matters of long-established custom have become interconnected with questions of piety and faith in ways which have caused confusion amongst outsiders and sometimes also amongst the faithful themselves.

It is important for non-Muslim Westerners (and indeed all Islamic adherents) to recognise that Islam is as diverse in its interpretations across the globe as, for instance, Christianity. There have been profound disagreements between Muslim communities and scholars about both the authenticity and the legitimacy of FGM,[38] with some (for example Sunni[39]) scholars continuing to insist it must be adopted.[40] The contentions extend both to *fatwas* (which are instructions about how adherents of Islam should or must conduct themselves[41]) and to *hadiths* or *sunna* (recommendations of varying 'strength' and origins about preferred behaviour[42]).

Claims are still made in some quarters that various forms of FGM or 'circumcision' are required on grounds of hygiene, beauty or piety.

These claims often rest on particular modern-day translations of Arabic words, and sometimes the requirement is said to be 'just a small nick', rather than 'serious' damage.[43] On this basis Type I 'sunna' cuts may not be perceived as FGM at all – making for even more confusion about clerical edicts, and difficulties for eradication, even though sunna too is in fact illegal in most countries.

But others point out both that there is no proof positive in any case that The Prophet required any surgery on female genitalia, and that this action is not allied with other substantive teachings of Islam.[44] The prohibition of FGM ('sunna' or 'circumcision'), as those promulgating it emphasise, is in line with modern secular law, just as FGM is now also banned under Islamic law in some states. Whether or not that law is observed, FGM of any sort is now forbidden in most practising countries.[45]

One Islamic religious position against FGM is also that, regardless of interpretations of the scriptures, the juncture to 'do no harm' must in any case override any other practice. Amongst those emphasising this aspect of the matter are the (US-based) Muslim Women's League – who are amongst the (apparently) few female Muslim formal organisations to have made their views widely known.[46]

The Muslim Women's League states without reservation that FGM is incompatible with the most basic and sacred tenets of their faith, which require upholding the integrity of the human being, in body and in spirit.

This position is further articulated by a range of Islamic scholars and religious leaders and organisations, amongst them the leading medical and theological authorities cited by the Women's League, as well as the London Central Mosque.[47]

Informed opinion amongst contemporary moderate Western-educated Muslims is thus very clear that FGM is harmful and unacceptable – a position finally confirmed in 2008 by the World Health Association,[48] reiterated in 2013 by the World Health Organization,[49] and definitively after many years of lobbying and debate also unanimously by the United Nations, on 20 December 2012.[50]

Nonetheless, and despite the evidence from history that female genital mutilation has multiple and ancient roots, many people still believe that FGM and certain faiths are fundamentally connected.

This continuing perception gives rise to several important issues, both about the practice of FGM itself and about wider public understandings and responses to it.

Amongst the most important of these issues in the British context are that:

- although the factual basis of their understanding is misjudged, some proponents of FGM believe sincerely that their faith requires girls and women in their communities to undergo the 'procedure';

- it can be expected that FGM is more likely to occur in some British communities than in others, but the correlation is far from exact, for either the adoption or the rejection of FGM; and
- the public (mis-)perception of the relationship between FGM and some religions has wider consequences for perceptions of diversity, general inter-community tolerance, and feelings of safety and acceptance across both 'sides' of the misunderstood divide.

The belief by some that FGM is a tenet of faith is increasingly being addressed directly within the British Muslim community itself, just as the Muslim Women's League in the USA has done.[51] The London Central Mosque statement (above) is one example of categorical rebuttal of FGM, but the same condemnation is now being voiced also by others.

Another example is the campaign by the British Arab Federation (BAF), which in late 2013 helped coordinate a parliamentary Early Day Motion (Number 365[52]) concerning FGM, calling for enforcement of the law and greater protection of vulnerable girls at risk.

The BAF then also arranged the UK's 'largest ever' (free) conference on FGM, in Birmingham,[53] bringing together individuals at risk of, or able to change opinions within their own communities about, FGM and assembling for the debate professionals from a range of experience and perspectives, to achieve an 'END 2 FGM' in the UK. The major outcome of this conference was a *Muslim Scholars Fatwa (Ruling) Against FGM*, issued on 12 December 2013.[54]

Sects and Witchcraft in the West

It has been suggested that FGM will in reality be easier to eradicate in places where the practice is based on religion, than in communities where the idea is fundamental to understandings about spirits and less formally articulated mythologies.

This position is derived from the idea that religious leaders can denounce and forbid FGM within a formal structure of authority, and without losing their status – something which is less likely to occur when witchcraft, with its much less visible hierarchies of influence, is involved.

The conjunctions between ancient beliefs, religions and witchcraft are complex. The formal hierarchies of the major world religions are relatively easy to discern, as are the lines of accountability of those who act as priests, imams and other religious leaders.

These lines of responsibility and communication are less overt, however, in some of the more recently developed faith movements. One important example of these which straddles both the developed and the developing world is fundamentalist religion, particularly Pentecostalism, with its focus on spirits and exorcisms, which may entail abuse, including that of children.[55]

The Pentecostal movement has grown rapidly in the UK. There were an estimated 3,900 Pentecostal churches in Britain in 2012, with more than 650 of these churches opening, many of them in London and other major cities, between 2005 and 2010.[56]

Alongside this rise has come an increasing concern about witchcraft and the possible procurement of body parts for this purpose.[57] There are several verified reports of child murder and mutilation in London in the first years of the twenty-first century[58] and there is also increasing concern that this may be linked to human trafficking and traditional harmful practices in other parts of the world.[59]

The extent of connection between fundamentalist religion, witchcraft and body parts in the UK is not known[60] but it is possibly linked to various aspects of witchcraft in Africa and elsewhere.

Reports exist of children being 'farmed' for subsequent sale, or trafficked for their body parts,[61] and in particular their sexual organs.[62]

These various fundamentalist beliefs, rumours and activities move a very long way from religious observance as the vast majority of people of all faiths understand it, and they are invisible in normal social life. They are taken seriously by the Metropolitan Police and London-based organisations such as AFRUCA,[63] Trust for London[64] and the Victoria Climbié Foundation.[65]

Whatever the perceptions and beliefs which fail to prevent it, child abuse of any sort is, quite straightforwardly, child abuse.

Discuss this chapter at http://nofgmukbook.com/2015/01/29/chapter-3-perceptions-and-beliefs/.

Endnotes

All weblinks accessed on 1 March 2015.

1   Gollaher, D.L. (2000) *Circumcision: A History of the World's Most Controversial Surgery*. New York: Basic Books, pp. xiv and 253.
2   Moore, V. (2010) A 'Ritual Nick' Too Far. *Sydney Morning Herald*, 25 January. Available at: http://www.smh.com.au/federal-politics/society-and-culture/a-ritual-nick-too-far-20100625-z8x2.html.
3   Lorenzi, R. (2012) How Did Female Genital Mutilation Begin? *Discover News*, 10 December. Available at: http://news.discovery.com/human/female-genital-mutilation-begin-121210.htm.

4   Global Alliance Against Female Genital Mutilation. (2015) *Historical Note.* Available at: http://www.global-alliance-fgm.org/Portal/AboutFGM/ HistoricalNote.aspx.

5   Global Alliance Against Female Genital Mutilation. (2015) *Historical Note.* Available at: http://www.global-alliance-fgm.org/Portal/AboutFGM/ HistoricalNote.aspx.

6   Elchalal, U., Ben-Ami, B., Gillis, R., Brzezinski, A. (1997) Ritualistic Female Genital Mutilation: Current status and future outlook. *Obstetrical & Gynecological Survey.* 52(10): 643–51 Available at: http://www.ncbi.nlm.nih.gov/pubmed/9326757.

7   Ansorge, R. (2008) *'You cannot change it in a day or night…' Female Genital Mutilation/Cutting in the Shanty Towns of Port Sudan.* MSc thesis, Charité Universitätsmedizin Berlin, Freie Universität and Humboldt Universität Berlin. Available at: http://www2.ohchr.org/english/bodies/cedaw/docs/cedaw_crc_ contributions/RoseAnsorge.pdf.

8   Lorenzi, R. (2012) How Did Female Genital Mutilation Begin? *Sott.net,* 10 December. Available at: http://www.sott.net/article/254571-How-did-female-genital-mutilation-begin.

9   Sherif, B. (1997-2001) Egypt. *The International Encyclopaedia of Sexuality 1-4.* Available at: http://www2.hu-berlin.de/sexology/IES/egypt.html.

10   Douglas, M. (1966) *Purity and Danger: An analysis of the concepts of pollution and taboo.* Psychology Press.

11   The Culture Trip. (2013) *Female Purity and Tradition.* Available at: http://theculturetrip.com/africa/articles/female-purity-and-tradition/.

12   Valenti, J. (2010) *The Purity Myth: How America's obsession with virginity is hurting young women.* Berkeley: Seal Press.

13   Jacobs Brumberg, J. (1997) *The Body Project: An intimate history of American girls.* New York: Random House.

14   Hirsi Ali, A. (2004) *The Caged Virgin: An emancipation proclamation for women and Islam.* New York: Free Press.

15   Moss, A. (2011) *Churching of Women in Medieval Times.* Available at: https://medievalchristianityd.wikispaces.com/Churching+of+Women.

16   Lightfood-Klein, H. (1989) The Sexual Experience and Marital Adjustment of Genitally Circumcised Females in The Sudan. *The Journal of Sex Research.* 26(3): 375–92. Available at: http://www.fgmnetwork.org/authors/Lightfoot-klein/ sexualexperience.htm.

17   Duffy, J. (1989) *A Nineteenth Century Answer to Masturbation. The Female Genital Cutting Education and Networking Project.* Available at: http://www.fgmnetwork. org/articles/duffy.htm.

18   Sheehan, E. (1981) Victorian Clitoridectomy: Isaac Baker Brown and his harmless operative procedure. *Med Anthropol Newsletter.* 12(4): 9–15. Available at: http://www.nci.nlm.nih.gov/pubmed/12263443.

19   Anonymous (1867) Clitoridectomy and Medical Ethics. *Medical Times and Gazette.* 1: 391–2. Available at: http://www.cirp.org/library/history/medicaltimes1867.

20 Ingenious (2014) *Clitoridectomy*. Available at: http://www.ingenious.org.uk/site. asp?s=RMA&ArticleID={971311AD-0810-483D-8F80-B97B6E8D9E44}.

21 Duffy, J. (1989) *A Nineteenth Century Answer to Masturbation*. The Female Genital Cutting Education and Networking Project. Available at: http://www. fgmnetwork.org/articles/duffy.htm.

22 Involuntary Foreskinectomy Awareness (2014) *America's Forgotten History of Female Circumcision*. Available at: https://sites.google.com/site/completebaby/ female.

23 McDonald, C.F. (1958) Circumcision of the Female. *GP*. 18(3): 98–9.

24 History of Circumcision (2014) *Circumcision of Females: Cultural and medical rationales*. Available at: http://www.historyofcircumcision.net/index. php?option=com_content&task=category&sectionid=13&id=76&Itemid=6.

25 See discussion in Chapter 5, pp. 132–5.

26 The Circumcision Reference Library (2012) *United States Circumcision Incidence*. Available at: http://www.cirp.org/library/statistics/USA/.

27 The Circumcision Reference Library (2006) *United Kingdom: Incidence of Male Circumcision*. Available at: http://www.cirp.org/library/statistics/UK/.

28 BBC (2013) Sheffield Circumcision Cuts Spark Backstreet Op. Fear. *BBC News*, 17 January. Available at: http://www.bbc.co.uk/news/uk-england-south-yorkshire-21057581.

29 NHS Choices (2014) *Circumcision*. Available at: http://www.nhs.uk/Conditions/ Circumcision/.

30 Chief Medical Officer Directorate (2008) *Religious Male Circumcision (Letter to Health Professionals in Scotland)*. Edinburgh: The Scottish Government. Available at: http://www.scotland.gov.uk/Resource/Doc/212548/0056530.pdf.

31 Rickwood, A., Kenny, S., Donnell, S. (2000) Towards Evidence Based Circumcision of English Boys: Survey of trends in practice. *BMJ*. 321(7264): 792–3. Available at: http://www.ncbi.nlm.nih.gov/pmc/articles/PMC27490/.

32 Daily Mail (2013) Israeli Mother Ordered to Pay Fine of $140 a Day for Refusing to Circumcise Her Son. *Daily Mail*, 26 November. Available at: http://www. dailymail.co.uk/news/article-2513892/Israeli-mother-ordered-pay-fine-140-day-refusing-circumcise-son.html.

33 Pool, G. (2012) Jewish Mum Speaks out about Circumcision. *Ending Unnecessary Male Circumcision in the UK*, 29 June. Available at: http://endmalecircumcision. blogspot.co.uk/2012/06/jewish-mum-speaks-out-against.html.

34 WHO (2007) *Male Circumcision: Global trends and determinants of prevalence, safety and acceptability*. Available at: http://apps.who.int/iris/ bitstream/10665/43749/1/9789241596169_eng.pdf.

35 Bill & Melinda Gates Foundation (2014) *What We Do: HIV Strategy Overview*. Available at: http://www.gatesfoundation.org/What-We-Do/Global-Health/HIV.

36 Yikoniko, S., Towindo, L. (2012) Were We Fooled? *Maravi*, 13 July. Available at: http://maravi.blogspot.co.uk/2012/07/sticky-sunday-mail-zw-were-we-fooled.html.

37 Doctors Opposing Circumcision (2008) *The Use of Male Circumcision to Prevent HIV Infection*. Available at: http://www.doctorsopposingcircumcision.org/info/HIVStatement.html.

38 Wikipedia (2015) *Religious Views on Female Genital Mutilation*. Available at: http://en.wikipedia.org/wiki/Religious_views_on_female_genital_mutilation.

39 Sunni Belief: the Tawhid (2015) Available at: https://sunnism.wordpress.com/.

40 Arora, V. (2014) Maldives: Cleric calls for FGM on Islamic grounds. *Lapidomedia*, 12 March. Available at: http://www.lapidomedia.com/node/3987.

41 Huda (2014) What Is a 'Fatwa'? *islam.about.com*. Available at: http://islam.about.com/od/law/g/fatwa.htm.

42 Keller, N. (1995) *What is the Distinction between Hadith and Sunna?* Available at: http://www.masud.co.uk/ISLAM/nuh/hadith.htm.

43 Wikipedia (2015) *Religious Views on Female Genital Mutilation*. Available at: http://en.wikipedia.org/wiki/Religious_views_on_female_genital_mutilation#Islam.

44 Topping, A. (2014) Muslim Youth Summit Told Female Genital Mutilation is not Part of Islam. *Guardian*, 8 October. Available at: http://www.theguardian.com/world/2014/oct/08/muslim-youth-summit-fgm-islam-gambia.

45 Wikipedia (2015) *Religious Views on Female Genital Mutilation*. Available at: http://en.wikipedia.org/wiki/Religious_views_on_female_genital_mutilation#Islam.

46 Muslim Women's League (1999) *Female Genital Mutilation*. Available at: http://www.mwlusa.org/topics/violence&harrassment/fgm.html.

47 ICC Services (2014) *Female Genital Mutilation: Religious, cultural and legal myths*. Available at: www.iccservices.org.uk/news_and_events/updates/female_genital_mutilation.htm.

48 WHO (2008) *Resolutions and Decisions: WHA 61.16 Female genital mutilation*. Available at: http://www.who.int/reproductivehealth/topics/fgm/fgm_resolution_61.16.pdf.

49 World Health Organization (2013) *Female Genital Mutilation*. Available at: http://www.who.int/topics/female_genital_mutilation/en/.

50 UN Women (2012) *United Nations Bans Female Genital Mutilation*. Available at: http://www.unwomen.org/en/news/stories/2012/12/united-nations-bans-female-genital-mutilation.

51 Muslim Women's League (1999) *Female Genital Mutilation*. Available at: http://www.mwlusa.org/topics/violence&harrassment/fgm.html.

52 Cunningham, J. (2013) *Early Day Motion 635: Female Genital Mutilation*. Available at: http://www.parliament.uk/edm/2013-14/635.

53 British Arab Federation (2013) *Female Genital Mutilation: Finding Answers*. Available at: http://end2fgm.com/events/end2fgm.

54 Armstrong, P.S. (2013) *Muslim Scholars Fatwa (Ruling on FGM)*. The Association of British Muslims, 12 December. Available at: http://www.aobm.org/muslim-scholars-fatwa-ruling-on-fgm/.

55 Metropolitan Police Service (2011) *Child Abuse Linked with a Belief Factsheet.* Available at: http://content.met.police.uk/cs/Satellite?blobcol=urldata&blobhead ername1=Content-Type&blobheadername2=Content-Disposition&blobheaderv alue1=application%2Fpdf&blobheadervalue2=inline%3B+filename%3D%22885 %2F75%2FSpirit+Possession+-+factsheet.pdf%22&blobkey=id&blobtable=Mung oBlobs&blobwhere=1283568747393&ssbinary=true.

56 Topping, A. (2012) Accusations of Witchcraft are Part of Growing Pattern of Child Abuse in UK. *Guardian,* 1 March. Available at: http://www.theguardian. com/uk/2012/mar/01/accusations-witchcraft-pattern-child-abuse.

57 Barnett, A., Harris, P., Thompson, T. (2002) Human Flesh 'on Sale in London'. *Guardian,* 2 November. Available at: http://www.theguardian.com/uk/2002/ nov/03/ukcrime.antonybarnett.

58 Bahunga, J. (2013) Tackling Child Abuse Linked to Faith or Belief. *Every Child Journal.* 3(3). Available at: http://www.afruca.org/wp-content/uploads/2013/07/ ECJ-3-4-Faith-based-abuse.pdf.

59 Crawford, A. (2013) Torso Case Boy 'Identified'. *BBC News,* 7 February. Available at: http://www.bbc.co.uk/news/uk-21365961.

60 Cobain, I. and Dodd, V. (2005) How Media Whipped up a Racist Witch-hunt. *Guardian,* 25 June. Available at: http://www.theguardian.com/uk/2005/jun/25/ children.pressandpublishing.

61 BBC News (2013) Nigerian 'Baby Factory' Raided in Imo State. *BBC News,* 10 May. Available at: http://www.bbc.co.uk/news/world-africa-22484318.

62 Kitabu, G. (2013) Police Probe New FGM Claims. *IPP Media,* 25 June. Available at: http://www.ippmedia.com/frontend/?l=56326.

63 AFRUCA (2013) Africans United Against Child Abuse. Available at: http:// www.afruca.org/.

64 Briggs, S., Bryan, A., Linford, H., Ludick, D., Ryan, E., Whittaker, A. (2011) *Safeguarding Children's Rights: Exploring issues of witchcraft and spirit possession in London's African communities.* Trust for London and Centre for Social Work Research. Available at: http://www.trustforlondon.org.uk/Safeguarding%20 summary.pdf.

65 VCF (2014) The Victoria Climbié Foundation UK. Available at: http://vcf-uk.org/.

4   Men, Women and Power

In the twentieth century female genital mutilation was a matter rarely discussed in polite Western society. Its immutable centrality in various traditional communities, even nations, was barely acknowledged in the more modern 'developed' world, where the very large majority of people had no idea that FGM is a fact of life for others, even sometimes a few others amongst their own compatriots.

The onset of the twenty-first century, however, has seen things change. FGM has started to be recognised as an issue in most cities in the Western world. People in Britain, mainland Europe, North America and, for instance, Australia have begun to ask how it is that such a bewildering and disturbing 'custom' can have become a feature of their own communities and society.

Two factors in particular stand out as partial answers to this question.

The first factor is that African and other diaspora have now become widely established in Western nations. The first small waves of migrants have been joined by second-, third- or even fourth-generation followers, as travel and economic opportunities have enabled people more easily to leave their place of origin for what they hope will be a better or more lucrative life. Diversity of place of birth and of custom and tradition is now unexceptional in most of the larger cities in the developed world.

But ease of travel is not the only very significant factor in the discovery of FGM in the West. A second massive factor is ease of communication. Technology has made it very simple for all of us to tell and share our stories day by day, through formal channels of information and social media, and in numerous other ways.

News of what happens in areas of the world previously almost inaccessible now reach other parts of the world through mobile telephones, television and social media such as Twitter. Journalists across the globe tell of these happenings via the same instantaneous media, as do charities and other organisations wanting to bring attention to particular issues; and concerned individuals reach out to friends, colleagues and acquaintances through Facebook, email and, increasingly significantly, e-petitions.

Whether or not those directly involved would wish to see traditional, sometimes secret, practices such as FGM exposed to international scrutiny, that is what twenty-first-century communications technologies have achieved.

And thus awareness of FGM has been sharpened in the developed countries. The first scarcely believed reports of FGM which emerged in Western nations in the 1970s[1] have now gained credence to become the basis of a global movement, expressed in diverse ways,[2, 3] to abolish this traditional harmful practice. One such example is the *Feminist Statement on Female Genital Mutilation*, published in 2013 by the present author and others (see the Appendix, pp. 323–9), and making the case that FGM is patriarchy.[4]

Thanks to easy intercontinental travel and the diaspora there are now many more people in the Western world with direct experience of FGM; and in the techno-ether the World Wide Web ensures that instantaneous modern communications reach and are transmitted from traditional developing areas as a matter of routine.

The Bigger Picture: Harmful Traditional Practices

These factors are relevant to contemporary understandings of FGM not only because they highlight matters hitherto almost invisible, but because they have arisen in parallel with other disclosures about the way societies perceive and shape the lives of their female members.

FGM is not alone in being a practice which physically and violently impinges on the intimate daily lives of women and girls.[5] Included along with FGM in the lexicons of 'harmful traditional practices' (HTPs) are various abuses (mostly gender-based, and directed more often at girls and women) listed by, for instance, the United Nations General Assembly,[6] the Inter-African Committee (IAC) on Traditional Practices,[7] the United Nations Virtual Knowledge Center to End Violence Against Women[8] and the Medical Research Council of South Africa.[9]

These organisations amongst others catalogue a range of HTPs, such as:

- beading[10] (in reality, culturally sanctioned paedophilia)
- breast ironing[11]
- domestic violence
- dowry-related violence[12]
- ebinyo (teeth-pulling) – four times more prevalent in female infants than in male[13]
- forced and child 'marriage'[14]
- 'honour' stoning and killing[15, 16]
- leblouh or gavage (forced fattening)[17]
- maltreatment of widows and wife/widow inheritance[18, 19, 20]
- okukyalira ensiko (labia elongation)[21, 22]
- sexual assault

- sexual harassment
- sex trafficking of women and girls[23]
- son preference and female feticide[24]
- twin infant killing and live burial of infants[25]
- witchcraft allegations[26] and 'spirit child' allegations.[27, 28]

The range and nature of these practices is still being revealed, as greater attention is paid to the various ways in which girls, especially, are the subject of HTPs (harmful traditional practices).[29]

It is impossible to be certain how often – or in some cases even if – various of these harmful traditional practices occur in Western countries such as Britain,[30] but there is no doubt that FGM at least is the experience of thousands of women and girls in the UK and other similar societies.

There is also substantive evidence that in some British communities a belief in witchcraft remains, as exemplified by the killings of 'Adam', Victoria Climbié and Kristy Bamu, and the torture with chilli peppers and knives of Child B – all of which became criminal cases heard in London in the years since the Millennium.[31, 32]

Even more recently, there have been several cases across Britain, for instance in Rotherham, Rochdale, Derby and Oxford, of men brought to trial for grooming young girls to have sex with them[33, 34] – a form of abuse connected with cultural understandings about the ages at which it is acceptable for girls to become sexually active: in some traditions girls undergo FGM or other rites of passage at the onset of puberty and are then married off, perhaps as additional wives, as soon as possible.

Whilst certainly not all grooming cases are underpinned by tradition-based beliefs (see for example Jimmy Savile[35] and Stuart Hall[36]), the connection with accepted expectations around premature sexual availability and child marriage in some communities is significant.

UK policing responses to these abuses of children have included Project Violet[37] and thereby an emerging understanding of difficult issues such as witchcraft[38, 39] (including possibly body parts and albinism[40]) as well as moves within various identified communities themselves to stop grooming and the serious harm it causes.[41] The evidence thus far, however, is that a fully joined-up public service approach to protecting children from serious harm and long-term trauma (even death) has by any measure yet to be established.[42]

In the meantime, FGM is one type of child abuse amongst a number which continue at least in part because of the connection with particular traditional community beliefs about the status, character and role of women in society.

It is possible also to make the case that similar, albeit less immovably trenchant, assumptions about girls and women have not helped in developing modern-day child protection services in Britain and elsewhere. If, as in Rochdale, girls reporting fears and concerns were not believed, it is obvious that they could not be safeguarded.

Education and Life Chances after Female Genital Mutilation

The underpinnings of FGM are fundamentally patriarchal. Whether it is done clandestinely or as part of an elaborate rite of passage, in infancy, as a girl reaches puberty or when as a young woman she reaches sexual maturity, the rationale behind the act is gendered oppression, suppression and limitation of autonomy. The tradition of FGM has as its basis the reduction of a woman's individuality and the requirement that the community comes first. She is, as some who have experienced FGM remark, above all else a bearer of babies.[43]

In this context it is unsurprising that those who experience FGM during puberty are said – research is required to establish the veracity and/or extent of this in the UK – often to drop out of, or perhaps simply disappear from, school shortly thereafter. (Such a course of action would be in line with patterns of school (non-)attendance demonstrated for example by young teenage girls who find themselves pregnant, whether in the UK[44] or in more traditional societies.[45] As in these cases, if dropout or disrupted education is confirmed, bespoke positive interventions on behalf of girls with FGM will need to be instituted to prevent this.)

Whilst a course of action now more frequently challenged than previously, withdrawing girls who have undergone FGM from school would probably be their parents' expectation in the country from which their heritage is drawn.[46, 47] Such a choice, albeit now actively opposed in many countries,[48] would traditionally be both the economic and the cultural norm and is therefore unremarkable even in Britain within the confines of family and local community.

This pattern of withdrawal from school after puberty is not restricted to girls undergoing FGM. It has also been the mode, for example, for working-class British-heritage girls whose families routinely expect young women to become pregnant in their early teens, but it is a critical constraint on an individual's prospects however and wherever it occurs,[49, 50] even though it may not add much to the level of disadvantage some girls from ethnic minority already experience.[51]

FGM does, however, add another sometimes massively negative dimension to the often low educational expectations and aspirations of affected girls and their families.

Beyond the issues in some diaspora and isolated communities of routine below-par academic attainment and/or the exhausting distractions of premature parenthood are real physical and psychological problems in everyday life.[52, 53]

Following the FGM 'procedure', girls are often in pain; and for some the most routine physiological functions may become perennially problematic. Menstruation may be excruciating, visits to the toilet may take hours, anaemia[54] may cause energy to dissipate. Even some normal physical movements (such as sitting cross-legged) can be difficult and uncomfortable.

Additionally, girls who have experienced FGM are prone to develop psychological conditions which, congruent with trauma arising from what has been done to them, have the effect of making them withdrawn and perhaps uncommunicative or distrustful. Like girls in other countries who drop out from school after FGM,[55, 56, 57] there are anecdotal reports (again, more research is needed) of teenage girls returning to the UK from 'holidays' abroad who were well adjusted to school before they went, but who fail to thrive in the learning environment after they return[58] – if indeed they ever return to school, or even to the UK, at all.

Although some girls and young women overcome all the disadvantages they may face after FGM, it may severely constrain formal academic advancement and social development. Future employment prospects and economic independence are compromised by the enduringly harmful consequences of FGM, and this is in some ways a self-fulfilling prophecy.

The cultural norm of female subjugation which offers the rationale for the abuse is in reality achieved by it being brutally imposed: the subjects of FGM may well by that very act lose their autonomy and become life-long dependent on men, and in particular their future husbands.

In some societies FGM is, literally, patriarchy incarnate.

Violence against Women and Girls

Violence against individuals in personal and intimate contexts can affect both men and women, but, whilst everyone has an equal right to personal safety and respect, the most usual scenario is that men inflict violence on women and girls. Violent behaviour by men may be to gain control and often originates from a sense of entitlement supported by sexist, racist, homophobic and other discriminatory attitudes.[59]

One in three women and girls across the globe has direct personal experience of physical and/or sexual violence,[60] yet this fact remains unremarked upon in most mainstream discussion. Invisibility is even greater for FGM.

The case for bringing violence against women and girls (hereafter: VAWG) and FGM specifically together in public awareness is strong.

As Betty Friedan observed half a century ago in *The Problem That Has No Name*,[61] her exploration of women's suppression (as unfulfilled 'housewives') to serve the interests of men, patriarchy is frequently unobserved, which feeds the secrecy in which intimate violence to the person thrives. Only by bringing things into the open can the abuse and limiting of women's potential be stopped.

Social taboos on the discussion of the harmful effects of violence are often deeply ingrained. If they were not, to give one entrenched example, it is unlikely that anyone would agree to go to war. Whole generations are traumatised by military action but rarely do societies recognise the damage to the collective psyche. Instead, nations over the centuries have polished and glamorised military action to the extent that its tawdry harm is usually put aside.[62]

It is no coincidence then that the rape and abduction of girls and women are in some instances the means by which military might is consolidated.[63] It is not enough to 'win' by military means. Victory must also be embedded at the individual, personal level, by conquering women and girls, as well as the men and boys who engaged as the enemy in actual combat.

These dark and difficult matters all point to the same core theme: male dominance and patriarchy are the underlying feature, just as they are with FGM. In some cases the violence is casual and impersonal – it matters not if the girl or woman concerned is known to her attacker – and in others it is planned and directed at closely targeted individuals.

In every instance, whether the act is perpetrated directly by men or indirectly for men, the result is the intimidation and subjugation of women to serve the interests of dominant males.

And this is also the reason that violence against the female person is such a hushed matter. Journalists, especially female journalists, in many parts of the world are grotesquely punished and harmed for reporting FGM and VAWG,[64, 65] politicians around the globe are wherever possible reluctant to acknowledge it,[66] sponsors and funders may find it more comfortable to support less embarrassing and challenging community work than combatting FGM.[67]

Added to this in the UK is the customary British reluctance to talk about intimate and sexual matters, even when the discussion is part of the school curriculum,[68, 69, 70] whilst sexual and other physical abuse is hardly acknowledged at all in decorous society[71] or even in the context of medical consultation.[72, 73]

The desire in some political quarters to evade the sex and relationships curriculum/education (SRE) exists in many places across the globe and its political divides. Modern Russia shares with, for example, many of the US

Deep South states a belief that childhood 'innocence' would be defiled by sex education beyond the 'abstinence only' discourse,[74, 75] even when the evidence suggests that knowledge is very important to personal outcomes and futures.[76]

It seems that some Western English-speaking cultures, albeit that they lead in rational discourse and cutting-edge high technology, remain as averse to plain-speaking in matters personal and intimate as do more technically oriented but traditionally authoritarian societies.

In communities where in addition science, technology and evidenced-based debate are generally absent, notions such as 'sex education' may therefore present a massive challenge to the status quo.

And in Western societies where techno-rational understandings are generally the norm, connections between sex, gender and patriarchy remain powerful undercurrents, permitting and enabling science and formalised knowledge to elide with masculinity in ways which remove the obligation (in the eyes of those who decide) to consider customs and practices of any or all kinds which throw into relief the power of men over women.[77]

Violence against women and girls, under cover of patriarchy, is found in almost every society, whether 'developed' or not. Absolute acceptance of this oppressive power may, however, hold even greater sway in communities where rational debate about personal and sexual matters is not encouraged.

Where beliefs favouring the interests of powerful men are handed down over generations without question, the 'facts' of science and the value of open discussion are unlikely, at least without counter-weighing and influential sponsors, to be persuasive. And so VAWG, and with it FGM in some communities, continues, often unchallenged.

Changing the Balance of Power

We have seen that VAWG, and specifically FGM, are aspects of patriarchy and the power of men over women. It is true that FGM is more often procured and performed by women than by men, but the claimed rationale for imposing this cruelty on female children is that men require it.

Girls who have not had FGM are held to be unclean, and perhaps sexually uncontrollable, until and unless they have FGM; they will not achieve a good dowry (bride price for their fathers), nor, it is held, will they be reliably subservient to the desires and control of their husbands. Education and knowledge – other than that received in some cases from the secret societies which deliver the FGM – is inappropriate for obedient wives, who may be 'married' very young indeed to much older men.

These young 'brides' – some of whom[78] will become in reality juvenile 'sex slaves'[79] – may have to share the beneficence (or otherwise) of their husbands with other wives, and will be totally dependent thereinafter on their husbands both for themselves and for their future children.

In such a setting the community in which the bride lives may consider formal education, which increases her prospects of later economic independence and personal autonomy, not just inappropriate, but actually subversive to the interests of the men who are in control.

It is therefore one of the ironies of FGM that, whilst enacting it lies within the remit of women, to prevent it requires a challenge to the status quo by men. Reports from various FGM-practising communities suggest, however, that often the men have, or affect to have, little idea of what is actually involved; or they may think FGM is 'only' circumcision (still a painful and sometimes very dangerous procedure to be borne stoically) such as they, the men, may also have endured.[80]

This disengagement is convenient. FGM directly plays to the (perceived) economic interests of men – the belief is that it keeps women chaste, subdues them, and supposedly ensures that children are in fact their father's. In effect it makes wives-as-objects the property of men; but allowing FGM to be moderated by women with no apparent instruction or direction from the men means this powerful arrangement is less visible.

Nonetheless, men and women alike can feel deep aversion to inflicting pain on others, especially their children. Nor do some (most?) men, despite their need to 'prove' themselves, actually want to hurt their brides on their wedding night[81] (albeit they must demonstrate their sexual prowess, so many rationalise what actually happened later on, and empathy may be in short supply[82]). In traditional times these feelings are usually dismissed because FGM is nonetheless believed ultimately to be in the best interests of the girl. Without it, she may be ostracised, perhaps even abandoned, because she has not adhered to the norms of the community and is therefore no longer part of it.

With Western culture, however, has come an increasing perception of every human being as an individual, an influence which may be at work even when this modern cultural perception is at a distance from the traditional culture of the FGM-practising community.

Whilst there is so far little real research to explain undercurrents in the shift towards men stopping FGM, if fathers and brothers see girls in a more individualised light they may begin to insist that the demands of the traditionally bound community come second to their daughters' entitlement to remain unharmed and intact.

Such a shift towards acknowledging the right of all children to protection from harm is important whether the harm arises from FGM or from other traditional harmful practices imposed on both girls and boys – albeit the contexts in these various practices may differ.

In Britain, for instance, 'grooming' is a crime which arises from the perception of girls as sexually available from a very young age. In this example, whilst FGM may or may not have occurred, it is deemed acceptable to take female children for sexual gratification from when the first signs of puberty arise, even though physical and psychological adulthood may still be years away.

The same might also be said of insisting that girls wear the niqab for reasons of 'modesty'. By inference, at a point when they are still really children, its adoption suggests, painfully, that these girls would otherwise be sexually available.[83]

Acknowledging and Taking Responsibility

Men within practising communities have a critical role in the cessation of FGM; and it is apparent that some of them understand this. There are repeated reports in various parts of the world of fathers, brothers and potential suitors refuting FGM, and even of threats by fathers to visit retribution upon anyone who attempts to inflict it without permission on a child.

But it is not only men in communities where FGM has been practised who have a critical role in its abolition.

Almost every nation in the world has legal statutes which directly or indirectly forbid FGM; in countries such as Britain the legal frameworks (and penalties) have been in place for many years. And the majority of people who uphold the law are men, just as are the majority of border control officers, policy-makers and so forth.

Men in the mainstream of modern societies – the police and lawyers, doctors, teachers, social and youth workers and many more – therefore have important parts to play, in both their professional and civic duties, in eradicating FGM.

Western societies are far from gender-equal, but the obligation to protect children from harm is a priority in all of them. FGM presents special difficulties because it concerns juvenile, physically intimate matters – issues from which male professionals especially may shy away.

Further, the majority of these male officers and professionals are probably also acutely aware that allegations of impropriety are an everyday hazard in their work. It is therefore centrally important that frameworks exist to ease the way to reporting without risk to the person with the concerns, when suspicions about FGM arise.[84]

Nonetheless, professional frameworks are not the only barrier to effective enforcement of the safeguarding obligation on all who must protect children from harm. Only quite recently, for example, have some in the police begun to recognise that violence against women, whether in the home or elsewhere, comprises, however it occurs, a criminal act.

This necessary shift in perceptions, it might be suggested, would have come earlier and more easily if law enforcement and other public services in Britain were routinely gender and ethnically diverse and sensitive to the range of concerns found in wider society.

Violence against women is not a 'domestic'; it is assault.

A similar consideration applies doubly in the case of FGM. It is not a 'cultural' matter or a 'women's issue'. It is criminal abuse and it requires formal, immediate and commensurate intervention.

These are not 'gendered' matters. They are fundamental issues of human rights and respect. Perhaps the extent of increasing involvement of men in fighting FGM is one indicator of moves towards gender equality and equity.

The effectiveness of measures to protect women and children from harm is similarly a very good indicator of the rule of law in both society overall and, more specifically, in any given community within that society. There is as yet a way to go.

Discuss this chapter at http://nofgmukbook.com/2015/01/29/chapter-4-men-women-and-power/.

Endnotes

All weblinks accessed on 1 March 2015.

1   Strain, K. (2013) The Unkindest Cut. *Cornell Alumni Magazine*. Available at: http://cornellalumnimagazine.com/index.php?option=com_content&task=view&id=1709&Itemid=56&ed=37.
2   New Vision (2013) Africa: Queens Declare War on HIV, FGM, Early Marriages. *AllAfrica Global Media*, 13 September. Available at: http://allafrica.com/stories/201309140263.html.
3   Forward UK (2014) *Child Marriage*. Available at: http://www.forwarduk.org.uk/key-issues/child-marriage.
4   Adeaga, T., Burrage, H., Ferrari, P., Levin, T., Sharp, L.M., Weil-Curiel, L. (2013) A Feminist Statement on the Naming and Abolition of Female Genital Mutilation. *Statement on FGM*, 28 August. Available at: http://statementonfgm.com/. Reproduced in the Appendix of this book.
5   London School of Hygiene and Tropical Medicine (2013) *Violence against Women a Global Health Problem of Epidemic Proportions*. 20 June. Available at: http://www.lshtm.ac.uk/newsevents/news/2013/gender_violence_report.html.

6   UN Office for the High Commissioner of Human Rights (1979) *Fact Sheet No. 23, Harmful Traditional Practices Affecting the Health of Women and Children.* Available at: http://www.ohchr.org/documents/publications/factsheet23en.pdf.

7   IAC-CIAF (2009) *The Inter-African Committee on Traditional Practices.* Available at: http://www.iac-ciaf.net/index.php?option=com_content&view=article&id=10 &Itemid=3.

8   End VAW Now (2014) *Legislation.* Available at: http://www.endvawnow.org/en/ modules/view/8-legislation.html#6.

9   Sexual Violence Research Initiative (2014) *Traditional Harmful Practices.* Available at: http://www.svri.org/female.htm.

10   Sarro, S. (2012) Female Circumcision in Samburu, Kenya: Where Culture is Above the Law. *KC Team,* 8 May. Available at: http://www.keycorrespondents. org/2012/05/08/female-circumcision-in-samburu-kenya-where-culture-is-above-the-law/#comment-154187.

11   Hall, A. (2013) Cameroon's Women Call Time on Breast Ironing. *New Internationalist Magazine,* 1 May. Available at: http://newint.org/ features/2013/05/01/tales-of-taboo/.

12   The Advocates for Human Rights (2014) *Dowry-Related Violence.* Available at: http://www.stopvaw.org/dowry-related_violence.

13   Bandyopadhyay, M. (2003) Missing Girls and Son Preference in Rural India: Looking Beyond Popular Myth. *Health Care Women Int.* 24(10): 910–26. Available at: http://www.ncbi.nlm.nih.gov/pubmed/16161877.

14   Forward UK (2014) *Child Marriage.* Available at: http://www.forwarduk.org.uk/ key-issues/child-marriage.

15   UN News Centre (2010) Impunity for Domestic Violence, 'Honour Killings' Cannot Continue – UN Official. *UN News Centre,* 4 March. Available at: http:// www.un.org/apps/news/story.asp?NewsID=33971#.Ub9UKkhwbcs.

16   Violence is not our culture (2014) *Frequently Asked Questions About 'Honour Killing'.* Available at: http://www.violenceisnotourculture.org/faq_honour.

17   Duval Smith, A (2009) Girls Being Force-Fed as Fattening Farms Revive. *The Guardian,* 1 March. Available at: http://www.theguardian.com/world/2009/ mar/01/mauritania-force-feeding-marriage.

18   Wikipedia (2015) *Widow Inheritance.* Available at: http://en.wikipedia.org/wiki/ Widow_inheritance.

19   Centre for Rights, Education and Awareness (2008) *Wife Inheritance: A death sentence behind the mask of culture.* Nairobi: Centre for Rights, Education, and Awareness.

20   UN News Centre (2010) Impunity for Domestic Violence, 'Honour Killings' Cannot Continue – UN Official. *UN News Centre,* 4 March. Available at: http:// www.un.org/apps/news/story.asp?NewsID=33971#.Ub9UKkhwbcs.

21   Admin (2012) ELONGATION: OKUKYALIRA ENSIKO, The Buganda Way of Enhancing Sexual Pleasure. *Ekimeeza Lifestyle,* 21 May. Available at: http://www. ekimeeza.com/2012/05/21/elongation-okukyalira-ensiko-the-buganda-way-of-enhancing-sexual-pleasure/.

22 Kakambo, T (2015) 'Okukyalita Ensiko' Similar to FGM, Say Lobbyists. *New Vision* , 2 January. Available at: http://www.newvision.co.ug/news/669249--okukyalira-ensiko-similar-to-fgm-say-lobbyists.html. Note 21 provides an illuminating alternative view.

23 Soroptimist (2014) *Sex Slavery/Trafficking: FAQ*. Available at: http://www.soroptimist.org/trafficking/faq.html.

24 Pande, R., Malhotra, A. (2006) *Son Preference and Daughter Neglect in India – What Happens to Living Girls?* Available at: http://www.unfpa.org/gender/docs/sexselection/UNFPA_Publication-39764.pdf.

25 Adeyemo, A (2013) In 2013, 40 Abuja Towns Still Kill Twins! A Missionary Recounts Bizarre Traditional Practices in the FCT. *Bella Niaja*, 23 March. Available at: http://www.bellanaija.com/2013/03/27/in-2013-40-abuja-towns-still-kill-twins-a-missionary-recounts-bizarre-traditional-practices-in-the-fct/.

26 Bataringaya, A., Ferguson, M., Lalloo, R. (2005) The Impact of Ebinyo, a Form of Dental Mutilation, on the Malocclusion Status in Uganda. *Community Dent Health.* 22(3): 146–50. Available at: http://www.ncbi.nlm.nih.gov/pubmed/16161877.

27 La Fontaine, J. (ed.) (2009) *The Devil's Children – From Spirit Possession to Witchcraft: New Allegations that Affect Children*. Farnham: Ashgate.

28 Schnoebelen, J. (2009) Witchcraft Allegations, Refugee Protection and Human Rights: A review of the evidence. *UNHCR New Issues in Refugee Research*, Research Paper No. 169. Available at: http://vcf-uk.org/safeguarding-childrens-rights-exploring-issues-of-witchcraft-and-spirit-possession-evaluation/.

29 Makoni, B. (16 June 2014) Top 20 Most Sexually Violent Harmful Cultural Practices the World Must Protect Girls From. *Girl Child Network Worldwide* Available at: http://www.girlchildnetworkworldwide.org/top-20-most-harmful-sexually-violent-harmful-cultural-practices-the-world-must-protect-girls-from/.

30 Dugan, E. (2013) 'Breast Ironing': Girls 'Have Chests Flattened Out' to Disguise the Onset of Puberty. *Independent*, 26 September. Available at: http://www.independent.co.uk/life-style/health-and-families/health-news/breast-ironing-girls-have-chests-flattened-out-to-disguise-the-onset-of-puberty-8842435.html.

31 Dangerfield, A. (2012) Government Urged to Tackle 'Witchcraft Belief' Child Abuse. *BBC News*, 1 March. Available at: http://www.bbc.co.uk/news/uk-england-london-17006924.

32 Crawford, A. (2013) Torso Case Boy 'Identified'. *BBC News*, 7 February. Available at: http://www.bbc.co.uk/news/uk-21365961. BBC News (2005) NSPCC Calls for Specialist Agency. *BBC News*, 3 June. Available at: http://news.bbc.co.uk/1/hi/uk/4607773.stm.

33 Penrose, J., Smith, V. (2013) Police Probe At Least 54 More Evil Child Sex Grooming Gangs. *Mirror*, 19 May. Available at: http://www.mirror.co.uk/news/uk-news/police-probe-least-54-more-1896991.

34 Dugan, E. (2013) Imams to Preach Against Grooming of Girls for Sex. *Independent*, 17 May. Available at: http://www.independent.co.uk/news/uk/home-news/imams-to-preach-against-grooming-of-girls-for-sex-8621655.html#.

35 BBC News (2013) Jimmy Savile: West Yorkshire Police Reveal Abuse Figures. *BBC News*, 30 May. Available at: http://www.bbc.co.uk/news/uk-england-leeds-22716302.

36 Bunyan, N. (2013) Stuart Hall Jailed for Indecently Assaulting Young Girls. *Guardian*, 17 June. Available at: http://www.guardian.co.uk/uk/2013/jun/17/stuart-hall-jailed-indecent-assault-girls.

37 Metropolitan Police (2014) *Abuse Linked with Spirit Possession.* Available at: http://content.met.police.uk/Article/Abuse-linked-with-spirit-possessi on/1400010000897/1400010000897.

38 Cobain, I., Dodd, V. (2005) How Media Whipped up a Racist Witch-hunt. *Guardian*, 25 June. Available at: http://www.guardian.co.uk/uk/2005/jun/25/children.pressandpublishing?.

39 Laville, S. (2012) Ritual Abuse of Children: A hidden and under-reported crime. *Guardian*, 1 March. Available at: http://www.guardian.co.uk/uk/2012/mar/01/witchcraft-ritual-abuse-hidden-crime?.

40 Smith, D. (2015) Tanzania Bans Witchdoctors in Attempt to End Albino Killings. *Guardian*, 14 January. Available at: http://www.theguardian.com/world/2015/jan/14/tanzania-bans-witchdoctors-attempt-end-albino-killings.

41 Dugan, E. (2013) Imams to Preach Against Grooming of Girls for Sex. *Independent*, 17 May. Available at: http://www.independent.co.uk/news/uk/home-news/imams-to-preach-against-grooming-of-girls-for-sex-8621655.html#. BBC News (2005) NSPCC Calls for Specialist Agency. *BBC News*, 3 June. Available at: http://news.bbc.co.uk/1/hi/uk/4607773.stm.

42 Weaver, M. (2014) Council Failings Putting Children at Risk of Abuse, Says Ofsted. *Guardian*, 19 November. Available at: http://www.theguardian.com/society/2014/nov/19/council-failings-child-sexual-exploitation-ofsted?CMP=EMCSOCEML657.

43 Okwonga, M. (2013) East African Muslim Women on Female Genital Mutilation: 'We were not meant to enjoy sex. We were supposed to be machines to have babies'. *Independent*, 9 April. Available at: http://blogs.independent.co.uk/2013/04/09/east-african-muslim-women-on-female-genital-mutilation-we-were-not-meant-to-enjoy-sex-we-were-supposed-to-be-machines-to-have-babies/.

44 Hosie, A. (2002) *Teenage Pregnancy in Young Women of School Age: An exploration of disengagement and re-engagement from the education system.* Paper presented at annual conference of the Society for the Study of Social Problems, Chicago. Available at: http://www.alisonhosie.co.uk/pdf/TPU_and_edu/Teenage_Pregnancy_in_Young_Women_of_school-age.pdf.

45 Grant, M., Hallman, K. (2006) *Pregnancy-related School Dropout and Prior School Performance in South Africa.* Available at: http://www.popcouncil.org/uploads/pdfs/wp/212.pdf.

46 Mulama, J. (2012) Giving Girls a Chance to be What They Want to be. *World Vision Kenya*, 23 September. Available at: http://wvi.org/kenya/article/giving-girls-chance-be-what-they-want-be.

47 Scanlon, L. (2012) 'They Have Put Down Their Knives' – Amref Health Africa's work against FGM. *Amref Health Africa*, 11 September. Available at: http://www.amrefuk.org/news/amref-newsroom/item/240-they-have-put-down-their-knives-amrefs-work-against-fgm.

48 BBC News (2014) Cows Offered to Keep Kenyan Girls in School in Laikipia. *BBC News*, 30 October. Available at: http://www.bbc.co.uk/news/world-africa-29834776.

49 NCSL (2014) Teen Pregnancy Prevention. *National Conference of State Legislatures*, 11 July. Available at: http://www.ncsl.org/issues-research/health/teen-pregnancy-prevention.aspx.

50 Teenage Pregnancy Independent Advisory Group (2010) *Teenage Pregnancy: Past successes – future challenges*. Available at: https://www.gov.uk/government/uploads/system/uploads/attachment_data/file/181078/TPIAG-FINAL-REPORT.pdf.

51 Department of Health Teenage Pregnancy Unit (2004) *Long-term Consequences of Teenage Births for Parents and their Children*. Available at: http://media.education.gov.uk/assets/files/pdf/b/briefing%201.pdf.

52 Burrage, H. (2013) What is Female Genital Mutilation? Why Does it Occur? What are its Health and Wellbeing Impacts? *Hilary Burrage Blog*, 15 January. Available at: http://hilaryburrage.com/2013/01/15/why-does-female-genital-mutilation-occur-and-what-are-its-impacts/.

53 Royal College of Nursing (2015) *Female Genital Mutilation – An RCN resource for nursing and midwifery practice (Second edition)*. Available at: http://www.rcn.org.uk/__data/assets/pdf_file/0010/608914/RCNguidance_FGM_WEB.pdf.

54 Chowdhury, K. (2011) India's Teen Girls Undernourished: UN. *India Today*, 26 February. Available at: http://southasia.oneworld.net/news/over-50-adolescent-girls-in-india-anaemic-unicef#.VGy5o4usWQw.

55 Girl Effect Team (2013) How Economics Can Change Thinking on FGM. *The Girl Effect*, 24 April. Available at: http://www.girleffect.org/news/2013/04/how-economics-can-change-thinking-on-fgm/.

56 Forward UK (2014) *Child Marriage*. Available at: http://www.forwarduk.org.uk/key-issues/child-marriage.

57 Schreiber, L. (2012) Avoid the Knife – FGM in Kenya. *Salt & Caramel*, 28 November. Available at: http://www.saltandcaramel.com/avoid-the-knife-fgm-in-kenya/.

58 Featherstone, L. (2014) Female Genital Mutilation: Guidelines to protect children and women. *Home Office, Department of Education*, 22 July. Available at: https://www.gov.uk/government/uploads/system/uploads/attachment_data/file/216669/dh_124588.pdf.

59 Women's Aid (2006) What is the Cause of Domestic Violence? *Women's Aid Federation of England*, 1 August. Available at: http://www.womensaid.org.uk/domestic-violence-articles.asp?section=00010001002200410001&itemid=1275.

60 World Health Organization (2013) Violence Against Women: A 'global health problem of epidemic proportions'. *World Health Organization*, 20 June. Available at: http://www.who.int/mediacentre/news/releases/2013/violence_against_women_20130620/en/index.html.

61 Napikoski, L. (2014) What Is the Problem That Has No Name? *womenshistory. about.com*. Available at: http://womenshistory.about.com/od/bettyfriedan/a/Problem-That-Has-No-Name.htm.

62 BBC News (2013) Repatriation Ceremonies for Fallen Personnel will not be Changed, says MoD. *BBC News*, 27 September. Available at: http://www.bbc.co.uk/news/uk-24296919.

63 Harvey, H. (2008) A Triumph for Women at the UN. *Guardian*, 25 June. Available at: http://www.guardian.co.uk/commentisfree/2008/jun/25/unitednations.warcrimes.

64 Lupick, T. (2012) *Journalists Intimidated for Reporting on Female Genital Mutilation in Liberia*. Available at: http://www.straight.com/news/travis-lupick-journalists-intimidated-reporting-female-genital-mutilation-liberia.

65 Wolfe, L. (2011) Documenting Sexual Violence Against Journalists. *Committee to Protect Journalists*, 16 February. Available at: http://cpj.org/blog/2011/02/documenting-sexual-violence-against-journalists.php.

66 Burrage, H. (2013) FGM: When the Deeply Personal is Fundamentally Political. *Hilary Burrage Blog*, 9 March. Available at: http://hilaryburrage.com/2013/03/09/fgm-when-the-deeply-personal-is-fundamentally-political/.

67 Humankind Foundation (2009) *Kamilika: Stop FGM*. Available at: http://www.humankindfoundation.org/sponsorship.html.

68 BBC News (2007) Britons Embarrassed about Condoms. *BBC News*, 5 August. Available at: http://news.bbc.co.uk/1/hi/health/6928266.stm.

69 Collins, N. (2010) Teachers Too Embarrassed to Teach Sex. *Telegraph*, 23 July. Available at: http://www.telegraph.co.uk/education/educationnews/7904538/Teachers-too-embarrassed-to-teach-sex.html.

70 Paton, G. (2010) General Election 2010: Compulsory sex education scrapped. *Telegraph*, 7 April. Available http://www.telegraph.co.uk/news/election-2010/7564034/General-Election-2010-compulsory-sex-education-scrapped.html.

71 The Belfast Telegraph (2010) Seek Help, Battered Women Urged. *Belfast Telegraph.co.uk*, 20 July. Available at: http://www.belfasttelegraph.co.uk/breakingnews/breakingnews_ukandireland/seek-help-battered-women-urged-28547946.html#ixzz1e6l10LFN.

72 Royal College of Nursing (2000) *Domestic Violence – Guidance for Nurses*. Available at: http://www.rcn.org.uk/__data/assets/pdf_file/0008/78497/001207.pdf.

73 Allard, C. (2013) Caring for People who Experience Domestic Abuse. *Emergency Nurse*. 21(2): 12–16.

74 Walker, S. (2013) Russian Literature is Best Sex Education for Young People, Says Ombudsman. *Guardian*, 19 September. Available at:

http://www.theguardian.com/world/2013/sep/19/russian-literature-sex-education-schools-childrens-ombudsman.

75 Bassett, L. (2013) Sex Education Programs for Teens Targeted by GOP Lawmakers. *Huff Post Politics*, 1 April. Available at: http://www.huffingtonpost.com/2013/04/01/sex-education-programs-gop_n_2993788.html?view=print&comm_ref=false.

76 Sex Education Forum (2004) 'Abstinence-only' Education, *National Children's Bureau*. Available at: http://www.ncb.org.uk/media/494613/forum_briefing_-_abstinence.pdf.

77 See for example: Leeson, J. (1978) *Women and Medicine (Tavistock women's studies)*. London: Tavistock Publications.

78 Forward UK (2014) *Child Marriage*. Available at: http://www.forwarduk.org.uk/key-issues/child-marriage.

79 Sharp, L.M. (2013) Parents Now in Kenya Bribing Chiefs to Secretly Mutilate Their Daughters in the Middle of Night, Girls between 11–14 years old and Marry Them, Sexual Slavery. *Mashua Voice for the Voiceless*, 26 August. Available at: http://mashuavoiceforthevoiceless.blogspot.co.uk/2013/08/parents-now-in-kenya-bribing-chiefs-to.html.

80 Hoegen, M. (ed.) (2013) *Engaging Men in the Abandonment of Female Genital Mutilation*. Deutsche Gesellschaft für Internationale Zusammenarbeit (GIZ) GmbH. Available at: http://www.intact-network.net/intact/cp/files/1375968625_giz2013-en-documentation-engaging-men-for-fgm-abandonment-4_final.pdf.

81 Nilsson, T. (2007) *The Impact of Empathy on the Realisation of Human Rights in General and Female Genital Mutilation in Particular*, p. 24. PhD Thesis: Lunds Universitet. Available at: http://lup.lub.lu.se/luur/download?func=downloadFile&recordOId=1319850&fileOId=1319851.

82 Nilsson, T. (2007) *The Impact of Empathy on the Realisation of Human Rights in General and Female Genital Mutilation in Particular*, p14. PhD Thesis: Lunds Universitet. Available at: http://lup.lub.lu.se/luur/download?func=downloadFile&recordOId=1319850&fileOId=1319851.

83 Cochrane, K. (2013) The Niqab Debate: 'Is the veil the biggest issue we face in the UK?' *Guardian*, 16 September. Available at: http://www.theguardian.com/world/2013/sep/16/veil-biggest-issue-uk-niqab-debate.

84 Burrage, H (2015) *UK Home Office Consultation on Mandatory Reporting – My Response*, 11 January. Available at: http://hilaryburrage.com/2015/01/11/uk-home-office-consultation-on-mandatory-reporting-of-fgm-my-response/.

5   Clinical Issues

Female genital mutilation, especially in its more extensive forms, is permanently scarring both physically and mentally. Its impacts are lifelong and often severe.

Sometimes FGM is fatal. Its victims do not always become 'survivors' in any sense of the word.

Some girls or women who undergo mutilation die in the immediate and short-term aftermath of the abuse, and later on more will die as a result of difficulties in childbirth or because of long-term conditions including fistula. Babies born to women with FGM are also at risk and sometimes die because of the obstetric complications it can cause.

The United Nations, the World Health Organization and many other international and professional bodies[1] are unanimous in asserting there is no positive benefit to FGM. They insist unequivocally that it must never be promoted or conducted as a medical procedure – which happens for instance in Kenya,[2] Indonesia,[3] Egypt[4] and Malaysia,[5] and which routinely puts the lives and well-being of those who undergo it at risk.

Impacts of FGM

There are four widely recognised types of FGM, of which Type I is the most 'mild', but rare because it is almost impossible to execute in conventional FGM settings without further damage, and Type III the most severe. (Type IV covers all genital mutilation not included in Types I to III and is therefore variable in its severity, see pp. 28–30.)

FGM has significant, often serious, lifelong negative impact on the well-being of those who experience it. It is always to some degree damaging, whether this be straightforwardly because of the trauma of enforced cutting (girls may agree and present themselves for the procedure, but they often do not realise exactly what it will entail, and they may also be pinned down brutally) or more immediately because of severe bleeding and shock, perhaps broken bones in a struggle, and thereafter sometimes lethal infection.

111

Later, the trauma may extend to permanent urinary and gynaecological problems and perhaps difficulties in conceiving or in achieving healthy obstetric outcomes.

Further, the damage may be social-psychological as well as physical. The trauma of the original procedure may result in states of mind found in many trauma victims, amongst them anxiety, fear and inability to trust or relax.

It is thought that the majority of women who have FGM experience the same levels of post-traumatic stress disorder (PTSD) as adults who have been subjected to early childhood abuse, and that 80 per cent suffer from affective (mood) or anxiety disorders;[6] and this may be exacerbated by a sense of betrayal when the girl or woman realises it was her own parent/s who initiated and insisted on FGM being performed.

The fact that FGM is 'culturally embedded' in the community is not on the evidence available a protection from PTSD and other psychiatric disorders.[7] Such perceptions can perhaps be made even worse by the later discovery that FGM is not the experience of the large majority of women outside the particular community in which it is the norm.

As noted in Chapter 1 (pp. 28–30), there are four generally agreed types of FGM; even so, precise diagnosis of type of FGM may be difficult for any particular individual.[8] Further details of the idealised typology of female genital mutilation are given by the WHO[9] as follows:

Types of female genital mutilation

Type I:

partial or total removal of the clitoris and/or the prepuce (clitoridectomy).

Subgroups:

Type Ia – removal of the clitoral hood (prepuce) only;

Type Ib – removal of the clitoris with the prepuce.

Type II:

partial or total removal of the clitoris and the labia minora, with or without excision of the labia majora (excision).

Subgroups:

Type IIa – removal of the labia minora only;

Type IIb – partial or total removal of the clitoris and labia minora;

Type IIc – partial or total removal of the clitoris, labia minora and labia majora.

Type III:

narrowing of the vaginal orifice with creation of a covering seal by cutting and appositioning the labia minora and/or the labia majora, with or without excision of the clitoris (infibulation).

Subgroups:

Type IIIa – removal and apposition of the labia minora;

Type IIIb – removal and apposition of the labia majora.

Re-infibulation is covered under this definition. This is a procedure to recreate an infibulation, for example after childbirth when de-infibulation is necessary.

Type IV:

unclassified – all other harmful procedures to the female genitalia for non-medical purposes, for example, pricking, piercing, incising, scraping and cauterization.

Source: WHO (2010)[10]

The impacts and consequences of FGM therefore vary between almost negligible to very severe and are obviously also shaped by the context in which the 'procedure' is carried out and by whom, as well as for instance the health of the girl or woman prior to FGM. Reports from organisations such as the World Health Organization (WHO)[11] as above confirm that a high percentage of those subjected to FGM suffer serious, sometimes fatal, consequences both in the short term and over time.

Whilst each type of FGM is likely to produce particular health and medical outcomes for any given girl or woman, there is also overlap in the effects which occur. Immediate and short-term (up to ten days) impacts include shock, haemorrhage, acute anaemia and infections (tetanus, urinary tract, urethral mucus/cystitis, septicaemia, vulvovaginitis).

Research by the WHO and many other bodies[12, 13, 14, 15] confirms that the consequences of female genital mutilation range from comparatively trivial (some pain, risk of infection and personal upset) to untimely death, whether immediately, in the short term, or even decades later, for the woman giving birth, her own death, and/or the death of her infant son or daughter.

As with any other trauma, the degree and extent of damage may also depend on the level of good health or otherwise of the person before the injury occurred. This is particularly important in the context of communities where malnutrition, lack of medical care and perhaps other adverse factors are already a reality.

Summary: Some Health Impacts of FGM

Impacts of FGM on physical health: immediate (up to ten days)

- abscesses and ulcers
- acute urinary retention (with pain and burning)
- fever
- gangrene
- haemorrhage
- infection of the wound
- septicaemia
- severe pain
- shock (sometimes death)
- tetanus
- urinary tract infection

Impacts of FGM on physical health: medium and longer term (after ten days)

- anaemia (and failure to thrive if malnourished child)
- anal incontinence
- bladder calculus/stone formation
- cheloids (abnormal growth of scar tissue)
- chronic back and pelvic pain
- chronic pelvic infection
- delay in wound healing due to infection, malnutrition and anaemia
- dysmenorrhoea/menstrual problems
- fibrosis (scarring at site of cutting)
- haematocolpos (accumulation internally of menstrual blood)
- hepatitis and other infections (because of poorly healed wounds)

- hypersensitivity of entire genital area, including neuroma on the dorsal nerve of the clitoris
- pain at sexual intercourse
- recto/vaginal fistulae (and often subsequent ostracisation by the community)
- synechia (abnormal fusion of labia)
- tissue rotation (abnormal scarring and retraction of anatomical zones)
- urinary problems/incontinence

Impacts of FGM on sexual health

- anxiety resulting in vaginal dryness
- dysparenuia/discomfort/spasm/pain during intercourse
- greater risk of HIV (because of cuts which bleed)
- infertility
- less (reported) sexual desire/lack of arousal
- less sexual satisfaction/difficult to reach orgasm
- morbidity due to anal intercourse, where vaginal access is difficult
- shame or embarrassment about intimacy

Impacts of FGM on psychological health (girls and women – specifics may depend on age)

- anger
- anxiety
- behavioural problems
- cognitive dissonance (where norms of FGM are not shared)
- confusion
- depression
- emotional distance
- fear
- flashbacks
- hyper-arousal
- hyper-vigilance
- inappropriate sense (in young girls) of entitlement to mature activity (for example child brides)
- lack of trust
- low self-esteem/sense of self-entitlement
- phobia
- post-traumatic stress disorder
- psychological disturbance
- psychological vulnerability
- psychosexual problems

- relationship difficulties or disorders
- sense of helplessness
- sleep disorders
- social isolation/dependent on group disconnected from the mainstream
- somatisation
- stigma

Impacts of FGM obstetrically: maternal

- caesarean section (sometimes this would have been unnecessary if the obstetrician had known beforehand)
- difficulties in performing good pelvic examination during labour (resulting in inadequate management of delivery)
- perineal lacerations
- perineal wound infections
- post-partum haemorrhage
- post-partum sepsis
- prolongation of second stage of labour
- repeated pregnancies because of infant mortality (amongst other factors)
- tearing and recourse to episiotomy
- torn uterus

Impacts of FGM obstetrically: paediatric

- cerebral palsy/brain damage
- death or serious incapacity of mother, so high risk also to child
- failure to thrive
- need for resuscitation
- neonatal distress and/or mortality
- stillbirth

The lists above are simply summaries of the currently available information garnered from many different sources about the impacts of FGM. Additional knowledge derived from clinical and psycho-sociological research is now forthcoming on a regular basis. All of it points to the human story of devastation which arises from this traditional harmful practice.

In the light of these known and deeply disturbing outcomes of female genital mutilation, it is unsurprising that as far back as 1994, a leading physician observer, Dr Nahid Toubia of Sudan and Egypt, remarked in the course of a detailed and learned review of FGM and its outcomes that it is only a matter of time before all forms of female circumcision in children will be made illegal in Western countries and, eventually, in Africa.[16]

Morbidity and Mortality Arising from FGM

A report by the FGM Cost Study Group of the World Health Organization[17] showed that almost every new girl subjected to FGM represents a future stream of preventable obstetric costs and/or a future death from obstetric complications, in addition to the risks attendant on undergoing FGM in the first place.

All the situations above present a significant risk of serious ill-health and even of premature death. Various surveys and reviews suggest that, depending on the severity of the original procedure, the risk of death for the girl or woman is at least one in forty and may be much higher than that,[18] perhaps between 10 per cent and even, in places such as rural Sudan, a third of those who undergo it.[19]

For those women and girls who survive the initial mutilation, there is still considerable risk, both from the chronic conditions (some of them listed above) which may arise, and especially from the extra peril when pregnant – though primary (and secondary) infertility may also be a hazard of FGM[20] – and giving birth.

We have already noted the risks associated with obstetric haemorrhage. To this must be added the risk of obstetric fistulae, immensely distressing and unpleasant conditions whereby the birth canal does not open adequately and obstructs the baby (who is thereby in grave danger – perhaps 90 per cent die) and then tears, resulting in damage to the urethra and/or rectum.[21]

Fistulae may occur in conjunction with FGM, and most frequently arise during the prolonged labour – typically more than three days – of very young women and girls, as a result of child and early marriage. Unless surgically repaired, the damage of fistula is traumatic: the 'leakage' is disturbing, offensive and continuous, and causes the woman to (be made to) withdraw from public life, carrying also the blame for the death of her child, if that occurs. Without surgery fistulae result in lifelong distress and socially isolating outcomes from pregnancy. This is obstetric morbidity of the highest order.

Mortality and general morbidity rates for infants born to mothers with FGM have also been observed to be significantly higher than the norm. It is estimated in one research study (see note 16) that an additional one to two babies per 100 deliveries die as a result of FGM. A 2006 research programme reported in the *Lancet*[22] found, as might be expected, that to a degree this depends on the type of FGM the mother has experienced.

The death rate among babies during and immediately after birth (neo-natal mortality rate) was similarly reported as much higher for those born to mothers with FGM: 15 per cent higher in those with FGM I, 32 per cent higher in those with FGM II, and 55 per cent higher in those with FGM III.

An increased need to resuscitate babies whose mother had had FGM (66 per cent higher in women with FGM III) was also reported.

Morbidity and mortality rates are, however, probably even higher than those above, because FGM tends to occur in areas and regions of the world where modern clinical intervention is unavailable, and, therefore, not only will FGM damage be less mitigated, but it may also go unobserved and unrecorded.

Of particular significance in this respect are reports in the UK of deaths during 'visits home' where it is said that a girl died from, perhaps, malaria or any other unidentified malaise. People in the relevant community may believe it was 'spirits' which caused death; others might suppose that the attentions of the local excisor were of more relevance.

Re-infibulation

Given the frequent severity of the outcomes of FGM, Western observers may be perplexed to learn that some women elect to undergo it as adults, either for the first time, just before marriage, or else again, post-partum (after delivery). Women sometimes specifically request that they be re-infibulated as part of their post-delivery care,[23] or they may approach a medically trained clinician for infibulation at some other point, assuring the operator that full adult consent will be given by the recipient of the procedure.

The reasons for such requests for infibulation and/or for re-infibulation are usually connected with community expectations and pressure to conform, either directly from the husband (or husband-to-be)[24] of the woman concerned, or from her family and other community members. But whatever the reason the request arises, and whatever assurances the woman herself gives, in almost all developed, and many developing, countries (re-)infibulation is illegal and cannot be undertaken, regardless of the qualifications of the intended operator.

Whatever the specific context, it is illegal in Britain and many other countries for FGM – infibulation or any other form – to be undertaken by medically trained personnel (or anyone else). In the UK such an act would probably result in a clinical practitioner being prosecuted, as well as struck from his or her professional register. (A prosecution on this issue in the UK found the defendants not guilty but the professional register issue is, as of February 2015, yet to be determined.[25])

But in various locations (such as Egypt – despite legal prohibition) the belief persists in some quarters that FGM performed by medically trained personnel is a better option than leaving a girl or woman to seek (re-)infibulation via a traditional operator (see note 4) with no proper clinical supervision, no asepsis and no anaesthetic; or clinicians may simply see performing FGM as a source of additional income.

The prime concern of those who work to eradicate FGM is to establish a global understanding that even reluctant, professional involvement in FGM[26] is a breach of medical ethics and may be perceived as legitimation of the 'procedure'. Regardless of the way the actual operation is done, with or without asepsis and anaesthesia, the likely future outcomes for the patient/victim remain perilous and should without exception be avoided.

'Medicalisation' of FGM

The position of the United Nations, the World Health Organization and other partners is clear: under no circumstances should FGM of any sort, either before marriage or post-partum, be placed within a 'clinical' context. The WHO produced a publication in 2010[27] which, in partnership with many other organisations, spells out the gravity of any such act:

Medical code of ethics
According to the World Medical Association's Declaration of Helsinki, 1964, it is the mission of the physician to safeguard the health of the people. Health professionals who perform female genital mutilation (FGM) are violating girls' and women's right to life, right to physical integrity, and right to health. They are also violating the fundamental ethical principle: 'do no harm'.

And yet, despite this position, it has been necessary, as above, for the WHO and others to conduct awareness campaigns to try to dissuade professional clinicians from carrying out FGM on minors, or on, for example, women post-partum who wish to be re-infibulated. The United Nations Population Fund (UNFPA) has made it very clear that there is never any medical reason to perform FGM and that whatever the mode of operation and by whomever the practice is carried out, its serious consequences, including sexual, psychological and obstetrical complications, still appertain. Another issue is that when clinicians are involved in the delivery of FGM, a false impression of legitimacy and benefit is given. The UNFPA[28] states categorically that performing FGM is a violation of the right to life, physical integrity and health (see note 16) and that:

FGM/FGC in any form should not be practised by health professionals in any setting – including hospitals or other health establishments. Unnecessary bodily mutilation cannot be condoned by health providers. FGM/FGC is harmful to the health of women and girls and violates their basic human rights and medicalization of the procedure does not eliminate this harm. On the contrary, it reinforces the continuation of the practice by seeming to legitimize it. Health practitioners should provide all necessary care and counseling for complications that may arise as a result of FGM/FGC.

Further, although most currently known instances of this medicalisation have occurred in African states, there is also a strong suspicion that the practice also occurs in Western nations – hence the 2012 'scandal' in Britain[29] when it was claimed that medical practitioners (none of whom was subsequently charged) had indicated that they would be willing to perform, or assist in securing, this practice. It has also been mooted that girls are sent for traditional methods of FGM to their (grand)parents' country of origin, or to Dubai or Singapore for surgical mutilation.

The trial of the first British clinician (a London doctor) for conducting FGM (re-infibulation) concluded in acquittal in early 2015 (see note 25). Similar criminal trials are also beginning to occur in other Western European countries (there have been many in France, with cases brought under wider legislation[30] by Linda Weil-Curiel of the Paris bar) and, for example, in North America and Australia.

Of direct converse concern is the possibility that a number of countries may choose to reverse their legal position on the medicalisation of FGM, arguing that enabling medically trained operators to undertake the 'procedure' makes it safer.[31] Not only is this directly contestable (it is thought clinicians may 'cut' more extensively; and the death occurred in 2013 of a child in Egypt, at an FGM 'clinic'[32]) but it may also encourage the growth in some locations of a legitimised 'FGM industry' within the remit of modern medical practice.

Such a possible outcome is viewed by some[33] as a major threat to the global eradication of female genital mutilation. There is an argument (considered below) that licensed genital cosmetic surgery is unacceptable for similar reasons.

Medicalisation of the abuse cannot be the way forward for reducing the harm of FGM.

Medical Care and Other Provision

The centrality of skilled health care in addressing female genital mutilation cannot be overstated; but this does not mean it is uniquely important. The very considerable skills and knowledge required for these tasks may not always be those required to develop a more general social strategy to eradicate FGM. Indeed, the normal medical focus on the individual patient might in some circumstances be seen as a distraction from this mission.

It would of course be unthinkable to downplay the many and critical roles of health care practitioners and clinical professionals, both in the prevention of FGM and in attending to the needs of those who have experienced it. It is most often health workers who see first-hand the realities of FGM. It is they who must know, immediately, what to do and say – and what not to do or say. This expert knowledge is self-evidently of a different sort than that required to develop overall policy on the eradication of FGM.

But in most places to date health care providers have, especially in the absence of other thought leaders, generally led the way. It is therefore critically important to be aware of the spheres of action for which clinicians and health workers have primary responsibility.

These areas include:

Clinical and personal care

- routine and emergency medical treatment for women and girls who have undergone FGM (routine and acute/trauma care, etc.);
- obstetric and neonatal-paediatric specialist care (of mothers and sometimes of their babies, if safe delivery of the infant was compromised by FGM);
- psychiatric and psychological treatment for girls and women who have undergone FGM – or been traumatised in their efforts to escape it;
- plastic and restorative gynaecological surgery to repair (and maybe reconstruct) FGM-damaged organs;
- referral of individual patients on to other non-health services.

Applications of professional knowledge, other than direct patient care

- diagnostic advice for legal enforcement and possible prosecution;
- information feeds and analysis for health service administrators and managers;
- preventative advice for parents (GPs, antenatal and child care clinics, etc.);
- educational and preventative work with children in schools and youth clubs, etc.;
- public health awareness campaigns;
- professional liaison and advice for colleagues in other public services;
- notification of the incidence and perceived risks of FGM;
- epidemiological studies, profiling and analysis of FGM risks and realities;
- training and in-service education of clinical and other health workers;
- training and in-service education of service providers and community activists working in fields outside health provision.

As these lists demonstrate, the range of responsibilities (and opportunities) which lie in the remit of health and medical services is very broad. As of the time of writing (early 2015) the personnel and material resources available do not remotely match the enormity of the task in hand, that is, the treatment of, and/or risk prevention for, many tens of thousands of girls and women in Britain. A recent study suggests that previous estimates of incidence seriously understate the prevalence of FGM in the UK.[34]

The reasons for the paucity of material support, and clinical skills and personnel in tackling FGM are many, but they include (at least until recently) widespread failure to understand, or even believe, the scale of the challenge, as well as other probable factors such as public aversion to issues perceived as relating to sexual medicine, the complex network of responsibilities (with no obvious lead or direction), and the reality of there being no requirement to develop new drugs or other medical products, such as would incentivise research and actively engage the commercial medical industry.

Nonetheless, a considerable literature now exists on the medical approaches to, and the clinical treatment of, FGM in both obstetric and gynaecological contexts, some of it deriving from the experience of midwives and other clinicians in countries where harmful traditional practices are common.

Internationally, this literature includes publications by the World Health Organization (WHO) on policy[35] and clinical curricula,[36] by the United Nations Population Fund (UNFPA), for example a general introduction to FGM[37] and its guidance on refugee situations,[38] and the *Position Statement on Female Genital Mutilation* of the International Confederation of Midwives.[39]

At the national level in the UK, direction and advice includes the UK Government's *Multi-Agency Practice Guidelines*,[40] the Royal College of Obstetrics and Gynaecologists Statement[41] and Guidance on management,[42] guidance for nurses and midwives by the Royal College of Midwives in the UK,[43] and the Royal College of Nursing,[44] and *FGM Treatment* guidelines by the FGM National Clinical Group,[45] as well as guidance issued by particular NHS hospital trusts, such as that of the Barking, Havering and Redbridge NHS Trust[46] or by, to give another example, Bristol Safeguarding Children Board.[47]

The extent to which awareness and concern about FGM has grown over the period since around 2012 is reflected in the NHS website entry and numerous weblinks to other professional posts and entries on the subject.[48] This website is a useful point of reference for those who wish to update themselves on the issues.

Remediation of FGM

The issue of FGM remediation is fraught with complexities. This is not simply a matter of reversing visible damage; it is about the whole girl or woman, her perception of herself and her expectation (or not) that she is entitled to a different bodily and – if for her such a perception or concept actually exists – sexual status.

Even if these matters are clear, the extent to which the consequences of FGM can be reversed still depends on many factors. Amongst these are:

- the level of understanding by the person with FGM of what has been done to her (especially bearing in mind that some children undergo FGM in infancy; and they may live in communities where it is the norm);
- the degree to which the harm of FGM is understood to relate to physical and/or psycho-sexual function;
- the degree to which (if at all), and why, the person concerned desires change;
- psychological and related personal readiness for change;
- the availability or otherwise of appropriate clinical expertise, skills and apparatus;
- the availability or otherwise of financial and other resourcing;
- the acceptability (or recognition) of reversal within the socio-economic milieu of the person concerned.

Given all these problematical issues, it is unsurprising that the idea of remediation is not universally welcomed. Firstly, the argument also applied against the medicalisation of FGM may be brought to bear – that is, there has been concern that focusing on reconstruction will prove to be an obstacle to eradication;[49] and secondly there is the fear that surgeons may lack required levels of operational skill, or that they will not be able adequately to support women going through this process, with its critical challenge to both physical and psychological stamina.

Another concern is the extent to which the remediation 'should' address both physical malaise – gynaecological and obstetric problems and so on – and/or psycho-sexual anxieties about lack of sensitivity and response during intercourse.

To a degree this debate centres on questions about the exact nature and shape or size of the clitoris. Knowledge about this organ has been scant but it is now understood to be much more extensive within the body than formerly supposed: the 'button' which is discernible is but a tip of a ring of tissue which encircles the vagina internally.

The French surgeon Pierre Foldes[50] undertook sonographic research on the clitoris in 2008[51] and has developed techniques to rebuild the front of FGM-damaged organs so there is a good chance of restoring sensitivity. Foldes' work[52] has been interrogated by Drs Sarah Creighton and Susan Bewley, as well as by the clinical psychologist Lih-Mei Liao,[53] all of London.

Foldes maintains his belief that the majority of women who undergo reconstruction benefit from this procedure, but one issue which remains unclear is the extent to which full sensation is possible if the front of the clitoris is removed very early and has therefore received no stimulation at all before the attempted reversal. It is accepted by most clinicians that restoration may in any case have benefits where it is actively desired by the individual concerned.[54]

To date the number of women who undergo surgical repair of labia, vulva or vagina after FGM is just a very tiny fraction of those who have the condition, and the number who are offered reconstruction of their clitoris (clitoriplasty) is much smaller still.

In some places, especially in France, where the restoration of damage and sensation is seen as a human rights issue, there is a developing expectation that remediation may be available and the state now pays for this treatment if the person concerned is a French national. Dr Pierre Foldes in Paris has operated on several thousand women, establishing techniques for repair and restoration which he has also taught to other (mostly also French) surgeons, and surgeons who have trained with him, such as Dr Barri Soldevila of Barcelona,[55] also now provide this service, often on a *pro bono* basis.

The year 2013 also saw the opening of the Desert Flower Centre clinic for restorative surgery and care in Berlin (Germany),[56] initiated by the campaigner Waris Dirie, who herself experienced FGM as a child aged five, with a clinical team led by Dr Cornelia Strunz.[57]

The first Australian FGM reversal clinic opened in 2011, at the Royal Women's Hospital in Melbourne, informal reports suggesting that at least initially there was considerable tension between the hospital and the community on this issue, the first operations all being performed on women who had come to Australia from North Africa.

Similar establishments can be found, for example, in San Francisco (USA),[58] where the lead surgeon is Dr Marci Bowers.[59] In this case, however, there is additional controversy because one of the clinicians, the counsellor Nadine Gary, belongs to the Raëlian sect,[60] a group whose beliefs include the idea that aliens they call Elohim – a Hebrew term for god/s but to the Raëlians meaning 'from the sky' – created human beings by genetic engineering for the purpose of striving for peace and enjoying sexual pleasure.

Such affirmation of the entitlement of all human beings to positive sexuality, regardless of how it is derived, is congruent with a clinical procedure designed to increase physical pleasure as well as remove gynaecological and obstetric malfunction. The Raëlians have created an organisation – Clitoraid[61] – to establish a remediation and clitoriplasty clinic in Burkina Faso, in defiance of traditional beliefs in that region (now being challenged also in more orthodox ways) about the 'need' for FGM.

More conventional restoration of damaged pudenda (external) and internal sexual parts is offered in Britain and other similar countries. One British surgeon, Dr Kamal Iskander,[62] is recorded as having performed clitoriplasty in the course of other FGM repairs, but most often surgery is performed straightforwardly to restore physical functions and/or to ease obstetric delivery.

But there is not as yet a British national strategy on surgical repair and reconstruction. Several clinics now provide services to reduce the pain, recurrent infections and other problems of FGM, but these provisions are dependent on trained, skilled operators, of whom there are only a few.

One aspect of the work of Dr Foldes is to encourage women, where they want to do so, to spread the message that FGM is not just unnecessary, but also deprives some of those who have it of significant aspects of their sexuality and sensory experience. This is an important aspect of prevention of FGM in the next generation.

Further, for some patients, FGM clinics – with or without restorative surgery or other treatment – afford the first opportunity ever to discuss the condition and its impact on their lives. The realisation that their condition compromises their health and personal well-being, and that, contrary to their community's belief, it is not a requirement of all adult women, can be revelatory.

But it can also be traumatic. The trauma is increasingly recognised as a clinical issue, and psychological approaches to the issues are emerging via the work of Professor Creighton and her colleagues, including the consultant clinical psychologist Lih-Mei Liao, who all see the need for integrated provision (as do Pierre Foldes and his colleagues) and a national action plan to tackle FGM.[63]

This is complicated territory. On the one hand, a dawning understanding that, with skilled medical and post-trauma/psychological support, things can be much better, is very significant in a positive way.

On the other hand, that realisation also requires recognition by the women concerned that FGM need not have happened in the first place – and with it the question of why FGM was inflicted by a mother, aunt or grandmother on a child, when (even if they were not aware that avoiding being mutilated brings great health benefit) that person knew from personal experience how much pain and psychological distress it would cause.

The resolution of these various revelations may be difficult. One response by clinicians (such as the London-based general practitioner

Dr Phoebe Abe, who also created the Dr Abe Foundation – see p. 318) may be to support informal groups of affected women so that they can talk between themselves and with others who may be able to help.

Discussions of this sort have several probable outcomes, amongst them being that the women affected may decide they will never permit FGM on their own daughters or on other young family members. It is emerging group consciousness of this nature, reinforced by newly acquired knowledge of the law and its increasing application, which will most likely bring FGM to a halt in Western nations.

But there is also a conundrum in this modern medical approach which divides Western and traditional understandings. The emphasis particularly on sensation, and if possible orgasm, may be interpreted in some quarters as evidence for the sexualised follies of the modern world. This is as we noted above especially evident in the disputed practice of clinicians in Africa and the USA who are trying to develop Clitoraid.

The damage caused by FGM is much more than 'just' a loss of sensation, and repairing the other harm – scarring, infection and so on – may be more important to some women (and, where discussed, to their husbands) than sexual pleasure as such. Nor as yet can we be sure it is true, as has been claimed, that the clitoris is the only organ with pleasure as its sole 'purpose': for instance, clitoral sensations also stimulate lubrication. Human physiology and endocrinology is rarely that simple.

There are many steps to be taken between recognising the dangers of FGM and finding ways to support women, on their own terms, to feel confident to challenge it and, if they wish, become physically 'whole' again. Recognition of the harm of FGM is only a part of the battle to make the practice history.

Estimates suggest, then, that the need for even basic female genital surgical repair after FGM is more widespread than previously thought. In London alone in the three years between 2010 and summer 2013, over 2,000 women and girls received hospital treatment to reduce pain and other damage, and of these almost 300 underwent surgical reversal of FGM.[64] The largest number (nearly 1,000 in just under three years) of these women and girls attended the Guy's and St Thomas' Hospital African Well Women's Clinic, where several of the patients were young girls. This clinic is led by Dr Comfort Momoh,[65] a consultant specialist midwife, who opened it in 1997 and has also trained other clinicians who work elsewhere.

In 2014 an additional dedicated FGM service was set up by Comfort Momoh and her colleagues, providing services specifically for girls and young women under 18. It offers both physical and psychological care.

The first African Well Women's Clinic in England for people with FGM was set up by the surgeon Harry Gordon at Northwick Park Hospital, North West London, in 1993. In 1997 Mr Gordon moved to the Central Middlesex

Hospital, where he continued to provide FGM reversal procedures, having completed over 100, mostly for Somali patients with Type III FGM, by the year 2000.[66]

There are now around 15 FGM-specialised clinics in England,[67] including five or six cities outside London with centres for the treatment specifically of FGM.[68, 69] Amongst them are Birmingham (Bordesley Green with 640 reported referrals),[70] Bristol (Frenchay and Southmead NHS Trust, with 117 women treated by the hospital or staff midwives),[71] Liverpool (237 maternity referrals in the three years to 2008),[72] and Nottingham (150 patients seen in two years 2011–13).[73] As of early 2015, neither Scotland nor Wales has a centre with specialist FGM focus.

Much more information is needed about where in Britain, in what communities, FGM occurs. Data to date is piecemeal; some hospitals and clinics have routinely provided it; many before later 2014 did not. Until 2014 there was no standard reporting code for cases of FGM to be recorded, nor was there any intention by the Department of Health until then to investigate the incidence of FGM in the UK.[74] The first more detailed, possibly regional, analyses of incidence were published in early 2015.[75]

NHS hospitals provided little information on FGM when diagnosed in patients (or about any family history of FGM, or if an FGM-related procedure has been carried out on a women (de-infibulation) before all acute hospitals in England and Wales were required to report newly diagnosed cases of FGM on a monthly basis from September 2014.[76]

This reporting will help to determine where resources should be focused, but even so it is only a partial response to the need for epidemiological data, because it does not include instances of FGM outside the acute hospital setting – and, even expected exclusions apart, it is also possible that parents and adult patients who are aware of the reporting regulations will choose to go elsewhere for medical advice.

Whether or not this happens, the patterns of incidence which arise from the available data will be a valuable guide to where efforts to combat FGM should be focused. Further information will also arise from the final report of the City University – Equality Now study to follow that cited earlier (p. 45).

Current thinking is that these figures may seriously understate the prevalence of FGM. This is in part because many women and girls with FGM do not seek medical advice or help, and in part because even when they do the consultation may not be recorded as being about FGM, or the clinician/s involved may have been unwilling to provide even anonymised overall data on these consultations. The changes as of September 2014 in reporting systems within the NHS[77] which make this reporting mandatory for acute hospitals, will produce more reliable data, as will the reporting by GPs and mental health trusts to be introduced in October 2015.[78]

Mandatory Reporting

There are at least two different sets of information with which clinicians are involved.

One set is reporting of the sort discussed above – the data which forms the epidemiological formulations behind any medical or public health issue. The reporting in such cases is anonymised and helps to shape policy and the focus of responses to the issue in question. The technical difficulties with this sort of reporting relate to professional training to identify the relevant condition, and the provision of standardised ways to report it.

The other set of data which may be required is not anonymised. In this instance the objective is to identify individuals who have experienced criminal violence/abuse to their person, that is, FGM.

The purpose of the reporting in this case is to identify individuals who have been harmed, in order to:

- enable 'victims' to receive appropriate clinical care;
- bring abusers to justice; and
- help in identifying children (girls whose mothers had FGM) and other young women who may be at risk in the future.

Recent debate has been about whether mandatory reporting of FGM and other child abuse should be brought into statute, given the very low levels of reporting to date under the voluntary and discretionary system of reporting. Mandating might be expected to apply to all those in regulated activity (that is, in occupations such as teaching, social work and clinical practice, which require formal registration by the state), but in the case of FGM it would fall particularly heavily on midwives, doctors and nurses.

Whilst in theory all the rationales for reporting are in line with professional ethics and good practice, in reality this reporting has seen resistance in some quarters, and the case for making it mandatory has not been accepted by all clinicians.[i]

Reasons for resistance vary, but include concerns:

- about breaking professional confidence and patient privacy (which the law also requires to be broken for some other matters around child safety and infectious disease);
- around building trust in relationships with patients (for example midwives may perceive themselves as maintaining a personal

---

i   See for instance the oral evidence from clinicians in session two of the Vaz Inquiry, p. 174, note 138.

relationship which includes advocacy for patients otherwise excluded from the mainstream);

- that legal interventions will obstruct clinical decisions;
- that diagnosis, especially of 'type', will be poor and will often be unnecessarily invasive;
- that reporting will drive FGM 'underground' (which others may say it is already);
- that patients will not seek professional clinical advice and support if they know FGM will be reported;
- that lawyers will have influence where doctors should be at liberty to determine action and outcomes (or vice versa) – a sort of professional turf war;[79]
- that 'historical' reporting will be required, such that patients who present with some entirely different current disorder will find their previous condition brought once more to the fore.

Some of these concerns will need to be addressed in the short term if mandatory reporting does become law. Clinicians will, for instance, require clear guidance on the typologies of FGM diagnosis, and about whether 'historical' reporting is required – and, if so, under what circumstances.

Other reservations are less persuasive. Decisions about what to do with or about law breakers are for the courts to make, not at the discretion of clinicians; and the argument that reporting will 'drive FGM underground' sits oddly with the evidence that it is already a crime conducted – like many others – in secret.

Most fundamentally, disputes about mandatory reporting seem, for FGM but self-evidently not for other forms of child abuse, to focus on the individual relationship between a woman and her midwife or physician. The discomfort around mandating for FGM has been made very clear by various medical bodies in evidence submitted, for instance, to the government consultation on mandatory reporting.[80]

The emphasis is on that personal link, and on the ways families are seen to function. There is sometimes less emphasis on the possibility that by reporting a woman or child's suspected FGM status her daughters or sisters may be protected from future damage. It remains to be seen how much legal pressure the Government will choose to apply in the light of different positions on the part of others seeking mandated reporting for child abuse, and resistance by clinicians and social workers.

Evidence and Examination

A more direct way to stem intentions to inflict FGM would be to introduce compulsory medical examination of girls thought to be at risk.

In France all children are examined until the age of six, unless the parent refuses the examination – which in itself would be regarded as indicative of a cause for concern – but routine medical examination of British children beyond infancy stopped some time ago, as the numbers of school nurses and doctors has decreased.

It may now be important to have the facility to require the examination of girls who are thought to have been taken for FGM on so-called 'vacation cutting' trips to their countries of origin or historical and cultural reference; but any such examination requires considerable training and skill if it is to produce meaningful findings with minimum distress for the person under scrutiny. The damage of FGM is not easily diagnosed, nor are accusations of discrimation or 'racial profiling' easily addressed.[81]

Whilst Alison Saunders, the current Director of Public Prosecutions, has held her counsel on this issue,[82] the head of the Metropolitan Police, Sir Bernard Hogan-Howe, has suggested that power to conduct compulsory examinations may in given instances be required.[83] It should in the meantime be noted that some provision for examination in cases of suspected child abuse is already available.[84]

In terms of prevention, it is important that parents and other carers be aware that a child may be taken into care and, after formal consultation with social services and/or the police, examined by an appropriately qualified clinician as an emergency, where there is serious concern that abuse may have occurred.

Psychological and Psychiatric Issues

As suggested above, the psychological and mental health issues attached to the experience of FGM are complex and of considerable significance.

At the present time knowledge of psychological and psychiatric outcomes is generally sketchy, with only a few researchers fully engaged in this medical field, but a consensus has already emerged. Almost all clinicians share the general view that FGM is a seriously traumatic and disturbing experience, sometimes with repercussions which last a lifetime.

Amongst those who have undertaken systematic study of the mental health and well-being issues around FGM is the psychologist Lih-Mei Liao of the FGM National Clinical Group. She reports[85] that, even where any language barriers can be overcome, research is complicated by the different meanings and understandings (or not) of concepts by women in or from different cultures: 'body image', for instance, is a largely Western idea, as indeed is the idea of 'therapy'.

Additionally, there is evidence that women with FGM may experience mental health problems, sexuality problems, family conflict and relationship problems and additional stress because, for instance, of unresolved status issues such as asylum seekers may encounter – few women seeking asylum voluntarily mention fears about FGM when they make their first claim; then when they mention it later the fear may be seen as sham. But a culture which demands modesty and reluctance to discuss intimate matters, especially in the presence of men who are strangers, may be the real reason FGM was not mentioned originally.

Recent moves have been made to begin to address these issues in a number of clinics and other locations.

Some of the provision is informal, such as that of the support groups provided by various general practitioners (GPs) such as Dr Phoebe Abe,[86, 87] and other support is available, for instance, at the Manor Gardens Community Centre (the Dahlia Project,[88] in conjunction with the Maya Centre) in Islington, London.[89]

Very importantly, new (as of late 2014) support provision and a clinic, specifically for girls and young women under 18, has now been established at the University College Hospital,[90] also in London.

The Preventative Approach

For all that preventative programmes can be built upon clinical and other support for FGM survivors, this is not the only or the optimum approach.

Community engagement through survivors who oppose FGM is a critical element in eradicating this harmful crime, but priorities in the care of survivors and the requirements for the abolition of FGM are by no means always co-terminous. Individuals personally affected by FGM require care and attention as people in their own right, regardless of whether or not they choose to be campaigners – although certainly all who campaign about such difficult matters should have access to specific support as well.

Epidemiologically, FGM can be theorised as a 'social disease' – a condition passed between people via social contact or contract, with underlying economic drivers, in which people's actions, beliefs and perceptions have causal effect, rather as these may do in, say, tuberculosis, sexually transmitted diseases, road traffic casualties or typhoid. Culturally variable behaviours will have different outcomes for transmission (or not) of the condition.

There is a well-established protocol in other disorders also for therapeutic engagement by patients with those who have already experienced and come to terms with a condition – drug or alcohol addiction, obesity, and post-natal depression are obvious examples of this approach, covering a range of different causations and clinical experiences – but strategies of this sort place considerable weight on the shoulders of sometimes already vulnerable people.

For these reasons (vulnerability and volunteering) amongst many, such approaches to the problem cannot be seen as cheap substitutes for more formal and structured ways forward. Community-based volunteers, whether or not themselves with FGM status, must have proper support and training, and strategic supervision. They are invaluable partners in the campaign to eradicate FGM, but they cannot do it alone.

Nor is the multi-agency approach of itself enough, as we shall see in Chapter 10. Some central organisation has to be in charge, taking an overview of the entire preventative programme, and in the case of 'social diseases' like FGM which affect people across the whole country and beyond, a national programme of action is the only feasible strategy.

The translation of national preventative programmes for use at the local level is greatly assisted by volunteers and others with local knowledge, understandings and vocabulary, but the general direction of travel must include proper data on distribution and developments concerning where FGM occurs, as well as standardised, national professional clinical and other training.

In these respects the UK has a huge advantage over some other countries. The National Health Service (NHS) affords almost universal coverage and capacity to address both individuals' health concerns and much wider public health challenges. It is therefore especially well placed to address many aspects of FGM eradication in Great Britain.

Consent, Cosmetic Genital Surgery and Gender Reassignment

Statistics on FGM are, however, only a part of the complete picture when it comes to the incidence of genital surgery in the UK and similar locations.

FGM itself is unequivocally illegal in Britain, but there is serious debate about whether the practice includes by definition all non-medically-essential female genital cosmetic surgery (FGCS) performed on consenting adults by qualified clinicians in appropriate locations. What exactly is meant by 'non-essential' is itself in question. Does 'essential' include 'required because a woman feels a psychological need', as well as 'must be done because of a physical threat to health'? Some of these questions were addressed in a 2013 report published by the UK's Royal College of Obstetricians and Gynaecologists, *Ethical Opinion Paper: Ethical considerations in relation to female genital cosmetic surgery (FGCS)*.[91]

More doubts still arise when the person undergoing the surgery is a minor, whatever the persuasiveness of her assertion that she wants the procedure.[92] British gynaecologist Sarah Creighton reported in her commentary on the film *Centrefold*[93] that she has seen girls as young as 11 undergoing labiaplasty.[94] In the USA federal law makes it an offence to perform any female genital cosmetic surgery on people under age 18,[95] as by inference from a letter of guidance does Scottish legislation.[96]

But English law has been perceived as more ambiguous, at least until the pronouncement by Home Secretary Theresa May in late 2014, to the effect that genital cosmetic surgery of any sort would probably be determined by the courts to be illegal.[97, 98]

Specifically, the question is whether, and if so why, clinical procedures such as labiaplasty[99] ('trimming', usually, the inner labia) and vaginoplasty[100] (in effect, vaginal tightening) are acceptable under the law. Whether or not this is so, the number of so-called 'designer vagina' surgical procedures is rising rapidly, in parallel also with increasing debate about the status of and rationales for labiaplasty and similar techniques.

In the UK in 2011, over 2,000 such operations were reported to have been performed on NHS patients – a five-fold increase since 2006[101] – and it is thought that many more cosmetic operations were performed privately, outside that service.

There is concern in some quarters that this increase has been fuelled by greater access to pornographic images,[102] of women with no genital hair who are presented as the ideal to which everyone should aspire – in much the same way that it is implied women should aspire to be size 8, like the models they see in clothes advertisements.

And over the same period there has been a growing awareness of FGM as such.

A 2013 report by the British Society for Paediatric and Adolescent Gynaecology, *Position Statement: Labial reduction surgery (labiaplasty) on adolescents*,[103] demonstrates growing – though not universal – consensus across the Western world that (unless otherwise medically essential) 'cosmetic' vulval surgery should not be undertaken on minors. But there is also discussion in some Western medical circles about whether, even when performed with full consent on adults, it is actually medicalised FGM.[104] This concern is compounded in that, whilst there may be a lesser degree of direct coercion in the traditional culture sense, clinicians record that their patients frequently report pressure or negative comment from sexual partners about the appearance of their vulva.

Is it a deceit to claim that this modern form of vulval surgery is sometimes medically 'required', to enable women to feel more comfortable in their minds as well as their bodies? Is the so-called designer vagina, as especially radical feminists claim,[105] actually a massive Western hypocrisy when set against the condemnation of FGM?[106]

Some commentators[107] have asked whether we can justly claim ('white') Western women's concerns about their body image are legitimate, whilst dismissing out of hand similar concerns expressed by ('black') women who seek or agree to undergo FGM in its traditional sense.[108]

The position taken by most clinicians performing genital cosmetic (that is, non-essential) surgery seems to be that these issues must be taken on a case-by-case basis: each individual seeking genital surgery should receive personal advice before she decides for herself whether she wishes to proceed.

Other doctors and clinical psychologists maintain that 'advice' at the initial stage is sometimes inappropriate or not enough.[109] They believe that surgery is becoming a substitute – often lucrative – for what would otherwise be painstaking therapeutic work to help women to feel at ease with their bodies. Yes, they concede, there are instances where anatomy is genuinely uncomfortable (in which case normal clinical judgements apply), but that does not account for the dramatic increase in rates of vulval surgery. Whilst knowledge of what comprises a 'normal' vulva is scant,[110] there is no likelihood that actual female anatomy has changed significantly in the early twenty-first century.

In other words, the case for designer vaginas (like, for instance, cosmetic breast reduction or enlargement) is challenged by some clinicians on very similar grounds to those applied in considering the medicalisation of FGM: the 'need' for it has come about through patriarchal pressure on women, acknowledged or not, to conform to perfect or 'pure' body images.

These matters are sometimes further complicated by indeterminate gender ('intersex') issues resulting from a lack of clarity about whether a child has been born male or female. Intersex infants may undergo gender (re-)assignment very early in their lives, both to enable them to develop a gender-defined persona, and to ease concerns on the part of their parents and others.

Some clinicians[111] and intersex activists[112] have challenged surgical intervention to allocate anatomical gender in childhood, asserting that this action is provoked by social and cultural stigma rather than a medical necessity to resolve the real issues. Responding to these concerns, in 2011 Australia added a third gender category, 'X', to its passports, so that a choice is available for intersex citizens or those undergoing gender assignment;[113] and in 2013 German law was amended to permit infants not to have their gender recorded, thereby lessening the impetus towards non-medically-necessary gender surgery.[114]

Critics of non-essential female genital surgery also observe that, whether traditional or modern Western practice is under scrutiny, the financial rewards to the practitioner of non-essential genital surgery or 'cutting' are in some cases (for example, in Britain, outside the NHS) significant.[115] Indeed, in both instances, variations on the idea of 'medical tourism' may also apply: for FGM, girls and women may be sent 'home' to parts of Africa. For designer vaginas they may visit dedicated clinics in locations such as Thailand.

It will probably prove difficult in the short or medium term to achieve consensus on these matters. The debate continues in, for instance, the UK[116] and Australia.[117] It must be noted, however, that the legality of female genital cosmetic surgery in the Western world will ultimately, as the UK Home Secretary observed (above), be resolved in court.[118] Already in the UK, opinions and guidance on the legal permissibility or otherwise of female non-essential genital surgery has been offered by various medical-legal professionals.[119, 120]

The usual guidance is to proceed, if at all, with extreme caution, and to ensure that all advice and consent is formally recorded. But consent, even if informed and adult, is relevant only to procedures which are legal. Whether consent and caution will prove adequate as defence with reference to genital cosmetic surgery remains to be seen.

Discuss this chapter at http://nofgmukbook.com/2015/01/29/chapter-5-clinical-issues/.

Endnotes

All weblinks accessed on 1 March 2015.

1   UNFPA, UNHCR, UNICEF, UNIFEM, WHO, FIGO, et al. (2010) Global Strategy to Stop Health-Care Providers from Performing FGM. *United Nations Population Fund.* Available at: http://www.unfpa.org/webdav/site/global/shared/documents/publications/2011/Global_strategy_for_health_providers.pdf.

2   Askew, I., Njue, C. (2004) Medicalization of Female Genital Cutting Among the Abagusii in Nyanza Province, Kenya. *Frontiers in Reproductive Health Program and Population Council.* Available at: http://www.who.int/reproductivehealth/topics/fgm/medicalization_fgm_kenya/en/#.

3   Smith, D. (2013) 'Medicalisation' Brings Setbacks for Anti-FGM Efforts. FIGO. Available at: http://www.figo.org/news/medicalisation-brings-setbacks-anti-fgm-efforts-0013639.

4   Farid, M. (2005) *No for Medicalization of FGM/FGC Case Study in Egypt.* UNFPA. Available at: www.unfpa.org/gender/fgm2007/documents/no_ medicalization_fgm.ppt.

5   Mohamed, F.J. (2013) Moves to Medicalize Female Mutilation Could Destroy 'Stop FGM' Advocacy. *Women's News Network,* 18 January. Available at: http:// womennewsnetwork.net/2013/01/18/medicalize-female-mutliation-destroy-fgm-advocacy/.

6   Keel, A. (2014) *Re: Female Genital Mutilation (Letter to Health Professionals in Scotland).* The Scottish Government. Available at: http://www.sehd.scot.nhs.uk/ cmo/CMO(2014)19.pdf.

7   World Health Organization (2014) *Health Complications of Female Genital Mutilation.* Available at: http://www.who.int/reproductivehealth/topics/fgm/ health_consequences_fgm/en/.

8   Creighton, S. (2014) *Female Genital Mutilation (FGM): Types and Identification.* UCLH NHS Foundation Trust. http://www.fgmnationalgroup.org/ documents/2014_dataset_sarah.pdf.

9   UNFPA, UNHCR, UNICEF, UNIFEM, WHO, FIGO, et al. (2010) Global Strategy to Stop Health-Care Providers from Performing FGM. *United Nations Population Fund.* Available at: http://www.unfpa.org/publications/global-strategy-stop-health-care-providers-performing-fgm.

10   WHO (2010) *Global Strategy to Stop Health-care Providers from Performing Female Genital Mutilation.* Available at: http://www.who.int/reproductivehealth/ publications/fgm/rhr_10_9/en/index.html.

11   WHO. *Female Genital Mutilation (FGM) and Harmful Practices.* Available at: http://www.who.int/reproductivehealth/publications/fgm/en/.

12   Bonhoure, I., Hechavarria, S., Kaplan, A., Martin, M. (2011) Health Consequences of Female Genital Mutilation/Cutting in the Gambia, Evidence into Action. *Reproductive Health.* 8: 26. Available at: www.reproductive-health-journal.com/content/8/1/26.

13   World Health Organization (2011) *An Update on WHO's Work on Female Genital Mutilation.* Available at: http://www.who.int/reproductivehealth/publications/ fgm/rhr_11_18/en/index.html.

14   World Health Organization (2008) *Eliminating Female Genital Mutilation: An Interagency Statement UNAIDS, UNDP, UNECA, UNESCO, UNFPA, UNHCHR, UNHCR, UNICEF, UNIFEM, WHO.* Geneva: WHO Press. Available at: http:// www.un.org/womenwatch/daw/csw/csw52/statements_missions/Interagency_ Statement_on_Eliminating_FGM.pdf.

15   UNFPA, UNHCR, UNICEF, UNIFEM, WHO, FIGO, et al. (2010) Global Strategy to Stop Health-Care Providers from Performing FGM. *United Nations Population Fund.* Available at: http://www.unfpa.org/publications/global-strategy-stop-health-care-providers-performing-fgm.

16 Toubia, N. (1994) Female Circumcision as a Public Health Issue. *New England Journal of Medicine*. 331: 712–16. Available at: http://www.nejm.org/doi/full/10.1056/NEJM199409153311106.

17 Adam, T., Bathija, H., Bishai, D., Bonnenfant, Y.T., Darwish, M., Huntingdon, D., et al. (2010) Estimating the Obstetric Costs of Female Genital Mutilation in Six African Countries. *Bulletin of the World Health Organization*, 20 January. Available at: http://www.who.int/bulletin/volumes/88/4/09-064808/en/index.html.

18 UNFPA (2011) *Female Genital Mutilation Overview*. Available at: http://www.unfpa.org/gender/practices3_2.htm.

19 Ali, N., Mohamud, A., Reymond, L. (1997) *The Facts: Female Genital Mutilation*. Seattle: PATH Publications. Available at: http://www.path.org/files/FGM-The-Facts.htm.

20 Almroth, L., Bergström, S., Elfadil, S.M., El Hadi, N., Elmusharaf, S., et al. (2005) Primary Infertility after Genital Mutilation in Girlhood in Sudan: A case-control study. *Lancet*, 366(9483): 385–91. Available at: http://www.ncbi.nlm.nih.gov/pubmed/16054938.

21 Forward UK (2014) *Obstetric Fistula*. Available at: http://www.forwarduk.org.uk/key-issues/fistula.

22 The Lancet (2006) New Study Shows Female Genital Mutilation Exposes Women and Babies to Significant Risk at Childbirth. *World Health Organization*, 2 June. Available at: http://www.who.int/mediacentre/news/releases/2006/pr30/en/index.html#.

23 Royal College of Nursing (2015) *Female Genital Mutilation – An RCN resource for nursing and midwifery practice (Second edition)*. Available at: http://www.rcn.org.uk/__data/assets/pdf_file/0010/608914/RCNguidance_FGM_WEB.pdf.

24 Muhammad, N. (2010) *Circumcised Girls Have Less Marriage Chance in Kurdistan*. RUDAW, 2 August. Available at: http://www.rudaw.net/english/culture_art/3074.

25 Bourne, T. (2015) The 'Dharmasena Case' Illustrates What is Wrong with Medical Regulation, the Review of Clinical Complications and Complaints. *BMJ*. 350: h703. Available at: http://www.bmj.com/content/350/bmj.h703/rr-2.

26 Shell-Duncan, B. (2001) The Medicalization of Female 'Circumcision': Harm reduction or promotion of a dangerous practice? *Social Science & Medicine*. 52(7): 1013–28. Available at: http://www.ncbi.nlm.nih.gov/pubmed/11266046.

27 UNFPA, UNHCR, UNICEF, UNIFEM, WHO, FIGO, et al. (2010) Global Strategy to Stop Health-Care Providers from Performing FGM. *United Nations Population Fund*. Available at: http://www.unfpa.org/publications/global-strategy-stop-health-care-providers-performing-fgm.

28 UNFPA (2014) *Frequently Asked Questions on Female Genital Mutilation/Cutting*. Available at: http://www.unfpa.org/gender/practices2.htm#19.

29 Press Association (2012) Doctors not to be Charged Following Female Genital Mutilation Investigation. *Guardian*, 20 September. Available at: http://www.guardian.co.uk/uk/2012/sep/20/doctors-not-charged-female-genital-mutilation.

30   European Institute for Gender Equality (2015) *Commission for the Abolition of Sexual Mutilations (Commission pour l'abolition des mutilations sexuelles)*. Available at: http://eige.europa.eu/content/commission-for-the-abolition-of-sexual-mutilationscommission-pour-l%E2%80%99abolition-des-mutilation.

31   Shell-Duncan, B. (2001) The Medicalization of Female 'Circumcision': Harm reduction or promotion of a dangerous practice? *Social Science & Medicine*. 52(7): 1013–28. Available at: http://www.ncbi.nlm.nih.gov/pubmed/11266046.

32   Beach, A. (2013) Egypt's Terrible FGM Death. *The Daily Beast*, 13 June. Available at: http://www.thedailybeast.com/articles/2013/06/13/egypt-s-terrible-fgm-death.html.

33   Mohamed, F.J. (2013) Moves to Medicalize Female Mutilation Could Destroy 'Stop FGM' Advocacy. *Women's News Network*, 18 January. Available at: http://womennewsnetwork.net/2013/01/18/medicalize-female-mutliation-destroy-fgm-advocacy/.

34   Doreknoo, E., Macfarlane, A. (2014) Female Genital Mutilation in England and Wales: Updated statistical estimates of the numbers of affected women living in England and Wales and girls at risk. *Equality Now, Interim report on provisional estimates*, 21 July. Available at: http://www.equalitynow.org/new_estimates_on_fgm_in_england_and_wales_by_equality_now_and_city_university_london.

35   World Health Organization (2011) *Female Genital Mutilation: The prevention and the management of the health complications – Policy guidelines for nurses and midwives*. WHO/FCH/GWH/01.5. Available at: http://www.who.int/reproductivehealth/publications/fgm/RHR_01_18/en/.

36   United Nations Population Fund (2001) *Female Genital Mutilation: Integrating the prevention and the management of the health complications into the curricula of nursing and midwifery*. Available at: http://www.who.int/reproductivehealth/publications/fgm/RHR_01_16/en/.

37   United Nations Population Fund (2015) *Female Genital Mutilation*. Available at http://www.unfpa.org/topics/genderissues/fgm.

38   United Nations Population Fund (2015) *Humanitarian Emergencies*. Available at: https://www.unfpa.org/emergencies/manual/7.htm#FGM.

39   International Confederation of Midwives (2005/2011) *Position Statement: Female Genital Mutilation*. Available at: http://internationalmidwives.org/assets/uploads/documents/Position%20Statements%20-%20English/PS2011_007%20ENG%20Female%20Genital%20Mutilation%20(FGM).pdf.

40   Featherstone, L. (2014) Female Genital Mutilation: Guidelines to protect children and women. *Home Office, Department of Education*, 22 July. Available at: https://www.gov.uk/government/uploads/system/uploads/attachment_data/file/216669/dh_124588.pdf.

41   Royal College of Obstetricians and Gynaecologists (2010) *RCOG Statement on the International Day of Zero Tolerance to Female Genital Mutilation*. Available at: https://www.rcog.org.uk/en/news/rcog-statement-on-the-international-

day-of-zero-tolerance-to-female-genital-mutilation/?_t_id=1B2M2Y8AsgTp
gAmY7PhCfg%3d%3d&_t_q=female+genital+mutilation+statement&_t_tag
s=language%3aen%2csiteid%3a39338ee9-cb61-4e10-a686-8f4a5e1b76d7&_t_
ip=71.190.138.149&_t_hit.id=EPiServer_Templates_RCOG_Models_Pages_
NewsArticleType/_1586d4e5-240e-4b38-8ef2-f918a017b8bc_en&_t_hit.pos=1.

42 Royal College of Obstetricians and Gynaecologists (2009) *Female Genital
Mutilation and its Management*. RCOG Green-top Guideline No. 53.
Available at: http://www.rcog.org.uk/files/rcog-corp/
GreenTop53FemaleGenitalMutilation.pdf.

43 Royal College of Nursing (2015) *Female Genital Mutilation – An RCN resource
for nursing and midwifery practice* (Second edition). Available at: http://www.
rcn.org.uk/__data/assets/pdf_file/0010/608914/RCNguidance_FGM_WEB.
pdf; https://www.rcn.org.uk/__data/assets/pdf_file/0012/78699/003037.pdf.

44 Royal College of Nursing (2015) *Female Genital Mutilation – An RCN resource for
nursing and midwifery practice (Second edition)*. Available at: https://www.rcn.org.uk/
__data/assets/pdf_file/0012/78699/003037.pdf.

45 FGM National Clinical Group (2015) *FGM Treatment*. Available at: http://www.
fgmnationalgroup.org/fgm_treatment.htm.

46 Homeyard, C., Hill, C. (2012) *Maternity Guideline for the Care of Women who have
been affected by Female Genital Mutilation*. Barking, Havering and Redbridge
University Hospitals Trust. Available at: http://www.nhs.uk/NHSEngland/
AboutNHSservices/sexual-health-services/Documents/FGM-guidelines.pdf.

47 Bristol Safeguarding Children Board (2011) *Female Genital Mutilation: Multi-
agency Guidelines*. Available at: https://www.bristol.gov.uk/sites/default/files/
documents/children_and_young_people/child_health_and_welfare/DRAFT%20
Revised%20%20Bristol%20FGM%20Multi%20Agency%20Guidance%20
FINAL011111.pdf.

48 NHS (2015) *Female Genital Mutilation*. Available at: http://www.nhs.uk/
Conditions/female-genital-mutilation/Pages/Introduction.aspx.

49 Bewley, S., Creighton, S., Liao, L.M. (2012) Reconstructive Surgery after Female
Genital Mutilation. *The Lancet* 380(9852): 1469. Available at: http://www.
thelancet.com/journals/lancet/article/PIIS0140-6736(12)61836-4/fulltext.

50 Wikipedia (2015) *Pierre Foldès*. Available at: http://en.wikipedia.org/wiki/
Pierre_Fold%C3%A8s.

51 Wikipedia (2015) *Clitoris*. Available at: http://en.wikipedia.org/wiki/Clitoris.

52 UnCut/Voices Press (2011) *Undoing FGM. Pierre Foldes, the Surgeon who restores
the clitoris*. Available at: http://uncutvoices.wordpress.com/2011/04/29/undoing-
fgm-pierre-foldes-the-surgeon-who-restores-the-clitoris/.

53 Bewley, S., Creighton, S., Liao, L.M. (2012) Reconstructive Surgery after Female
Genital Mutilation. *The Lancet* 380(9852): 1469. Available at: http://www.
thelancet.com/journals/lancet/article/PIIS0140-6736(12)61836-4/fulltext.

54 FGM National Clinical Group (2015) *About Us*. Available at: http://www.
fgmnationalgroup.org/about_us.htm.

55   BBC4 (2013) Spain: Operation FGM. *Crossing Continents*, 29 July. Available at: http://www.bbc.co.uk/programmes/b037706f.

56   The Local (2013) First Female Genital Mutilation Clinic Opens. *The Local DE*, 10 September. Available at: http://www.thelocal.de/20130910/51851.

57   Dirie, W. (2013) I Am Proud of Our New Desert Flower Center. *Desert Flower – The Blog*, 14 November. Available at: http://warisdirie.wordpress.com/ 2013/11/14/i-am-proud-of-our-new-desert-flower-center/.

58   Walters, J. (2013) High Hopes: The UFO cult 'restoring' the victims of female genital mutilation. *Guardian*, 25 August. Available at: http://www.theguardian. com/society/2013/aug/25/surgery-for-female-genital-mutilation.

59   Bowers, M. (2015) *Marci L. Bowers, M.D.* Available at: http://www.marcibowers.com/.

60   Wikipedia (2015) *Raëlism*. Available at: http://en.wikipedia.org/wiki/ Ra%C3%ABlism.

61   Clitoraid, Inc. (2015) *Clitoraid: Restoring a sense of dignity and pleasure*. Available at: http://www.clitoraid.org/.

62   Trustplus (2015) *Mr Kamal Shehata-Iskander*. Available at: http://www.trustplus. co.uk/consultant/mr-kamal-shehata-iskander.

63   BMJ (2013) Tackling Female Genital Mutilation in the UK. *The BMJ*, 4 December. Available at: http://www.bmj.com/content/347/bmj.f7150.

64   Bentham, M. (2013) True Number of FGM Victims in Capital is 'Far More than Figures Show'. *London Evening Standard*, 6 September. Available at: http:// www.standard.co.uk/news/health/true-number-of-fgm-victims-in-capital-is- far-more-than-figures-show-8801826.html.

65   Rix, J. (2005) Comfort Momoh. *Guardian*, 9 November. Available at: http:// www.theguardian.com/society/2005/nov/09/genderissues.

66   The BMJ (2000) Concern Mounts over Female Genital Mutilation. *BMJ*. 321(7256): 262. Available at: http://www.ncbi.nlm.nih.gov/pmc/articles/PMC1118273/.

67   EIGE (2015) *African Well Woman Clinics*. Available at: http://eige.europa.eu/ content/african-well-woman-clinics.

68   FORWARD (2013) *Female Genital Mutilation – Information Services & Support Guide*. Available at: http://www.forwarduk.org.uk/wp-content/ uploads/2014/12/ISSGuide-Forward.pdf.

69   Daughters of Eve (2015) *Resources and Links*. Available at: http://www.dofeve. org/resources-and-links.html.

70   Varma, A. (2013) Birmingham Hospital Treats 640 Females for Genital Mutilation. *Birmingham Mail*, 25 June. Available at: http://www.birminghammail. co.uk/lifestyle/health/birmingham-hospital-treats-640-females-4709664.

71   BBC News (2013) Female Genital Mutilation: Bristol study finds 117 cases. *BBC News Bristol*, 13 March. Available at: http://www.bbc.co.uk/news/uk- england-bristol-21766729.

72   Liverpool Daily Post (2008) UK: Hundreds of Liverpool Girls 'Mutilated' in African Ritual. *Liverpool Daily Post*, 5 February. Available at: http://www. wunrn.com/news/2008/02_08/02_04_08/020408_uk2.htm.

73 Garfitt, J. (2013) The Horrific Secret that Leaves Some Young Girls Scarred for Life. *Nottingham Post*, 3 July. Available at: http://www.nottinghampost.com/horrific-secret-leaves-young-girls-scarred-life/story-19463330-detail/story.html.

74 Gillen, S. (2011) Reversing a Brutal Act. *Nursing Standard*. 25(41): 62–3, 15 June. Available at: http://rcnpublishing.com/doi/full/10.7748/ns2011.06.25.41.62.p5609.

75 Health & Social Care Information Centre (2014) Female Genital Mutilation (FGM) Prevalence Dataset, 16 October. Available at: http://www.hscic.gov.uk/catalogue/PUB15711/fgm-sep-2014-exp-qual.pdf (p7).

76 Department of Health (2014) *New FGM measures launched to 'care, protect, prevent'*. Gov.UK, 22 July. Available at: https://www.gov.uk/government/news/new-fgm-measures-launched-to-care-protect-prevent.

77 Sibeko, S. (2014) *Female Genital Mutilation (FGM) Prevalence Dataset*. Available at: http://www.fgmnationalgroup.org/documents/2014_dataset_sam.pdf.

78 Department of Health, Home Office, Department for Education (2015) New Measures to End FGM on International Day of Zero Tolerance. *Gov.UK*, 6 February. Available at: https://www.gov.uk/government/news/new-measures-to-end-fgm-on-international-day-of-zero-tolerance.

79 Burrage, H. (2015) *Preventing FGM: Beware A Turf War Between Medicine and the Law*, 7 March. Available at: http://hilaryburrage.com/2015/03/07/preventing-fgm-beware-a-turf-war-between-medicine-and-law/.

80 Royal College of Paediatrics and Child Health (2015) *Response to Home Office Consultation – Introducing mandatory reporting for female genital mutilation*. Available at: http://www.rcpch.ac.uk/system/files/protected/consultation/RCPCH%20Final%20Response%20Jan%202015.pdf.

81 Ellison, K. (2013) *Karen Ellison: FGM – Can The Law Protect Our Children?* Available at: http://nofgm.org/2013/09/01/karen-ellison-fgm-can-the-law-protect-our-children/. Lien, I. and Schultz, J. (2014) *Interpreting Signs of Female Genital Mutilation Within a Risky Legal Framework*. Available at: http://lawfam.oxfordjournals.org/content/28/2/194.full.

82 Travis, A. (2014) Reporting Female Genital Mutilation should be Legally Required. *Guardian*, 25 March. Available at: http://www.theguardian.com/society/2014/mar/25/female-genital-mutilation-fgm-reporting-legally-required-cps.

83 Press Association (2014) Met Chief Says UK May Turn to Mandatory Medical Tests for FGM. *Guardian*, 9 May. Available at: http://www.theguardian.com/society/2014/may/09/fgm-met-chief-medical-tests.

84 Tidy, C. (2012) Safeguarding Children – Referral and Management of an Abused or At-risk Child. *EMIS*, 20 November. Available at: http://www.patient.co.uk/doctor/safeguarding-children-referral-and-management-of-an-abused-or-at-risk-child.

85 FGM National Clinical Group (2015) *Psychological Aspects*. Available at: http://www.fgmnationalgroup.org/psychological_aspects.htm.

86 Karma Nirvana (2014) *Conference on Legal Changes to Forced Marriage and Female Genital Mutilation*. Available at: http://www.karmanirvana.org.uk/wp-content/uploads/2014/05/thames-valley-roadshow-170614.pdf.

87   Burrage, H. (2014) NoFGM Fringe Event at 2014 Labour Party Conference: Some Outcomes. *Hilary Burrage, 26 September.* Available at: http://hilaryburrage.com/2014/09/26/nofgm-fringe-event-at-2014-labour-party-conference-some-outcomes/.

88   The Maya Centre (2015) *Dahlia Project for Survivors of FGM.* Available at: http://www.mayacentre.org.uk/dahlia-project-survivors-fgm/.

89   Manor Gardens (2015) *Female Genital Mutilation (FGM) Special Initiative.* Available at: http://www.manorgardenscentre.org/fgm-initiative/.

90   University College London Hospital (2014) UCLH to Open First Paediatric FGM Clinic. *UCLH,* 18 August. Available at: https://www.uclh.nhs.uk/News/Pages/UCLHtoopenfirstpaediatricFGMclinic.aspx.

91   RCOG Ethics Committee (2013) Ethical Considerations in Relation to Female Genital Cosmetic Surgery (FGCS). *RCOG,* October. Available at: https://www.rcog.org.uk/globalassets/documents/guidelines/ethics-issues-and-resources/rcog-fgcs-ethical-opinion-paper.pdf.

92   Real Self (2010) *How Old Do You Have to Be to Get Labiaplasty?* Available at: http://www.realself.com/question/how-old-do-you-be-get-labiaplasty.

93   Centrefold (2015) *The Centrefold Project.* Available at: http://www.thecentrefoldproject.org/.

94   Roberts, R. (2013) #FGM: The 'Designer Vagina' isn't the Same as Female Genital Mutilation, but it is Comparable. *Independent,* 6 March. Available at: http://www.independent.co.uk/voices/comment/fgm-the-designer-vagina-isnt-the-same-as-female-genital-mutilation-but-it-is-comparable-8522466.html.

95   Bacquet-Walsh, C., Jordan, S., Moneti, F. (2012) Female Genital Cutting Fact Sheet. *Office of Women's Health,* 16 July. Available at: http://www.womenshealth.gov/publications/our-publications/fact-sheet/female-genital-cutting.html.

96   Keel, A. (2014) *Re: Female Genital Mutilation (Letter to health professionals in Scotland).* The Scottish Government. Available at: http://www.sehd.scot.nhs.uk/cmo/CMO(2014)19.pdf.

97   O'Connor, R. (2014) Designer Vagina Surgery could be as Illegal as FGM, Theresa May Warns. *Independent,* 10 December. Available at: http://www.independent.co.uk/news/uk/politics/designer-vagina-surgery-could-be-as-illegal-as-fgm-theresa-may-warns-9915466.html#.

98   UK Government (2014) *Female Genital Mutilation: The case for a national action plan.* Available at: https://www.gov.uk/government/uploads/system/uploads/attachment_data/file/384349/FGMresponseWeb.pdf.

99   Stern (2015) *Before and After Patient Photos of Labia Surgery (Labiaplasty).* Available at: http://www.labiaplastysurgeon.com/labiaplasty-photos.html#.UpIzYcRdXUw.

100 The Gynae Centre (2015) *Vaginoplasty.* Available at: http://www.gynae-centre.co.uk/our-services/vaginoplasty/.

101 Hogenboom, M. (2012) The Rise in Women Seeking a Perfect Vagina. *BBC News,* 24 July. Available at: http://www.bbc.co.uk/news/health-18947106.

102 Davis, R. (2011) Labiaplasty Surgery Increase Blamed on Pornography. *Guardian*, 26 February. Available at: http://www.theguardian.com/lifeandstyle/2011/feb/27/labiaplasty-surgery-labia-vagina-pornography.

103 British Society for Paediatric and Adolescent Gynaecology (2013) *Position Statement: Labial Reduction Surgery (Labiaplasty) on Adolescents*. Available at: https://www.rcog.org.uk/globalassets/documents/news/britspag_labiaplastypositionstatement.pdf.

104 Dingle, S. (2012) Medicare-funded Labiaplasty on the Rise. *ABC*, 4 October. Available at: http://www.abc.net.au/worldtoday/content/2012/s3603589.htm.

105 Radfem Hub (2010) British Women Protest FGM (Female Genital Mutilation). *Radfem Hub*, 10 December. Available at: http://radicalhubarchives.wordpress.com/2011/12/10/british-women-protest-fgm-female-genital-mutilation/.

106 Laurance, J. (2006) West is Accused of Double Standards on Female Circumcision. *Independent*, 17 July. Available at: http://www.independent.co.uk/life-style/health-and-families/health-news/west-is-accused-of-double-standards-on-female-circumcision-408248.html.

107 Olujobi, G. (2009) Designer Vaginas: Is female circumcision coming out of the closet? *Truth Dig*, 2 July. Available at: http://www.truthdig.com/report/page3/20090702_designer_vaginas_is_female_circumcision_coming_out_of_the_closet.

108 Nurka, C. (2012) Female Genital Cosmetic Surgery: A labial obsession. *The Conversation*, 28 August. https://theconversation.com/female-genital-cosmetic-surgery-a-labial-obsession-9119.

109 Davis, R. (2011) Labiaplasty Surgery Increase Blamed on Pornography. *Guardian*, 26 February. Available at: http://www.theguardian.com/lifeandstyle/2011/feb/27/labiaplasty-surgery-labia-vagina-pornography.

110 Andrikopoulou, M., Creighton, S.M., Liao, L.M., Michala, L. (2013) The Normal Vulva in Medical Textbooks. *Journal of Obstetrics and Gynaecology*. 33(7): 648–50. Available at: http://www.ncbi.nlm.nih.gov/pubmed/2412794.5.

111 Creighton, S. (2001) Surgery for Intersex. *Journal of the Royal Society of Medicine*. 94(5): 218–20. Available at: http://www.ncbi.nlm.nih.gov/pmc/articles/PMC1281452/.

112 Intersex Society of North America (2008) *Our Mission*. Available at: http://www.isna.org/.

113 Australian Government Department of Foreign Affairs and Trade (2015) *Sex and Gender Diverse Passport Applicants*. Available at: https://www.passports.gov.au/web/sexgenderapplicants.aspx.

114 Paramaguru, K. (2013) Boy, Girl, or Intersex? *Time*, 12 November. Available at: http://world.time.com/2013/11/12/boy-girl-or-intersex/.

115 Lord, R. (2013) More Women Undergo Surgery in Quest for 'Designer Vaginas'. *South China Morning Post*, 26 February. Available at: http://www.scmp.com/lifestyle/health/article/1158305/more-women-undergo-surgery-quest-designer-vaginas.

116 Kennedy, C. (2013) Cosmetic Surgery: Royal College of Surgeons guidance is welcome, but regulation is required. *Clinical Negligence Law Blog*, 19 February. Available at: http://www.kingsleynapley.co.uk/news-and-events/blogs/clinical-negligence-law-blog/cosmetic-surgery-royal-college-of-surgeons-guidance-is-welcome-but-regulation-is-required.

117 Brell, R (2013) How FGM Legislation Applies to Cosmetic Procedures. *Avant*, 1 July. Available at: http://www.avant.org.au/News/20130701-how-fmg-legislation-applies-to-cosmetic-procedures/.

118 Johnsdotter, S. (2009) *The FGM Legislation Implemented: Experiences from Sweden*. Malmö University. Available at: http://www.uv.es/cefd/17/Johnsdotter.pdf.

119 Kelly, B., Foster, C. (2012) Should Female Genital Cosmetic Surgery and Genital Piercing be Regarded Ethically and Legally as Female Genital Mutilation? *BJOG*. 119: 389–92. Available at: http://onlinelibrary.wiley.com/doi/10.1111/j.1471-0528.2011.03260.x/pdf.

120 McCabe, F. (2013) *The Female Genital Mutilation Act and Its Relation to Female Genital Cosmetic Surgery*. Mills & Reeve. Available at: http://www.mills-reeve.com/files/Publication/e023b495-a726-4241-b4dc-5d607f22d2f4/Presentation/PublicationAttachment/efa6e8e7-14e1-498d-9496-5fc0bde49384/FGMA_Oct13.pdf.

6 Legislation and Governance

The UK Parliament has been sporadically concerned with female genital mutilation for almost a century, and British statute goes back three or more decades; but as of early 2015 there still has not been a single successful prosecution concerning any aspect of FGM. The circumstances which have produced this situation are complex, and, as the 2014 Report of the UK Parliament Home Affairs Select Committee[1] (the 'Vaz Report') demonstrates, responsibility for upholding the law has frequently seemed to be regarded as someone else's to resolve, whenever any public service professional is asked.

Thus we find ourselves in a position where the UK Parliament has pondered FGM for generations, but still some issues around legislation are unresolved. Frustration at the snail's pace of effective legal positions has been shared by many, from way back in time – amongst those impatient with progress being Sophie Ramsay, great-great-niece of Katherine Atholl who co-chaired the first parliamentary committee, in 1929.[2]

And the global legal community has also been overtly concerned about FGM since at least the end of the Second World War. The illegality of female genital mutilation is grounded in the 1948 *Universal Declaration of Human Rights*,[3, 4] as well as in formal international law and in the explicit legislation of many nations around the world, including the United Kingdom.

International Legislation, Protocols and Reports

Leaders across the international community have registered concerns about FGM on many occasions since the second half of the twentieth century.[5] A number of the major developments concerning the eradication of FGM run parallel to the development of that international community as it matured in the post-Second World War era.

This development arose via the historic creation of, and subsequent collaborations between, the United Nations (formally established on 24 October 1945,[6] only seven weeks after the final cessation of the Second World War on 2 September 1945 – now celebrated annually as United

145

Nations Day), the World Health Organization (whose constitution came into force on 7 April 1948 – now World Health Day[7]), and collaborations, for example, between the nations of the African continent.

The instruments of the international human rights framework are the *Universal Declaration of Human Rights* (10 December 1948)[8, 9] and the six core human rights treaties[10] including:

1. International Covenant on Economic, Social and Cultural Rights (1966)[11]
2. Convention on the Rights of the Child (1989)[12, 13, 14]
3. Convention Against Torture and Other Cruel, Inhuman or Degrading Treatment or Punishment (1984)[15]
4. International Convention on the Elimination of All Forms of Racial Discrimination (1965)[16]
5. Convention on the Elimination of All Forms of Discrimination against Women (CEDAW) (1979).[17]

Every country in the world has ratified at least one of these, and many have ratified most of them. These treaties are important tools for holding governments accountable for the respect for, protection of and realisation of the rights of individuals in their country.[18]

Detailed information about some elements of legislation and timelines around the world can be found elsewhere,[19, 20, 21, 22, 23] but what follows demonstrates something of the complexities and enduring efforts over the last century to make FGM history in many different nations:

- 1948: the United Nations sets a common standard on human rights with the adoption of the *Universal Declaration of Human Rights*.[24]
- 1965, 21 December: *International Convention on the Elimination of All Forms of Racial Discrimination*[25] adopted by the United Nations General Assembly (above).
- 1966, 16 December: *International Covenant on Civil and Political Rights* (multilateral treaty)[26] adopted by the United Nations General Assembly to ensure to all individuals (their human) rights without distinction of any kind, such as race, colour, sex, language, religion, political or other opinion, national or social origin, property, birth or other status.
- 1966, 16 December: *International Covenant on Economic, Social and Cultural Rights* (multilateral treaty)[27] adopted by the United Nations General Assembly, committing parties to work towards the granting of economic, social, and cultural rights (ESCR) to individuals, including labour rights and the right to health, the right to education, and the right to an adequate standard of living. As of 2013, the Covenant had 160 parties. A further seven countries, including the United States of America, had signed but not yet ratified the Covenant.

- 1975, 9 December: the *Declaration on the Protection of All Persons from Being Subjected to Torture and Other Cruel, Inhuman or Degrading Treatment or Punishment*[28] (the 'Torture Declaration') by the General Assembly of the United Nations.
- 1975: the United Nations gives 1975 the title *International Women's Year* (IWY) – thereafter always celebrated on 8 March as *International Women's Day*[29] – a date which has been celebrated variously across the world from the beginning of the twentieth century.[30] This year (1975) was also designated the beginning of the United Nations Decade for Women.
- 1975–85: the United Nations Decade for Women.[31]
- 1979: the *Convention on the Elimination of All Forms of Discrimination against Women* (CEDAW),[32] often known as an 'international bill of rights for women' is adopted by the United Nations General Assembly. Consisting of a preamble and 30 articles, it defines what constitutes discrimination against women and sets up an agenda for national action to end such discrimination. The Convention defines discrimination against women as

   > ... any distinction, exclusion or restriction made on the basis of sex which has the effect or purpose of impairing or nullifying the recognition, enjoyment or exercise by women, irrespective of their marital status, on a basis of equality of men and women, of human rights and fundamental freedoms in the political, economic, social, cultural, civil or any other field.

   The Convention is the only human rights treaty which affirms the reproductive rights of women and targets culture and tradition as influential forces shaping gender roles and family relations. It affirms women's rights to acquire, change or retain their nationality and the nationality of their children. Parties to the Convention also agree to take appropriate measures against all forms of traffic in women and exploitation of women. Countries that have ratified or acceded to the Convention are legally bound to put its provisions into practice. They are also committed to submit national reports, at least every four years, on measures they have taken to comply with their treaty obligations.[33]
- 1979, February: the American feminist writer Fran Hosken (1920–2006) presents her research – *The Hosken Report: Genital and sexual mutilation of females*[34] – to the WHO's first 'Seminar on Harmful Traditional Practices Affecting the Health of Women and Children', after which African women from several countries at the conference lead a vote to end FGM.
- 1984, 10 December: *Convention Against Torture and Other Cruel, Inhuman or Degrading Treatments or Punishments* adopted by the General Assembly of the United Nations (resolution 39/46).[35] The Convention entered into force on 26 June 1987 after it had been ratified by 20 states.

- 1984: formation of the *Inter-African Committee on Traditional Practices Affecting the Health of Women and Children*.[36] These practices include female genital mutilation (FGM), early and forced marriages, son preference, and the dowry systems, many of which have serious consequences for the girl child's physical, emotional, and psychological development.[37] The IAC is an African non-governmental organisation (NGO) regional umbrella body. It was formed by African delegates to a United Nations seminar, with support from UNFPA, UNICEF, WHO and the Ministry of Health of Senegal, at a time when FGM was a highly controversial and 'sensitive' issue with a critical need for an African regional voice in the international campaign against the practice.
- The IAC's headquarters are in Addis Ababa, Ethiopia, plus a liaison office in Geneva. It has two main objectives:
  1. to prevent and eliminate traditional practices that are harmful to or impede the health, human development and rights of women and girls and advocate for care for those who suffer the health consequences of harmful practices; and
  2. to promote and support those traditional practices that improve and contribute to the health, human development and rights of women and children.
- The IAC has national committees, in 29 African countries and links to African population groups in the diaspora through its global affiliates (for example in Belgium, France, United Kingdom, Spain, Germany, Sweden, Norway, Italy, Canada, USA, New Zealand, Japan).
- 1990: United Nations *Convention on the Rights of the Child* (article 24.3): adopted and opened for signature, ratification and accession by General Assembly resolution 44/25 of 20 November 1989, entry into force 2 September 1990.[38]
- 1990: African Charter on the Rights and Welfare of the Child,[39] unique in that it focuses on a specific continent and, whilst building on the same basic principles as the UN Convention on the Rights of the Child, highlights issues of special importance in the African context.
- 1990: Inter-African Committee on Traditional Practices Affecting the Health of Women and Children begins to refer to *'female genital mutilation'*, rather than *'female circumcision'*.[40, 41]
- 1991: the WHO recommends that the UN use the same term (that is, female genital mutilation).[42, 43]
- 1993, June: UN World Conference on Human Rights passes the *Vienna Declaration*[44, 45] recognising the rights of women and girls, and classifying FGM as a human-rights violation: United Nations *Declaration on the Elimination of Violence against Women* (Res. 48/104, 48 U.N. GAOR).
- 1994: International Conference on Population and Development (ICPD) (Cairo),[46] where it was affirmed that the equality and empowerment

of women is a global priority, both from the perspective of universal human rights, and also as an essential step towards eradicating poverty and stabilising population growth. Reproductive health and rights are declared a cornerstone of women's empowerment, as well as being the key to sustainable development.

- 1995: United Nations 4th World Conference on Women (Beijing),[47] which recognises that the status of women has advanced in the previous decade but that progress has been uneven, with inequalities, particularly increasing poverty, continuing to affect the lives of the majority of the world's people, especially women and children.
- 1996: the WHO adopts new FGM classification. The *Note on Terminology*[48] explains that use of the word 'mutilation' reinforces the fact that the practice is a violation of girls' and women's rights and so, in view of its significance as an advocacy tool, all United Nations agencies have agreed to use the single term 'female genital mutilation'.
- 1997: WHO *Regional Plan of Action to accelerate the elimination of FGM*[49] covering the 20-year period 1996–2015 in three phases (1996–8, 1999–2006 and 2007–15), with a 'sharp focus' towards the end of 2005, when a comprehensive evaluation of the first and second phases has been made.
- 1997: Joint WHO/UNFPA/UNICEF *Statement for the elimination of FGM* (updated in 2008),[50] which notes (2008) that communities engaged in collective decision-making have been able to abandon the practice; if they decide themselves to abandon female genital mutilation, the practice can be eliminated very rapidly.
- 1998: the *Banjul Declaration*[51] is published following the first of four symposia for religious leaders organised by the Inter-African Committee (IAC), in The Gambia, via a Network of African Religious Leaders against FGM and for Development.[52] This network offers practical guidance for advocacy and sensitisation on female genital mutilation. Other symposia are subsequently held in 2001 (Dar-es-Salaam, Tanzania), in 2005 (Egypt and Burkina Faso) and in 2007 (Abidjan, Côte d'Ivoire).
- 1998: Susan Izett and Nahid Toubia of RAINBO write report, *Female Genital Mutilation: An overview*, for the World Health Organization (WHO),[53, 54] offering guidance to activists, international agencies, and non-governmental organisations on available research and ways forward to end FGM.
- 1999: United Nations Educational, Scientific and Cultural Organization (ECOSOC) Resolution A/RES/53/117 on FGM,[55, 56] which welcomes the *Ouagadougou Declaration*,[57] adopted on 6 May 1999 at the Regional Workshop on the Fight against Female Genital Mutilation in the countries that are members of the West African Economic and Monetary Union, and reaffirms that such traditional or customary

practices constitute a definite form of violence against women and girls and a serious form of violation of their human rights.

- 2000: the Inter-African Committee facilitates young people from its 29 member countries to create an African Regional Network of Youth for the elimination of female genital mutilation (FGM).[58]
- 2003, 6 February: first United Nations International Day of Zero Tolerance to Female Genital Mutilation when the Inter-African Committee organises an International Conference entitled 'Zero Tolerance to Female Genital Mutilation' that leads to three major outcomes:[59]
  1. the adoption of 6 February by the UN as an International Day of Zero Tolerance to Female Genital Mutilation (FGM);[60]
  2. a call on African heads of state requesting their personal commitment and involvement in the struggle for the elimination of female genital mutilation (FGM);
  3. joining efforts between different actors (governments, UN institutions, parliamentarians, legislators, policy-makers, NGOs…) in order to coordinate their approaches and harmonise activities under the coordination of the Inter-African Committee.
- 2003, May–June: 33rd Session and publication of General Comment No. 4 on *Adolescent Health and Development in the Context of the Convention on the Rights of the Child.*[61]
- 2003, July: African Union ratifies the *Maputo Protocol* (Protocol to the African Charter on Human and Peoples' Rights, on the Rights of Women),[62, 63] guaranteeing certain rights for women, including an end to FGM.
- 2005: General Assembly of the IAC issues the *Bamako Declaration*[64, 65] demanding that respect be shown towards the international agreement, led by the African community, that FGM be known in formal contexts as 'mutilation', rather than by any euphemism.
- 2008: the WHO adopts new classification of FGM.[66]
- 2012, 20 December: United Nations General Assembly votes unanimously to take all necessary steps to end FGM, with the 54 nations of the African Group introducing the resolution.[67, 68]

Legislation, Protocols and Reports in Known FGM-practising Countries

Individual African and some countries in the Middle East and parts of Asia[i, 69] have also challenged FGM for many years:

---

i   FGM is most common in the western, eastern, and north-eastern regions of Africa,

- 1906: Protestant missionaries in Kenya complain about FGM;[70]
- 1920s: Egyptian Doctors' Society call for a ban on FGM;[71]
- 1924: Pharaonic circumcision becomes an issue for the British in Sudan;[72]
- 1928, December: Egyptian surgeon Ali Ibrahim Pasha, director of Cairo University, speaks out against FGM;[73]
- 1929–31: Kenyan circumcision controversy;[74, 75, 76]
- 1937: Elaine Hills-Young; campaign against FGM in Sudan;[77]
- 1945: Society for the Abolition of Female Circumcision founded in Sudan;[78]
- 1946, February: law in Sudan enacted;
- 1946, September: Rufa'a riots against new law in Sudan;[79]
- 1956: council of male elders (the Njuri Nchecke) in Meru, Kenya, announce ban on clitoridectomy;[80]
- 1956–9: *Ngaitana*: over 2,000 girls in Kenya charged with having circumcised themselves in protest;[81]
- 1957–8: Egyptian women's magazine, *Hawwaa*, publishes series of critical articles about it;[82]
- 1959: becomes illegal to perform infibulation in Egypt's state-run health facilities;[83]
- 1965: FGM becomes illegal in Ghana, amended 2007;[84]
- 1965: FGM becomes illegal in Guinea, amended 2000;[85]
- 1966: FGM becomes illegal in the Central African Republic (amended 1996);[86, 87]
- 1975–85: United Nations Decade for Women;[88]
- 1977: publication of *The Hidden Face of Eve: Women in the Arab World*, highly critical of FGM, by Egyptian physician Nawal El Saadawi (and with Asma El Dareer[89]);
- 1982: publication of *Woman, Why Do You Weep?* (1982), highly critical of FGM, by Sudanese physician Asma El Dareer;[90]
- 1994–5: Egypt reverses its 1959 ban to allow doctors to perform FGM;[91]
- 1995: FGM becomes illegal in Djibouti, amended 2009;[ii]
- 1996: FGM becomes illegal in Burkina Faso;
- 1998: FGM becomes illegal in Cote d'Ivoire;
- 1998: FGM becomes illegal in Togo;
- 1998: FGM becomes illegal in United Republic of Tanzania;
- 1999–2006: FGM becomes illegal in several states in Nigeria;
- 1999: FGM becomes illegal in Senegal;
- 2001: FGM becomes illegal in Kenya, amended 2011;
- 2001: FGM becomes illegal in Yemen;

---

some countries in Asia and the Middle East, and among migrants from these areas.

ii   For all following national legislative bans, please see lists of legislation above.

- 2003: FGM becomes illegal in Benin;
- 2003: FGM becomes illegal in Chad;
- 2003: FGM becomes illegal in Niger;
- 2004: FGM becomes illegal in Ethiopia;
- 2005: FGM becomes illegal in Mauritania;
- 2007: FGM becomes illegal in Eritrea;
- 2008: FGM becomes illegal in Egypt again;
- 2008–9: FGM becomes illegal in Somalia;
- 2010: FGM becomes illegal in Uganda;
- 2011: FGM becomes illegal in Guinea-Bissau;
- 2011: FGM becomes illegal in Iraqi Kurdistan;
- 2012: FGM becomes illegal in Somalia.

Legislation, Protocols and Reports in (non-UK) Western Nations

Various other Western nations as well as Britain have also began to recognise that they must address FGM:

- 1975: Rose Oldfield Hayes publishes influential paper in the *American Ethnologist* about infibulation in north Sudan;[92]
- 1979, February: Fran Hosken reads her report to the WHO's first 'Seminar on Harmful Traditional Practices Affecting the Health of Women and Children', which voted to end FGM (above);
- 1982: FGM becomes illegal in Sweden, the first traditionally non-practising country to pass dedicated legislation;[93]
- 1982: two girls die after FGM in France, leading to a series of prosecutions under France's penal code;[94]
- 1994: Canada becomes first country to recognise FGM as a form of persecution; grants refugee status to Khadra Hassan Farah, who fled Somalia with her 10-year-old daughter to avoid FGM;[95]
- 1996: United States recognises FGM as form of persecution; grants asylum to Fauziya Kasinga, who fled Togo to escape FGM;[96]
- 1997: FGM becomes illegal in the United States;[97]
- 2012, 20 December: United Nations General Assembly votes unanimously to take all necessary steps to end FGM, with the 54 nations of the African Group introducing the resolution (above).

This 2012 United Nations position is particularly significant as it will facilitate a wider global response to FGM, which is articulated as a blight of truly epidemic proportions across many nations, traditional and Western, on communities' health and well-being.

Legislation, Protocols and Reports in Britain

British concerns about FGM also extend back (in parallel with many other nations) even further, since the mid-Victorian era, including as we have seen several contributions to the debate which have international dimensions:

- 1867: Isaac Baker Brown, who promoted clitoridectomy, expelled from the British Obstetrical Society;[98]
- 1906: Protestant missionaries in Kenya complain about FGM (as above);
- 1924: Pharaonic circumcision becomes an issue for the British in Sudan (as above);
- 1929–31: Kenyan circumcision controversy (as above);[99]
- 1929, December: debate in House of Commons about FGM in Sudan; Katharine, Duchess of Atholl, and Eleanor Rathbone head all-party committee;[100]
- 1930: Jomo Kenyatta, Kenya's future prime minister, defends FGM in letter to the *Guardian*;[101]
- 1943: Eleanor Rathbone (MP for the Combined English Universities) publishes *Child Marriage: The Indian Minotaur – An object lesson from the past to the future*,[102] which comprises a sociological report, based on the 1933 Indian Census, CEFM and similar subjects closely related to FGM;
- 1944: Elaine Hills-Young report on FGM given to parliament (as above);
- 1949: 26 January: House of Commons debate on pharaonic circumcision in Sudan;
- 1985, 16 July: The *Prohibition of Female Circumcision Act 1985*[103] is introduced to the British House of Lords by Wayland Young, 2nd Baron Kennet (1923–2009; a British writer, Labour Party and later SDP politician[104]), the first reading being on 2 March 1983 (volume 439 c1141). The Act, which applies to the whole of the United Kingdom, makes it a criminal offence to perform the act on any person, or to aid, abet, counsel or procure the performance of the act by another person of any of those acts on that other person's own body. The Act is presented and sponsored in the Commons by the Conservative Dame Marion Audrey Roe, then MP for Broxbourne;[105]
- 2003–5: it becomes illegal in the UK to arrange FGM overseas on a British resident or citizen. The legislation is introduced as a Private Members Bill by Ann Clwyd, Labour MP for Cynon Valley.[106]

The Legal Position in the UK in Early 2015

As previously noted, there is already legislation concerning female genital mutilation in United Kingdom statute, some of it going back three or more decades; but as of early 2015 there has not been a single successful prosecution concerning any aspect of FGM. The circumstances which have produced this failure are complex,[107] and responsibility for upholding the law has frequently seemed, at least until very recently, to be regarded as someone else's to resolve, whenever any public service professional is asked.

Nor was this organisational buck-passing helped by the abandonment in early 2011 of the previous government's introduction of a national FGM coordinator position,[108] whereby policy and practice would be brought together with a view to developing an FGM unit or group. Instead, focus was redirected towards a multi-agency approach, which has had some effect in formal terms, but probably less on the ground. Tellingly, in December 2014 the Home Office announced the creation of a new FGM unit.[109]

From 2012 onwards, however, things have begun to change, with the introduction for example of national phone helplines[110] and a parliamentary inquiry into FGM and UK law,[111] plus previous parliamentary debates and also the first criminal charges concerning FGM in the UK.

During 2013 increasing pressure from a number of sources[112] was brought to bear to secure a direct reporting and consultation phone line for British concerns around FGM, there having previously been no national point of reference. In June 2013 the NSPCC set up such a line (for adult enquirers)[113, 114] and since that time there has been a steady trickle of reports and requests for information and advice – 153 calls in the first eight months[115] – a considerable number of them relating to the concerns of separated parents who fear their ex-partner/spouse will subject their daughters to FGM.[116]

A focus on FGM in the UK politics and Parliament also developed in 2012–13. In September 2011 (and also in 2012), as evidence that FGM remains a serious issue in the UK was becoming clearer, it was raised as a substantive issue at the Labour Party Women's Conference[iii] and elsewhere within the party.

Then, in January 2013 Karl Turner, a Labour MP and barrister, led a parliamentary debate[117] in which he called for a national action plan to address FGM in the UK.[118] This action plan should, he said, be led by the Ministry of Justice and also include the collection and collation of data on the prevalence and geographical location of the crime as well as a single national agency to take responsibility for moving forward.

---

iii By the current writer, and subsequently also by others.

A few months later, in October 2013, Jane Ellison, Conservative MP for Battersea, was appointed Minister for Public Health and announced that FGM would be a significant focus of her work in that role.[119] Previously, Ms Ellison had introduced and chaired an All Party Parliamentary Group (APPG) on FGM,[120] continuing the focus brought to that issue by the APPG on Population, Development and Reproductive Health,[121] which under leadership of its Chair, Labour MP Christine McCafferty[122] (Calder Valley), had supported the 2003 FGM Ten Minute Bill successfully introduced by Ann Clwyd MP[123] (Labour, Cynon Valley).

And again, in 2014, FGM was subject to serious discussion at the Labour Party Annual Conference, in Manchester. This time there was debate at a *Make FGM History* fringe event[124] (held outside the police cordon, so that people not attending the full conference could join the discussions), sponsored by the North-West TUC[125] and arranged by the present writer. An indication of the level of concern is that speakers included Sir Keir Starmer QC,[126] the previous Director of Public Prosecutions, Shadow Ministers Luciana Berger (Public Health) and Seema Malhotra (in the new post of Shadow Minister for Preventing Violence Against Women and Girls[127]), Richard Watts as Leader of Islington Council, Professor Hazel Barrett of REPLACE2, and Dr Phoebe Abe,[128] as well as survivors, including Hibo Wardere, who also led some of the discussion. There was consensus on the analysis presented by Keir Starmer that the 'FGM debate' is entering a new phase which will focus more closely on resolving real challenges, both within traditionally practising communities, and in or between public services which seek to bring an end to this abuse.

Plan UK and other organisations also held meetings at various party conferences in 2014, to draw attention to FGM and CEFM. A new UK national political agenda was developing: it would be necessary not 'just' to seek, as some headlining politicians urged, the eradication of FGM in traditionally practising (parts of) nations, but also to erase the problem at home. The emerging evidence demonstrated that the UK too faces a very serious, and possibly growing, domestic challenge.

And so another major development also came about in 2014, when the UK Parliament Home Affairs Committee, chaired by Keith Vaz MP (Labour, East Leicester) with cross-party membership,[129] delivered a wide-ranging report on why there have – as of the date of publication of their report – been no successful prosecutions for FGM in Britain. Testimony to the Committee was presented by interested parties from the UK and also wider afield, representing many different aspects of the issue, from expert professional observations (legal, medical, and so on) through academic perspectives[130] and also the direct experience of community activists, from organisations both large and small.

The conclusions of the Committee, with MP members from across the political spectrum, were challenging.[131] They welcomed the recent publication of multi-agency guidelines,[132, 133] but also highlighted the lack of coordination between organisations on the ground in tackling the issues, as well as the general unpreparedness and lack of relevant training of professionals and other practitioners who might encounter FGM in their everyday work.

The Committee (and particularly its chair) was scathing about the failure of various professional colleges and bodies, such as those of the chief constables (police), the medical general practitioners and the obstetricians, to take a serious lead on the subject. As a result of this very public critique it is likely that a greater degree of leadership will henceforth become evident.

Other areas which the 'Vaz Report'[134] addressed included the issue of mandatory reporting, that is, the possibility of legislation to require all those engaged in regulated activity (registered professionals such as teachers and doctors working in positions of trust with children[135]) to report concerns that FGM – or other child abuse – may have occurred or might occur.[136]

The Committee's recommendation on mandatory reporting was weak – that legislation be introduced to compel reporting of concerns by professionals in regulated activity if this is not routinely happening after a year – but it did put the issue firmly on the agenda. Since then the Home Office has set up a consultation on mandatory reporting,[137] with the Home Secretary's recommendation[138] that this course of action (direct to the police) be required only in limited circumstances constrained by lack of certainty, matters of professional confidentiality and limited resources. There is also outright opposition without discussion by the Home Office to the idea of routine examination of children – a position at odds with the French experience.[139]

The outcomes of the mandatory reporting consultation, which relates to consideration of an FGM National Action Plan (as above, proposed by the Home Affairs Committee, and before that by Karl Turner) will become clearer during 2015. Whilst other professionals may be less positive, mandatory reporting has already been endorsed by the Bar Human Rights Committee of England and Wales, in their submission to the Vaz Inquiry.[140] Some respondents, this writer amongst them,[141] consider, however, that the specific proposals on mandatory reporting are too narrowly focused (on 'just' FGM, not on FGM as one type of child abuse) and do not examine the case for a tiered national system of reporting which would prevent children falling through the net if, as diaspora residents may do, they move to another location in the UK.

One way forward would be to have a small number of Abuse Reporting Officers who make decisions on action in much the same way as in France, and who maintain records of reported suspicions for all children and adults at risk of, or experiencing, abuse, forced marriage, and so on.

This data could be used in conjunction with that derived from the HSCIC records on FGM, to help develop a clearer picture of prevalence and at-risk factors in Britain.

In any case, as Keith Vaz pointed out to one of the obstetricians who gave evidence at the inquiry,[142] the decision about whether legal action might be appropriate should be taken by lawyers, not clinicians. Prosecution initiated by the police, social services, clinicians, and so on (and taken forward by the Crown Prosecution Service) would emphasise upholding the law. Severity and type of punishment of anyone found guilty is a separate matter, decided by the courts.

And on another issue too, the political, cross-party composition of the Home Affairs Committee made for some equivocation. An enthusiasm for prevention and, to at least a degree, prosecution had in the course of its enquiries become evident across Westminster, but the means by which these aims might be secured remained at that point less clear.

As we saw, in early 2011 in the Conservative–Liberal Democrat Coalition Government abolished the sole national coordinator post to be replaced by wider portfolios across government departments – a decision which the Vaz Committee did not scrutinise. The evidence which was presented to the Home Affairs Committee by implication suggested strongly, however, that this alternative wider cross-departmental approach has not been successful; and in December 2014 a new national FGM Unit was launched, following the earlier introduction of a similar Unit for CEFM.

Details of various of the UK Government developments, including some information about senior officials involved, have been published in the *Civil Service Quarterly*.[143]

The Vaz Report confined itself to pleas for coordination and collaboration, and did not examine the question of how, and with what finance or extended budget, this might be achieved. Of such fudges is serious politics necessarily comprised.

Developments since the publication of the Home Affairs Committee Report have nonetheless been rapid.

On 22 June 2014 the UK Prime Minister, David Cameron, co-hosted with UNICEF the first *Girl Summit*.[144] This very high-profile international event, held in London, showcased many global leaders and celebrities in the fight against FGM and CEFM, the related deeply harmful traditional practice of so-called 'child marriage' – in reality economically based, culturally endorsed paedophilia.

The aims of the *Girl Summit*, which the UK Prime Minister and UNICEF hosted, 'bringing together community leaders, grassroots organisations, governments, international organisations and the private sector to support a global movement to end FGM and CEFM in a generation, everywhere, forever', were:

Sharing what works:

- learning and celebrating success: successful action by community leaders, governments and others, discussions between professionals to share and embed effective practice, and funding new research to inform and support action to end FGM and CEFM.

Agreeing an agenda for change:

- securing commitments to action: a declaration to end FGM and CEFM within a generation, announcing new actions by governments, civil society groups and private sector organisations to tackle FGM and CEFM, and increased funding (from governments, NGOs and private business) to tackle these issues.

Engaging people for change:

- inspiring a generation to declare support to end CEFM and FGM, launching a global social media campaign to raise awareness, signpost support and gather pledges, and hosting a UK youth pre-event to engage young people.

The *Girl Summit* was the fourth annual Department for International Development (DfID) event to address issues concerning international development. Previous themes were:

- nutrition (2013; the UK committed an additional £375 million of core funding and £280 million of matched funding from 2013 to 2020);[145]
- family planning (2012; the UK Government and the Bill & Melinda Gates Foundation together launched a ground-breaking effort to make affordable, lifesaving contraceptives, information, services, and supplies available to an additional 120 million women and girls in the world's poorest countries by 2020);[146] and
- vaccination against disease (2011; the UK Government committed to match donations to an agreed limit, potentially raising £100 million over the next five years to pay for vaccinations for children against diseases including pneumonia, Hepatitis B and rotavirus, which causes potentially fatal diarrhoea).[147]

Many international and British organisations worked with the DfID to deliver the 2014 *Girl Summit*, but it was deemed by various observers insufficiently inclusive of the full range of established UK activists against FGM. There was a feeling in some quarters[148] that the high-profile ambitions of some involved in the event were at the expense of many who had worked on the issues for years, even decades, and that more effort might have been put into consulting widely – and offering substantive support to – those on home ground, before moving to the international arena.

This sentiment is probably not uncommon in matters where the interplay of unmet local need and the larger desire for substantial coverage, with the advantage it brings both to the cause and to those who promote it, become entangled. The local sentiment is valid and must be heard, but the event certainly gained considerable news time around the world, raising the profile of the problems of FGM and CEFM significantly as it did so.

How this will impact on efforts in domestic but (relatively) isolated communities in UK towns and cities remains to be seen. To date direct funding for work to stop FGM in Britain remains comparatively modest, and the direction of programmes is largely hands off.

This diversity of understandings and perspectives was illustrated for instance by the views of one organisation, Plan-UK, the chief executive of which has a professional background in international development and the leadership of non-governmental organisations (NGOs). She has emphasised her belief that FGM in Britain will not be erased until it is also eradicated elsewhere[149] – the belief also of Home Secretary Theresa May and reiterated in March 2015 in the informative Ministry of Justice / Home Office *Serious Crime Act 2015 Factsheet* on FGM.[150] The view that FGM cannot be erased in the UK before it is eliminated 'in Africa' is not however shared by all.[151]

Current UK Government Initiatives

As the event approached, and then in association with *Girl Summit* partners, Prime Minister David Cameron announced a number of new measures related to legal aspects of FGM prevention. These included:

- publication of a UK cross-government strategy, *A Call to End Violence Against Women and Girls*, and a supporting action plan,[152] which includes abolition of FGM;
- UK law enforcement measures:[153] bring forward legislation via the 2014–15 Serious Crime Bill[154] to make the law clearer on parents' or guardians' liability for failing to prevent their child from being subjected to FGM, to grant victims of FGM lifelong anonymity and to extend the reach of the extra-territorial offences in the FGM Act 2003 to habitual (as well as permanent) UK residents;
- consulting on how best to introduce mandatory reporting for FGM;

- consulting on a new civil protection order to work alongside criminal legislation to protect potential victims of FGM;
- liaising with the College of Policing on professional practice to tackle FGM;
- supporting frontline UK professionals: £1.4 million in the 2014 financial year to set up a national FGM Prevention Programme in partnership with NHS England;
- (re)establishment in December 2014 of a specialist FGM unit for nationwide outreach with criminal justice partners, children's services, healthcare providers and affected communities,[155] some four years after the previous nascent body was foreclosed;
- training and professional standards packages for social workers and safeguarding practitioners;
- development of a PSHE briefing for use in schools;
- preventing abuse in the UK: a Home Office communications campaign to raise awareness of FGM and to signpost the NSPCC FGM Helpline;
- £90,000 from the Department of Communities and Local Government (DCLG) for community engagement projects to tackle FGM;
- £30,000 from the DCLG to support a network of community champions to tackle FGM and forced marriage;
- engagement of faith leaders in declaring that FGM is not religiously required and is child abuse;
- DfID support for international programmes (announcements in 2013–14): £35 million for a central programme (announced in March 2013) to help fight FGM;[156]
- £25 million (announced at the *Girls Summit*) for a new UN multi-country programme to end CEFM[157] (plus nation-specific contributions);
- £31 million (also announced at the *Summit*) a longitudinal research programme, the *Global Girls Research Initiative*, to generate new evidence on 'what works' to transform the lives of poor adolescent girls – this to include, but not only about, consideration of FGM and of CEFM.[158]

Local Government

Increasingly also local government has played a part in the development of programmes to prevent and address FGM. Pioneers, amongst them Manchester, Islington and Bristol, have been working on the problem for some years, and in late 2014 the Local Government Association – which includes almost every local authority and some other services – held a conference and published formal guidance and further references on the issues.[159]

But action remains at best piecemeal, and sometimes almost non-existent. This has led Sir James Munby, the most senior family court judge in England and Wales, to say in January 2015 that local authorities need to be more proactive and vigilant in protecting girls from the 'great evil' of FGM.[160]

To an extent this may be a matter of severe constraints on budgets and a lack of knowledge until recently of what sort of measure may be required, but it is also likely to be in part because of the reluctance by the national government to introduce formal requirements for tackling FGM, whilst at the same time making other additional demands on local government.

The now emerging HSCIC figures[161] on verified incidence in acute hospitals in England at least should help local councils to understand the extent to which specialised FGM services are required (or can be shared with other local authorities). Mandatory reporting, if the legislation goes through in early 2015 (which, or in what form, is uncertain[162] – there is opposition by bodies such as the Royal College of Paediatrics and Child Health (RCPCH) to mandated involvement of the police, rather than their preferred option, social services) should also be a helpful indicator, but other recent government initiatives may not be so facilitating.[163]

One question which has arisen from these initiatives is the extent to which the decision in effect to address FGM and CEFM in one programme, without reference to other forms of child abuse, makes sense.

It is of course evident that both types of abuse are (generally) inflicted on girls and women, reflecting the lesser status of females in the eyes of some in their communities; and both arise most often in or from harmful traditional practices which started in other nations than Britain. Further, in terms of government administration, both of these harmful practices are now the focus of support for their eradication from the DfID (Department for International Development), the body which instigated the actual *Girl Summit*.

On the other hand, grooming and other harmful practices such as breast ironing, about which we in the UK are only just beginning to learn – and about the incidences of which we currently have no real idea[164] – also arise from powerful social norms which devalue women; and conversely FGM and CEFM are but two examples of the many different and very damaging ways in which children, boys as well as girls, are abused.

FGM and CEFM in Britain

Even if we confine the programmes of action to 'traditional culture', including 'only' further harmful practices such as honour killing, the issues are complex. For instance (to give a few examples from amongst the multitude which might be cited):

- whilst FGM may be followed by CEFM, it is sometimes done many years before even child marriage is likely to occur; and conversely it may be carried out well after a woman is married, perhaps at the time of her giving birth;
- 'honour' killings do not occur (intentionally, as opposed to as a consequence of FGM) in many communities where FGM is the norm; but they do occur in some (not all) communities which tolerate grooming;
- (as in the case of male genital mutilation or circumcision) early and forced marriage can be imposed on young men as well as on young women, and the consequences of this for overall prohibition programmes remain largely yet to be resolved;
- issues around the ideal age at which marriage should be permitted – often suggested to be 18; perhaps the age of consent to then be different from that for marriage? – will not easily be resolved, when even in nations like Britain that age is 16.[iv] How to address that challenge, with all the legal, social, political, cultural and economic nuances it brings, is too multidimensional to be addressed as a side issue.

FGM and CEFM, like 'honour' killings, are all very serious crimes under UK law. This is the case whatever the age of the girl or woman (or boy or man) involved. The importance of that legal fact in ensuring the safety of young women (and young men) must not be put aside; the law is clear and must be enforced when an offence has occurred, albeit appropriate sanction of the offender/s are thereafter at the discretion of the court.

It will be critical, as the UK (rightly) supports international programmes to end FGM, that the fundamental necessity to stop many sorts of abuse of children at home is not lost to public view. That is one reason why high-profile events which focus on global issues must also address very openly the challenge where, as in this case, it also exists domestically, in the host nation.

Different government departments may be involved in different aspects of these challenges, but a joined-up approach in domestic matters is as important as in international ones.

The goodwill of all those involved on the ground is vital to success in the UK; but, despite the understandable claims to the contrary, it is probable that FGM can in fact be brought to an end in Britain before it is history everywhere, as long as there is sufficient support for activists and engagement between them and the national government. Eradication in

---

iv People aged 16 and over may marry without parental consent in Scotland, but require it in England, Wales and Northern Ireland. Anyone aged 18 or over may marry without the consent of others in any part of the UK.

the UK, regardless of what happens elsewhere, is a matter of political will, but very likely possible given sufficient insight and determination. (It is puzzling that the UK Government continues in this context to refer to FGM being eradicated 'in Africa'; FGM occurs in many other locations as well as Africa.)

Nations such as Burkina Faso seem almost to have abolished FGM,[165] so the UK, with vastly more formal resources and a long-established administrative and legal infrastructure, can surely do so as well, if the governmental will is there.

2014 and Beyond

Following on from these initiatives it seems some form of mandatory reporting will become statutory, some funding is being made available for domestic programmes, and a national unit to coordinate UK programmes against FGM has begun to be established alongside the significant monies to be dispensed internationally by the Department for International Development.

New legal measures are also being introduced to close the loophole in the 2003 legislation which (probably unwittingly) excluded FGM performed on girls who are not 'ordinarily' resident in the UK and, as recommended by the UK Bar Human Rights Committee to develop civil powers[166] to help the court protect girls at risk of FGM in the UK.

All these measures have received a welcome, to whatever degree cautiously, from others engaged in stopping FGM. This caution was, however, nourished by the context in which they emerged. Whilst no one disputed that the desire to make FGM history is genuine, these 'female-friendly' developments were observed by some to be aligned with the desire of the Coalition Government to demonstrate a greater concern for women, evidenced also by the appointment in the same time period (prior to the beginning of a General Election campaign) of several women to a decidedly male UK Cabinet.

For some this alignment of new approaches prompted a level of cynicism,[167] but most commentators, at least in public, took the view that any media focus and government action around the abolition of FGM should be welcomed unequivocally – whilst also in some cases noting that the *Girl Summit* was a closed, invitation-only event which excluded significant numbers of established British activists (whilst not all invited turned up). What transpires next will for most be the true test of declared determination to deliver.

But the Vaz Inquiry was not the only new development of early 2014.

In 2013 the then Director of Public Prosecutions, Sir Keir Starmer QC, brought to bear a focus on violence against women, acknowledging the failure thus far to take advantage of the various legislative opportunities to identify and prosecute the perpetrators of FGM in Britain. Starmer emphasised that FGM should be seen as a crime in parallel with other child abuse and domestic violence[168] and noted that some progress had been made in this general area, albeit FGM itself requires further attention.[169]

These moves also followed a consultation on revision of the Code for Crown Prosecutors for the Crown Prosecution Service (CPS)[170, 171] and campaigning from many quarters[172, 173] to secure robust action towards prosecution of those who perpetrate FGM in the UK – campaigns not always welcomed by the powers that be.[174] Since that time a new DPP, Alison Saunders, has been appointed[175] and she has continued work along these lines.[176] Several potential FGM prosecutions, previously dropped, were re-examined and just before the start of the Vaz Inquiry formal charges were laid against Dr Dhanuson Dharmasena and Hasan Mohamed[177] in connection with allegations of illegal post-partum procedures on a woman who had a baby at Wittington Hospital in London. Those accused were found not guilty in early 2015.[178]

It is likely that other legal cases around FGM will also arise within the foreseeable future, as previous files are revisited and new ones are reported. There was, however, regret that ten of the twelve cases of alleged involvement in FGM which were reassessed by the CPS in autumn 2014 have been discontinued, possibly in some instances because the suspected acts fell outside the explicit law as it currently stands.[179]

But as noted above on another front progress is about to be made. When she became CPS Alison Saunders joined others in making the case for mandatory reporting to the police by healthcare, educational and social work staff (those working in 'regulated activities') of suspected cases of FGM.[180] This is also the position of lobbying organisation Mandate Now[181] and of many human rights and other lawyers.[182] Although it was initially opposed by, for example, the NSPCC, there has been some movement from them[183] towards legislation to require mandatory reporting, and the Vaz Report has also proposed, as above, that mandating may well be necessary. The Children's Commissioner for England and the College for Social Work[184] are, however, amongst those who remain, like the RCPCH (above) largely unconvinced.[185]

So why has FGM become a highly visible legal issue in the period beginning 2012–13 until the present?

Part of the answer lies in the very much higher incidence in the UK of FGM, with increasing immigration from parts of the world where this harmful practice traditionally occurs.

Part of it lies in the growing realisation, with more accurate, not euphemistic, naming ('mutilation', not 'circumcision'), that FGM is a gross infringement in many respects of human rights; and partly there has been a tipping point in respect of policing and legal focus, as the relevant agencies have grappled also with the previously unmet challenges of domestic violence, rape and crimes such as grooming and forced marriage.

And another aspect of the greatly increased concern in Britain and some other nations about FGM is that social media have brought the story forward in authentic and convincing ways. We can now know precisely what people elsewhere are experiencing or worried about, and how they intend to address these concerns; and we can find out too who else has an interest in any given matter.

Until quite recently those who spoke up about FGM and other abuses were at best seen, by anyone who actually knew about them, as lone worthy voices; and at worst as interfering people with too much imagination and time on their hands. Now, thanks to the media, both formal and social, we know the truth about FGM and the horror it brings.

With continued pressure from activists against FGM and related crimes, the impetus to address these crimes and human rights abuses formally by upholding the law will not abate.

Discuss this chapter at http://nofgmukbook.com/2015/01/29/chapter-6-legislation-and-governance/.

Endnotes

All weblinks accessed on 1 March 2015.

1   House of Commons (2014) *Home Affairs Committee – Second Report, Female genital mutilation: the case for a national action plan.* Available at: http://www.publications.parliament.uk/pa/cm201415/cmselect/cmhaff/201/20102.htm.

2   Mohamed, F. (2014) Tell Schools to Teach Risks of Female Genital Mutilation before the Summer. *Change.org,* February. Available at: https://www.change.org/p/educationgovuk-tell-schools-to-teach-risks-of-female-genital-mutilation-before-the-summer-endfgm.

3   United Nations (1948) *Universal Declaration of Human Rights.* Available at: http://www.ohchr.org/EN/UDHR/Pages/Introduction.aspx.

4   United Nations (1948) *Universal Declaration of Human Rights.* Available at: http://www.ohchr.org/EN/UDHR/Pages/Introduction.aspx.

5   Wikipedia (2015) *Female Genital Mutilation.* Available at: https://en.wikipedia.org/wiki/Female_genital_mutilation.

6   United Nations (2015) *History of the United Nations.* Available at: https://www.un.org/en/aboutun/history.

7   WHO (2015) *History of WHO*. Available at: http://www.who.int/about/history/en.

8   United Nations (1948) *Universal Declaration of Human Rights*. Available at: http://www.un.org/en/documents/udhr/.

9   United Nations (2015) *History of the Document*. Available at: http://www.un.org/en/documents/udhr/history.shtml.

10   UN OCHCR (n.d.) *Pamphlet No.4 of the UN Guide for Minorities*. Available at: http://www.ohchr.org/Documents/Publications/GuideMinorities4en.pdf.

11   UN OCHCR (1976) *International Covenant on Economic, Social and Cultural Rights*. Available at: http://www.ohchr.org/en/professionalinterest/pages/cescr.aspx.

12   UNICEF (2015) *Convention on the Rights of the Child*. Available at: http://www.unicef.org/crc/.

13   UNICEF (2014) *FACT SHEET: A summary of the rights under the Convention on the Rights of the Child*. Available at: http://www.unicef.org/crc/files/Rights_overview.pdf.

14   UNICEF (2015) *20 Years: The Convention on the Rights of the Child*. Available at: http://www.unicef.org/rightsite/.

15   UN OCHCR (1987) *Convention Against Torture and Other Cruel, Inhuman, or Degrading Treatment or Punishment*. Available at: http://www.ohchr.org/EN/ProfessionalInterest/Pages/CAT.aspx.

16   UN OCHCR (1969) *International Convention on the Elimination of All Forms of Racial Discrimination*. Available at: http://www.ohchr.org/EN/ProfessionalInterest/Pages/CERD.aspx.

17   UN Women (2009) *Convention on the Elimination of All Forms of Discrimination against Women, Overview of the Convention*. Available at: http://www.un.org/womenwatch/daw/cedaw/.

18   UNICEF (2014) *Convention on the Rights of the Child, Human Rights Approach*. Available at: http://www.unicef.org/crc/index_framework.html.

19   Wikipedia (2015) *Female Genital Mutilation*. Available at: https://en.wikipedia.org/wiki/Female_genital_mutilation.

20   IRIN (2005) *Gabon: Links and References for FGM*. Available at: http://www.irinnews.org/report/53327/gabon-links-and-references-for-fgm.

21   IRIN (2015) *Humanitarian News and Analysis* (Various resources). Available at: http://www.irinnews.org/indepthmain.aspx?InDepthId=15&ReportId=62479.

22   No Peace without Justice (2015) *Status of African Legislations on FGM*. Available at: http://www.npwj.org/FGM/Status-african-legislations-FGM.html.

23   About FGM (2011) *References*. Available at: http://about-fgm.co.uk/references/.

24   United Nations (1948) *Universal Declaration of Human Rights*. Available at: http://www.un.org/en/documents/udhr/.

25   UN OCHCR (1969) *International Convention on the Elimination of All Forms of Racial Discrimination*. Available at: http://www.ohchr.org/EN/ProfessionalInterest/Pages/CERD.aspx.

26   UN OCHCR (1976) *International Covenant on Civil and Political Rights*. Available at: http://www.ohchr.org/en/professionalinterest/pages/ccpr.aspx.

27 UN OCHCR (1976) *International Covenant Economic, Social, and Cultural Rights.* Available at: http://www.ohchr.org/EN/ProfessionalInterest/Pages/CESCR.aspx.

28 United Nations (1975) *Declaration on the Protection of All Persons from Being Subjected to Torture and Other Cruel, Inhuman or Degrading Treatment or Punishment.* Available at: http://www1.umn.edu/humanrts/instree/h1dpast.htm.

29 African Development Bank (2015) *International Women's Day.* Available at: http://www.internationalwomensday.com/.

30 African Development Bank (2015) *About International Women's Day (8 March).* Available at: http://www.internationalwomensday.com/about.asp.

31 United Nations (2015) *Women.* Available at: http://www.un.org/en/ globalissues/women.

32 UN Women (2008) *Convention on the Elimination of All Forms of Discrimination against Women, Overview of the Convention.* Available at: http://www.un.org/ womenwatch/daw/cedaw.

33 UN Women (2008) *Convention on the Elimination of All Forms of Discrimination against Women, Text of the Convention.* Available at: http://www.un.org/ womenwatch/daw/cedaw/cedaw.htm.

34 Rafti, P. (2009) The Hosken Report: Genital/Sexual Mutilation of Females. Fran. P. Hosken. *Medical Anthropology Newsletter.* 11(1): 19–20. Available at: http://onlinelibrary.wiley.com/doi/10.1525/maq.1979.11.1.02a00200/abstract.

35 UN OCHCR (1987) *Convention against Torture and Other Cruel, Inhuman, or Degrading Treatment or Punishment.* Available at: http://www.ohchr.org/EN/ ProfessionalInterest/Pages/CAT.aspx.

36 Inter-African Committee on Traditional Practices (2009) *Welcome to Inter-African Committee, Girls' and Women's Rights First!* Available at: http://www.iac-ciaf.net/.

37 Ras-Work, B. (2006) *The Impact of Harmful Traditional Practices on the Girl Child.* United Nations. Available at: http://www.eldis.org/go/ home&id=24304&type=Document#.VQsB2I6sWQw.

38 UN OCHCR (1990) *Convention on the Rights of the Child.* Available at: http:// www.ohchr.org/en/professionalinterest/pages/crc.aspx.

39 African Committee of Experts on the Rights and Welfare of the Child (2011) *The African Charter on the Rights and Welfare of the Child.* Available at: http:// acerwc.org/the-african-charter-on-the-rights-and-welfare-of-the-child-acrwc/.

40 UNICEF (2008) *Changing a Harmful Social Convention: Female Genital Mutilation/Cutting.* Florence, Italy: UNICEF. Available at: http://www.unicef-irc.org/publications/pdf/fgm_eng.pdf.

41 El Dareer, A. (1983) *Woman, Why Do You Weep?: Circumcision and Its Consequences.* London: Zed Books.

42 Rushwan, H. (2013) Female Genital Mutilation: A tragedy for women's reproductive health. *African Journal of Urology* 19(3): 130–33. Available at: http://www.sciencedirect.com/science/article/pii/S1110570413000520.

43 WHO (2008) *Eliminating Female Genital Mutilation: An interagency statement OHCHR, UNAIDS, UNDP, UNECA, UNESCO, UNFPA, UNHCR, UNICEF,*

UNIFEM, WHO. Geneva: World Health Organization. Available at:
http://www.un.org/womenwatch/daw/csw/csw52/statements_missions/
Interagency_Statement_on_Eliminating_FGM.pdf.

44   UN OCHCR (1993) *Vienna Declaration and Programme of Action.* Available
at: http://www.ohchr.org/en/professionalinterest/pages/vienna.aspx.

45   Coomaraswamy, R. (2003) *Integration of the Human Rights of Women and
the Gender Perspective: Violence Against Women.* New York: United Nations
Economic and Social Council. Available at: http://www.coe.int/t/dg2/
equality/domesticviolencecampaign/Source/PDF_UN_Sp_Rapp_general_
report_1994-2003.pdf.

46   UNFPA (2015) *International Conference on Population and Development.* Available
at: http://www.unfpa.org/public/icpd.

47   UN Women (1995) *Fourth World Conference on Women.* Available at: http://www.
un.org/womenwatch/daw/beijing/fwcwn.html.

48   WHO (2008) *Eliminating Female Genital Mutilation: An interagency statement
OHCHR, UNAIDS, UNDP, UNECA, UNESCO, UNFPA, UNHCR, UNICEF,
UNIFEM, WHO.* Geneva: World Health Organization. Available at: http://
www.un.org/womenwatch/daw/csw/csw52/statements_missions/Interagency_
Statement_on_Eliminating_FGM.pdf.

49   Inter-African Committee on Traditional Practices (2014) *Farewell Pioneers
Anti-FGM/ Adieu Pionnières anti-MGF.* Available at: www.iac-ciaf.net/index.
php?option=com_content&view … id.

50   WHO (2008) *Eliminating Female Genital Mutilation: An interagency statement
OHCHR, UNAIDS, UNDP, UNECA, UNESCO, UNFPA, UNHCR, UNICEF,
UNIFEM, WHO,* Geneva: World Health Organization. Available at: http://
www.un.org/womenwatch/daw/csw/csw52/statements_missions/Interagency_
Statement_on_Eliminating_FGM.pdf.

51   Symposium for Religious Leaders and Medical Personnel on Female Genital
Mutilation as a Form of Violence (1998) Banjul Declaration on Violence Against
Women. *Women's International Network News.* 24(4): 27. Available at: http://
connection.ebscohost.com/c/articles/1210076/banjul-declaration-violence-
against-women.

52   Symposium for Religious Leaders and Medical Personnel on Female Genital
Mutilation as a Form of Violence (1998) Symposium for Religious Leaders and
Medical Personnel: Banjul, the Gambia, July 22, 1998. *Women's International Network
News.* 24(4): 27. Available at: http://connection.ebscohost.com/c/articles/1210075/
symposium-religious-leaders-medical-personnel-banjul-gambia-july-22-1998.

53   WHO (1998) Female Genital Mutilation: An Overview. *World Health
Organization.* Available at: http://books.google.co.uk/books/about/Female_
Genital_Mutilation.html?id=rn-FQgAACAAJ&redir_esc=y.

54   Wikipedia (2015) *RAINBO.* Available at: http://en.wikipedia.org/wiki/RAINBO.

55   United Nations (2000) *Resolution Adopted by the General Assembly [on the report of
the Third Committee (A/54/598 and Corr.1 and 2)] 54/133. Traditional or customary*

practices affecting the health of women and girls. New York: United Nations Economic and Social Council. Available at: http://www.worldlii.org/int/other/ UNGARsn/1999/265.pdf.

56   UNESCO (1999) *Recent Decisions and Activities of the Organization of the United Nations System of Relevance to the Work of UNESCO.* Paris: United Nations Educational, Scientific, and Cultural Organization. Available at: http://unesdoc. unesco.org/images/0011/001158/115847e.pdf.

57   UN Women (2012*) Sources of International Human Rights Law on Female Genital Mutilation.* Available at: http://www.endvawnow.org/en/articles/645-sources-of-international-human-rights-law-on-female-genital-mutilation.html.

58   Inter-African Committee on Traditional Practices (2003) *Report of the International Conference on 'Zero Tolerance to FGM'.* Available at: http://www. african-women.org/documents/Zero_Tolerance.pdf.

59   Inter-African Committee on Traditional Practices (2009) *About IAC.* Available at: http://www.iac-ciaf.net/index.php?option=com_content&view=article&id=1 0&Itemid=3.

60   Timeanddate.com (2015*) International Day of Zero Tolerance to Female Genital Mutilation.* Available at: http://www.timeanddate.com/holidays/un/zero-tolerance-day-female-genital-mutilation.

61   United Nations (2003) *General Comment No. 4 (2003) Adolescent health and development in the context of the Convention on the Rights of the Child.* Available at: http://tb.ohchr.org/default.aspx?Symbol=CRC/GC/2003/4.

62   African Commission on Human and Peoples' Rights (July 2004) *Protocol to the African Charter on Human and Peoples' Rights on the Rights of Women in Africa* (The Maputo Protocol) Available at: http://www.achpr.org/instruments/ women-protocol/.

63   African Commission on Human and Peoples' Rights (2003*) Protocol to the African Charter on Human and Peoples' Rights on the Rights of Women in Africa.* Maputo: African Commission on Human and Peoples' Rights. Available at: http://www.achpr.org/files/instruments/women-protocol/achpr_instr_ proto_women_eng.pdf.

64   Inter-African Committee on Traditional Practices (2005) *DECLARATION: on the Terminology FGM; 6th IAC General Assembly, Bamako, Mali: Inter-African Committee on Traditional Practices.* Available at: http://umarfeminismos.org/images/stories/ mgf/Bamako%20Declaration%20on%20the%20Terminology%20FGM_%20 6th%20IAC%20General%20Assembly_4%20-%207%20April%202005.pdf.

65   Ellison, K. (2014) The Bamako Declaration: Female Genital Mutilation Terminology (Mali, 2005). *NoFGM (UK) blog.* Available at: http://nofgm. org/2014/11/12/the-bamako-declaration-female-genital-mutilation-terminology-mali-2005/.

66   WHO (2008) *Eliminating Female Genital Mutilation: An interagency statement OHCHR, UNAIDS, UNDP, UNECA, UNESCO, UNFPA, UNHCR, UNICEF, UNIFEM, WHO.* Geneva: World Health Organization. Available at:

http://www.un.org/womenwatch/daw/csw/csw52/statements_missions/
Interagency_Statement_on_Eliminating_FGM.pdf.

67 66   United Nations General Assembly (2012) *General Assembly Strongly Condemns Widespread, Systematic Human Rights Violations in Syria, as It Adopts 56 Resolutions Recommended by Third Committee.* Available at: http://www.un.org/press/en/2012/ga11331.doc.htm.

68 UNFPA, UNICEF (2013) *Joint Evaluation UNFPA-UNICEF Joint Programme on Female Genital Mutilation/Cutting: Accelerating Change 2008–2012.* New York: UNFPA UNICEF. Available at: http://www.unicef.org/evaluation/files/FGM-report_11_14_2013_Vol-I.pdf.

69 WHO (2014) *Female Genital Mutilation Fact Sheet No. 241.* Available at: http://www.who.int/mediacentre/factsheets/fs241/en/.

70 Wikipedia (2015) *Hulda Stumpf.* Available at: http://en.wikipedia.org/wiki/Hulda_Stumpf.

71 UNICEF (2013) *Female Genital Mutilation/Cutting: A statistical overview and exploration of the dynamic of change.* New York: UNICEF. Available at: http://www.unicef.org/publications/index_69875.html.

72 Broddy, J. (2007) *Civilizing Women: British Crusades in Colonial Sudan.* Princeton: Princeton University Press.

73 UNICEF (2013) *Female Genital Mutilation/Cutting: A statistical overview and exploration of the dynamic of change.* New York: UNICEF. Available at: http://www.unicef.org/publications/index_69875.html.

74 Karanja, J. (2009) *The Missionary Movement in Colonial Kenya: The Foundation of Africa Inland Church.* Gottingen: Cuvillier Verlag Gottingen.

75 Wikipedia (2015) *Campaign Against Female Genital Mutilation in Kenya, 1929–32.* Available at: http://en.wikipedia.org/wiki/Female_circumcision_controversy_%28Kenya,_1929%E2%80%9332%29.

76 Pittman, D. (2015) *British Women's Roles in Colonial Policy-Making: Female Circumcision and Female Education in Kenya, 1929–1939.* Thesis: Loyola Marymount University. Available at: https://www.academia.edu/8197680/British_Women_s_Roles_in_Colonial_Policy-Making_Female_Circumcision_and_Female_Education_in_Kenya_1929-1939.

77 Durham University (2015) *Catalogue of the Papers of Miss Elaine Hills-Young.* Available at: http://endure.dur.ac.uk:8080/fedora/get/UkDhU:EADCatalogue.0309/PDF.

78 Broddy, J. (2007) *Civilizing Women: British Crusades in Colonial Sudan.* Princeton: Princeton University Press.

79 Mahmoud, M. (2007) *Quest for Divinity: A Critical Examination of the Thought of Mahmud Muhammad Taha,* Syracuse: Syracuse University Press.

80 Wikipedia (2015) *Female Genital Mutilation.* Available at: http://www.wikipedia.or.ke/index.php/Female_genital_mutilation.

81 Wikipedia (2015) *Female Genital Mutilation.* Available at: http://www.wikipedia.or.ke/index.php/Female_genital_mutilation.

82 UNICEF (2013) *Female Genital Mutilation/Cutting: A statistical overview and exploration of the dynamic of change.* New York: UNICEF. Available at: http://www.unicef.org/publications/index_69875.html.

83 Wikipedia (2015) *Female Genital Mutilation.* Available at: http://en.wikipedia.org/wiki/Female_genital_mutilation.

84 Ali, F. (2013) FGM in Ghana: What local African organisations are doing to eliminate female genital mutilation. *Independent,* 18 March. Available at: http://www.independent.co.uk/voices/comment/fgm-in-ghana-what-local-african-organisations-are-doing-to-eliminate-female-genital-mutilation-8537898.html.

85 UNICEF (2013) *In Guinea, One Girl's Story of Violence Reveals a Commonplace Nightmare.* Available at: http://www.unicef.org/infobycountry/guinea_71072.html.

86 No Peace Without Justice (2015) *Status of African Legislations on FGM.* Available at: http://www.npwj.org/FGM/Status-african-legislations-FGM.html.

87 Ras-Work, B. (2009) *Legislation to Address the Issue of Female Genital Mutilation (FGM).* Addis Ababa: United Nations. Available at: http://www.un.org/womenwatch/daw/egm/vaw_legislation_2009/Expert%20Paper%20EGMGPLHP%20_Berhane%20Ras-Work%20revised_.pdf.

88 Ras-Work, B. (2009) *Legislation to Address the Issue of Female Genital Mutilation (FGM).* Addis Ababa: United Nations. Available at: http://www.un.org/womenwatch/daw/egm/vaw_legislation_2009/Expert%20Paper%20EGMGPLHP%20_Berhane%20Ras-Work%20revised_.pdf.

89 Wikipedia Kenya (2015) *Female Genital Mutilation.* Available at: http://www.wikipedia.or.ke/index.php/Female_genital_mutilation.

90 El Dareer, A. (1983) Epidemiology of Female Circumcision in the Sudan. *Tropical Doctor.* 13(1): 41–5.

91 Equality Now (1997) *Egypt: Court Asserts Doctors' Right to Perform Female Genital Mutilation (FGM).* Available at: http://www.equalitynow.org/node/131.

92 Oldfield Hayes, R. (1975) Female Genital Mutilation, Fertility Control, Women's Roles, and the Patrilineage in Modern Sudan: A Functional Analysis. *American Ethnologist.* 2(4): 617–33. Available at: http://paellapolitica.files.wordpress.com/2012/05/female-genital-mutilation-fertility-control0dwomens-roles-and-the-patrilineage-in-modern-sudan-0da-functional-analysis-pd.pdf.

93 Trousson, P. (2003) *Female Genital Mutilation.* European Commission. Available at: http://www.african-women.org/documents/article-fgm.pdf.

94 Rowling, M. (2012) France Reduces Genital Cutting with Prevention, Prosecutions – Lawyer. *Thomson Reuters Foundation,* 27 September. Available at: http://www.trust.org/item/?map=france-reduces-genital-cutting-with-prevention-prosecutions-lawyer/.

95 Wikipedia (2015) *Female Genital Mutilation.* Available at: http://www.wikipedia.or.ke/index.php/Female_genital_mutilation.

96 Equality Now (1996) *United States: Political Asylum for Fear of Female Genital Mutilation – The Kasinga Case.* Available at: http://www.equalitynow.org/node/143.

97 mgmbill.org (2014) *US FGM Law*. Available at: http://mgmbill.org/usfgmlaw.htm.

98 Anonymous (1867) Clitoridectomy and Medical Ethics. *Medical Times and Gazette*. 1867(1): 391–2. Available at: http://www.cirp.org/library/history/medicaltimes1867/.

99 Pittman, D. (2015) *British Women's Roles in Colonial Policy-Making: Female Circumcision and Female Education in Kenya, 1929–1939*. Thesis: Loyola Marymount University. Available at: https://www.academia.edu/8197680/British_Women_s_Roles_in_Colonial_Policy-Making_Female_Circumcision_and_Female_Education_in_Kenya_1929-1939.

100 Simkin, J. (1997) *Katherine Stewart-Murray, the Duchess of Atholl*. Available at: http://spartacus-educational.com/PRstewartmurray.htm.

101 Wikipedia (2015) *Campaign against Female Genital Mutilation in Kenya, 1929–32*. Available at: http://en.wikipedia.org/wiki/Female_circumcision_controversy_%28Kenya,_1929%E2%80%9332%29.

102 Rathbone, E. (1934) *Child Marriage: The Indian Minotaur An Object-Lesson from the Past to the Future*. Reading: George Allen & Unwin.

103 UK Government (1985) *Prohibition of Female Circumcision Act 1985*. Available at: http://www.legislation.gov.uk/ukpga/1985/38.

104 Wikipedia (2014) *Wayland Young, 2nd Baron Kennet*. Available at: http://en.wikipedia.org/wiki/Wayland_Young,_2nd_Baron_Kennet.

105 HC Deb (1984–5) *Prohibition of Female Circumcision*, 17 January 1985 vol 71 cc525-6. Available at: http://hansard.millbanksystems.com/commons/1985/jan/17/prohibition-of-female-circumcision#S6CV0071P0_19850117_HOC_250.

106 Staff and agencies (2003) Prison for Female Circumcision 'Holidays'. *Guardian*, 21 March. Available at: http://www.theguardian.com/politics/2003/mar/21/immigrationpolicy.women.

107 Dias, D., Gerry, F., Burrage, H. (2014) 10 Reasons Why Our FGM Law Has Failed – and 10 Ways to Improve It. *Guardian*, 7 February. Available at: http://www.theguardian.com/commentisfree/2014/feb/07/fgm-female-genital-mutilation-prosecutions-law-failed.

108 IKWRO (2011) *Snip, snip, snip. That's right, the coalition's still cutting away at women's rights…* Available at: http://ikwro.org.uk/2011/03/snip-snip-snip-thats-right-the-coalitions-still-cutting-away-at-womens-rights/.

109 Home Office (2013) Female Genital Mutilation. *GOV.UK*, 22 March. Available at: https://www.gov.uk/government/collections/female-genital-mutilation.

110 4Viewers (2015) *Support Organisations – Abuse, FGM, Exploitation and Trafficking*. Available at: http://www.channel4.com/4viewers/help-support/child-abuse-exploitation-and-trafficking.

111 Burrage, H. (2014) UK Parliament Home Affairs Committee Report on Female Genital Mutilation (FGM): My Response. *Hilary Burrage blog*, 3 July. Available at: http://hilaryburrage.com/2014/07/03/uk-parliament-home-affairs-committee-report-on-female-genital-mutilation-fgm/.

112 Burrage, H. (2013) Needed Right Now: A 'Keep Safe' Phone-Line to Stop Female Genital Mutilation in Britain. *Hilary Burrage blog*, 15 May. Available at: http://hilaryburrage.com/2013/05/15/needed-right-now-a-keep-safe-phone-line-ksl-to-stop-female-genital-mutilation-in-britain/.

113 Topping, A. (2013) NSPCC Launches Helpline to Protect Girls from Female Genital Mutilation. *Guardian*, 23 June. Available at: http://www.theguardian.com/society/2013/jun/24/nspcc-helpline-girls-female-genital-mutilation.

114 NSPCC (2015) *Female Genital Mutilation (FGM) – At a glance*. Available at: http://www.nspcc.org.uk/preventing-abuse/child-abuse-and-neglect/female-genital-mutilation-fgm/.

115 Anonymous (2014) NSPCC Reports Growing Number of FGM Helpline Calls. *Journal of Family Health Care*, 12 February. Available at: http://www.jfhc.co.uk/nspcc_reports_growing_number_of_fgm_helpline_calls_25769807478.aspx.

116 Anonymous (2014) NSPCC Reports Growing Number of FGM Helpline Calls. *Journal of Family Health Care*, 12 February. Available at: http://www.jfhc.co.uk/nspcc_reports_growing_number_of_fgm_helpline_calls_25769807478.aspx.

117 Turner, K. (2013) Female Genital Mutilation. *TheyWorkForYou.com*, 8 January. Available at: http://www.theyworkforyou.com/whall/?id=2013-01-08a.27.0.

118 Burrage, H. (2015) So What Have Politicians Done for the UK 'End FGM' Campaign in 2014? *Hilary Burrage blog*, 1 January. Available at: http://hilaryburrage.com/2015/01/01/so-what-have-politicians-done-for-the-uk-end-fgm-campaign-in-2014/.

119 Bentham, M. (2013) My Blueprint for Preventing FGM, by New Health Minister Jane Ellison. *London Evening Standard*, 25 October. Available at: http://www.standard.co.uk/news/uk/my-blueprint-for-preventing-fgm-by-new-health-minister-jane-ellison-8904147.html.

120 AllParty.org (2012) *Female Genital Mutilation*. Available at: http://www.allparty.org/all-party-groups/genital-mutilation.

121 APPG on Population, Development and Reproductive Health (2015) *Home*. Available at: http://www.appg-popdevrh.org.uk/.

122 Wikipedia (2014) *Christine McCafferty*. Available at: http://en.wikipedia.org/wiki/Christine_McCafferty.

123 APPG on Population, Development and Reproductive Health (2003) *Female Genital Mutilation*. Available at: http://www.appg-popdevrh.org.uk/Publications/FGM/FGM.html.

124 Burrage, H. (2014) NoFGM Fringe Event at 2014 Labour Party Conference: Some Outcomes. *Hilary Burrage blog*, 26 September. Available at: http://hilaryburrage.com/2014/09/26/nofgm-fringe-event-at-2014-labour-party-conference-some-outcomes/.

125 TUC North West (2015) *About North West TUC*. Available at: http://www.tuc.org.uk/north-west.

126 Doughty Street Chambers (2015) *Sir Keir Starmer, KCB, QC*. Available at: http://www.doughtystreet.co.uk/barristers/profile/sir-keir-starmer-kcb-qc.

127 Malhotra, S. (2015) *Seema Malhotra MP Appointed First Ever Shadow Minister for Preventing Violence Against Women and Girls*. Available at: http://www.seemamalhotra.com/seema-malhotra-mp-appointed-first-ever-shadow-minister-for-preventing-violence-against-women-and-girls/.

128 Dr Abe Foundation (2015) *About Dr Abe*. Available at: http://drabefoundation.com/drabe.php.

129 Commons Select Committee (2013) *Home Affairs Committee – membership*. Available at: http://www.parliament.uk/business/committees/committees-a-z/commons-select/home-affairs-committee/membership/.

130 Commons Select Committee (2014) *Immediate Action Needed to Tackle FGM in the UK*. Available at: http://www.parliament.uk/business/committees/committees-a-z/commons-select/home-affairs-committee/news/140703-fgm-rpt-pubn/.

131 Commons Select Committee (2014) *Immediate Action Needed to Tackle FGM in the UK*. Available at: http://www.parliament.uk/business/committees/committees-a-z/commons-select/home-affairs-committee/news/140703-fgm-rpt-pubn/.

132 Home Office, Department for Education, Featherstone, L. (2011) Female Genital Mutilation: Guidelines to protect children and women. *GOV.UK*, 20 April. Available at: https://www.gov.uk/government/publications/female-genital-mutilation-guidelines.

133 HM Government (2014) *Multi-Agency Practice Guidelines: Female Genital Mutilation*. Available at: https://www.gov.uk/government/uploads/system/uploads/attachment_data/file/355044/MultiAgencyPracticeGuidelines.pdf.

134 Commons Select Committee (2014) Immediate Action Needed to Tackle FGM in the UK. *www.parliament.uk*, 3 July. Available at: http://www.parliament.uk/business/committees/committees-a-z/commons-select/home-affairs-committee/news/140703-fgm-rpt-pubn/.

135 Disclosure & Barring Service (2012) *DBS Referrals Guide: Summary of regulated activity with children*. Available at: https://www.gov.uk/government/uploads/system/uploads/attachment_data/file/377519/DBS_referrals_guide_summary_of_regulated_activity_with_children_v2.2.pdf.

136 Australian Institute of Family Studies (2014) Mandatory Reporting of Child Abuse and Neglect. *Australian Government*, August. Available at: https://www3.aifs.gov.au/cfca/publications/mandatory-reporting-child-abuse-and-neglect.

137 Home Office, Featherstone, L. (2014) Introducing Mandatory Reporting for FGM. *GOV.UK*, 5 December. Available at: https://www.gov.uk/government/consultations/introducing-mandatory-reporting-for-fgm.

138 Home Office (2014) Introducing Mandatory Reporting for Female Genital Mutilation – A consultation. *GOV.UK*, December. Available at: https://www.gov.uk/government/uploads/system/uploads/attachment_data/file/383075/Mandatory_Reporting_for_FGM_Consultation_Framework_v6.pdf.

139 Burrage, H. (2015) UK Home Office Consultation on Mandatory Reporting of FGM – My Response. *Hilary Burrage blog*, 11 January. Available at: http://hilaryburrage.com/2015/01/11/uk-home-office-consultation-on-mandatory-reporting-of-fgm-my-response/.

140 Bar Human Rights Committee (2014) *BHRC Submits Report to the Parliamentary Inquiry into Female Genital Mutilation (FGM)*. Available at: http://www.barhumanrights.org.uk/node/415.

141 Burrage, H. (2015) UK Home Office Consultation on Mandatory Reporting of FGM – My Response. *Hilary Burrage blog*, 11 January. Available at: http://hilaryburrage.com/2015/01/11/uk-home-office-consultation-on-mandatory-reporting-of-fgm-my-response/.

142 Commons Select Committee (2014) Committee to Hold Final Evidence Session on Female Genital Mutilation. *www.parliament.uk*, 6 May. Available at: http://www.parliament.uk/business/committees/committees-a-z/commons-select/home-affairs-committee/news/140501-fgm-ev/.

143 Ditchburn, L. and O'Brien, J. (2014) Voice, Choice and Control. *Civil Service Quarterly*, 15 July. Available at: https://quarterly.blog.gov.uk/2014/07/15/voice-choice-and-control/.

144 Department for International Development (2014) Girl Summit 2014: How you can get involved. *GOV.UK*, 25 June. Available at: https://www.gov.uk/government/news/girl-summit-2014-how-you-can-get-involved.

145 Department for International Development, Greening, J. (2013) Nutrition for Growth: Beating Hunger through Business and Science. *GOV.UK*, 8 June. Available at: https://www.gov.uk/government/news/nutrition-for-growth-beating-hunger-through-business-and-science.

146 Department for International Development (2012) Family Planning: London summit, 11 July 2012. *GOV.UK*, 11 July. Available at: https://www.gov.uk/government/news/family-planning-london-summit-11-july-2012.

147 Department for International Development (2011) Vaccine Summit Saves Four Million Lives in Four Hours. *GOV.UK*, 13 June. Available at: https://www.gov.uk/government/news/vaccine-summit-saves-four-million-lives-in-four-hours.

148 Otoo-Oyortey, N. (2014) Where Were the Grassroots Voices at the Girl Summit? *Guardian*, 30 July. Available at: http://www.theguardian.com/global-development-professionals-network/2014/jul/30/where-were-grassroots-voices-girl-summit.

149 147Barron, T. (2014) We Must End FGM Everywhere, Not Just in the UK. *Guardian*, 3 July. Available at: http://www.theguardian.com/society/2014/jul/03/we-must-end-fgm-everywhere.

150 Ministry of Justice/Home Office (2015) *Serious Crime Act 2015 Factsheet – Female Genital Mutilation*. March (28): 5. Available at: https://www.gov.uk/government/uploads/system/uploads/attachment_data/file/416323/Fact_sheet_-_FGM_-_Act.pdf.

151 Burrage, H. (2014) So What Have Politicians Done for the UK 'End FGM' Campaign in 2014? *Hilary Burrage blog*, 1 January. Available at: http://hilaryburrage.com/2015/01/01/so-what-have-politicians-done-for-the-uk-end-fgm-campaign-in-2014/#more-6728.

152 Home Office (2014) A Call to End Violence Against Women and Girls: Action Plan 2014. *GOV.UK*, 8 March. Available at: https://www.gov.uk/government/publications/a-call-to-end-violence-against-women-and-girls-action-plan-2014.

153 Ministry of Justice (2014) Serious Crime Bill: Fact sheet – Female Genital
Mutilation. *GOV.UK*, November. Available at: https://www.gov.uk/
government/uploads/system/uploads/attachment_data/file/371024/Fact_
sheet_-_Female_Genital_Mutilation_-_Commons_Intro.pdf.

154 UK Government (2015) *Serious Crime Act 2015*. Available at: http://services.
parliament.uk/bills/2014-15/seriouscrime.html.

155 Home Office, Featherstone, L., William, S. (2014) Government Launches
Consultation into Mandatory Reporting of FGM. *GOV.UK*, 5 December.
Available at: https://www.gov.uk/government/news/government-launches-
consultation-into-mandatory-reporting-of-fgm.

156 Department for International Development, Featherstone, L. (2013) UK to Help
End Female Genital Mutilation. *GOV.UK*, 6 March. Available at: https://www.
gov.uk/government/news/uk-to-help-end-female-genital-mutilation.

157 Featherstone, L. (2014) Written Ministerial Statement: Tackling violence against
women and girls overseas. *Department for International Development*, 16 October.
Available at: http://www.parliament.uk/documents/commons-vote-office/2014-
October/16%20October/15.DIFID-Tackling-Violence-Against-Women-and-
Girls-Overseas.pdf.

158 Department for International Development (2015) *Global Girl Research Initiative:
What works to transform girls' lives?* Available at: http://devtracker.dfid.gov.uk/
projects/GB-1-203529/.

159 Local Government Association (2015) *Female Genital Mutilation (FGM)*.
Available at: http://www.local.gov.uk/community-safety/-/journal_
content/56/10180/6510834/ARTICLE.

160 Press Association (2015) Councils Must Be More Proactive to Prevent FGM,
says Top Judge. *Guardian*, 14 January. Available at: http://www.theguardian.
com/society/2015/jan/14/councils-proactive-prevent-fgm-judge.

161 Health & Social Care Information Centre (2015) *Female Genital Mutilation
Datasets*. Available at: http://www.hscic.gov.uk/fgm.

162 HC Deb (2014–15) 29 January 2015: Col. 335WH. Available at: http://
www.publications.parliament.uk/pa/cm201415/cmhansrd/cm150129/
halltext/150129h0001.htm.

163 RCPCH (2015) RCPCH Warns Current Plans on FGM May Deter Families
and Abused Children From Visiting Doctors *RCPCH*, 19 January. Available
at: http://www.rcpch.ac.uk/news/rcpch-warns-current-plans-fgm-may-deter-
families-and-abused-children-visiting-doctors.

164 Ramesh, R. (2014) Rotherham Child Sexual Abuse Scandal is Tip of the Iceberg,
says Police Chief. *Guardian*, 15 October. Available at: http://www.theguardian.com/
society/2014/oct/15/rotherham-child-sexual-abuse-scandal-tip-iceberg-police-chief.

165 Juggapah, S. (2014) Ending FGM in Burkina Faso: How communities are leading
the way. *One.org*, 10 July. Available at: http://www.one.org/international/blog/
ending-fgm-in-burkina-faso-how-communities-are-leading-the-way/.

166 Dias, D. (2014) Bar Human Rights Committee Report to the Parliamentary Inquiry into FGM. *JusticeBrief.com*, 1 November. Available at: http://justicebrief.com/2014/11/01/bar-human-rights-report-to-the-parliamentary-inquiry-into-fgm/.

167 Gold, T. (2014) David Cameron's FGM Drive Cannot Obscure his Dismal Record on Vulnerable Women. *Guardian*, 23 July. Available at: http://www.theguardian.com/commentisfree/2014/jul/23/david-cameron-fgm-women.

168 CPS (2015) *Violence Against Women and Girls*. Available at: http://www.cps.gov.uk/Publications/equality/vaw/index.html.

169 CPS (2013) *DPP's FGM Action Plan*. Available at: http://www.cps.gov.uk/Publications/equality/vaw/dpp_fgm_action_plan.pdf.

170 CPS (2015) *A Public Consultation on a Revision of the Code for Crown Prosecutors*. Available at: http://www.cps.gov.uk/consultations/code_2012_consultation_index.html.

171 Burrage, H. (2012) The Crown Prosecution Service Finally Responds to the Horrors of Female Genital Mutilation in the UK. *Hilary Burrage blog*, 23 November. Available at: http://hilaryburrage.com/2012/11/23/the-crown-prosecution-service-finally-responds-to-the-horrors-of-female-genital-mutilation-fgm-in-the-uk/.

172 HM Government (2013) *Epetition: STOP Female Genital Mutilation (FGM/'cutting') in Britain*. Available at: http://epetitions.direct.gov.uk/petitions/35313.

173 Burrage, H. (2014) *UK Government: Enforce the UK law which forbids Female Genital Mutilation (FGM)*. Available at: https://www.change.org/p/uk-government-enforce-the-uk-law-which-forbids-fgm-female-genital-so-called-cutting.

174 Pink Politika (202) HM Government E-petition on FGM Rejected. *Pink Politika blog*, 29 May. Available at: http://pinkpolitika.com/2012/05/29/h-m-government-e-petition-on-fgm-rejected/.

175 Bowcott, O. (2013) Director of Public Prosecutions Alison Saunders Ready to Roll Up Her Sleeves. *Guardian*, 8 November. Available at: http://www.theguardian.com/law/2013/nov/08/director-public-prosecutions-alison-saunders-profile.

176 Rustin, S. (2014) Alison Saunders, Director of Public Prosecutions: 'I think women have had, as witnesses and victims, a raw deal'. *Guardian*, 2 May. Available at: http://www.theguardian.com/law/2014/may/02/alison-saunders-director-public-prosecutions-interview.

177 Topping, A. (2014) FGM: First suspects to be charged appear in court. *Guardian*, 15 April. Available at: http://www.theguardian.com/society/2014/apr/15/fgm-first-suspects-charged-court.

178 Laville, S. (2015) First FGM Prosecution: How the case came to court. *Guardian*, 4 February. Available at: http://www.theguardian.com/society/2015/feb/04/first-female-genital-mutilation-prosecution-dhanuson-dharmasena-fgm.

179 Bentham, M. (2014) Fight against FGM Suffers a Blow as More Cases are Dropped Without Charges. *London Evening Standard*, 17 November. Available at: http://www.standard.co.uk/news/uk/fight-against-fgm-suffers-a-blow-as-more-cases-are-dropped-without-charges-9865025.html.

180 Travis, A. (2014) Reporting Female Genital Mutilation Should Be Legally
    Required – CPS Chief. *Guardian*, 25 March. Available at: http://www.
    theguardian.com/society/2014/mar/25/female-genital-mutilation-fgm-
    reporting-legally-required-cps.
181 Available at: http://mandatenow.org.uk/.
182 LeighDay (2014) *Mandatory Reporting of Child Abuse 'Only Way Forward',
    According to Leading Lawyers.* Available at: http://www.leighday.co.uk/
    News/2014/October-2014/%E2%80%8BMandatory-reporting-of-child-abuse-
    %E2%80%98only-way-forw.
183 NSPCC (2014) *Strengthening Duties on Professionals to Report Child Abuse –
    NSPCC Policy Briefing.* Available at: http://www.nspcc.org.uk/globalassets/
    documents/information-service/policy-briefing-strengthening-duties-
    professionals-report-child-abuse.
184 The College of Social Work (2014) *The College of Social Work Response to the
    Home Office Consultation on Introducing Mandatory Reporting for Female Genital
    Mutilation.* Available at: https://www.tcsw.org.uk/uploadedFiles/TheCollege/
    CollegeLibrary/Easy_read_documents/2015.01.12%20FGM%20Mandatory%20
    Reporting.FINAL.pdf.
185 18Office of the Children's Commissioner (2015) *OCC Response to the Home
    Office Consultation: Introducing Mandatory Reporting for Female Genital Mutilation.*
    Available at: http://www.childrenscommissioner.gov.uk/content/publications/
    content_914.

7 Prevention –
Formal Approaches

The available instruments of enforcement in eradicating female genital mutilation are both formal and informal. Whilst the prevention of FGM is self-evidently a matter for the legal authorities, this is by no means the only way in which upholding the law is – or should be – enforced.

Despite occasional attempts by some proponents of specific approaches to make the issue 'either/or', the effectiveness of any one prevention strategy is likely in the end to be enhanced (or just occasionally to be hampered) by the others.

The tools of enforcement include community engagement, education via schools, clinics and other public facilities, working with the transport and migration authorities, media programmes, briefing of professionals and ultimately the legal process itself.

Even all these strategies cannot, however, ensure prevention, especially when the fundamental meanings of FGM are still perceived differently by different elements of the practising communities, the preventative public and voluntary services, and the general public.

The 'Meanings' of FGM

We have already noted that even the nomenclature for FGM remains contested. Very broadly, it might be said that those who, despite current recommendations and requirements, insist that FGM is 'cutting' even in formal discussion are also those who place less emphasis or even oppose legal enforcement as a substantive element in prevention.[1]

For these people the way forward is 'respect' for perpetrators, on the grounds that they inflict the mutilation on girls and young women as an 'act of love'. This view has been explored here already in the Introduction and is for some activists of value only insofar as it enables those seeking to eradicate FGM to identify, understand and address stumbling blocks to that aim.

Of course it is sometimes necessary at the initial stages of discussion to employ vocabulary which those in practising communities will recognise; cultural sensitivity and good manners do not negate the requirement that, for children to be protected effectively from the harm of FGM, that harm may need to be referred to in understood (common usage or euphemistic) terms before it can be formally articulated as mutilation. Clinical professionals frequently use informal terminology when conversing with patients ('down there', 'water works', and so on) but they do not employ those terms in case conferences or when presenting papers to colleagues.

Whilst total respect for every human being is a basic requirement in any open society, the 'respect' approach to FGM as such is therefore put aside by those (this author amongst them) who promote, and perceive a universal trend towards, the belief that each individual, and especially each child, is entitled not only to respect as a concept, but also to physical and psychological safety, bodily integrity and protection from harm and unnecessary trauma, regardless of cultural mores and beliefs. In modern society there is no place for harmful traditional practices or other cruelty to children (or women and men), and FGM must be called out for what it is.

The advantages of straightforward plain-speaking are that clarity can with care be achieved and everyone has the same perception of what FGM actually is. Nonetheless, some apologists and cultural relativists continue to promote alternative, more ambivalent or euphemistic terminologies. There is little conclusive evidence as yet – research is needed – but confusion of terms may be one of the reasons why UK (and other nations') legislation forbidding it is not seen as relevant by some of those who practise FGM.

There are many informal words which refer to FGM[2] and because the formal naming has not in some communities been used, various people may never have heard the correct formal terminology, or understand how it relates to harmful traditional practices. As one example: the word 'sunna' (Arabic for 'custom' thought to be required by the Prophet) originally referred to the removal – in theory, though very rarely in practice – of simply the tip of the prepuce of the clitoris, and now sunna is erroneously not considered to be FGM by some followers of Islam. But, conversely, the term is also deemed by some to include all types of FGM.[3] Such confusions illustrate why precise vocabulary is required.

Public and Professional Perceptions

Confusions or ambivalence about the meanings of FGM infuse public and professional understandings as well as those in communities where it occurs. It is obviously more difficult to insist on observance of the law when uncertainty or total ignorance about it pertains. Is there, some wonder, any legal constraint on the action or practice as I know it to be named, and if so how does it apply?

Many accounts exist of girls and young women who say they had no idea that their mutilation was illegal,[4] and there is also evidence that professionals in relevant roles may not always understand what FGM comprises,[5] even if they are teachers[6] or clinicians.[7]

This ignorance probably arises in part from the clandestine (and to many unlikely) nature of FGM, in part from the repeated claims that some people believe cultural practices are different from activities requiring legal constraint, and in part from embarrassment about the anatomical knowledge required to understand the act of genital mutilation.

But whatever the explanation for the failure to perceive FGM as it is, the upshot probably inhibits both discussion and intervention. It is not only small children who cannot be expected to report their harm, or fears of harm, at police stations; many members of the general public may be equally unlikely to do so, even if they have an adequate understanding of what FGM comprises to have concerns about a child's safety.

In short, the vocabulary around FGM is sometimes confusing, and by its very nature tends to inhibit referral to legal enforcement authorities, whether by the general public or by responsible professionals. Both general public information programmes and professional training need to find ways to secure enforcement of the prohibition of FGM.

Securing Convictions, Dissuading Others

Enforcement of the law on FGM cannot, however, be 'all carrot and no stick'. There has been serious concern, expressed in many ways, about the continuing failure of the authorities to secure even one successful prosecution for this serious crime in the three decades (and for many more even before that, via general statute) that FGM has been illegal in Britain.

Indeed, in the minds of some members of the British public now there may be a *quid pro quo* on this matter: they are willing to see public money spent on protecting children from FGM, and its eradication, as long as those who break the law are seen to be punished for so doing.

This implicit 'social contract', insofar as it may exist, is rarely if ever discussed but may be an underlying factor in the reluctance of some public leaders, at a time when no prosecutions have been obtained, to engage meaningfully in the issues.

It is easier to dismiss or simplify a problem when 'they' – the other – are to 'blame', than it is to focus on the complex community development requirements (for example overcoming social and economic marginalisation) to achieve the public health and many other benefits long term of addressing a harmful act before it occurs.

Petitions to encourage enforcement of the law have been one way that citizens have sought to encourage action on the part of the legal authorities. There has, however, been resistance on the part of some in government. Thus, an e-petition (with which the current writer was with several others involved) submitted to the HM Government website in early 2012[8] was held without any official response for a considerable time and then, in the words of the Cabinet Office, 'not accepted', on the suggested grounds that it might:

- contain information which may be protected by an injunction or court order
- contain material that is potentially confidential, commercially sensitive or which may cause personal distress or loss....

The full text of the rejected petition was:

> STOP Female Genital Mutilation (FGM: 'cutting' or circumcision) in Britain
>
> Over 20,000 children in Britain are estimated to be at risk annually of female genital mutilation (FGM or 'cutting') – more than 50 girls and babies every day, or 2+ every hour.
>
> It is a child protection scandal of massive dimension that even now (May 2012) no-one in the UK has been fully sanctioned by the law for performing or allowing FGM in the UK, or on UK minors.
>
> The legal position is clear and is not, even remotely, being upheld.
>
> There can be no 'taboo' issues in law.
>
> The embarrassment of carers and others responsible for safe-guarding children, or community unwillingness to intervene 'for cultural reasons', cannot excuse inaction on child cruelty.
>
> Criminal abuse of children must not be ignored because those who enforce the law are uncertain how to deal with perpetrators and their victims.
>
> This scandalous professional neglect, with 20,000+ children in the UK at risk, must be remedied forthwith. Full enforcement of the law must be brought to bear immediately.

The e-petition was subsequently published on the HM Government website after considerable correspondence and with slight amendment,[9] including reference to the 'disbanding' of the role of national FGM coordinator by the Government in April 2011, when a new cross-disciplinary approach was introduced with (initially) just £50,000 funding.

The e-petition further insisted that £50,000 is direly inadequate to address the risk of harm across Britain to thousands of girls, and that that sum should be significantly increased, and the FGM coordinator role must be reinstated immediately, to ensure effective national delivery of safe-keeping.

As it was, plans which had been afoot as early as 2009 and 2010[10] were very likely deferred or put aside. A London Safeguarding Children Board document in January 2010[11] reports that a new national FGM forum, led by the cross-government coordinator appointed the previous year (whose role the Coalition shortly thereafter abolished in favour of various committees) was working at that time to produce a set of national guidelines and resources largely modelled on the London approach.

It is not surprising therefore that, without any external support, the revised version of the 2012 e-petition protesting against this regressive positioning gained nearly 3,000 signatories whilst it was live.

The initial unexpected rejection and following delays nonetheless nurtured in the minds of various observers at the time the idea that there was more enthusiasm in the Cabinet Office to protect professionals than to engage with the public on protecting children. By this point, however, other arms of the new government were beginning to become more aware of the issues and how important public involvement would be.

Community and Public Information

Returning to the idea of an unspoken 'social contract', evidence suggests that the general public's awareness and concern about a topic like FGM relates to how effectively it can be stopped.[12] Such deterrence is likely to have greater effect if the weight of the law, as well as public opinion, is brought to bear on the offence, as FGM prosecutions in France appear to indicate.

It is therefore obvious that community engagement in developing understanding of FGM is critical. The example of the 2014 *Guardian* e-petition[13] to secure action by the Education Secretary, then Michael Gove, to alert children and staff in schools before the summer season for mutilation (the so-called 'cutting season') demonstrates how, once awareness has been raised, literally hundreds of thousands of people can become involved, in and beyond any given country, if the media positioning is effective.

The repercussions of such engagement can be many. This sort of approach reaches far beyond what can be achieved with normal awareness-raising in communities and it repositions public perceptions in a way which may make law enforcement more straightforward: the greater the grasp people in mainstream and minority communities have of the dangers of FGM, the easier (comparatively) it becomes for the authorities to tackle this crime.

And, with accurate naming to reflect the nature of the crime, the easier it also becomes for those in practising communities who would like to bring

FGM to an end. Firstly, there is a very good reason to persuade others in the social group not to do it – permitting FGM may (if the law is properly applied) result in a long term of imprisonment. This is not always seen as a disincentive when people refuse to believe the punishment will be applied, but it is a powerful tool in the rationale for persuading friends and neighbours to report their fears, or children to speak with their teachers, before the harm is done: if parents can be turned away from damaging their daughters, they will not go to jail.

Likewise, in the wider community, reporting concerns about serious child abuse, in this case FGM, is very different from sharing concerns about a 'cultural practice'. The shift to recognising that FGM is clear-cut child cruelty is gaining traction, and, with it, generally misplaced worries about (Westerners) appearing racist or insensitive to other traditions will probably also diminish – as will concerns about actually inciting racism, especially against people in the diaspora, because of disclosures about FGM. The crime of child abuse, of which FGM is one example, is very serious; and it is not restricted to any single cultural tradition or creed.

One commentary of the reasons why the UK legal system has been slow to respond is that by Dias, Gerry and Burrage.[14] There is, as noted in this discussion, no doubt that many different approaches are required if FGM is to be eradicated. Karen Ellison, a medical doctor and lawyer, has also considered the interplay and tensions between the legal and medical care approaches.[15] All are agreed, however, that the complexities (of which there are many, as the January 2015 Family Court judgment amply demonstrates[16]) do not excuse the necessity to uphold the law.

Prevention of Criminal 'FGM Tourism'; the FGM 'Passport'

Whilst much of the work to prevent FGM can be undertaken in schools and health care settings, there are also some contexts which offer very specific scope for prevention. Prime amongst these are travel venues and migration facilities, especially those which are associated with 'holidays' when FGM may be the main purpose of the journey. In line with terminology for instrumental, planned visits to other places for health and medical treatment (which FGM emphatically is not), this might in one sense be termed 'FGM tourism'.

The child (or baby) may herself be taken to a location where FGM is traditionally performed, perhaps as one individual amongst a number whose mutilation (and sometimes rite of passage) will be 'celebrated' by her family's community of origin; or the intending mutilator may travel to a venue where, in probability, several girls may have been assembled for a so-called 'cutting party'.[17] The initial focus for action in the UK is therefore either airports[18] which offer eventual destinations in sub-Saharan Africa, or the Eurostar train running between London Kings Cross and Paris (France).

In the first instance the Metropolitan Police are now arranging, with volunteers from relevant communities, to talk to families travelling with girls, both when they depart and when they return, in the hope of preventing or detecting FGM activity.[19] Details of an arrangement whereby girls thought to be at risk can have their passports confiscated are also being thought through[20] and Protection Orders[21] will be instituted to this effect.

In addition, the Home Office has now emulated the Dutch scheme[22] for the 'Health Passport' or 'FGM Passport',[23] a small document in various languages[24] which can be given to girls and their families by community volunteers or the police (or for example in schools before the holidays begin) and which makes clear why FGM must not occur.

The FGM Passport offers the opportunity to emphasise the illegal and harmful nature of FGM, and it also provides a way to break the conventional and well-observed silence on the subject, even within practising families. Further, it is intended to be useful as a way for parents and (older) girls to demonstrate to their traditional communities and family members that permitting FGM will have serious consequences for any responsible person when they return to the UK.

The other major approach which has been taken to what might be termed FGM tourism is vigilance around travel between France and the UK. There have been claims that Britain is the 'FGM capital' of Europe because of its failure to bring prosecutions. For this reason it is thought that mutilators travel from, for instance, Paris to London to inflict FGM on groups of girls brought together for that purpose. Just as with the airports, police and activists – including those in France, such as Isabelle Gillette-Faye of GAMS[25] – sometimes patrol the points of departure and arrival. There are reports that at least a few children have been spared FGM as a result of this intervention.[26]

These interventions also point to another important aspect of FGM prevention. It is an international issue which will not go away until cross-border collaboration is the routine order of the day. This applies whether simply in the context of crossing the Channel to and from mainland Europe to Britain, or whether the connections are intercontinental.

It is probable that the communities in Britain where girls are most at risk of FGM are:[i]

---

i   Approximate figures: calculations by the author, on the basis of various reports.

- Somalia (UK population around 115,000, of which 98 per cent of women and girls, perhaps 56,000, are vulnerable);
- Kenya (203,000, of which perhaps 27 per cent vulnerable: 27,000);
- Nigeria (154,000, of which perhaps 27 per cent vulnerable: 21,000);
- Eritrea (40,000, of which perhaps 89 per cent vulnerable: 18,000); and
- Egypt (25,000, of which perhaps 91 per cent vulnerable: 11,000).

Surveillance of passengers – whether vulnerable girls or possible mutilators – travelling between the UK and these countries should be a particular priority for national border authorities.

But it cannot be assumed that travel is along predictable routes. Not only is there potential complication because of the increasing illegal entry of immigrants from Africa to southern Europe,[27, 28] but also girls being taken from, for example, the UK are not now necessarily going to their familial 'homeland': it is thought that instead some are taken to countries such as Egypt, or Dubai and Singapore, where the mutilation is delivered by health professionals,[29] albeit without specific training in FGM 'procedures', and with the possibility that the excision may even be more severe[30] than when done by untrained excisors.

Tackling this wider context around the FGM agenda requires international collaboration between numbers of public service, non-governmental and enforcement agencies. Amongst the non-statutory bodies are the World Health Organization (WHO),[31] the United Nations Population Fund (UNFPA)[32] and various African and European specific bodies such as the Inter-African Committee on Traditional Practices (IAC), the END FGM European Campaign[33] run by Amnesty International,[34] the Daphne REPLACE2 programme[35] and various NGOs, the African Women's Organization[36] and Equality Now.[37]

On the governmental side are national, European and global collaboration organisations concerned with migration and border control, crime (including trafficking, slavery and child abuse) and health.

Cooperation between these many bodies is complex and necessarily also further complicated by the variations in statutes and judicial systems between different states. Nonetheless, FGM and other human rights crimes do not stay within national borders, and must therefore be tackled as global (and European) cross-border issues.

Beyond the obvious preventative and crime-solving collaborations required even within a given country, there are also, however, UK enforcement challenges of a more particular nature.

(More) Girls may be Subjected to FGM at a Younger Age

One of these is attempts by those who practise FGM to reduce the age at which it is inflicted, both because this may be perceived as more 'humane' (assuming she survives, the child 'forgets' what happened) and because the act cannot be resisted or reported by her, and it is in any case easier to keep a pre-school child out of the public eye.

There is some evidence that FGM does occur earlier in some instances when surveillance by the authorities increases.[38] This is then used by some parties to argue for a more informal approach to stopping FGM, with increased communication and reduced policing.

But whilst the call for more communication and education is always valid, this position (informal, not formal, enforcement) can be countered by the observation that FGM is in the category of crime – premeditated and planned – which is most amenable to formal enforcement.[39]

Perhaps a case can be made for customs being emotionally compelling or apparently 'inevitable' in much the same way as crimes of passion (which are not premeditated acts), but this case is less persuasive in the contexts of modern communications and wider exposure to the outside world.

Further, it can be argued that there are often some extra casualties (sadly, in this case mutilated girls) whilst a new order is being imposed; but in the long run the logic of the situation suggests that more children will benefit from hastening the final eradication of FGM than may suffer because of shifts in behaviour/response to new enforcement in the interim.

It is expected that empirical evidence of the efficacy of greater legal enforcement will be forthcoming if or when confirmation studies of reduced levels of FGM in France, where there have been multiple prosecutions and convictions, become available.[40]

The concerns about mutilation at a very early age are, however, regarded by some[41] as further evidence that the medical examination of young girls should, as in France,[42, 43] be routine, at least – despite reservations by reluctant parties – for infants deemed at risk. (Why not for all children, again as in France, as a measure which promotes good health?)

Mandatory Reporting: Is the Priority the 'Victim' Now, or Others in the Future?

These probabilities are muddled and confounded, however, by the 'warm hearts versus hard head' issues which clinicians especially must confront almost daily. There is currently considerable resistance, even by some professionals, to this longer-term preventative perspective and the requirement which comes with it formally to report suspected cases of FGM. This may (but does not always) apply especially to professionals such as midwives, obstetricians and social workers who have immediate, intimate and close responsibility for women survivors and their families.

Medical/clinical personnel are likely to give more weight to requirements for immediate personal patient confidentiality, and less to theoretical modelling and future outcomes based on legal action and epidemiological predictions – as was indicated by some responses from clinicians during the Home Affairs Committee enquiry into FGM, when the Chair, Keith Vaz MP, enquired about their views on mandatory reporting.[44] The responsibility to report immediately any fears that a child might be at risk of FGM was in principle accepted; but (as we saw in Chapter 6) patient confidentiality was for some clinicians their chosen over-riding consideration – or occasionally justification? – if a woman consulted later on about medical conditions arising from that FGM, or for any other reason.

Clinicians, and other professionals in the UK such as teachers, may also give substantial weight to concerns around family breakdown, if historical FGM is noted or when there is only vague and circumstantial evidence that it may occur. It was to address these concerns that a Consultation on Mandatory Reporting[45] was conducted in late 2014/early 2015.

The opposition to mandating expressed in their responses to that consultation by the Children's Commissioner,[46] the College of Social Work[47] and the Royal College of Paediatrics and Child Health[48] demonstrates some of the evidence-based uncertainties and practice concerns which a range of professionals continue to have, despite the established requirement, for example, for doctors to report certain medical conditions.[49, 50] As observed in Chapter 6 (above), the scope and need for development of pan-professional information-sharing, research and thoughtful, listening dialogue is clear, when these equivocal responses are compared with, for example, those of the Bar Human Rights FGM Committee or the views of the Director of Public Prosecutions. And the pathways for reporting still need considerable clarification; neither the current arrangements (social services) nor the proposed new one (the police) is ideal.

There is a reluctance in some quarters to involve the enforcement authorities because of the disruptions to children's lives which may ensue. This failure to report was, according to various parties speaking during the second Vaz Inquiry hearing,[51] one of the reasons that the police have been unable to proceed to significant numbers of prosecutions. It may, however, arise from a misunderstanding.

Clinicians and others have on occasion overlooked the reality that the courts alone may decide on guilt and outcomes. The role of the police and prosecutors is separate. Police and prosecutors simply discern whether, once initial evidence has been presented, there is a viable case to present for trial. They then, if appropriate, take the case forward to court.

It is not the responsibility of the police (or other professionals) to determine punishments or sentences if convictions are secured. The tariff for being party to FGM in the UK is potentially steep – the 2003 Act enables imprisonment for up to 14 years – but determining what will happen to anyone found guilty is the task of the courts, taking into consideration all aspects of context if misdemeanour is proven.

Those on the front line who may detect a risk (or the possible actuality) of FGM have no say in what happens if a perpetrator or aider is found guilty. Decisions about 'breaking up the family' are not for clinicians, teachers, social workers or even police officers to make.

Nonetheless, the current guidance on how to report concerns around FGM, even should a professional decide or feel obliged to do so, is not helpful. Here is the recently published statutory guidance for schools:[52]

> Warning signs that FGM may be about to take place, or may have already taken place, can be found on pages 11–12 of the Multi-Agency Practice Guidelines[53] referred to previously. Staff should activate local safeguarding procedures, using existing national and local protocols for multi-agency liaison with police and children's social care.

… advice which various professionals in the field have interpreted as telling them to find out the contact details for themselves, should they be worried about a child who may be harmed or at risk. The guidance is, as some who seek mandatory reporting have suggested, 'flat pack', unconstructed advice.

It is, however, important, regardless of the formal advice, to put issues such as mandatory reporting into a wider context than 'just' FGM alone. There are, as this writer amongst others has stressed,[54] many different forms of child abuse, and FGM should not in the view of a wide range of commentators[55] be seen as any different from other sorts of cruelty to children (or adults), all of which require mandatory reporting, at least by professionals involved in regulated activity.[56]

False Accusation; Fear of Repercussions or Reprisals

Another concern which holds back reporting and enforcement is the possibility or fear of false accusation,[57, 58] especially as the reality is so difficult to establish and responsibility for acts in pursuance of delivering FGM can so easily be passed from one party to another. Mothers and fathers may each claim that the other parent is responsible and there is also the possibility that girls (or a disaffected relative or friend) might claim someone wants to make them undergo FGM when that is not the case.

These considerations are further compounded by traditions such as forced and child 'marriage', which can be related issues. The upholding of family 'honour' underscores many customs in some traditional societies and the first consideration within such communities may be an imperative to impose silence, not only with the outside world, but also between those with active roles in upholding these traditions. Men, women and children alike, no-one is permitted to discuss the situation. As previously noted, all are expected to go about their business unquestioningly for the supposed common good.

And there is also one particular aspect of enforcing the law on FGM which is often put aside: there are (even some highly visible) activists against FGM who have themselves undergone it, but who are unequivocally unwilling to take the law to their own parents and/or other perpetrators.[59]

These 'victims' or 'survivors' may in some instances also fear for their personal safety: whilst honour killing is not usually part of the culture of traditional FGM-practising communities, murder for other 'reasons', and physical assault such as flogging for suspected adultery or perhaps other perceived 'betrayals', may be.[60]

Whilst a reluctance to expose one's own family members to the might of the law is understandable in human terms, it has also brought about accusations by others in affected communities of hypocrisy. If activists are unwilling to tell on their own family members, why should anyone else now do so? Some traditionally practising communities have been helped to find ways to address this critical obstacle to progress: support is given towards family reconciliation after a girl has found it necessary to escape FGM, or to bring her parents to account for it.[61]

These are complex issues – apart from anything else, it is not necessarily a matter of choice on the part of 'victims' when other evidence of a crime is also available and a prosecution goes ahead. The proposal in the UK Serious Crimes Bill to introduce 'lifelong' anonymity for girls and women who give evidence against violators may help,[62] but, despite the necessity to enact such a measure, it is currently difficult to see how it will always operate in close-knit communities when the intended FGM perpetrator is a family member.

In autumn 2014 the UK Government published a summary of responses to its proposal to introduce measures enabling civil protection orders[63] to keep safe girls and women at risk of being taken abroad or otherwise subjected to FGM. Most respondents indicated support for this proposal, many of them saying it should be interpreted widely; the legislation is therefore now going through Parliament, also as an element of the 2015 Serious Crimes Bill.

Both the legislation to guarantee lifelong anonymity and that to grant civil protection orders were proposed and endorsed by the Bar Human Rights FGM Group[64] in its submission to the Vaz Inquiry.

Greater clarity about many aspects of the protection and care of the child victim and her future is, however, required. In this it would, as Keith Vaz suggested in his inquiry, be useful to consider the French model (explained by Linda Weil-Curiel from the Paris Bar[65]) where the child has her own '*guardian ad litem*-type'[66] protector from the very start – and that person takes responsibility for many aspects of her care, including control of the financial damages she has been paid by her mutilators, where this occurs, until she reaches her majority.

Risk, Guilt and Punishment

One aspect of this will be a clear understanding that, in crimes such as FGM, criminal guilt and decisions about punishment are separate matters. Ignorance is not an excuse under the law, but it may in some circumstances mitigate punitive outcomes. Despite several attempts to prosecute in the UK,[67] there are as of very early 2015 no convictions or successful cases on which to base a judgment, but repeat and 'commercial' offenders (that is, paid mutilators) may reasonably expect heavy sentences. The quest for successful prosecutions which may provide opportunities to make this point continues.[68]

For many reasons such issues must come into the open and be addressed. 'Victims', professionals concerned about the outcomes of required FGM reporting and the general public all need reassurance that the law must be upheld without fear or favour.

In such circumstances it is unsurprising that UK enforcement agencies find their work challenging. The problems become clear when the number of successful prosecutions in the UK (none, as of the end of 2014) is compared with the dozens of cases which police authorities have considered in recent years.[69] The issue was previously considered in 2012 by the All Party Parliamentary Group on Population, Development and Reproductive Health, when members met with the Director of Public

Prosecutions (then, Keir Starmer) to discuss how to make better headway in prosecuting perpetrators of FGM, and set up roundtable discussions on the same theme.[70] The Population APPG also produced a report, including specifically the UK contexts, on Child Marriage and FGM etc. in 2012.[71] The APPG looked for ways of discouraging child marriage in the long term, both by further legislation in this country and by encouraging other countries to follow.

And so, whilst progress is slow, increasingly professionals with enforcement responsibilities agree that the silence must be broken. To date each sector has been eager to pass responsibility onto another of the enforcement and protection professions, but there is a growing recognition that, because of this lethargy, girls continue to be harmed; it will not do.

Over time the authorities have begun to confront such gendered and intimate crime on behalf of those whom the law deems to be at risk; and sometimes the law itself has had to change – as in, to give another thorny and contentious example, halting backstreet abortion[72] – to accommodate a better informed position. This process is now slowly beginning to come about also in respect of FGM, especially since the UK Home Affairs Committee Inquiry ('Vaz Report') on FGM, of early 2014. As we noted (in Chapter 6), legislation is likely soon to update the 2003 and 2005 (Scotland) law concerning FGM.

But formal enforcement is nonetheless critical, and much more could be done to achieve it, as has been recognised by Keir Starmer, then Director of Public Prosecutions, who instigated the 2012 round table discussions and in 2013 introduced an FGM Action Plan[73] to bring together the various aspects of work by the Crown Prosecution Service, the National Policing Leads and, for example, the Local Safeguarding Children Boards.[74]

This position has been taken forward also by the current (2015) Director of Public Prosecutions, Alison Saunders, who has confirmed her view that reporting concerns about FGM must be legally required, that is, mandatory.[75]

Policing

One development following the CPS moves was a raised awareness of the issues within the police, and liaison between the National Policing Lead for Honour-Based Violence, Forced Marriage and FGM, Commander Mak Chishty, and the Chief Executive of the College of Policing, Chief Constable Alex Marshall, to increase police training and in 2014 to conduct an internal consultation[76] on development of guidance for policing and FGM.

At about the same time (February 2014) the London Assembly Police and Crime Committee also made an investigation into safeguarding in London.

A document supplied for the enquiry[77] by Metropolitan Police Assistant Commissioner Mark Rowley provides considerable insight into the incidence of child abuse and developments on FGM, VAWG and other harmful traditional practices policing and public health provision, including Project Azure, African Well Woman Clinics, Guidance for Schools and social care strategies.

It is of note that many of these programmes have arisen from the work undertaken in 2009–10 by the London Safeguarding Children Board,[78, 79] the Metropolitan Police and the then-FGM national coordinator, whose post was subsequently abolished in early 2011.

The policing of FGM has now developed to include not only awareness-raising and other crime prevention measures such as Home Office posters and leaflets[80] but also, as Commander Chishty emphasised during the 2014 police consultation, the detection of those who practise FGM in the UK, as well as those who aid, abet, counsel or procure it. This might include money lenders who help families take or send girls abroad to be mutilated, travel agents who arrange trips knowing the purpose of the travel, and even the taxi driver who takes them to the airport knowing what will happen when they reach their eventual destination.

The police are currently developing their intelligence and networks, as they would for other sorts of crime, and other statutory agencies must recognise their own critical roles in providing knowledge or suspicions which can inform this work.

Gendered Crime and Diversity

Traditionally in parts of British society there has been a reluctance by some enforcers to become involved in matters of sexual activity, whether this has been (historically) with back street abortions, or with domestic violence or child sexual abuse.

Likewise, there is a growing realisation, as also came about earlier for domestic violence, that FGM, like forced marriage, 'grooming' of young girls and child 'marriage', is violence against girls and women, and a gross infringement of human rights.

Senior police officers now emphasise that it is not 'racist' to confront such infringements;[81] indeed, it is effectively racist not to do so if the crime affects some parts of the community more than others. In the UK this realisation has been substantially reinforced by the work of bodies such as the Bar Human Rights Committee,[82] which submitted a response to the Vaz Inquiry.[83]

Enforcement cannot supplant other approaches to ending FGM.[84] Education is crucial and so are genuine opportunities to engage for those in displaced or minority socio-economic positions. But nonetheless formal enforcement is and will at various points be required.

One important aspect of this is the diversity in the personnel of police forces. Officers need deep and personal experience of a wide variety of communities, if all parts of society are to be policed both effectively and fairly.[85] On-the-ground intelligence requires a thorough knowledge of a community and how it operates. Some measures to achieve this objective have been implemented, but it will only come about to a significant degree when national political and policy leaders demand unequivocally that it must happen; but how such effectiveness and a greater diversity of officers at all levels will be achieved is as yet to be agreed.

Next Steps

One matter as yet to be determined in the UK is what will happen if a person is found guilty of FGM. The sentencing (up to 14 years' imprisonment)[86] may be severe, especially if the perpetrator was paid, is medically trained or is a repeat offender. Anecdotal evidence from France suggests that, even in the case of parents themselves (who have self-evidently failed very seriously in their duty of care), severe punishment is necessary to make it clear to everyone that FGM will in no circumstances be 'understood' or tolerated.

The Serious Crime Bill[87, 88] will become law in 2015. This bill includes provision across the United Kingdom to include (Section 5: Protection of Children etc.):

> [67] Offence of female genital mutilation: extra-territorial acts;
> [68] Anonymity for victims of female genital mutilation;
> [69] Offence of failing to protect girl from risk of genital mutilation;
> [70] Female genital mutilation protection orders.

Importantly, these matters are also as of late 2014 being taken up consultatively by the Northern Ireland Assembly.[89]

There was also a proposal in autumn 2014 by Baroness Walmsley that the bill include mandatory reporting,[90] but this was withdrawn[91] to await further consultation (and reinstatement) as above. Baroness Walmsley did, however, stress before withdrawing her amendment that stated concerns about a high volume of malicious reporting have not been supported by evidence from elsewhere; for instance, although the absolute numbers of reports went up in Australia when mandatory reporting was introduced, the relative number of malicious reports remained at about 20 per cent.

The next stage in making FGM history in the UK may be to articulate what is likely to happen after enforcement of the law, which will be a matter for careful consideration by the courts of the circumstances of the crime (if committed); and alongside that to develop clear pathways for support and reinforcement of deterrence if, as is always infinitely to be preferred, FGM has been prevented.

Mandatory reporting is a critical move in the right direction for the prevention (and where necessary exemplary punishment) of all child abuse, but at present there is a sense in some quarters that it constitutes a step into the unknown, or an invasion of carefully guarded professional territory. Significant numbers of (public) service providers concerned with FGM and similar harmful traditional practices and child abuse were evidently unhappy about the proposals.

There is still a reluctance by many in professional roles to share across disciplines. Multi-agency approaches are promoted by those in authority; but there is little acknowledgement of the nuances of interpretation between professionals in different fields (let alone of the pressures to serve disciplinary self-interest, whether perceived or not) when it comes to matters of confidentiality and resource-sharing.

Similarly, in January 2015 the first local authority care order concerning FGM in the Family Court[92] fell for lack of expert consensus. More insight into how possible harm occurred (a fingernail, not a knife?) might have been available via a medical anthropologist.

The conflicting interests and modes of operation of professionals in different specialities which may obstruct progress on FGM, and child abuse in general, will only be overcome by top-level facilitation and structures to make shared intelligence and resourcing formally required. To date that has not happened.

The pathways (or preferably just one, across the whole of Britain) for reporting suspicions about FGM remain convoluted; they must be signposted unambiguously as a matter of urgency, with no room at the local level for ambiguity. And the various consequences of, and fears about, reporting also require clear articulation as soon as possible.

UK-wide law requires UK-wide, uniform interpretation and application across the many professional disciplines involved. When professionals in their different roles are confident that they are acquainted with, and are conducting matters in, the approved and required fashion, positive outcomes in terms of eradicating FGM in Britain can be expected.

Discuss this chapter at http://nofgmukbook.com/2015/01/29/chapter-7-prevention-formal-approaches/.

Endnotes

All weblinks accessed on 1 March 2015.

1   Direnfield, G. (2014) Discussing Female Genital Mutilation Non-Judgementally. *Gary Direnfield blog*, 22 November. Available at: http://garydirenfeld.wordpress. com/2014/11/22/discussing-female-genital-mutilation-non-judgementally/.
2   FORWARD (2015) *FGM*. Available at: http://www.forwarduk.org.uk/key-issues/ fgm/definitions.
3   FORWARD (2015) *FGM*. Available at: http://www.forwarduk.org.uk/key-issues/ fgm/definitions.
4   ITV (2014) Police Target 'High Risk' Flights in Fight against FGM. *ITV News*, 9 May. Available at: http://www.itv.com/news/update/2014-05-09/gp-a-lot-of-girls-dont-know-fgm-is-against-the-law/.
5   Robertson, P. (2013) *UK Authorities 'Lack Knowledge of FGM'*. FIGO. Available at: http://www.figo.org/news/uk-authorities-lack-knowledge-fgm-0010783.
6   FORWARD (2013) FORWARD Statement on NSPCC Teacher FGM Awareness Study. *FORWARD*, 25 March. Available at: www.forwarduk.org.uk/628/.
7   ITV (2014) ITV New Central: FGM special investigation. *ITV News*, 5 February. Available at: http://www.itv.com/news/central/2014-02-05/itv-news-central-fgm-special-investigation/.
8   Burrage, H. (2012) H.M. Government e-petition on FGM rejected. *Hilary Burrage blog*, 29 May. Available at: http://pinkpolitika.com/2012/05/29/h-m-government-e-petition-on-fgm-rejected/.
9   HM Government (2013) *Epetition: STOP Female Genital Mutilation (FGM/'cutting') in Britain*. Available at: http://epetitions.direct.gov.uk/petitions/35313.
10   London Safeguarding Children Board (2015) *FGM: National FGM Resources*. Available at: http://www.londonscb.gov.uk/fgm/.
11   London Safeguarding Children Board (2010) *London Board Update – January 2010*. Available at: http://www.londonscb.gov.uk/about_the_london_safeguarding_children_board/.
12   Barron, T. (2014) Half of Britons Think Punishment is Key to Ending FGM. *Family Law Week*, 14 August. Available at: http://www.familylawweek. co.uk/site.aspx?i=ed131573.
13   Mohamed, F. (2014) Tell Schools to Teach Risks of Female Genital Mutilation before the Summer. *Change.org*. Available at: https://www.change.org/p/ educationgovuk-tell-schools-to-teach-risks-of-female-genital-mutilation-before-the-summer-endfgm.
14   Dias, D., Gerry, F., Burrage, H. (2014) 10 Reasons Why Our FGM Law Has Failed – and 10 Ways to Improve It. *Guardian*, 7 February. Available at: http:// www.theguardian.com/commentisfree/2014/feb/07/fgm-female-genital-mutilation-prosecutions-law-failed.

15 Ellison, K. (2013) FGM – Can The Law Protect Our Children? *NoFGM (UK)*, 1 September. Available at: http://nofgm.org/2013/09/01/karen-ellison-fgm-can-the-law-protect-our-children/.

16 Munby, J. (2015) [2015] EWFC 3, Case no: LJ13C00295. *Royal Courts of Justice*, 14 January. Available at: http://www.judiciary.gov.uk/wp-content/uploads/2015/01/BandG_2_.pdf.

17 Topping, A., Carson, M. (2014) FGM is Banned but Very Much Alive in the UK. *Guardian*, 6 February. Available at: http://www.theguardian.com/society/2014/feb/06/female-genital-mutilation-foreign-crime-common-uk.

18 RT (2014) Female Genital Mutilation 'Cutters' Targeted by UK Border Control. *RT.com*, 11 September. Available at: http://rt.com/uk/186928-fgm-cutters-uk-boder/.

19 Laville, S. (2014) Anti-FGM Campaign at UK Airports Seeks to Stop Mutilation of Girls. *Guardian*, 9 May. Available at: http://www.theguardian.com/society/2014/may/09/anti-fgm-airports-heathrow-met-action-nigeria-sierra-leone/print.

20 Topping, A. (2014) UK to Introduce Measures to Stop Girls being Taken Abroad for FGM. *Guardian*, 20 October. Available at: http://www.theguardian.com/society/2014/oct/20/uk-introduce-measures-stop-girls-taken-abroad-fgm.

21 Ministry of Justice, Penning, M. (2014) Vulnerable Girls to be Protected from FGM. *GOV.UK*, 20 October. Available at: https://www.gov.uk/government/news/vulnerable-girls-to-be-protected-from-fgm.

22 RNW (2011) New Dutch Campaign against Female Circumcision. *Radio Netherlands Worldwide*, 10 March. Available at: http://www.rnw.nl/english/article/new-dutch-campaign-against-female-circumcision.

23 https://www.gov.uk/government/policies/ending-violence-against-women-and-girls-in-the-uk/supporting-pages/female-genital-mutilation.

24 Home Office, Featherstone, L. (2012) Statement Opposing Female Genital Mutilation. *GOV.UK*, 23 November. Available at: https://www.gov.uk/government/publications/statement-opposing-female-genital-mutilation.

25 Women NGOs (2014) *Fédération nationale GAMS*. Available at: http://www.womenngos.eu/2013/06/fr-federation-nationale-gams-national.html.

26 Lloyd Roberts, S. (2012) Hidden World of Female Genital Mutilation in the UK. *BBC News*, 23 July. Available at: http://www.bbc.co.uk/news/health-18900803.

27 Sherwood, H., Smith, H., Davies, L., Grant, H. (2014) Europe Faces 'Colossal Humanitarian Catastrophe' of Refugees Dying at Sea. *Guardian*, 2 June. Available at: http://www.theguardian.com/world/2014/jun/02/europe-refugee-crisis-un-africa-processing-centres.

28 Mabilia, M. (2013) FGM or FGMo? Cross-cultural dialogue in an Italian minefield. *Anthropology Today*, 10.1111/1467-8322.12030. Available at: http://onlinelibrary.wiley.com/doi/10.1111/1467-8322.12030/abstract.

29 Davies, A. (2014) British Girls Flown to Singapore and Dubai for 'Medicalised' FGM. *London Evening Standard*, 14 May. Available at: http://www.standard.co.uk/

news/world/british-girls-flown-to-singapore-and-dubai-for-medicalised-fgm-9369122.html.

30 UNFPA (2008) *Global Consultation on Female Genital Mutilation/Cutting – Technical Report.* Available at: http://www.unfpa.org/sites/default/files/pub-pdf/fgm_2008.pdf.

31 Available at: http://www.who.int/.

32 Available at: http://www.unfpa.org/.

33 Available at: http://www.endfgm.eu/en/.

34 Available at: http://www.amnesty.i.e./.

35 Available at: http://www.replacefgm2.eu/.

36 Available at: http://www.african-women.org/.

37 Available at: http://www.equalitynow.org.

38 Bentham, M. (2014) FGM Parents 'are having Girls Cut at Younger Age'. *London Evening Standard*, 27 May. Available at: http://www.standard.co.uk/news/health/fgm-parents-are-having-girls-cut-at-younger-age-9440144.html.

39 Dias, D., Gerry, F., Burrage, H. (2014) 10 Reasons Why Our FGM Law Has Failed – and 10 Ways to Improve It. *Guardian*, 7 February. Available at: http://www.theguardian.com/commentisfree/2014/feb/07/fgm-female-genital-mutilation-prosecutions-law-failed.

40 Burrage, H. (2012) The UK Can Learn from France on Female Genital Mutilation Prosecutions. *Hilary Burrage blog*, 28 November. Available at: http://hilaryburrage.com/2012/11/28/the-uk-can-learn-from-france-on-fgm-prosecutions/.

41 Refuge (2014) *Refuge Response to Consultation on Proposals to Introduce a Civil Protection Order for Female Genital Mutilation.* Available at: http://www.refuge.org.uk/files/FGM-consultation-August-2014.pdf.

42 Lichfield, J. (2013) The French Way: A better approach to fighting FGM? *Independent*, 15 December. Available at: http://www.independent.co.uk/news/world/europe/the-french-way-a-better-approach-to-fighting-fgm-9006369.html.

43 Burrage, H. (2015) UK Home Office Consultation on Mandatory Reporting of FGM – My Response. *Hilary Burrage blog*, 11 January. Available at: http://hilaryburrage.com/2015/01/11/uk-home-office-consultation-on-mandatory-reporting-of-fgm-my-response/.

44 HOC Home Affairs Committee (2014) Female Genital Mutilation. *www.parliament.uk*, 6 May. Available at: http://www.parliamentlive.tv/Main/Player.aspx?meetingId=15385.

45 Home Office, Featherstone, L. (2014) Consultation Outcome – Introducing mandatory reporting for FGM. *GOV.UK*, 5 December. Available at: https://www.gov.uk/government/consultations/introducing-mandatory-reporting-for-fgm.

46 Office of the Children's Commissioner (2015) *OCC Response to the Home Office Consultation: Introducing Mandatory Reporting for Female Genital Mutilation.* Available at: http://www.childrenscommissioner.gov.uk/content/publications/content_914.

47 The College of Social Work (2014) *The College of Social Work response to the Home Office consultation on Introducing Mandatory Reporting for Female Genital Mutilation*. Available at: http://www.tcsw.org.uk/uploadedFiles/TheCollege/CollegeLibrary/Easy_read_ documents/2015.01.12%20FGM%20Mandatory%20Reporting.FINAL.pdf.

48 Boffey, D. (2015) Theresa May's New FGM Reporting Rules 'Will Stop Families Seeking Help'. *Guardian*, 17 January. Available at: http://www.theguardian.com/ society/2015/jan/17/theresa-may-fgm-rules-doctors-stop-victims-seeking-help.

49 General Medical Council (2009) *Confidentiality: Disclosing information about serious communicable diseases*. Available at: http://www.gmc-uk.org/Confidentiality_ disclosing_info_serious_commun_diseases_2009.pdf_27493404.pdf.

50 General Medical Council (2015) *Confidentiality Guidance: Disclosures required by law*. Available at: http://www.gmc-uk.org/guidance/ethical_guidance/ confidentiality_17_23_disclosures_required_by_law.asp.

51 HOC Home Affairs Committee (2014) Female Genital Mutilation. *www.parliament.uk*, 29 April. Available at: http://www.parliamentlive.tv/Main/ Player.aspx?meetingId=15337.

52 Department for Education (2014) *Keeping Children Safe in Education*. Available at: https://www.gov.uk/government/uploads/system/uploads/attachment_data/ file/354151/Keeping_children_safe_in_education_Information_for_staff.pdf.

53 Home Office, Department for Education, Featherstone, L. (2011) Female Genital Mutilation: Guidelines to protect children and women. *GOV.UK*, 20 April. Available at: https://www.gov.uk/government/publications/female-genital- mutilation-guidelines.

54 Burrage, H. (2015) UK Home Office Consultation on Mandatory Reporting of FGM – My Response. *Hilary Burrage blog*, 11 January. Available at: http:// hilaryburrage.com/2015/01/11/uk-home-office-consultation-on-mandatory- reporting-of-fgm-my-response/.

55 National Secular Society (2012) *A Response from the National Secular Society to the Scottish Government Consultation on a Proposed Children and Young People Bill*. Available at: http://www.secularism.org.uk/uploads/nss-response-scottish- government-consultation-on-a-proposed-children-and-young-people-bill.pdf.

56 Mandate Now (2015) *Why We Exist*. Available at: http://mandatenow.org.uk/ why-we-exist/.

57 Burnett, R. (2012) Co-ordinating Developments to Stop FGM. *NoFGM.org*, 4 July. Available at: http://nofgm.org/2012/07/04/co-ordinating-developments- to-stop-fgm-by-ros-burnett/.

58 Dias, D., Gerry, F., Burrage, H. (2014) 10 Reasons Why Our FGM Law Has Failed – and 10 Ways to Improve It. *Guardian*, 7 February. Available at: http:// www.theguardian.com/commentisfree/2014/feb/07/fgm-female-genital- mutilation-prosecutions-law-failed.

59 Ahmed, B. (2014) Why Laws Couldn't Protect This 13-Year-Old Girl Who Died from Female Genital Mutilation. *Think Progress*, 21 November. Available at: http://thinkprogress.org/world/2014/11/21/3595399/fgm-egypt/.

60 Women Living Under Muslim Laws (2013) *East Africa Report* Available at: http://www.wluml.org/taxonomy/term/85.

61 Wakahiu, J. (2014) A Safe Haven for Girls Escaping FGM in Kenya. *Global Sisters Report*, 16 September. Available at: http://globalsistersreport.org/ministry/safe-haven-girls-escaping-fgm-kenya-11011.

62 Ministry of Justice, Penning, M. (2014) Vulnerable Girls to be Protected from FGM. *GOV.UK*, 20 October. Available at: https://www.gov.uk/government/news/vulnerable-girls-to-be-protected-from-fgm.

63 Ministry of Justice (2014) *Female Genital Mutilation: Proposal to Introduce a Civil Protection Order*. Available at: https://consult.justice.gov.uk/digital-communications/female-genital-mutilation-proposal-to-introduce-a/results/female-genital-mutilation-consultation-response.pdf.

64 Bar Human Rights Committee of England and Wales (2014) *Report of the Bar Human Rights Committee of England and Wales To the Parliamentary Inquiry into Female Genital Mutilation*. Available at: http://www.barhumanrights.org.uk/sites/default/files/documents/news/bhrc_fgm_submission_12_feb_2014.pdf.

65 Burrage, H. (2012) The UK Can Learn from France on Female Genital Mutilation Prosecutions. *Hilary Burrage blog*, 28 November. Available at: http://hilaryburrage.com/2012/11/28/the-uk-can-learn-from-france-on-fgm-prosecutions/.

66 Guardian Ad Litem. (2008) *West's Encyclopedia of American Law, edition 2*. Available at: http://legal-dictionary.thefreedictionary.com/Guardian+Ad+Litem.

67 Bentham, M. (2014) Fight against FGM Suffers a Blow as More Cases are Dropped without Charges. *London Evening Standard*, 17 November. Available at: http://www.standard.co.uk/news/uk/fight-against-fgm-suffers-a-blow-as-more-cases-are-dropped-without-charges-9865025.html.

68 Vaz, K. et al. (2015) Domestic Abuse. *TheyWorkForYou*, 10 February. Available at: http://www.theyworkforyou.com/debates/?id=2015-02-10a.610.4&s=female+genital+mutilation#g611.1.

69 BBC (2014) FGM: UK police investigate 'dozens' of cases since 2011. *BBC News*, 7 August. Available at: http://www.bbc.com/news/uk-28685854.

70 Tonge, B. (2013) Female Genital Mutilation – Question for Short Debate. *TheyWorkFOrYou*, 4 December. Available at: http://www.theyworkforyou.com/lords/?id=2013-12-04a.305.0.

71 UK All-Party Parliamentary Group on Population, Development and Reproductive Health (2012) *A Childhood Lost*. Available at: http://www.appg-popdevrh.org.uk/UK%20APPG%20on%20PDRH%20-%20A%20Childhood%20Lost.pdf.

72 Furedi, A., Hume, M. (2007) Abortion Law Reformers – Pioneers of Change. *British Pregnancy Advisory Service*. Available at: http://www.bpas.org/js/filemanager/files/abortion_pioneers.pdf.

73 CPS (2012) *Female Genital Mutilation Action Plan Launched*. Available at: http://cps.gov.uk/news/latest_news/female_genital_mutilation_action_plan_launched/.

74 Director of Public Prosecutions (2013) DPP's FGM Action Plan – October 2013. *Crown Prosecution Service.* Available at: http://www.cps.gov.uk/publications/ equality/vaw/dpp_fgm_action_plan.pdf.

75 Travis, A. (2014) Reporting Female Genital Mutilation Should Be Legally Required – CPS Chief. *Guardian,* 25 March. Available at: http://www. theguardian.com/society/2014/mar/25/female-genital-mutilation-fgm-reporting-legally-required-cps.

76 Baker, M. (2014) Consultation on New Police Guidance to Tackle Female Genital Mutilation Launched. *College of Policing.* Available at: http://college. pressofficeadmin.com/component/content/article/45-press-releases/768.

77 Rowley, M. (2014) Letter to Joanna McCartney AM. *London.gov,* 17 January. Available at: http://www.london.gov.uk/moderngov/documents/s33348/ Appendix%202.pdf.

78 London Safeguarding Children Board (2015) *FGM: National FGM Resources.* Available at: http://www.londonscb.gov.uk/fgm/.

79 London Safeguarding Children Board (2010) *London Board Update – January 2010.* Available at: http://www.londonscb.gov.uk/about_the_london_ safeguarding_children_board/.

80 Davies, C. (2014) Female Genital Mutilation Poster Campaign Targets Mothers and Carers. *Guardian,* 2 June. Available at: http://www.theguardian.com/ society/2014/jun/02/female-genital-mutilation-fgm-poster-campaign-mothers.

81 Glendinning, A. (2014) FGM Must Be Classed as Child Abuse – not Seen as a Race Issue, says Top Police Officer. *Manchester Evening News,* 12 November. Available at: http://www.manchestereveningnews.co.uk/news/greater-manchester-news/fgm-must-classed-child-abuse-8098828.

82 Bar Human Rights Committee of England and Wales (2014) *Report of the Bar Human Rights Committee of England and Wales To the Parliamentary Inquiry into Female Genital Mutilation.* Available at: http://www.barhumanrights.org.uk/ sites/default/files/documents/news/bhrc_fgm_submission_12_feb_2014.pdf.

83 Home Affairs Committee (2014) Female Genital Mutilation: The case for a national action plan. *www.parliament.uk,* 3 July. Available at: http://www. publications.parliament.uk/pa/cm201415/cmselect/cmhaff/201/20104.htm.

84 Garavelli, D. (2014) How Best to Stamp out FGM? *The Scotsman,* 20 February. Available at: http://www.scotsman.com/news/dani-garavelli-how-best-to-stamp-out-fgm-1-3467796.

85 AFRUCA (2014) *AFRUCA Submission to London Assembly on FGM.* Available at: http://www.afruca.org/wp-content/uploads/2014/04/London-Assembly-Evidence-on-FGM-AFRUCA-Submission.pdf 3.1.3.

86 The Crown Prosecution Service (2015) *Female Genital Mutilation Legal Guidance.* Available at: http://www.cps.gov.uk/legal/d_to_g/female_genital_ mutilation/#annexc.

87 House of Lords (2015) Serious Crime Bill [HL] 2014–15. *www.parliament.uk.* Available at: http://services.parliament.uk/bills/2014-15/seriouscrime.html.

88 UK Parliament (2015) Serious Crime Bill (HC Bill 116). *www.parliament.uk*. Available at: http://www.publications.parliament.uk/pa/bills/cbill/2014-2015/0116/cbill_2014-20150116_en_1.htm.

89 Northern Ireland Assembly Executive Committee (2014) Serious Crime Bill: Legislative Consent Motion. *TheyWorkForYou*, 8 December. Available at: http://www.theyworkforyou.com/ni/?id=2014-12-08.3.3&s=female+genital+mutilation.

90 HL Deb (2014–15) 28 October 2014: Col. 1059. Available at: http://www.publications.parliament.uk/pa/ld201415/ldhansrd/text/141028-0001.htm.

91 HL Deb (2014–15) 28 October 2014: Col. 1059. Available at: http://www.publications.parliament.uk/pa/ld201415/ldhansrd/text/141028-0001.htm.

92 LexisNexis Blog (2015) *What can be learnt from the first FGM case?* Available at: blogs.lexisnexis.co.uk/family/what-can-be-learnt-from-the-first-fgm-case/.

8 Prevention – Communities

Female genital mutilation is a complex business. It involves deeply entrenched beliefs, real and resolute social and economic forces, human agency of a particularly intimate nature, brutality and secrecy. It is also held by large numbers of those involved, and perhaps also by the recipient of the action, to be in the best interests of the person who experiences it.

These are not easy issues to unpick, and the path towards understanding and arresting the practice is further complicated by the gulf between the traditions and beliefs which engender and enable, even ennoble, FGM, and those which proclaim it without exception to be abhorrent abuse.

Collectivism and Individuality Varies in Diaspora Communities

The divide in understandings is vast, but in its fundamentals easily perceived. Put very simply (and with significant loss of nuance), traditional, embedded communities tend to value social cohesion far more than they value the individual – if the concept of 'individual' is actually a part of the collective consciousness at all.

Notions about individuals, each striving to meet their own personal 'potential' and to be 'autonomous', have developed in any general way only comparatively recently. Ideas of this sort usually arise only when conditions permit more than simply a struggle for physical survival. They are therefore much more common in wealthier, modern, Western and open societies than in communities where major investment of time, resources and effort is required simply to stay alive. In such contexts the interests and concept of the individual are often deemed irrelevant, if not incomprehensible.

For most people in traditional societies, survival of the group is the paramount, sometimes only, consideration. If individuals who stand out are an encumbrance or challenge age-old understandings and conventions fall by the wayside, that's the price which must be paid to sustain the status quo.

In such traditional communities the emphasis is on upholding time-honoured social mores. Human empathy may well exist but such sentiments must be put aside for the common good and to maintain established values. Thus, for instance, whilst mothers may not wish to hurt their daughters, they are nonetheless obliged to insist on FGM because that is the way to ensure a young woman's purity (and thereby her future 'worth' and prospects) within the community.

Plus, few adult women who have undergone FGM would wish to believe their mothers intentionally harmed them; it would be painful for women who have FGM to consider the possibility that what their mothers (or other relatives) permitted was wrong and unnecessary. FGM must have been done for the common good of the group, and so must continue.

Conversely, however, modern, technocratic and rapidly changing communities may value the individual more than they value 'society'. The rationale of social interest, that of the common good, does exist; but it is set within a dialogue which emphasises the over-arching priority of human rights and the entitlement of each person to determine her or his own destiny.

In this context the individual and fundamental human right to 'bodily integrity' renders unacceptable any deliberate and clinically unnecessary action to alter, invasively and permanently, the physical form (or mental state or social standing) of a child. A focus on a girl's virginity ('purity'), for instance, may still be important in some parts of Western society, but these anxieties do not provide exemption from the legal prohibition on physical invasion of her person, at the very least until she reaches her majority and can (within limits) legally decide for herself.

It is important nonetheless to note that even modern societies give some leeway in respect of specific communities. One much-debated example is the continuing toleration of male genital cutting, often known as 'circumcision' by its proponents, and as 'mutilation' by those who oppose it: some of these traditions do remain, largely unchallenged, even in legal-technical nations. Likewise, genital cosmetic surgery – though mostly demanded because of socially imbued body image concerns – is still generally permitted, or at least has not actually been stopped, by Western governments, sometimes even on minors. (Chapter 5 considers these matters in more detail.)

The sway of individual autonomy and self-determination is, then, nowhere completely universal. There is therefore some degree of malleability between the 'old', immutable precedence of social mores, and the 'new' focus on individual human rights.

Opportunities for Dialogue

It is the space between these two opposed sets of value that offers prospects for dialogue on FGM.

It is significant that traditions like FGM are located within 'communities' rather than 'societies'. Thus, we find that mutilation is practised in some parts of various African and Middle Eastern nations, but not usually – there are a few exceptions – in all locations within any given country. An example of this is the very strongly traditional Maasai tribe (mainly found in Kenya and Tanzania) where FGM continues, albeit with modest but growing resistance, across a number of relatively recent national borders.

Specific local communities across the world may hold beliefs and values in common which are not similarly held elsewhere. The difference between traditional and modern ones is, however, that, in the former, local values may take precedence over formal, national ones, whilst in the latter national statute has absolute precedence – and variation from it, at least in theory, is not tolerated.

But the old collective values are not always paramount, even in nations where harmful traditional practices are the norm. There are increasingly frequent reports of prosecutions for FGM (cutters and parents) in places in the world such as Kenya and Uganda where the practice has hitherto been accepted for centuries.

Nonetheless, it is likely that some local communities will continue harmful practices, against the grain of national moves to modernise (protect individual well-being and rights), when state controls are relatively weak, whilst the converse should apply where nationwide governance is strong and the authorities have coherent strategies to ensure the crime is stopped.

It is also, however, important to recognise that not all leaders of nations in the developing world are keen to align their enthusiasm for modern technologies with a parallel move towards democracy and human rights. Technologies can be used by the powerful to restrain citizens as easily as they can be used to enable freedoms; and such restraint may sit comfortably with covert encouragement to exercise particular control over women through patriarchal violence.

Modern technological dominance does not always lie easily with the values of individualism. In this context governments in the Middle East which embrace Sharia law, or elements of it, may illustrate the point. Large swathes of, for instance, signifcantly advanced nations such as Nigeria or Egypt, in both of which FGM remains very prevalent,[i] show that it would be a mistake to assume modern technologies always see ancient traditions swept aside.

---

i   FGM was first made illegal in Egypt in 1997 but was not prohibited in Nigeria until 2015.

It is unlikely – though we do not know for sure – that the situation is initially much different in traditionally facing diaspora communities from that of the historic populations which those in the diaspora left.

It may be, however, that, at least in some contexts, with each generation of a diaspora, allegiance to the old ways weakens.[1] A study in France (2009), reported by the Scottish Refuge Council,[2] suggests that women who arrived from an FGM practising country less than 15 years ago still present high risk, those who arrived more than 15 years ago are medium risk, and those whose parents came from high-risk countries but were themselves born in Europe are low risk. Other studies have, however, suggested that FGM may become a symbol of allegiance/adherence to tradition, and that diasporians returning 'home' may actually push for the retention there of FGM in acknowledgement of shared heritage, even if the practice was being abandoned – although the contrary situation may also arise, with diaspora groups, having seen that FGM is not always the norm, then arguing for abandonment in their country of origin.[3]

Finding a Way Forward

Somehow, those who want to secure the end of FGM must devise a way through all the conflicting ideas and beliefs.

There is self-evidently a place in these endeavours for enforcement of the legislation, found across the developed world and in much too of the developing world, which forbids FGM.

But law alone is not enough. Some observers even see it as an obstacle to real progress. They fear that it will drive FGM activity underground and leave the children of imprisoned offenders without support. In traditionally practising countries the introduction of alternative rites of passage (ARP)[4, 5] and related discussions may be the preferred way forward for various campaigners, along with recognition that FGM, sometimes euphemistically named an 'act of love', is actually a very dangerous form of harm – an understanding and perspective which it may be difficult to establish in the face of centuries of a different view.

Others, however, insist that, in modern democratic nations, there can be no excuse for ignoring acts which, by any criteria, constitute bodily harm and child abuse. As the practice continues and the incidence of FGM may even be increasing in the UK and elsewhere, the second position is gaining favour in some quarters. There is a sense that only punitive and public action will bring this persisting very serious crime to a halt.

And then, as we saw in Chapters 5 and 7, there is the issue of mandatory reporting. Should, or should not, professionals and others with formal child safeguarding responsibilities be required by law to report the risk of, or actual harm to, children and women through some formal mechanism?

Again, on the one hand there is the fear that reporting will drive FGM underground (as if it were not already), and on the other hand that failure to report FGM puts even more girls at risk in the future. A temporary increase in stealthy underground activity may in reality be the price (so harmfully paid by its victims) of a longer-term trend towards cessation.

Negotiating a balance between these positions is not an academic exercise. It is a matter of judgement between knowns and unknowns, with real implications for real people. How significant, it must be asked, is the possibility of future undetected underground FGM activity? How likely is it that widely publicised enforcement of the law will actually reduce the future incidence of FGM?

The truth is, as at 2015, no one really knows. Estimates are possible, but are they realistic, and what do they really tell us, beyond reflecting the views of those who propose them?

But available knowledge is all we have, and therefore what policy and strategy in areas such as FGM must be based on. Risk management grounded in what currently can be learned is the only way forward.

Evaluating Risks and Strategies

The eradication of FGM in Britain is not at present (early 2015) a thought-through, fully coordinated effort. As correspondence between the then Minister, Lynne Featherstone, and Louise Ellman MP shows, work instigated by the previous Labour government to bring public services together via a nascent national FGM Unit[6] was halted in 2011,[7] when the Coalition Government came to power. Multi-agency guidelines and training planned back then have only subsequently been made available on official government department websites. But inter-departmental liaison alone is not enough, and a new formally constituted FGM Unit[8] was finally instituted in December 2014.

As at early 2015 the Home Office coordinates initiatives across government and provides outreach support to local areas.[9] Significantly, its 'collection' of material on FGM lists two items (a poster and a leaflet) in early 2011, none in 2012, one, a case study, in 2013, and then a significant volume of information for 2014, as media activity and the momentum once again picked up. The human cost from 2010/11 of this arrested institutional development can only be imagined.

Whilst these moves meet some of the requirements for professional practice, they are unlikely adequately to encompass the plethora of (mostly small) organisations and even individuals who strive to stop FGM within their own communities, and sometimes elsewhere.

Ideally, each element of the movement towards eradication of FGM might be identified to understand the role and task/s for which it is best suited within a framework of evaluated risk management and opportunities for progress. This ideal situation (rarely achieved in any case, whatever the matter under review) is some long way off.

What we have is numerous activities in the field, with often little convergence beyond the desire to make FGM history.

Probably for most, this concern is simply a matter of additional professional duty alongside many others. For others, it's a single, narrowly focused agenda, driven variously by personal experience, by concern for children's vulnerability, or by a determination to uphold human rights. It does not follow that any of these groups has adequate over-arching insight, or indeed connection with the other.

These various sorts of focus are not exclusive or necessarily conflicting, but they do lead to different understandings and to different ways of doing things; and at present no one knows definitively which approaches and understandings in the UK will have the most positive impact.

There are some moves towards evaluating formal UK programmes of action (such as the European REPLACE2 programme,[10] or as part of the work of Rosa[11] or Options[12]) but as yet not even much clarity about who the many people working in the field are, or what exactly they are doing.

Global evaluations of FGM programmes (such as by the WHO and UNFPA[13]) are becoming more nuanced, as are some European ones, but there is still considerable scope for further evaluation in the UK.

The first challenge if FGM is to be stopped in Britain is therefore to ascertain which sorts of action are most likely to be effective in which contexts, and what opportunities and risks appertain in each case.

The second challenge is to discern which sorts of activists will, in each case, deliver these actions most effectively – and to discover who, what and where these activists are. It is this question to which we now turn.

Voluntary Agencies and Community Activism in Britain

As in many aspects of action in civil society, when it comes to FGM there are overlapping activities and gaps, (a few) issues which are clearly defined and dealt with accordingly – and a lot where the various requirements and responsibilities remain diffuse.

Clear procedures have, as discussed in Chapter 5, been put in place to care for those who have undergone FGM and are now pregnant. There are protocols to guide obstetric professionals and there is an understanding that these are extremely sensitive matters.

Usually, however, midwifery is provided in the UK by the National Health Service and such issues become a matter for other (often NGO) agencies only when the woman concerned seeks support and/or surgery for reconstruction. (A decision to go ahead with restoration usually comes via voluntary enablement and/or contact with others who have experienced FGM and reversal.)

This sort of intervention, necessarily associated with voluntary action as well as high-level professional expertise, is currently at the least visited end of the community activity spectrum.

Community activism

Outside the more formal and institutionally led endeavours, much voluntary and NGO activity is led by women who have themselves experienced, or know of others who have experienced, FGM in their own right. Perhaps the majority of them will be people who have joined the diaspora in the UK from their heritage or 'homeland' nation.

Some of these activists may well be in Britain because they sought refuge from danger or even life-threatening harm elsewhere. Some will speak English well or as their native language; others may still communicate largely in their mother or heritage tongue.

Especially at the beginning of their advocacy against FGM, almost all of these activists are likely to be unpaid and working in their own time, at their own expense. When they start they are often acting in isolation from others, and have little knowledge of larger, more orchestrated and mainstream campaigns.

This direct engagement is invaluable; but it also presents challenges in a number of respects.

Evident advantages in the campaign against FGM to be gained from the engagement of deeply community-based and local activists include these:

- Those at the forefront of the campaign can claim legitimacy, in that they often share common ground with the people whose behaviour and perspectives they wish to change.
- The activists usually know their communities well. They know who has the greatest influence and who is most likely to support or obstruct their efforts.

- They know how to approach the influencers and who not to alienate.
- The activists also know how to 'read' their communities; they are more likely to be aware of the signs that events are about to occur, or that opinions are shifting, whether for better or worse.
- Local (women) activists can talk about intimate matters to their sisters, daughters, female neighbours, health workers, and others as required.
- Efforts to engage faith leaders (almost always male) may be more effective via community-based activists, and may also then engage even more men within the community.
- Activists are well placed to explain and 'interpret' their local community positions and views to others in the mainstream.

On the other hand, immersion by campaigners against FGM in their local culture can have drawbacks:

- Activists may be compromised, even intimidated, by their community links. Where FGM has been conducted in seclusion or secretly for hundreds of years it is unlikely that those most actively involved will be comfortable with the message that it has to stop.
- It may be actually dangerous to campaign against FGM in one's own community. Sometimes death or other threats compromise campaigners' safety, or that of their families or other connections.
- There may be serious, perhaps permanent, conflicts of loyalty between activists' wish to stop FGM and their wish to maintain close relationships with their families.
- Activists may also be compromised or limited by their only modest understandings and connections with mainstream society; a concern to stop FGM does not necessarily arise alongside mainstream engagement.
- Because a person wants to stop FGM does not necessarily also mean that they want to collaborate with mainstream authorities of activists. Resentment about poor liaison and differences in perceptions may arise on either or both 'sides'.
- Community activists may be regarded as betraying their family and community and so lose local credibility by their engagement in the campaign, with the result that, especially if it is not well supported externally, the impact of their work is reduced.
- Local activists, especially women, may find it difficult to converse with men – often the *de facto* community influencers – about personal and private matters; and men may not discuss such matters at all.
- Campaigners whose messages have influence in some spheres may be alienating to those in other contexts.

For all these reasons and more it is important that campaigning and education programmes within FGM-practising communities are taken forward jointly between mainstream and local activists. Both need to have input and support from the other.

Unless, however, the community activity is driven by an organisation such as a properly endowed local association, church or mosque (all of which options have both benefits and dis-benefits) the onus to initiate and support will largely lie with external mainstream bodies; and this in turn requires already well-established communication and liaison in both directions.

Voluntary and non-governmental organisations

Amongst those with a long record of work to eradicate FGM primarily in Britain are both FGM-dedicated and more general voluntary organisations and NGOs (non-governmental organisations). Some of these are relatively large national organisations, others are much smaller and have a local focus; the range is wide.

What follows is a list of some of the organisations, also listed in more detail on pp. 317–22, which campaign in the UK specifically against FGM, naming it clearly as mutilation:

- 28 Too Many
- Agency for Culture and Change Management (ACCMUK)
- Afruca (Africans Unite Against Child Abuse)
- Amnesty International (UK)
- Asylum Aid
- Black Women's Health and Family Organisation
- Campaign Against Female Genital Mutilation (CAGeM)
- Churches' Child Protection Advisory Service (CCPAS)
- Daughters of Eve
- Dignity Alert and Research Forum (DARF)
- Dr Abe Foundation
- END FGM European Campaign
- Equality Now
- FGM National Clinical Group
- Foundation for Women's Health Research and Development (FORWARD)
- Greater Manchester FGM Forum
- Hawa Trust
- Iranian and Kurdish Women's Rights Organisation (IKRWO)
- Integrate Bristol
- Justice for FGM Victims UK

- Manor Gardens (FGM Special Initiative)
- Ms Rose Blossom
- Muslim Women Network UK
- National Society for the Prevention of Cruelty to Children (NSPCC)
- One True Voice
- OPTIONS End FGM/C Social Change Campaign
- Plan UK
- REPLACE2
- Research, Action and Information Network for the Bodily Integrity of Women (RAINBO)
- Rosa (The UK Fund for Women and Girls)
- Roshni
- Safe World for Women
- Soroptimist International of Great Britain and Ireland (SIGBI)
- Scottish Refugee Council
- Trust for London
- Victoria Climbié Foundation.

Similar organisations and campaigners in other English-speaking nations which address FGM in their own (Western) communities as well as elsewhere include:

- Action for Women and Child Concern (AWCC) (USA and Somalia)
- AHA Foundation (Ayaan Hirsi Ali) (USA)
- Desert Flower Foundation (Waris Dirie) (Austria, Germany and Switzerland)
- Healthy Tomorrow/Sini Sanuman (USA and Mali)
- Ifrah Ahmed (Ireland and Somalia)
- Lucy Mashua: independent activist against FGM, and Voice for the Voiceless (USA)
- No FGM Australia (Australia)
- REPLACE2 (European-wide)
- Safe Hands for Girls (Jaha Dukureh) (USA)
- Sanctuary for Families (USA)
- UnCUT Voices (Germany).

FGM voluntary and NGO typologies

It is immediately clear that such an array of organisations, even just within the UK, all with different levels of complexity and formality, different legal bases, and arising from very different experiences, rationales and understandings, will also have widely different modes of operation, outcomes and impact.

Broadly speaking, these organisations can be sorted into a number of (overlapping) groups:

- organisations (small, or originally small) initiated by women with first-hand or immediate experience of FGM, for example: Daughters of Eve, Dr Abe Foundation, Hawa Trust;
- organisations concerned about violence against women and girls, for which FGM has become one of a number of central issues, for example: Dignity Alert and Research Forum (DARF);
- organisations concerned with minority ethnic health or human rights, such as asylum, for which FGM has become an acknowledged issue, for example: Research, Action and Information Network for the Bodily Integrity of Women (RAINBO), Iranian and Kurdish Women's Rights Organisation (IKROW) and Asylum Aid;
- organisations involved in child safeguarding and safety, framing FGM as an abuse from which they must receive protection via the formal and state health, social, welfare, educational and legal services, for example: AFRUCA and National Society for the Prevention of Cruelty to Children (NSPCC);
- organisations promoting equality and women's rights, and who see FGM as one amongst many oppressions, sometimes viewed through the lens of patriarchal analysis, for example: Soroptimist International of Great Britain and Ireland (SIGBI).

It is unlikely that the activities of this array of organisations could be fully coordinated. Various activists and workers in them have different perspectives, understandings and priorities, ranging from direct support for individuals who have experienced (or are at risk) of FGM, through to bodies which emphasise research, public education or lobbying about policy. If any co-ordination of activities is achieved, it is likely to be funding-led, that is, directed from 'above' as a result of grant-aid regimes which require certain objectives to be delivered, rather than through articulated consensus between all the organisations concerned. Inter-agency formal discussions and collaboration do occur, facilitated by both government and large NGOs, but necessarily only to a limited extent.

Some of these organisations rely on individual volunteers and giving, some seek finance for larger-scale research and policy development, and some themselves disperse funds, on the basis of widely varying criteria, to other voluntary national and local agencies, or to community organisations.

In the light of so many complexities it is obvious that issues around coordinating all these bodies' efforts to best effect must be met indirectly.

Whilst individual organisations and agencies may sometimes challenge the government, and all have their own ways of doing things, it is essential that formal pathways (legal, public service provision, and so on) are uniform, unambiguous, fully signposted and easy to access.

In that respect there is a long way still to go.

Local government and state agencies

Local government engagement with communities affected by FGM have varied enormously. Councils such as Bristol,[14] Islington,[15, 16] Newham[17, 18] (and some other London Boroughs[19]), as well as Liverpool[20] and Greater Manchester[21] (10 boroughs) in England, and some cities in Wales and Scotland, have developed forums and agreed procedures with partners, and are finding ways to reach out into the community, but this is not as yet true of all local authorities.

Ways to address the issues are, however, being developed across Britain. In the final few weeks of 2014 the Local Government Association[22] produced a guide[23] for councillors in England and Wales, published on its website, alongside much other information and a number of case studies which it has collated. Some of this material relates to community engagement, for example work being undertaken in Lambeth.[24] The LGA also held a conference in October 2014 on councils' roles in tackling FGM, with a particular focus on the role of health visitors and school nurses.[25]

The formal agencies of the state likewise have a critical role to play at the level of community interventions to tackle FGM.

These state agencies include:

- Department for Communities and Local Government[26]
- Department for Education[27]
- Department of Health[28] and the National Health Service[29] (including the African Well Women's Service[30])
- Home Office
- Department for International Development[31]
- Ministry of Justice.[32]

Community and public involvement

A Home Office research programme in 2013 investigated 'what works' in community engagement towards eradicating FGM.[33] The ensuing report, published in July 2014, confirms that interventions are becoming more effective and nuanced, with increasing community understanding and acceptance of interventions against FGM by the authorities – although the report also opines that legal messages may sound 'punitive and threatening', and work to develop understanding of FGM as a form of child abuse continues to be required. A growing willingness by both men and women within relevant communities to discuss the matter is noted.

It was also noted that interventions are best effected on the basis of multiple stakeholders, including community groups, working together at the local level. The Pan-London FGM Forum is cited as one example of this approach (the Greater Manchester FGM Forum[34] might be another).

The researchers conducting this investigation found, however, that not all interventions were equally effective. Whilst useful work had been undertaken to encourage men (and women) faith leaders to dismiss the perceived religious basis for some forms of FGM, working with young people to empower them directly to speak out had been more effective than trying to change the opinions of older people, who often held deeply entrenched views.

An increasing emphasis on work in schools is therefore important as a way to inform vulnerable girls about the risks of FGM. Part of this strategy is to ensure that all children (boys and girls) should be aware of the issues, so that girls at risk are not isolated in their concerns. The strategy therefore reaches out to parents and wider family, as well as to school staff.

One catalogue of materials, published in July 2014, is the Home Office FGM Resource Pack,[35] which lists a variety of publications, case studies, films and other resources which review safeguarding and education information requirements.

But schools alone cannot address the perils of FGM; the whole community must be aware. One example of the active interplay between concerned citizens in general, and schools specifically, is the early 2014 campaign by the *Guardian* to persuade Secretary for Education Michael Gove MP to require that all head teachers ensure their students are informed about FGM and know what to do to prevent it happening.

To this end a change.org e-petition – headed up by 17-year-old schoolgirl Fahma Mohamed, with support from United Nations Secretary General Ban Ki-moon[36] and (when she had learned about FGM) Malala Yousafzai[37] – was launched to 'Tell schools to teach risks of female genital mutilation before the summer'.[38] The summer date is critical because the biggest so-called 'cutting season' occurs then,[ii] with girls away from school in Britain for long enough to undergo the mutilation, often back in their country of cultural origin.

---

ii   Another high-risk period in some countries is December; the deciding factor regarding timing has, by tradition, often been when the harvest occurs (when families hope to have money to pay for such activities).

As previously noted, within a few weeks 234,375 people had signed the *Guardian*-promoted petition and, after a period of resistance and a meeting with Fahma Mohamed,[39] Michael Gove agreed to send a letter to all schools in England.[40] His counterparts in Scotland (Michael Russell MSP)[41] and Wales (Huw Lewis AM)[42] also, and with less initial hesitation, undertook to contact their schools on the subject.

Here then is an example of community engagement resulting in significant action. The combination of genuine citizen concern, high-profile backers, intense media exposure (other media outlets also supported the *Guardian* initiative, some of them overtly[43]) and political positioning brought about a positive response with national ongoing impact. The next steps after the agreement to contact all schools included greater emphasis on issues of professional training and a commitment to further curricular development.

But equally importantly, this campaign probably secured a greater degree of awareness of the UK's position on FGM in the population as a whole and, specifically, amongst some of the British-based communities where it is practised. Many of the most publicly (media) visible activists in the campaign were schoolgirls from such communities, taking the opportunity, with support from their teachers, to express fundamental opposition to FGM.

This message resonated within their own homes and social groups, as well as in the wider society, and is one way forward. Since then the Department for Communities and Local Government has released modest funding (£40,000 in total for each)[44] to support national networks of 'community champions' to tackle both FGM and forced marriage, beginning in March 2015. Funding has also been made available (similarly, by tender) for some other small-scale community programmes, for example £80,000 to work with 'faith leaders'.[45]

These funds may assist in developing a greater understanding of what works in such interventions, not least because their outputs will be monitored. It is important to acknowledge, however, that many contributions by community leaders and activists have been made at no cost to the public purse; organisations as diverse as the Dr Abe Foundation, ACCMUK, the British Arab Federation, the Hawa Trust and Roshni have campaigned against FGM as a commitment, not a commission.

But this does not mean that formal funding, and the opportunity it permits for (supportive) monitoring to learn more and improve, is unimportant. A report by the Scottish Refugee Council (December 2014)[46] confirms that FGM activists and volunteers may feel they are taken for granted, and perhaps unsupported, even to the extent that they move on and the impetus they have established is dissipated.

Acknowledging long-time campaigners

This sense of being taken for granted must not be ignored, at either the interpersonal or more collective levels. The internet has facilitated great changes in how we all connect and what we can achieve, but communities remain places where people most often interact at first hand. Direct personal campaigning to stop FGM, as noted earlier, has now been a reality through several generations.

There is a risk in the age of the World Wide Web that activists coming into the field as concerned professionals in relevant disciplines, or even as brave survivors, will not know that the fight to eradicate FGM has been going on for many decades in both traditionally practising countries and in the West; and nor will they know that there is still much to be learned from their predecessors.

Unless generous acknowledgement of campaigners who worked long and hard without the benefit of the internet is forthcoming, knowledge and wisdom gained at considerable cost may be squandered.

The African (men and) women who have struggled, and continue to fight, often in peril, in their homeland nations and within their own diaspora communities demand respect, recognition and support. Acknowledgement of what has gone before is a sensitive issue in this context.

Similarly, there are Western campaigners who have worked unsung, perhaps for decades, some of whom would have given much for the advantages which the internet now so easily provides. They too have invaluable knowledge, experience and insights to share.

In the post-millennium world the internet has changed the way that everyone communicates with and relates to each other; and this is at least as true of campaigns to eradicate FGM as it is of any other aspect of contemporary life.

To have genuine and long-lasting impact, moves to stop FGM, whether in traditionally practising countries or in the diaspora, must acknowledge the past and its lessons, as well as looking to the future.

Sustaining the progress achieved by previous generations of campaigners may yet prove to be a significant challenge in the fight against FGM.

Including men

Amongst other possible pitfalls along the way to eradication is to ignore or underestimate the influence of men in practising communities.

As noted above, some attention is being focused on faith leaders, many of whom are male, but how best to take this approach forward is currently uncertain.

Traditional community leaders will vary in their willingness to accept messages about the dangers and illegality of FGM. Their authority may rest on demanding that the old ways continue without question; but alternatively they may recognise the evidence of harm and be keen to support moves to secure eradication.

Intense debate continues in some parts of the world, for instance, about the rulings of the Qur'an in this matter amongst (very largely male) scholars in the Islamic faith – although by no means all FGM is associated in any way with Islam, even given that different interpretations of that scripture continue to hold sway.

Further, whilst faith and other traditional community leaders are usually men, it may (and quite possibly often does) not follow that they represent the community as a whole. It can be difficult to ascertain the extent to which people of prominence are self-appointed, especially in communities where the roles of women are often restricted to the domestic sphere.

Nonetheless, numbers of faith leaders (such as those of the London Central Mosque, the Ahmadiyya Muslim Community and Afruca) have demonstrated very serious intent to stop FGM, and full support for these leaders – still more likely to be men than women – is one obvious way forward.

This support is particularly important because leaders in some diaspora communities who step outside the traditional ways of thinking may find themselves sidelined, in which case more overall is lost than gained; and the risk of negative outcomes is increased when few in the community (in this instance specifically adult males) understand why speaking out is necessary.

For this reason amongst others, working with young people is particularly critical. Children in school, boys as well as girls, are now beginning to learn about FGM and other harmful practices in a safe and supportive environment, as part of their normal curriculum. This is an ideal way to break the silence which enables FGM to continue.

When boys and young men know what FGM entails and how dangerous it is, they are often willing, wherever they are, to expose the reality behind the secrecy and conventions which uphold the practice. Brothers, friends and potential husbands can be enabled to protect their sisters and girlfriends before harm is done.

Similarly with adult men, there are many opportunities to provide information and to secure collaboration in preventing FGM. Male professionals in the relevant occupations have a significant role to play and in this respect it may be that more attention will now be paid to diversity within the appropriate roles: whilst for example most women from diaspora communities would prefer (or require) female clinicians, it may be that men from the same communities are more willing to discuss previously unspoken matters with other men.

Further, the lessons of public health education in other difficult topics have yet to be applied to FGM. Smoking, sexually transmitted disease, substance abuse, alcohol problems and mental health are all conditions which have required that those seeking to reduce incidence go out to reach men (as well as women) in the community, rather than the community going to the professional in the first instance.

The direct causations of these various problems and disorders may be different, but the same generic approach is in order: if men, as less likely regular users of the health service, are to be informed and engaged, active and appropriate ways to reach them must be devised.

In this respect, as in many others, the experience, drawing on parallel areas of concern, which public and community health practitioners have of engaging men particularly is very relevant.

Discuss this chapter at http://nofgmukbook.com/2015/01/29/chapter-8-prevention-communities/.

Endnotes

All weblinks accessed on 1 March 2015.

1 Browne, E. (2014) Harmful Traditional Practices in Diaspora Communities, *GSDRC Helpdesk Research Report*, 16 May 2014. Available at: http://www.gsdrc.org/docs/open/HDQ1108.pdf.

2 Baillot, H., Murray, N., Connelly, E., Howard, N. (2014) Tackling Female Genital Mutilation in Scotland – A Scottish model of intervention. *London School of Tropical Medicine & Scottish Refugee Council*, December. Available at: http://www.scottishrefugeecouncil.org.uk/assets/0000/9054/Tackling_FGM_in_Scotland_Report_2014_W.pdf.

3 International Organisation for Migration (IOM) (n.d.) Supporting the Abandonment of Female Genital Mutilation in the Context of Migration Available at: http://www.iom.int/jahia/webdav/shared/shared/mainsite/projects/documents/fgm_infosheet.pdf.

4 Njeri Chege, J., Askew, I., Liku, J. (2001) An Assessment of the Alternative Rites Approach for Encouraging Abandonment of Female Genital Mutilation in Kenya. *Frontiers in Reproductive Health*, September. Available at: http://www.popcouncil.org/uploads/pdfs/frontiers/FR_FinalReports/Kenya_FGC.pdf.

5   Jacob, M. (2015) Tanzania: Girls Get Training On FGM in Mugumu. *Tanzania Daily News*, 9 January. Available at: http://allafrica.com/stories/201501091033.html.

6   London Safeguarding Children Board (2015) *FGM: National FGM Resources.* Available at: http://www.londonscb.gov.uk/fgm/.

7   IKWRO (2011) *Snip, Snip, Snip. That's right, the coalition's still cutting away at women's rights.* Available at: http://ikwro.org.uk/2011/03/snip-snip-snip-thats-right-the-coalitions-still-cutting-away-at-womens-rights/.

8   Home Office (2014) Female Genital Mutilation. *GOV.UK*, 5 December. Available at: https://www.gov.uk/government/collections/female-genital-mutilation.

9   Home Office (2014) Female Genital Mutilation. *GOV.UK*, 5 December. Available at: https://www.gov.uk/government/collections/female-genital-mutilation.

10   Available at: http://www.replacefgm2.eu/.

11   Rosa (2013) *Tackling FGM in the UK: What works in community-based prevention work.* Available at: http://www.rosauk.org/tackling-fgm-in-the-uk-what-works-in-community-based-prevention-work.

12   Options (2014) *The Girl Generation to End FGM.* Available at: http://www.options.co.uk/our-programmes/end-fgmc-social-change-campaign-mobilising-a-global-movement.

13   Evaluation Office UNFPA, Evaluation Office UNICEF (2013) *UNFPA-UNICEF Joint Evaluation of the UNFPA-UNICEF Joint Programme on Female Genital Mutilation/Cutting (FGM/C): Accelerating Change.* Available at: http://www.unfpa.org/admin-resource/unfpa-unicef-joint-evaluation-unfpa-unicef-joint-programme-female-genital.

14   The Voice (2014) *Bristol Launches Campaign to Stop Female Genital Mutilation.* Available at: http://www.voice-online.co.uk/article/bristol-launches-campaign-stop-female-genital-mutilation.

15   Islington Borough Council (2015) *Female Genital Mutilation (FGM).* Available at: http://www.islington.gov.uk/services/policing-safety/how/domesticviolence/affected/Pages/money.aspx.

16   Islington Borough Council (2012) *Female Genital Mutilation (FGM) in Islington: A Statistical Study.* Available at: http://www.islington.gov.uk/publicrecords/library/Community-safety-and-emergencies/Publicity/Public-notices/2013-2014/%282013-04-18%29-FGM-In-Islington-A-Statistical-Study.pdf.

17   Newham Council (2015) *Female Genital Mutilation (FGM).* Available at: http://www.newham.gov.uk/Pages/ServiceChild/Female-Genital-Mutilation-%28FGM%29.aspx.

18   Manor Gardens (2015) *Newham FGM Prevention Service.* Available at: http://www.manorgardenscentre.org/fgmnewham/.

19   Mayor of London (2013) Mayor to Challenge Agencies to Share Information to Help Prevent Violence against Women and Girls in the Capital. *London.gov.uk*, 27 November. Available at: https://www.london.gov.uk/media/mayor-press-releases/2013/11/mayor-to-challenge-agencies-to-share-information-to-help-prevent.

20 FGM Liverpool (2015) *Female Genital Mutilation*. Available at: http://www.fgm-liverpool.org.

21 Local Government Association (2014) *Greater Manchester*. Available at: http://www.local.gov.uk/web/guest/community-safety/-/journal_content/56/10180/6593489/ARTICLE.

22 Available at: http://www.local.gov.uk/.

23 Local Government Association (2014) *Female Genital Mutilation (FGM): A Councillor's Guide*. Available at: http://www.local.gov.uk/documents/10180/5854661/L14-567+FGM+guidance+for+councillors_09.pdf/7196465e-4b63-4b58-b527-a462f5b5cc9d.

24 http://www.local.gov.uk/web/guest/community-safety/-/journal_content/56/10180/6593409/ARTICLE.

25 Local Government Association (2014) *London Borough of Lambeth*. Available at: http://www.local.gov.uk/documents/10180/6632833/Working+with+partners+-+Pauline+Watts.pdf/f182573c-6cbe-4bd4-a6e9-db1c552a74ab.

26 Available at: https://www.gov.uk/government/organisations/department-for-communities-and-local-government.

27 Available at: https://www.gov.uk/government/organisations/department-for-education.

28 Available at: https://www.gov.uk/government/organisations/department-of-health.

29 Available at: http://www.nhs.uk/Pages/HomePage.aspx.

30 Available at: http://www.nhs.uk/NHSEngland/AboutNHSservices/sexual-health-services/Pages/fgm-health-services-for-women.aspx.

31 Available at: https://www.gov.uk/government/organisations/department-for-international-development.

32 Available at: https://www.gov.uk/government/organisations/ministry-of-justice.

33 Home Office (2014) Main Findings from the 2013 FGM Initiative. *GOV.UK*, 22 July. Available at: https://www.gov.uk/government/publications/fgm-suppport-materials/main-findings-from-the-2013-fgm-initiative.

34 Greater Manchester Safety Partnership (2013) *Greater Manchester FGM Forum*. Available at: http://www.gmsafeguardingchildren.co.uk/newsroom/greatermanchesterfgmforum.

35 Home Office (2014) Female Genital Mutilation: Resource pack. *GOV.UK*, 22 July. Available at: https://www.gov.uk/government/publications/female-genital-mutilation-resource-pack/female-genital-mutilation-resource-pack.

36 Topping, A. (2014) Ban Ki-moon Puts UN Weight Behind Guardian-backed FGM Campaign. *Guardian*, 6 March. Available at: http://www.theguardian.com/society/2014/mar/06/ban-ki-moon-un-guardian-fgm-campaign-fahma-mohamed.

37 Topping, A. (2014) Ban Ki-moon Puts UN Weight behind *Guardian*-backed FGM Campaign. *Guardian*, 6 March. Available at: http://www.theguardian.com/society/video/2014/feb/24/fgm-malala-yousafzai-supports-guardian-campaign-video.

38 Mohamed, F. (2014) Tell Schools to Teach Risks of Female Genital Mutilation before the Summer. *Change.org*. Available at: http://www.change.org/en-GB/petitions/educationgovuk-tell-schools-to-teach-risks-of-female-genital-mutilation-before-the-summer-endfgm.
39 Department for Education, Gove, M. (2014) Michael Gove: Guidance for schools on female genital mutilation. *GOV.UK*, 25 February. Available at: https://www.gov.uk/government/news/michael-gove-guidance-for-schools-on-female-genital-mutilation.
40 Topping, A. (2014) Michael Gove Writes to Every School in England about Dangers of FGM. *Guardian*, 10 April. Available at: http://www.theguardian.com/politics/2014/apr/11/michael-gove-writes-schools-dangers-female-genital-mutilation/.
41 Topping, A., Mason, R., Harvey, E. (2014) Michael Gove Writes to Every School in England about Dangers of FGM. *Guardian*, 8 February. Available at: http://www.theguardian.com/society/2014/feb/07/female-genital-mutilation-scotland-schools-headteacher-fgm.
42 Welsh Government (2014) *Welsh Ministers Take Hard Line to End FGM in Wales*. Available at: http://wales.gov.uk/newsroom/educationandskills/2014/140310fgmletter/?lang=en.
43 Burrage, H. (2014) Islam Channel Television Examines FGM in the UK. *Hilary Burrage blog*, 24 April. Available at: http://hilaryburrage.com/2014/04/24/islam-channel-tv/.
44 Department for Communities and Local Government, Government Equalities Office (2014) Community Projects to Tackle Female Genital Mutilation and Forced Marriage. *GOV.UK*, 31 October. Available at: https://www.gov.uk/government/publications/community-projects-to-tackle-female-genital-mutilation-and-forced-marriage.
45 Department for Communities and Local Government et al. (2014) Funding to Prevent Female Genital Mutilation and Forced Marriage. *GOV.UK*, 11 October. Available at: https://www.gov.uk/government/news/new-funding-for-female-genital-mutilation-and-forced-marriage-prevention.
46 Baillot, H., Murray, N., Connelly, E., Howard, N. (2014) Tackling Female Genital Mutilation in Scotland – A Scottish model of intervention. *London School of Tropical Medicine & Scottish Refugee Council*, December. Available at: http://www.scottishrefugeecouncil.org.uk/assets/0000/9054/Tackling_FGM_in_Scotland_Report_2014_W.pdf.

9 Prevention – Information and Education

The most obvious opportunity to tackle FGM, alongside health and medical contexts, is in schools. Almost every child attends school, whatever her or his background, and even in 2015 the Department for Education and Ofsted[1] (the Inspectorate) remain influential.

Working in Schools

It is for this reason, as we saw in Chapter 8, that the *Guardian* newspaper campaign[i] in early 2014 to raise awareness of the pending summer so-called 'vacation cutting' (also known as the FGM 'season') focused on the then Secretary of State for Education, Michael Gove. A change.org petition was launched,[2] and reached almost a quarter of a million signatures within weeks. After some hesitation, Mr Gove gave an undertaking that:

> … guidance will be sent out by Easter (2014) and it will specifically include material that will enable everyone working with young people to tackle female genital mutilation. That material will cover:
>
> - what we know about the prevalence of female genital mutilation, in the UK and abroad
> - factors which heighten the risk of a schoolchild in the UK becoming a victim of female genital mutilation
> - indications that a child may have been a victim of female genital mutilation
> - statutory safeguarding duties of teachers and other school staff in relation to female genital mutilation

---

i   With which the present writer was closely associated.

> It [will also carry] links to external expert advice on specific safeguarding
> issues from the NSPCC. I will write to all headteachers to draw their attention
> to the updated schools safeguarding guidance and to reiterate that all teachers
> should familiarise themselves with it.[3]

This communication on guidance from the Secretary of State was sent out
in April 2014.[4, 5] It comprised, however, only a brief, routine emailed letter
to head teachers which mentioned in short measure safeguarding children
from a wide range of perils comprising 'female genital mutilation, child
sexual exploitation, cyberbullying, mental health, and radicalisation'.

The full guidance is available as *Keeping Children Safe in Education.*[6]
It refers not only to FGM, but to child abuse overall, including in extended
detail child sexual exploitation, cyberbullying, faith abuse, forced marriage,
gender-based violence (VAGW), mental health, radicalisation, teenage
relationship abuse and trafficking.[7]

These and other forms of abuse must all be addressed. Nonetheless, the
context of the advice on FGM is diluted by being set alongside the other
stated concerns about radicalisation and the Government's 'Channel'
programme,[8] which focuses on protecting people from radicalisation into
terrorism, and most significantly from the threat of al-Qa'ida (and, latterly,
emerging similar groups), and which was perhaps also shaped by emerging
concerns arising from the 'Trojan Horse'[9] allegations in Birmingham schools.

But radicalisation, whilst an extremely serious matter, is a far cry from
the contexts in which FGM may arise – terrorism happens when individual
people are persuaded, or decide, to depart the mainstream; FGM occurs
when communities (in Western countries) are already positioned as a
group outside the prevailing conventions. How this conflation of risks was
received in schools is not known.

In any case, the impact of the Gove email, even though it contained
important instructions about how to protect children, did not reach large
numbers of head teachers. A Freedom of Information enquiry revealed a few
weeks later that the letter had not been read by the majority of recipients;
by 30 April 2014, of the 31,600 addressees in 25,035 schools, 43 per cent had
opened the email, and 30 per cent of recipients had clicked through to the
website offering guidance on safeguarding.[10]

It might seem, therefore, that other ways of engaging schools in the
fight against FGM are also required. One informal suggestion was that
schools not reading (or at least not opening) emailed communications
from the Department for Education should suffer financial sanctions on
discretionary budgets; a more straightforward, less hostile or alienating,
approach comprises including essential elements of the educational offer
in the statutory national curriculum, and as a compulsory part of initial
teacher training and updates.

Safeguarding Children, and Personal, Social and Health Education (PSHE)

Campaigns to ensure that the Personal, Social, Health and Relationships Curriculum (PSHRE – more often referred to simply as PSHE) is included in the core curriculum go back a long way, and have been centre stage since at least the 1980s.[11] The issues then were around the appropriateness (or not) of information on sex, HIV and homosexuality, and in every case there was considerable resistance from some politicians and various religious groups.

Often this resistance seemed to centre more on the personal unease of the people refuting the need for PSHE than on the entitlement of young people to understand and take responsibility for their own bodies and actions. Over time, however, there has been a growing realisation that the social and health curriculum is essential to equip children for the modern world. Amongst other conditions, teenage pregnancy, illness and psychiatric problems (for example the suicide of young men who believe they are gay) all arise more frequently when information about physical and other personal issues and how to handle them is denied.

Overall, and despite setbacks, considerable progress has been made since the 1980s.

As of September 2014, PSHE remains a non-statutory element of the school curriculum, but section 2.5 of the National Curriculum framework, along with the Department for Education guidance,[12] does require that:

> Schools should seek to use PSHE education to build, where appropriate, on the statutory content already outlined in the national curriculum, the basic school curriculum and in statutory guidance on: drug education, financial education, sex and relationship education (SRE) and the importance of physical activity and diet for a healthy lifestyle.

The Statutory Safeguarding Guidance for England (published in April 2014[13]) is for head teachers, teachers and education staff, governing bodies and proprietors, and relates to the care of all children (aged under 18) in maintained schools and colleges, independent schools, academy schools, free schools, alternative provision academies and free schools, pupil referral units, further education colleges and sixth-form colleges.

The guidance requires schools and colleges to work with social care, the police, health services and other services to promote the welfare of children and protect them from harm, and also requires that each school and college have a designated safeguarding lead to provide support to staff members to carry out their safeguarding duties and to liaise closely with other services such as children's social care.

It is essential that school governors are aware of their responsibility to ensure that appropriate training and safeguarding measures are in place.[14]

The guidance also states that under the Teacher Standards 2012[15] teachers, including head teachers (and other staff), must seek to:

- safeguard children's well-being and maintain public trust in the teaching profession as part of their professional duties;
- provide a safe environment in which children can learn;
- identify children who may be in need of extra help or who are suffering, or are likely to suffer, significant harm;
- take appropriate action, working with other services as needed; and also support social workers to take decisions about individual children.

Additionally, all schools must fulfil their wider statutory duties. This includes opportunities for children to learn about themselves and their environments. That Ofsted (the English Office for Standards in Education, Children's Services and Skills[16]) takes this requirement very seriously is illustrated by the 2013 report, *Not Yet Good Enough: Personal, social, health and economic education in schools*.[17]

Ofsted's focus also is in line with section 2.1 of the National Curriculum, which states that:

Every state-funded school must offer a curriculum which is balanced and broadly based and which:

- promotes the spiritual, moral, cultural, mental and physical development of pupils at the school and of society
- prepares pupils at the school for the opportunities, responsibilities and experiences of later life.

This is a curriculum requirement based on the (amended) 2002 Education Act[18] and the 2010 Academies Act.[19] Well-being and safeguarding are also addressed via the Children Act 2004,[20] as is community cohesion (Education Act 2006[21]).

Whilst the Department for Education decided in 2013 not to take forward new statutory requirements for PSHE, the underlying rationales remain. As for instance the Sex Education Forum explains,[22] children have a right to know about their own bodies and how to cope with the social world in which they exist; and they have a right to knowledge about how they can thrive and avoid harm.

The requirement that education be one element of safeguarding for children was further articulated by Lord Laming in his inquiry into the events and professional negligence culminating in the death in London in 2000 of 8 year old Victoria Climbié:[23] 'The support and protection of children cannot be achieved by a single agency. ... Every Service has to play its part. All staff must have placed upon them the clear expectation that their primary responsibility is to the child and his or her family' (Lord Laming in the Victoria Climbié Inquiry Report,[24] paragraphs 17.92 and 17.93).

In this tragic context – repeated also in the instances of a number of other children – it is impossible to maintain that schools do not have a responsibility to protect children from harmful practices, including FGM. Further, it is self-evident that PSHE has a role in providing this protection.

Amongst those continuing to insist that PSHE, and particularly sex and relationships education, becomes an expressly required part of the curriculum is the Sex Education Forum, an organisation with a wide range of agency members,[25] hosted by the National Children's Bureau, which also provides up-to-date lists of suitable materials for children at various stages in their school careers.[26]

FGM-specific Curriculum and Concerns

The campaign to secure required status for PSHE, and an element covering FGM within this, continues. One film making the case includes school children involved in the Integrate programme;[27] and others, bringing to bear professional expertise, who are pressing for compulsory PSHE and sex/FGM education include the PSHE Association, as articulated by Joe Hayman, its chief executive, at the 2013 annual conference.[28]

FGM-specific curriculum has been developed by various professional bodies, including the PSHE Association in collaboration with the Home Office and the Department for International Development.[29] A number of English local authorities have developed curriculum specifically to address FGM. These include Bristol (involving Somali parents,[30] and the Integrate programme, including music and other popular media approaches developed by young people to raise awareness of FGM[31]), Islington (PSHE materials for Key Stages 3 and 4[32]) and Greater Manchester (*End the Fear* leaflets[33] and professional training for teachers and others, via the internet;[34, 35] see also the Against Violence and Abuse (AVA) e-learning website for training material on domestic and sexual abuse, and so on[36]). The *End the Fear* training website on FGM is freely accessible and provides detailed information and guidance on many aspects of the practice and its prevention.

The Home Office has recently introduced a Virtual College online training for frontline professionals, including teachers,[37] and the London Safeguarding Children Board has also produced a substantial compilation of materials, starting with its 2009 FGM Resource Pack, launched in Southwark.[38]

Other materials now produced to help girls at risk include films with child actors, such as the Metropolitan (London) Police production *CUT – Some Wounds Never Heal*,[39, 40] made by the Kids Taskforce with pupils at Lilian Baylis Technology School, Kennington and aimed at 11–17-year-olds. It also features the anti-FGM human rights activist Waris Dirie, who created the Desert Flower Foundation.

Similar strategies and materials are available for Scotland and Wales. The Scottish Education Authority had produced guidance[41] and learning materials[42] as have the Welsh authorities,[43] including, as in Scotland,[44] a letter to schools.[45]

Ireland has also seen developments in schools to prevent children being taken abroad for FGM.[46]

All these developments and materials have heightened awareness of FGM in schools, and enabled more teachers to address it in age- and context-appropriate ways. Nonetheless, as FORWARD told the UK Education Select Committee when they undertook an Inquiry into Child Protection,[47] much work remains to be done to ensure that every child receives and can use the information required to ensure her or his personal safety.

Further, there is a growing recognition that materials and strategies must not address only girls directly at risk. Brothers, friends, other family members and neighbours can often provide first-instance support (and warnings) to children under threat.

This area of the curriculum remains difficult. There are still parents, from almost all religious backgrounds and politics, who find everything concerning personal and health issues challenging or even unacceptable. Sometimes they are aware of the issues but don't want them discussed for any of a number of different reasons; sometimes they themselves lack awareness of the information which PSHE offers.

Either way, these parents can present serious obstacles to the learning to which any child is entitled, if she or he is to be protected from dangerous and avoidable risks. Earlier examples of these sorts of challenge include, for example, the Gillick case, 1980–86, where Mrs Victoria Gillick did not want her under-16 daughters to receive medical advice or treatment around contraception. The House of Lords ultimately ruled that such advice was lawful, upholding the position of the DHSS that contraceptive medical care for under 16s may in appropriate cases be provided.[48]

This ruling also has relevance, for example, for sex education in schools. In summary, any young person deemed competent (that is, able to understand and foresee the possible consequence) may consent to medical attention and/or advice, including that relating to sexual and reproductive health.

Parental consent in receiving or seeking this advice is encouraged but not required. Further, young people are owed duties of care and confidentiality in the same way as adults. Confidentiality may, however, be broken when the safety, welfare or health of that person (or of others) could without that breach of confidence be gravely at risk.

This position is clearly important if a child discloses that she, or another child, is at risk of, or has already undergone, FGM. PSHE is obviously one context in which that situation might occur.

In some schools the head teacher will decide on a low-level approach on school policy, perhaps just a note about PSHE in the context of a general report for parents. In other schools the head may choose to refer the issues to the board of governors. Some schools will post detailed information about their social curriculum on a website. But however the issues are addressed, addressed they must be.

Schools – a critical source of knowledge for people of all sorts in their host communities – must also seek to enable their social curriculum to encourage others to be alert and able to assist in escaping FGM. One example of such an approach, with carefully thought-through materials for classroom use and scope for wider discussions, has been developed by the Islington Healthy Schools Team.[49]

PSHE and related studies must encompass the perils of FGM and other dangers in a general way, as well as directly to those most at risk.

Detecting and Preventing the Risk of FGM

Staff in schools are often ideally placed to know when a child is at risk of FGM. They know the children concerned and are familiar with their communities and normal routines.

Advice on the warning signs, and guidance, is available from a number of organisations, such as the National Health Service,[50] the PSHE Association,[51] the Metropolitan Police,[52] FORWARD,[53] the NSPCC[54] and others.

Indications that a girl may be about to undergo FGM include:

- talk of a 'special party' (either in the UK or abroad);
- plans for a girl 'becoming a woman';
- vaccinations or other preparations to visit a country of cultural reference or origin in which FGM occurs;
- requests for significant time off school for travel;

- preparations for a special event, such a buying traditional clothes or other items;
- vague discussion by girls of a forthcoming secret event;
- a family history of girls and women undergoing FGM, especially if close relatives are thought to have had it.

Alternatively, it may be feared that a child has already undergone FGM. Indications that this may be so include:

- prolonged absence from school, or a visit abroad;
- changed moods or withdrawal, or evidence of anxiety or other upset;
- frequent visits by the girl to the bathroom;
- the child is apparently in pain or frequently seems/feels unwell;
- unwillingness to join in sports, swimming or other physical activity which may be difficult or cause hurt;
- talk of having had something special or secret done;
- discomfort if the child has to sit on the floor or in other potentially painful positions.

Any of these indicators must be taken very seriously. The indications can arise in many different contexts, formal or informal,[55] and all school and related personnel need to receive training in what steps to take if the possibility of a child undergoing, or having undergone, FGM arises.

The immediate required action in an educational context is to report the concern to the school's designated safeguarding lead[56] – who must be formally trained[57] – or, if he or she is not available, to a senior member of staff. This step is not optional.[58] The person who became aware of the risk or possible crime is required to report it, and the report must be formally noted.

It is important too that the original person listens carefully to what the child says, taking notes as soon as possible. A commitment to treating the information as confidential may be offered, but expressly not a promise to tell absolutely no one else.

Where possible this commitment to confidentiality but not secrecy should be explained clearly to the child, but discretion about what to say, within the boundaries of not promising secrecy, needs to be used. The primary consideration must always be the safety of the child, which explains both why secrecy, as opposed to confidentiality, is not possible and why care must be taken in explaining to the child what will happen next.

The advice for schools on disclosure and confidentiality, from the *UK Government Multi-Agency Practice Guidelines: Female Genital Mutilation*,[59] is clear, albeit not always straightforward to act upon in the real world:

If there is an indication that the child or young person is at risk of FGM or has undergone FGM, or she has expressed fears of reprisals or violence, the information must be shared with both the police and children's social care. [School] staff should:

- talk about FGM in a professional and sensitive manner, in line with Section 4.2;
- explain that FGM is illegal in the UK and that they will be protected by the law;
- recognise and respect their wishes where possible, but child welfare must be paramount. FGM is child abuse and against the law. If a member of staff believes that the girl is at risk of FGM, or has already undergone FGM, the police and social services must be informed even if this is against the girl's wishes. If you do take action against the student's wishes, you must inform them of the reasons why;
- activate local safeguarding procedures, using existing national and local protocols for multi-agency liaison with the police and children's or adults' social care;
- ensure that the girl is informed of the long-term health consequences of FGM to encourage her to seek and accept medical assistance;
- liaise with the designated teacher with responsibility for safeguarding children;
- refer the student, with their consent, to appropriate medical help, counselling and local and national support groups;
- ensure that safeguarding and protection is considered for any female family members. [9.2]

The *Multi-Agency Practice Guidelines* also emphasise to school staff that speaking to the student's parents about intended actions may place the student at risk of emotional and/or physical harm. Contacting the family must be avoided; it may expedite any travel arrangements and hasten plans to carry out FGM.

In general terms this advice holds whether the girl in question is thought to be at risk of FGM or whether the suspicion is that she has already been subjected to it.

Beyond this things may, however, become uncertain.

Safeguarding Referrals

Advice from organisations such as the police and FORWARD identifies a number of agencies which can be approached by members of the public, the school safeguarding officer or other professionals/practitioners to secure the safety of girls at potential risk of FGM. These include:

- the local Social Services Department (telephone number from the Town Hall);
- the local Police Child Protection Unit (or 999 in an emergency);
- the NSPCC (0800 028 3550 – for adults seeking general advice or referral on FGM);
- ChildLine (0800 1111 – for concerned or anxious children);
- the Local Safeguarding Children Board;
- and, if there are fears that a girl may be taken abroad for FGM, the Foreign and Commonwealth Office (020 7008 1500).

It is no surprise that very few formal referrals about FGM are made in the UK, when the pathways to referral are so confusing and poorly identified.[60] Even those with a direct professional responsibility for FGM safeguarding are presented with a plethora of options for how (or if) to report their concerns, and they may also have little information available to guide their preference. Some institutions articulate these complexities clearly on their websites.[61]

As at the January 2015 Consultation the Government is proposing mandatory reporting of suspected FGM or risk of FGM in very limited circumstances to the police. The range of responses to this proposal has been wide (from outright rejection of the idea to embracing required reporting much more widely as the way forward).

This writer's position[62] is that mandating is essential, but that decisions on whether to report to the police should be made by specially trained abuse reporting officers (AROs) who receive all initial indications of concern. Having received training to evaluate the degree of danger and/or level of likelihood before formal referral, officers would operate a coordinated nationwide network to establish in each case levels of risk, thereby avoiding both excessive numbers of escalated formal reports to the police, and, through the national network, the danger that children in mobile families or communities may fall through the net.

Such a system (referral to proposed abuse reporting officers) would also reduce the degree of conflict some concerned professionals might have because they, too, in a previous time, have experienced FGM or other child abuse or personal trauma. Unless these professionals consciously chose to become AROs they would not be required to make any decisions or deliver anything except the initial referral, when it arose. The reality that some professionals working with children and vulnerable adults will themselves have experience of abuse – and that their work can be valuably informed by this – must be acknowledged and managed, supportively and effectively.

The current situation and proposals are, however, unsatisfactory at both the strategic and the operational level. It is also made even more complex by the range of contexts in which disclosure or suspicions of risk may occur.

Beyond the formal parameters of school itself, children who may experience FGM are also to be found in nurseries, other early years settings, youth clubs, church groups and many more locations. Whilst, at last, school teachers are increasingly likely to receive training in what to do about FGM when the issue arises – or at least, who to tell in the first instance about concerns – other practitioners working with children may be less acquainted with their responsibilities.

The inter-agency approach and the NSPCC 'helpline' are (as at early 2015) not producing reports from the public of FGM at remotely the frequency which estimates of FGM occurrence would suggest might be expected; and in any case it is very unclear how reporting should be done.

Some developments to address the complexities, and challenges to public service providers, of FGM are, however, taking shape. These will be discussed in Chapter 10.

Informal Approaches to Information Sharing: Creative Responses

As we have noted, it is not only via the formal school curriculum that children and thereafter others in their communities and further afield learn about FGM.

The subject is one which easily adapts to a creative response. Children in schools, adults in (performing) arts colleges and organisations, members of informal drama and fine arts clubs, literary writers, professional painters, poets, film-makers and others all contribute to awareness-raising and debates about FGM. Skilfully managed, art and music, as one example, may deliver the message (or identify the problem), especially for children, more effectively than the formally spoken or printed word.

Discuss this chapter at http://nofgmukbook.com/2015/01/29/chapter-9-prevention-information-and-education/.

Endnotes

All weblinks accessed on 1 March 2015.

1   Available at: https://www.gov.uk/government/organisations/ofsted.
2   Mohamed, F. (2014) Tell Schools to Teach Risks of Female Genital Mutilation before the Summer. *Change.org*. Available at: http://www.change.org/en-GB/ petitions/educationgovuk-tell-schools-to-teach-risks-of-female-genital-mutilation-before-the-summer-endfgm.
3   Department for Education, Gove, M. (2014) Michael Gove: Guidance for schools on female genital mutilation. *GOV.UK*, 25 February. Available at: https://www.gov.uk/government/news/michael-gove-guidance-for-schools-on-female-genital-mutilation.
4   Gove, M. (2014) Letter to Headteachers. *GOV.UK*, 2 April. Available at: https://www.gov.uk/government/uploads/system/uploads/attachment_data/file/309593/KCSiE_letter.pdf.
5   Topping, A. (2014) Michael Gove Writes to Every School in England about Dangers of FGM. *Guardian*, 10 April. Available at: http://www.theguardian.com/politics/2014/apr/11/michael-gove-writes-schools-dangers-female-genital-mutilation/.
6   Department for Education (2014) *Keeping Children Safe in Education – Information for all school and college staff*. Available at: https://www.gov.uk/government/uploads/system/uploads/attachment_data/file/354151/Keeping_children_safe_in_education_Information_for_staff.pdf.
7   Press Association (2014) Michael Gove Urges Schools and Colleges to Watch for Signs of Abuse. *Guardian*, 8 May. Available at: http://www.theguardian.com/politics/2014/may/08/michael-gove-schools-children-radicalisation-abuse-fmg.
8   HM Government (2012) *Channel: Protecting vulnerable people from being drawn into terrorism*. Available at: https://www.gov.uk/government/uploads/system/uploads/attachment_data/file/118194/channel-guidance.pdf.
9   Clarke, P. (2014) *Report into Allegations Concerning Birmingham Schools Arising from the 'Trojan Horse' Letter*. Available at: https://www.gov.uk/government/uploads/system/uploads/attachment_data/file/340526/HC_576_accessible_-.pdf.
10 Bentham, M. (2014) The Secretary of State's Letter to Schools Regarding Female Genital Mutilation (Freedom of Information request to Department for Education). *WhatDoTheyKnow*, July. Available at: https://www.whatdotheyknow.com/request/the_secretary_of_states_letter_t.
11 Burrage, H. (2013) Personal, Social and Health Education (PSHE), Citizenship and Sex and Relationships Education (SRE) are Essential Curriculum Entitlements. *Hilary Burrage blog*. Available at: http://hilaryburrage.com/pshe-factass/.
12 Department for Education (2013) Personal, Social, Health and Economic (PSHE) Education. *GOV.UK*, 11 September. Available at: https://www.gov.uk/

government/publications/personal-social-health-and-economic-education-pshe/
personal-social-health-and-economic-pshe-education.

13 Department for Education (2014) Keeping Children Safe in Education. *GOV.
UK*, 15 October. Available at: https://www.gov.uk/government/publications/
keeping-children-safe-in-education?campaignkw=keepingchildrensafestatguid
ance&campaignkw=Keepingchildrensafe.

14 The Key for School Governors (2015) *Keeping Children Safe in Education:
Summary*. Available at: http://schoolgovernors.thekeysupport.com/sample-
articles/keeping-children-safe-in-education-summary.

15 Department for Education (2013) Teachers' Standards. *GOV.UK*, 7 March.
Available at: https://www.gov.uk/government/collections/teachers-standards.

16 Ofsted (2015) About us. *GOV.UK*. Available at: http://www.ofsted.gov.uk/
about-us.

17 Ofsted (2012) *Not Yet Good Enough: Personal, social, health and economic education
schools*. Available at: http://www.surreyhealthyschools.co.uk/downloads/not_
yet_good_enough_pshe_ofsted_2013.pdf.

18 UK Government (2002) *Education Act 2002*. Available at: http://www.legislation.
gov.uk/ukpga/2002/32/contents.

19 UK Government (2010) *Academies Act 2010*. Available at: http://www.legislation.
gov.uk/ukpga/2010/32/contents.

20 HM Government (2007) Statutory Guidance on Making Arrangements to
Safeguard and Promote the Welfare of Children under Section 11 of the
Children Act 2004. *Department for Education*. Available at: http://webarchive.
nationalarchives.gov.uk/20130401151715/https:/www.education.gov.uk/
publications/eOrderingDownload/DFES-0036-2007.pdf.

21 UK Government (2006) *Education and Inspections Act 2006*. Available at: http://
www.legislation.gov.uk/ukpga/2006/40/contents.

22 Brook, PSHE Association and Sex Education Forum (2014) *Sex and
Relationships Education (SRE) for the 21st Century*. Available at: http://www.
sexeducationforum.org.uk/media/17706/sreadvice.pdf.

23 Batty, D. (2002) Background to the Victoria Climbié Inquiry. *University of
Huddersfield*. Available at: http://victoriaclimbie.hud.ac.uk/background.html.

24 House of Commons Health Committee (2003) The Victoria Climbié Inquiry
Report. *House of Commons*, 5 June. Available at: http://www.publications.
parliament.uk/pa/cm200203/cmselect/cmhealth/570/570.pdf.

25 Sex Education Forum (2015) *List of Members*. Available at: http://www.
sexeducationforum.org.uk/members/list-of-members.aspx.

26 Sex Education Forum (2012) Resources List. *National Children's Bureau*, April.
Available at: http://www.sexeducationforum.org.uk/media/4465/resource_list_
primary_-_in_new_template.pdf.

27 The Pixel Project (2013) A Pixel Project Inspirational Interview: FGM In the
UK – An Interview with Integrate Bristol. *YouTube*, 31 October. Available
at: http://www.youtube.com/watch?v=Q9uz0rSNO_A.

28 Hayman, J. (2013) Keynote at 2013 Annual Conference – 'Tackling sensitive issues in a time of change'. *PSHE Association*, 27 June. Available at: https://www.pshe-association.org.uk/content.aspx?CategoryID=1155.

29 PSHE Association (2014) *Addressing FGM in Schools: Teaching, learning and support*. Available at: https://www.pshe-association.org.uk/content.aspx?CategoryID=1193.

30 PSHE Association (2012) *Somali Parent Engagement in Inner-City Secondary School*. Available at: http://www.sexeducationforum.org.uk/practice/parents-sre/somali-parent-engagement-in-inner-city-secondary-school.aspx.

31 Integrate Bristol, Zed Productions, Buck, R., Rose, N. (2014) Use Your Head (Official Music Video). *Integrate Bristol*, 26 June. Available at: http://integratebristol.org.uk/2014/06/26/the-most-uplifting-thing-you-will-watch-this-summer-useyourhead-support-our-new-music-video/.

32 Islington Healthy Schools Team (2014) *KS3 FGM Lesson*. Available at: https://www.pshe-association.org.uk/resources_search_details.aspx?ResourceId=494&Keyword=&SubjectID=0&LevelID=0&ResourceTypeID=4&SuggestedUseID=0&campaignkw=SREcoveredlisting.

33 EndTheFear.co.uk (2014) *Information Sheet: Female genital mutilation*. Available at: http://www.endthefear.co.uk/wp-content/uploads/2010/06/FGM-leaflet.pdf?563068.

34 EndTheFear.co.uk (2015) *E-learning*. Available at: http://www.endthefear.co.uk/practitioners/e-learning/.

35 EndTheFear.co.uk (2015) *Female Genital Mutilation (FGM) Resources*. Available at: http://www.endthefear.co.uk/media/uploads/fgm/story.html.

36 AVA (2015) *Our Courses*. Available at: http://elearning.avaproject.org.uk/.

37 SAFE (n.d) *Free Online Training for Frontline Professionals in Helping Girls at Risk of FGM*. Available at: http://www.safenetwork.org.uk/news_and_events/news_articles/Pages/free-home-office-fgm-elearning.aspx.

38 London Safeguarding Children Board (2015) *FGM: National FGM Resources*. Available at: http://www.londonscb.gov.uk/fgm/.

39 Metropolitan Police (2011) *CUT – Some Wounds Never Heal*. Available at: http://content.met.police.uk/News/CUT--Some-Wounds-Never-Heal/1260269158604/1257246745756.

40 Values vs Violence (2015) *FGM*. Available at: http://vvvuk.com/fgm/.

41 The Scottish Government (2010) *National Guidance for Child Protection in Scotland 2010*. Available at: http://www.scotland.gov.uk/Publications/2010/12/09134441/0.

42 Education Scotland (2014) *Female Genital Mutilation Resource*. Available at: http://www.educationscotland.gov.uk/resources/f/fgm.asp.

43 Jones, C. (2011) All Wales Protocol – Female Genital Mutilation (FGM). *All Wales Child Protection Procedures Review Group*, March. Available at: http://www.awcpp.org.uk/wp-content/uploads/2014/03/Female-Genital-Mutilation.pdf.

44 Russell, M., Robinson, S. (2014) Letter Issued to Schools around Female Genital Mutilation. *Scottish Government*, 21 March. Available at: http://www.gov.scot/Resource/0044/00446674.pdf.

45 Learning Wales (2014) A Letter to Schools – Help eradicate female genital mutilation in Wales. *Welsh Government*, 9 June. Available at: http://learning.wales.gov.uk/news/sitenews/letter-to-schools-eradicate-female-genital-mutilation/?lang=en.

46 Finn, C. (2014) More Training Needed for Teachers on Female Genital Mutilation to Identify Children at Risk. *the journal.i.e.*, 25 July. Available at: https://uk.news.yahoo.com/more-training-needed-teachers-female-genital-mutilation-identify-214154800.html#5W3y8Tp.

47 FORWARD (2012) Education Committee – Children first: the child protection system in England – Written evidence submitted by FORWARD. *www.parliament.uk*, 16 November. Available at: http://www.publications.parliament.uk/pa/cm201213/cmselect/cmeduc/137/137vw51.htm.

48 FPA (2009) *Under-16s: Consent and confidentiality in sexual health services factsheet.* Available at: http://www.fpa.org.uk/factsheets/under-16s-consent-confidentiality.

49 Healthy Schools Islington (2014) SRE Covered. *PSHE Association*. Available at: https://www.pshe-association.org.uk/resources_search_details.aspx?ResourceId=494.

50 NHS (2014) Female Genital Mutilation. *GOV.UK*, 27 June. Available at: http://www.nhs.uk/Conditions/female-genital-mutilation/Pages/Introduction.aspx.

51 PSHE Association (2014) *Addressing FGM in Schools: Teaching, learning and support.* Available at: https://www.pshe-association.org.uk/content.aspx?CategoryID=1193.

52 Metropolitan Police (2014) *Met Briefing Note: Female genital mutilation.* Available at: http://www.met.police.uk/docs/female-genital-mutilation.pdf.

53 Kunze, K. (2013) Responding to Female Genital Mutilation – A guide for key professionals. *Terre des Femmes, FORWARD*. Available at: http://www.forwarduk.org.uk/wp-content/uploads/2014/12/CHANGE-Responding-to-FGM-A-Guide-for-Key-Professionals.pdf.

54 NSPCC (2015) *Female Genital Mutilation (FGM) – At a glance.* Available at: http://www.nspcc.org.uk/Inform/resourcesforprofessionals/minorityethnic/female-genital-mutilation_wda96841.html#factors.

55 Burrage, H. (2014) Schools Must Safeguard Girls from FGM; But How? *Hilary Burrage blog*, 26 July. Available at: http://hilaryburrage.com/2014/07/26/schools-must-safeguard-girls-from-fgm-but-how/.

56 The Key for School Leaders (December 2014) *Role of the Designated Safeguarding Lead.* Available at: https://schoolleaders.thekeysupport.com/pupils-and-parents/safeguarding-children/procedures/child-protection-designated-person.

57 The Key for School Leaders (2015) *Safeguarding: Training requirements.* Available at: https://schoolleaders.thekeysupport.com/pupils-and-parents/safeguarding-children/procedures/child-protection-training-guidance.

58 Michelon, K. (2013) FGM and School's Safeguarding Duties. *Optimus Education,* 16 October. Available at: http://www.optimus-education.com/fgm-and-schools-safeguarding-duties.

59 Home Office, Department for Education, Featherstone, L. (2014) Female Genital Mutilation: Guidelines to protect children and women. *GOV.UK,* 22 July. Available at: https://www.gov.uk/government/uploads/system/uploads/attachment_data/file/216669/dh_124588.pdf.

60 Burrage, H. (2014) Let's Drop the Clichés: Mandatory Reporting and Simple Protocols are Essential to Prevent FGM and Other Child Abuse. *Hilary Burrage blog,* 7 April. Available at: http://hilaryburrage.com/2014/04/07/lets-drop-the-cliches-mandatory-reporting-and-simple-protocols-are-essential-to-prevent-fgm-and-other-child-abuse/.

61 Carlton Bolling College (2014) *Child Protection & Safeguarding Policy.* Available at: http://www.carltonbolling.co.uk/home/policies-statements/child-protection-safeguarding/.

62 Burrage, H. (2015) UK Home Office Consultation on Mandatory Reporting of FGM – My Response. *Hilary Burrage blog,* 11 January. Available at: http://hilaryburrage.com/2015/01/11/uk-home-office-consultation-on-mandatory-reporting-of-fgm-my-response/.

10 Prevention – Social Services and Multi-agency Work

Progress is now (early 2015) being made, but the removal by the new Coalition Government in 2011 of the post of national coordinator of action to eradicate female genital mutilation was a serious blow to the UK programme. As noted in Chapter 7, progress was interrupted for some while: whilst the post was fairly new, its potential value is indicated by the fact that, more than three years and much vigorous activist positioning and campaigning later, in 2014, discussion of how to implement a meaningful national action plan again came onto the agenda.

In the meantime, as recent studies have shown, the number of women and girls with, or at risk of, FGM in Britain has probably increased significantly. It is impossible to know precisely how many individuals could have been spared FGM if the emerging 2011 national coordinator role had continued, but an estimate of this number would be instructive as part of a study of the impact of nationally integrated service provision or the converse.

Nonetheless, there is now understanding and acceptance across the UK public service sector that FGM is, and must be tackled as, gross child abuse.

In line with this, various developments have occurred, amongst them, in 2014, the plan in acute hospitals to begin data collection on the incidence of FGM,[1] the letter by the then Secretary of State for Education instructing schools to ensure that the hazard of so-called 'vacation cutting' is addressed,[2] and, in 2013, the introduction of a charity phone line to advise adults who are concerned about children at risk of FGM.[3]

In addition, a number of professional bodies have joined with the Department of Health to produce the multi-agency guidelines on FGM,[4] bringing together more formally the perspectives of most of the relevant organisations.

But still support and training for public sector professionals such as teachers and social care workers is weak, if it exists at all. As has become clear from cases such as Baby P,[5] or from recent historic disclosures about child abuse by 'celebrities'[6] and in (especially, boys' boarding) schools,[7] and, for example, in the 'grooming' cases in Rochdale and Oxford of the early 2000s,[8] high-level guidance around child protection to date has not in general been translated by any measure effective into work on the ground, in the classroom and in the connections between medical and social services.

This is the advice on disclosure and confidentiality from the *UK Government Multi-Agency Practice Guidelines: Female Genital Mutilation*:[9]

> IN ALL CASES:
> If you are worried about someone who is at risk of FGM or has had FGM, you must share this information with social care or the police. It is then their responsibility to investigate and safeguard and protect any girls or women involved. Other professionals should not attempt to investigate cases themselves. [Preface, 4.1]
>
> Under section 47 of the Children Act 1989, anyone who has information that a child is potentially or actually at risk of significant harm is required to inform social care or the police. Initially, the professional will refer the potential victim as a child in need and social services will assess the risk. This definition of harm has been extended in the Adoption and Children Act 2002, which includes where someone sees or hears of the ill treatment of another. Specifically, this relates to situations where there may not be direct disclosure of FGM being performed.
>
> To safeguard children and young people as required by UK law, it may be necessary to give information to people working in other agencies or departments. For some professionals, this can pose dilemmas when it involves going beyond the normal boundaries of confidentiality. Nonetheless, both law and policy allow for disclosure where it is in the public interest or where a criminal act may have been perpetrated.
>
> There may also be the perception that passing on information can damage the relationship of trust built up with families and communities. However, it is crucial that the focus is kept on the best interests of the child as required by law. [4.6]

Beyond the critical clarity of the statement that the best interests of the child are paramount lies considerable confusion about how to proceed.

The Multi-agency Approach

After a slow start the principle of multi-agency working is now well established. *Female Genital Mutilation: Multi-agency practice guidelines*[10] were published in 2011 by the Department of Health in active collaboration with most of the relevant professional bodies.

The Royal College of Midwives (RCM) has also published (2013) an important and detailed set of guidelines, *Tackling FGM in the UK: Intercollegiate recommendations for identifying, recording and reporting*.[11] These recommendations arose from the joint deliberations, with the RCM, of the Royal College of Obstetricians and Gynaecologists (RCOG), the Royal College of Nursing (RCN), Equality Now and the Community Practitioners and Health Visitors Association (CPHVA), the UK's leading professional organisation for health visitors, school nurses, nursery nurses and other community nurses working in primary care.

The *Intercollegiate Recommendations* summarise required action for tackling FGM in the UK[12] as:

1. Treat it as Child Abuse: FGM is a severe form of violence against women and girls. It is child abuse and must be integrated into all UK child safeguarding procedures in a systematic way.

2. Document and collect information: The NHS should document and collect information on FGM and its associated complications in a consistent and rigorous way.

3. Share that information systematically: The NHS should develop protocols for sharing information about girls at risk of – or girls who have already undergone – FGM with other health and social care agencies, the Department for Education and the police.

4. Empower frontline professionals: Develop the competence, knowledge and awareness of frontline health professionals to ensure prevention and protection of girls at risk of FGM. Also ensure that health professionals know how to provide quality care for girls and women who suffer complications of FGM.

5. Identify girls at risk and refer them as part of child safeguarding obligation: Health professionals should identify girls at risk of FGM as early as possible. All suspected cases should be referred as part of existing child safeguarding obligations. Sustained information and support should be given to families to protect girls at risk.

6. Report cases of FGM: All girls and women presenting with FGM within the NHS must be considered as potential victims of crime, and should be referred to the police and support services.

7. Hold frontline professionals accountable: The NHS and local authorities should systematically measure the performance of frontline health professionals against agreed standards for addressing FGM and publish outcomes to monitor the progress of implementing these recommendations.

8. Empower and support affected girls and young women (both those at risk and survivors): This should be a priority public health consideration; health and education professionals should work together to integrate FGM into prevention messages (especially those focused on avoiding harm,

e.g. NSPCC 'Pants' Campaign, Personal, Social and Health Education, extracurricular activities for young people).

9. Implement awareness campaign: The government should implement a national public health and legal awareness publicity campaign on FGM, similar to previous domestic abuse and HIV campaigns.

Another critical front-line body, the Royal College of General Practitioners (RCGP), was not involved in the original publication, but is now liaising with the other Royal Colleges to take this agenda forward.

In evidence to the Vaz Inquiry (2014) the RCGP reported that GPs have a specific code for recording FGM and have a duty to refer patients to the relevant bodies such as the police, social services and mental health support, but also explored a number of potential barriers to FGM identification and intervention by GPs, including cultural sensitivities, the need to maintain patient confidentiality and concerns about the consequences of referral to the police and other agencies in cases where there is room for doubt – a concern which, it was suggested by the Home Affairs Select Committee,[13, 14] lies squarely with the law enforcement agencies, not clinicians.

In general accordance with the *Intercollegiate Recommendations*, the RCGP also proposes the following strategies to move forward,[15] some of which (for example engaging in communities and developing the evidence base) are already being actioned:

-   developing specific care pathways for FGM that involve health, education and social services;
-   developing a way for general practice and other relevant health bodies to identify those at risk from FGM;
-   engaging with affected communities by identifying and supporting people to work in a culturally sensitive way within the affected communities;
-   making culturally sensitive specialist FGM services available, especially for long-term psychological consequences, including post-traumatic stress disorder;
-   publicising available support services such as the dedicated NSPCC helpline;
-   improving the evidence base through research into the epidemiology of FGM in the UK, its association with other forms of child abuse, long-term outcomes for those affected, and the effectiveness of interventions.

Despite this plethora of expert recommendations, however, achieving cohesion to ensure that children's interests and safety are always the core rationale for everything which is done remains a challenge. Dr Maureen Baker, then Chair of the RCGP, expressed this failure of coordination clearly in her 2014 statement:

> The RCGP views FGM as child abuse and believes that it should be treated as such by all governmental agencies. But we do not yet feel that child protection and combating FGM are properly strategically aligned.
>
> We also have significant concerns over the lack of detailed data on the prevalence of FGM within the UK, as planning of services cannot be adequately undertaken without knowledge of the scale of the problem.[16]

The evidence to date (early 2015) continues to illustrate a considerable gap between ambition and reality, sometimes still in general child protection as well as, more specifically, in regard to FGM.

All the relevant agencies would assert sincerely that their work maintains children's interests centre stage, but they do not all identify and prioritise these interests in the same way; nor do they all share similar operational regimes.

Health, education, law, welfare, social services and many other elements must come into play in taking care of children, but these elements are not all the same. Legal status, funding sources, management structures, training requirements and accountability, to give just some examples, may vary considerably between different institutions and bodies. The principle – safeguarding – is agreed, but how to effect that is a complex matter as yet not resolved.

Connecting Front-line Services to Protection and Enforcement

In all circumstances where FGM is suspected, or a possible risk, the police and social services are the agencies with formal powers to protect or take forward allegations of FGM, but they are rarely the agencies which first learn about the suspected risk or crime. Staff in schools or clinics are more likely to be the first to know.

The problem then, as generally identified, is how to connect the suspicions or fears of front-line professionals in health and education with those other professionals who have direct legal and formal powers to deal with them.

The complexities of this connection have been noted previously. As noted (p. 232), amongst those who may or should be notified of concerns around child abuse, and FGM specifically, are:

- the local Social Services Department (telephone number from the Town Hall);
- the local Police Child Protection Unit (or 999 in an emergency);
- the NSPCC (0800 028 3550 – for adults seeking general advice or referral on FGM);
- ChildLine (0800 1111 – for concerned or anxious children);
- the Local Safeguarding Children Board;
- and, if there are fears that a girl may be taken abroad for FGM, the Foreign and Commonwealth Office (020 7008 1500).

The mechanisms for prevention, protection and prosecution all exist, but how are these best applied in the context of FGM, a crime or risk rarely if ever reported by those exposed to it? The summary pathways, both for children at any sort of risk (for example[17]), and for FGM,[18] have been clearly articulated by a number of bodies, and are freely available for reference online – if one is aware they exist, and knows how and where to search for them.

The Coram Children's Legal Centre CP System provides a clear flow-chart and further detail of referral paths.[19]

Essentially, the pathways involve an assessment of the immediacy of the risk (or potential seriousness of the suspected act) and then a series of steps, often including a Section 47 Investigation[20] to establish the circumstances within which it is feared a child is at risk of 'significant harm'.[21] Section 47 Investigations are one of the duties placed by the Children Act 1989[22] on local authorities. They take the form of an in-depth assessment of the nature of a child's needs, and of parental ability to meet those needs.

Normally, a 'strategy discussion'[23] will be held between the social (children's) services, education, health and other relevant agencies and then, if the concerns are deemed plausible, a Child Protection Conference[24] must be held within 15 days.

In the case of a potential and serious emergency (such as the risk to a girl of FGM during a 'holiday') a Family Court can be asked under Section 31 of the Children Act 1989 to place a Care Order,[25] or the local authority (or any other authorised person such as an NSPCC officer, a designated police officer or concerned citizen) can apply to the Family Court for an Emergency Protection Order (EPO);[26] but this is regarded as an emergency measure only to be applied where essential to the immediate safety of the child. (We noted in Chapter 8 that the planned Civil Protection Orders[27] to make safe girls at risk of FGM, alongside those at risk of CEFM, may be a way forward.)

Similarly, under Section 46 of the Children Act 1989, the police can apply Police Protection Powers[28] to take or retain a child in a place of safety (a foster carer's home, or a hospital), but these powers are only for very short-term actions and responsibility for the child is normally passed immediately to the relevant local authority.

The Border Agency may also be alerted as a matter of urgency if there is a risk of the child being taken out of the country for FGM.[29] In this case the immediate risk to the child will be addressed by the Border Force Safeguarding and Trafficking authorities via (in 2014) 'Operation Limelight', a proactive airside operation looking at inbound and outbound flights to 'countries of prevalence' for FGM.[30]

Similar arrangements may be put in place where it is thought a girl has already undergone FGM, either in the UK – where she must receive immediate medical and social care – or for investigations to be undertaken as she returns via Immigration from abroad.

In all these cases it would be expected – and will probably soon, should mandatory reporting become law, be legally required – that the police are also notified, via the guidance already in place and the anticipated pathways shortly to be introduced.

Making the System Work

But expectations of multi-agency engagement have proven very difficult to meet in the current contexts. Various pilot schemes are therefore being set up to bridge that gap, including one involving up to six London boroughs over two years.[31]

This pilot programme,[32] initiated in 2014, involves liaison between Children and Families Across Borders (CFAB), the London Mayor's Office for Policing and Crime (MOPAC),[33] the Metropolitan Police, NHS England, the Royal College of Midwives and some non-governmental organisations (Equality Now, FORWARD, Imkaan and the NSPCC). It aims to develop practical mechanisms for social work intervention, using powers already available for example under the Children Act 1989, to improve FGM child protection investigations and prosecutions.

The initial focus is maternity clinics and data about patients. Medical staff are well placed to know which expectant mothers have had FGM and which have daughters – who are potentially at risk because women with FGM are often more likely to inflict it also on their own daughters. The task, shared by health and social workers, will then be to establish referral pathways and to pilot development with the local authorities of a dedicated risk assessment protocol that recognises FGM-specific protective and aggravating factors.

All families within the identified cohort will receive literature about the damage FGM causes and about the penalties for inflicting it.

The families believed to be most likely to impose FGM will receive direct attention from social workers, who will escalate matters with the police and, if appropriate, the Crown Prosecution Service, should they suspect that FGM is scheduled or may have occurred. The next step may be alerting the Border Agency if there are fears the girl may be taken abroad, or a request for a child protection medical examination to ascertain whether she has had FGM.

At the very least it is hoped the development of this model will increase Section 47 interventions to help protect girls and infants potentially at risk; and that it will also identify more actively women who have already had FGM and require support, both for themselves and in their decision not to permit FGM on their daughters.

Local Safeguarding Children Boards

Whilst, however, pilot programmes are valuable and can inform good practice, the core challenge remains how to ensure that the full potential of all available strategies against child abuse (and the abuse of vulnerable adults) is brought to bear. The UK record in this respect to date, as the numbers of women and girls at risk increases annually, is abysmal.

Delivering competent and effective protection from, and care for those who have, FGM must sit fully and overtly within the context of formal mechanisms which address abuse. To many of those engaged in FGM eradication the issues are moral and engagement driven, but in governance terms they must also be about professional delivery, resourcing, coherence and accountability.

It is therefore very important that programmes to prevent FGM in the UK are fundamentally located within the formal frameworks which exist to prevent all forms of, especially, child abuse.

The Local Safeguarding Children Boards (LSCBs)[34] – one for each local authority in England and Wales – were set up in 2006 as a result of the Children Act 2004.[35] This Act was in part a response to the publication of the 2003 report[36] by Lord Laming (former chief inspector of the Social Services Inspectorate[37]) on his inquiry,[38, 39] into the torture and murder at the hands of an aunt and her partner of eight-year-old Victoria Climbié in London in 2000.

LSCBs have subsequently become key at the local authority level in establishing partnerships to safeguard and promote the welfare of children. LSCB partners are required (at least in theory) to hold each other to account and ensure that safeguarding children remains high on the agenda of every locality of the country.

In her report, *The Munro Review of Child Protection: A child-centred system* (2011),[40] Professor Eileen Munro concluded that, to avoid future tragedies, instead of 'doing things right' (that is, following procedures), the system must be focused on 'doing the right thing' (that is, checking whether children and young people are being helped). She added that Local Safeguarding Children Boards are 'well placed to identify emerging problems through learning from practice and to oversee efforts to improve services in response'.

Professor Munro also challenged some beliefs about the child protection system, which she identified as including the mistaken opinion that the complexity and associated uncertainty of child protection work can be eradicated; a readiness, in high-profile public inquiries into the death of a child, to focus on professional error rather than on the underlying causes of the error; and the undue importance given to performance indicators and targets which provide only part of the picture of practice, so drawing attention to process over the quality and effectiveness of help given.

It would be reasonable to think that the factors mitigating against general good practice in protecting children from abuse apply also to some aspects of the prevention of FGM in the UK. Thus, the mapping by LSCBs of local organisations, including voluntary and community services, is essential in protecting children from FGM as much as from any other harm. This is especially so as the government becomes increasingly committed to multi-agency and multi-funding arrangements which require voluntary and community sector organisations to be much more involved in the running of public services.

It is important, however, to note also the findings for instance of the 2011 Care and Social Services Inspectorate Wales (CSSIW) *Joint Inspection of Local Safeguarding Children Boards*.[41] The CSSIW acknowledges that the 'huge amount of work' and 'significant legislative, organisational and practice change' since Lord Laming's Inquiry was published in 2003 means that children are now better safeguarded and protected.

The CSSIW inspectors found that generally LSCBs were 'not effectively fulfilling their responsibilities as set out in Section 31 (1) of the Children Act 2004'.[42] The report examines the reasons for this failure to deliver in some detail, but they may be summarised as relating to leadership, governance and accountability, strategic direction, structures, funding, performance management and quality assurance and citizen engagement – engaging with children, young people and others.

The commentary here on funding is similar to that implicit in the references to more widely based funding above. The CSSIW inspectors expressed their concerns thus:

> To function effectively LSCBs need to be supported with sufficient and reliable resources. The Children Act 2004 places an obligation on statutory

LSCB partners to support the operation of the LSCB either through direct funding or through the provision of staff, goods, services, accommodation or other resources. LSCB member organisations are together responsible for determining what resources are needed and how they will be provided. In practice, few LSCBs had agreed long term appropriate funding formulae and budgetary mechanisms. Many relied too heavily on the local authority to fund its activities. This is unsustainable and further reinforces the misconception that LSCBs are primarily the responsibility of local authorities. The funding arrangements for LSCBs have been a source of tension and dispute since their creation and this inspection confirmed that this continues to be the case. For LSCBs to function effectively there is a need to have in place secure arrangements which ensure appropriate levels of funding and resourcing to enable them to fulfil their responsibilities. (para 15)

This concern resonates with the National Assembly for Wales Health, Wellbeing and Local Government Committee's *Inquiry into Local Safeguarding Children Boards in Wales* view[43] that in order for LSCBs to operate effectively, their funding arrangements need to be secure; and that the creation of a funding formula is the best way to ensure that partnership (paras 171, 172).

And, returning to the CSSIW inspectorate, we find a similar position:

There is a need for clear strategic direction at a national level with well defined objectives and outcomes, which also facilitate local decision making to meet the needs of children in their local communities. LSCBs must be enabled to effectively harness the collective resources, professional skills and knowledge of all agencies in safeguarding and protecting children. In return they must become clearly and publically accountable for their work to their local communities and nationally. (para 23)

Similar findings seem in early 2015 to be emerging from work by the English-based Association of Independent Chairs of LSCBs.[44] There is little reason to suppose that the findings for Wales would not also apply to England. If that is so, the LSCBs, it seems, have very considerable overall potential to deliver safeguarding, but they are not as yet producing the evidence to demonstrate substantial effectiveness. Their governance is fragile, their financial position precarious and their influence weak.

Taking cognisance of the inter-agency and intercollegiate documentation, what applies to the LSCBs in respect of safeguarding overall may be even more the case in respect of the prevention of FGM. In the immediate interim, however, LSCBs remain the best prospect for achieving progress in programmes against FGM, if they can be empowered, structured, helped and funded to find ways to deliver effectively.

Varying Professional Perspectives

Secure, nationally supported, properly accountable UK-wide public health and other strategies to eradicate FGM are required as a matter of urgency: the current commitment to a national action plan will be a start, but alone not enough. Considerable work remains to be done, and a number of fundamental difficulties must be resolved, to bring about a convincing narrative on the implementation, meaningfully, of the much-promoted multi-agency approach.

Amongst the challenges is the reconciling of different professional perspectives. These differences are starkly illustrated by the variance in views about mandatory reporting, whether of FGM or other types of child abuse. As we have seen, whilst for instance human rights lawyers promote strongly the requirement for reporting, others on the ground (midwives, social workers, general practitioners and paediatricians and so on) are resistant; and these disparities are made even more complex by the wider differences in positioning of, say, adults who were abused when at school (pro-mandating, seeking prosecutions) and many of those in Britain who as a child underwent FGM at the hands of close relatives (often very unwilling to name, or instigate legal action against, their own families).

To a degree, differences on the professional front can be explained (as again we have noted) by the immediacy or distance between the subject of concern and the advocate for one course of action or another; it is easier to demand reporting in the abstract than to do it in respect of a real person who has come for support.

Victims who have experienced abuse by teachers, priests, or others who have betrayed children in an official capacity usually seek to establish distance and retribution; those who are abused by their own families in the name of 'love' are less – though not always – likely to see this as a way forward. Justice and prevention do not always sit easily together.

On another level, there is the inevitability of professional and organisational turf wars. Each interest seeks to protect its influence and resources, to establish boundaries which permit those with the interest to operate as freely (and, in their own terms, effectively) as possible; and this is especially so when feelings run high and/or when resources and leeway are scant.

For all these reasons it is critical that rules of conduct and engagement are, with due regard to all concerned, established clearly and at a high level of applicability by legislators and those who implement the legislation.

As past events so sadly demonstrate, 'guidelines' alone will not protect children from harm. Only crystal-clear legislation backed by serious resourcing, training and support can begin to do that.

Discuss this chapter at http://nofgmukbook.com/2015/01/29/chapter-10-prevention-social-services-and-multi-agency-work/.

Endnotes

All weblinks accessed on 1 March 2015.

1   Home Office et al. (2014) New Government Measures to End FGM. *GOV.UK*, 6 February. Available at: https://www.gov.uk/government/news/new-government-measures-to-end-fgm.

2   Gove, M. (2014) Letter to Headteachers. *GOV.UK*, 2 April. Available at: https://www.gov.uk/government/uploads/system/uploads/attachment_data/file/309593/KCSiE_letter.pdf.

3   Topping, A. (2013) NSPCC Launches Helpline to Protect Girls from Female Genital Mutilation. *Guardian*, 23 June. Available at: http://www.theguardian.com/society/2013/jun/24/nspcc-helpline-girls-female-genital-mutilation.

4   Home Office, Department for Education, Featherstone, L. (2014) Female Genital Mutilation: Guidelines to protect children and women. *GOV.UK*, 22 July. Available at: https://www.gov.uk/government/uploads/system/uploads/attachment_data/file/216669/dh_124588.pdf.

5   Batty, D. (2009) Timeline: Baby P case. *Guardian*, 7 October. Available at: http://www.theguardian.com/society/2009/may/22/baby-p-timeline.

6   Pitas, C. (2014) UPDATE 2 – UK Kids' TV Star Rolf Harris Jailed for Child Abuse. *Reuters*, 4 July. Available at: http://www.reuters.com/article/2014/07/04/britain-harris-idUSL6N0PF2NU20140704.

7   Norfolk, A. (2014) 130 Private Schools in Child Abuse Scandal. *The Times*, 20 January. Available at: http://www.thetimes.co.uk/tto/news/uk/article3980201.ece.

8   Vallely, P. (2013) The Oxford Child Sex Abuse Verdict Highlights a Cultural Problem, but not a Specifically Muslim One. *Independent*, 15 May. Available at: http://www.independent.co.uk/voices/commentators/the-oxford-child-sex-abuse-verdict-highlights-a-cultural-problem-but-not-a-specifically-muslim-one-8616370.html.

9   Home Office, Department for Education, Featherstone, L. (2014) Female Genital Mutilation: Guidelines to protect children and women. *GOV.UK*, 22 July. Available at: https://www.gov.uk/government/publications/female-genital-mutilation-multi-agency-practice-guidelines.

10   Home Office, Department for Education, Featherstone, L. (2014) Female Genital Mutilation: Guidelines to protect children and women. *GOV.UK*, 22 July. Available at: https://www.gov.uk/government/publications/female-genital-mutilation-multi-agency-practice-guidelines.

11 RCM, RCN, RCOG, Equality Now, UNITE (2013) *Tackling FGM in the UK: Intercollegiate recommendations for identifying, recording, and reporting*. London: Royal College of Midwives. Available at: https://www.rcm.org.uk/sites/default/files/FGM_Report.pdf.

12 RCM, RCN, RCOG, Equality Now, UNITE (2013) *Tackling FGM in the UK: Intercollegiate recommendations for identifying, recording, and reporting*. London: Royal College of Midwives. Available at: https://www.rcm.org.uk/sites/default/files/FGM_Report.pdf.

13 House of Commons Home Affairs Committee (2014) Female Genital Mutilation: The case for a national action plan. *House of Commons House of Commons London: The Stationery Office Limited*, 25 June. Available at: http://www.publications.parliament.uk/pa/cm201415/cmselect/cmhaff/201/201.pdf.

14 Bentham, M. (2014) Keith Vaz Accuses GPs of Failing Girl Victims. *London Evening Standard*, 8 May. Available at: http://www.standard.co.uk/news/health/keith-vaz-accuses-gps-of-failing-girl-victims-9336401.html.

15 RCGP (2014) *Female Genital Mutilation is Child Abuse and should be Dealt with as Safeguarding Issue, says GPs*. Available at: http://www.rcgp.org.uk/news/2014/february/female-genital-mutilation-is-child-abuse-and-should-be-dealt-with-as-safeguarding-issue.aspx.

16 RCGP (2014) *Female Genital Mutilation is Child Abuse and should be Dealt with as Safeguarding Issue, says GPs*. Available at: http://www.rcgp.org.uk/news/2014/february/female-genital-mutilation-is-child-abuse-and-should-be-dealt-with-as-safeguarding-issue.aspx.

17 Coram Children's Legal Centre (2015) *CP System*. Available at: http://www.protectingchildren.org.uk/cp-system/.

18 EndTheFear.co.uk (2015) *Female Genital Mutilation (FGM) Resources*. Available at: http://www.endthefear.co.uk/media/uploads/fgm/story.html.

19 Coram Children's Legal Centre (2015) *CP System*. Available at: http://www.protectingchildren.org.uk/cp-system/.

20 Coram Children's Legal Centre (2015) *Section 47 Investigation*. Available at: http://www.protectingchildren.org.uk/cp-system/initial-assessment/s47-investigation/.

21 Coram Children's Legal Centre (2015) *Child Likely to Suffer Significant Harm*. Available at: http://www.protectingchildren.org.uk/cp-system/initial-assessment/child-likely-to-significant-harm/.

22 UK Government (1989) *Children Act 1989*. Available at: http://www.legislation.gov.uk/ukpga/1989/41/contents.

23 Coram Children's Legal Centre (2015) *Strategy Discussion*. Available at: http://www.protectingchildren.org.uk/cp-system/initial-assessment/strategy-discussion/.

24 Coram Children's Legal Centre (2015) *Initial Child Protection Case Conference*. Available at: http://www.protectingchildren.org.uk/cp-system/initial-assessment/initial-child-protection-case-conference-and-recommendation/.

25   Coram Children's Legal Centre (2015) *Care Orders*. Available at: http://www. protectingchildren.org.uk/cp-system/proceedings-process/care-order/.

26   Coram Children's Legal Centre (2015) *Appropriate Emergency Action*. Available at: http://www.protectingchildren.org.uk/cp-system/child-in-need/appropriate-emergency-action.

27   Ministry of Justice (2014) *Female Genital Mutilation: Proposal to introduce a civil protection order*. Available at: https://consult.justice.gov.uk/digital-communications/female-genital-mutilation-proposal-to-introduce-a.

28   Coram Children's Legal Centre (2015) *Police Protection Powers*. Available at: http:// www.protectingchildren.org.uk/cp-system/child-in-need/police-protection-powers/.

29   The Afro News (2014) Specialist Border Force Teams Deployed to UK Airports and Ports to Fight FGM. *TheAfroNews.eu*, 24 July. Available at: http://www. theafronews.eu/news/uk-news/3070-specialist-border-force-teams-deployed-to-uk-airports-and-ports-to-fight-fgm.html.

30   Border Force (2014) FGM: Border Force Targets 'High Risk' Flights at Heathrow to Stop Female Genital Mutilation. *GOV.UK*, 9 May. Available at: https:// www.gov.uk/government/news/fgm-border-force-targets-high-risk-flights-at-heathrow-to-stop-female-genital-mutilation.

31   CFAB (2014) *FGM and Statutory Child Protection – a briefing for Independent LSCB Chairs*. Available at: www.lscbchairs.org.uk/sitedata/files/FGM_briefing_Feb2014.docx.

32   Puffett, N. (2014) Major Crackdown on FGM to Launch in London. *Children & Young People Now*, 11 April. Available at: http://www.cypnow.co.uk/cyp/news/1143389/major-crackdown-fgm-launch-london.

33   Available at: https://www.london.gov.uk/priorities/policing-crime.

34   Safe Network (2015) *Find out about what Local Safeguarding Children Boards (LSCBs) are*. Available at: http://www.safenetwork.org.uk/training_and_awareness/pages/lscbs.aspx.

35   UK Government (2004) *Children Act 2004*. Available at: http://www.legislation. gov.uk/ukpga/2004/31/contents.

36   Laming, L. (2003) The Victoria Climbié Inquiry Report. *House of Commons Health Committee*, 5 June. Available at: http://www.publications.parliament.uk/pa/cm200203/cmselect/cmhealth/570/570.pdf.

37   Social Services Inspectorate (2003) The Social Services Inspectorate – Who we are and what we do 2003 edition. *Department of Health*. Available at: http://webarchive. nationalarchives.gov.uk/20130107105354/http:/www.dh.gov.uk/prod_consum_dh/groups/dh_digitalassets/@dh/@en/documents/digitalasset/dh_4011303.pdf.

38   BBC News (2002) The Victoria Climbié Inquiry: Inquiry Conclusions. *BBC*, 9 June. Available at: http://news.bbc.co.uk/1/hi/in_depth/uk/2002/victoria_climbie_inquiry/default.stm.

39   Laming, L. (2003) The Victoria Climbie Inquiry Report. *The Stationery Office*, January. Available at: https://www.gov.uk/government/uploads/system/uploads/attachment_data/file/273183/5730.pdf.

40 Munro, E. (2011) The Munro Review of Child Protection: Final Report. *Department for Education*, May. Available at: https://www.gov.uk/government/uploads/system/uploads/attachment_data/file/175391/Munro-Review.pdf.

41 Health, Wellbeing and Local Government Committee (2010) Inquiry into Local Safeguarding Children Boards in Wales. *National Assembly for Wales*, November. Available at: http://www.assemblywales.org/cr-ld8312-e.pdf.

42 Health, Wellbeing and Local Government Committee (2010) Inquiry into Local Safeguarding Children Boards in Wales. *National Assembly for Wales*, November. Available at: http://www.assemblywales.org/cr-ld8312-e.pdf.

43 Health, Wellbeing and Local Government Committee (2010) Inquiry into Local Safeguarding Children Boards in Wales. *National Assembly for Wales*, November. Available at: http://www.assemblywales.org/cr-ld8312-e.pdf.

44 http://www.lscbchairs.org.uk/ (report due April 2015).

11 UK Politics and the Media

There are various participants in the journey to end female genital mutilation in the UK. Most, but certainly not all, would align with the declared, socially progressive assumptions of this text. All except the most radical apologist or traditionalist seek somehow to eradicate FGM. The commonality of aim but discrepancies of perspective do, however, come into sharp relief when issues of politics, media and culture are considered.

The central players seeking directly to end FGM in the UK can be characterised as:

- people who become active because they have experienced, or know about people who have experienced, FGM;
- people who are already community activists and become aware through their involvement generally that FGM must be stopped;
- people who have professional or other formal roles in communities and the public sector (teachers, nurses, youth and faith leaders, police and others in public service) who must address FGM as a part of their wider responsibilities;
- people who become directly involved in campaigns through academic or policy research;
- people who have a direct professional responsibility to eradicate FGM (obstetric, other clinical, public health, education, social work and legal experts in this specific field).

Alongside these, there are others who have become involved in less 'hands on' direct ways. Such people include:

- voluntary and community group/NGO personnel in wider fields who lobby and take forward action to stop FGM;
- authors, playwrights, artists and others who write or produce fictional or semi-factual books, theatrical productions, films and other artistic/cultural materials to portray the realities of FGM, using in their productions either community volunteers or professionals;

- academics and policy researchers who produce reports, papers, books and other evidence and research-based materials which include aspects of FGM;
- journalists (print and other media) who report and/or campaign for the eradication of FGM;
- politicians (local and national) who choose, or are urged, to address the issues.

It is obvious that the nature and degree of engagement by all these different people will vary.

Some of them will perceive FGM as a public health (epidemiological) and educational or enforcement preoccupation; others may view it as a personal obligation, crusade or as a socio-cultural matter, with little interest in the wider and generic issues.

And whatever the perception, almost all these perspectives are to some degree context bound. The same beliefs, observations or acts may have different significance and outcomes, depending on the location and position of the person involved. People will see things variously, in different lights.

Ideas and actions mean different things in different places; but the translations and re-interpretational aspects of context in the challenge to eradicate FGM are often overlooked.

This can give rise to problems; or it may indeed open up opportunities to make progress.

Thus, as we saw in Chapter 3 'Perceptions and Beliefs Over Time', rational–legal and scientific arguments against FGM are quite literally 'meaningless' within deeply traditional communities, but the same positions may – though as the evidence about levels of 'readiness' in different places for change[1] tells us, not always – become persuasive in the right, facilitating context if people from those communities have had formal Western-style education or a range of other experiences beyond traditional ways of life. In changed circumstances those who previously endorsed FGM may, with support, become ambassadors for eradication.

To take advantage of a given situation, you have to be aware of it; and to be aware you need to have had different experiences to compare. Even in countries like the UK, such exposure to differing considerations has not been and still is not available to all who experience, practise, resist or even work against FGM. We do not start from a level playing field, let alone the exact same one.

Nor are the reasons for engagement, beyond the desire to address issues around FGM, the same for everyone. Some of the different objectives of those involved may be:

- to identify and support women and girls in the UK who resist FGM;
- to support women and girls in traditionally practising countries who resist FGM;
- to identify and support women and girls in the UK who have experienced FGM;
- to support women and girls in other places who have experienced FGM;
- to lobby and/or secure services which address the harm of FGM in the UK;
- to lobby and/or secure services which address the harm of FGM elsewhere;
- to acknowledge and/or address issues which arise from having experienced FGM;
- to inform practising communities about the nature and hazards of FGM;
- to inform society at large about the nature and hazards of FGM;
- to encourage research (medical, psychological or social) about FGM;
- to increase community leadership influence or gain political kudos;
- to earn a living or create work for others;
- to develop or extend one's professional skills or markets, whether as students or as experienced practitioners;
- to find and report 'news' or stories about FGM as a journalist;
- to make a statement or illustrate a point about different sorts or categories of people.

Many of these objectives are consistent – multiple reasons for engagement are probably common – but they do encourage different ways of looking at the challenges to which FGM gives rise. Some reasons are humanitarian and some are much more instrumental.

With FGM as with all other concerns there is often a mixture of high-mindedness, personal positioning and economics. Of necessity, motives are generally complicated.

The study of FGM is not as yet a properly acknowledged, cohesive field of work or research. The very fact that even now every news report, policy paper or discussion has to start with an introduction explaining what FGM entails demonstrates the immaturity of the topic in popular, public and policy discourse.

Identikit general introductions on every occasion do not occur in the discourse of established specialist disciplines.

But FGM as a field of study and endeavour is still in its infancy; it does not to date have a recognised paradigm. An articulated framework for analysis, development and implementation continues to be elusive.

The announcement in May 2013 of plans for the first university chair in FGM,[2] to be held in Paris with support from the Global Alliance against FGM

(GA-FGM)[3, 4] and GIZ, the German Agency for International Cooperation,[5] represents a big step forward, as are the REPLACE/DAPHNE[6] programmes (the 2013–15 REPLACE2[i] has been led by a team from Coventry University[7]), but there remains a long way to go to establish FGM as a mainstream field for academic research and development.

In UK communities where FGM continues, people not directly affected, even those with responsibilities to protect the vulnerable, may still in 2015 be unclear about what FGM entails.

Sending out the Message

All these factors play their part in shaping the ways in which FGM is seen. There is no well-defined, distinct or settled picture, and this makes for a variety of difficulties when working with the media or trying to develop policy and plans.

Simply agreeing what to call FGM may become a problem; disputes about nomenclature are not uncommon. Accusations of disrespect or even of racism between survivors, community activists and professionals may also arise over terminology, resourcing and other more detailed matters. Basic issues such as whether certain colloquial terms for FGM are in some contexts admissible (as 'translation', to ease understanding), or are inadmissible (because they might seem to promote acceptability) are not to date fully resolved.

The question of the various statuses of women who have experienced FGM continues also to be challenging. Clearly they were initially 'victims' of a crime, but for many who later speak out it is personally critical that they be referred to as 'survivors' – a choice which is absolutely theirs courageously to make. But does this speak to uninformed observers in the same way it speaks to those in the know?

Does it suggest to some observers that FGM is something, like many medical conditions, from which those who wish to can 'recover', rather than delivering unambiguously the message that FGM is a criminal act perpetuated on defenceless children? How can we best publicly articulate, for those who must unequivocally be told, that the 'FGM status' of a brave and determined adult woman is very different from that of a powerless small girl?

At this point in developments, and to a degree, all this is inevitable. FGM is a hothouse of cultural disparities, people who have experienced the trauma of FGM, sometimes ill-informed and sometimes unsupported public

---

i   For which the present writer is a member of the advisory board.

sector workers, media and political pundits with a variety of motives, and confused members of the general public.

Outside the professional bodies and, to an extent, the NGOs, there is little overall consensus about what to think or where to go next. Should the UK priority for eradication be punishment or prevention? Is the problem religion or culture? How close is the connection with immigration? Why is the UK involved in international efforts to stop FGM? Any or all of these questions may arise from a cursory glance at the news.

And, crucially, can FGM be eradicated in the UK before it is eradicated globally?

Tanya Barron, chief executive of Plan UK (one of the organisations which has (in 2014/15) taken a lead in the UK charge against FGM), has suggested that FGM will not stop in Britain until it has stopped 'in Africa'; and this has also been the message, shared by Home Secretary Theresa May, of Lynne Featherstone,[8] in 2014 the Minister for International Development.[9] Others, this writer included, might draw on evidence elsewhere[10] to suggest this is not necessarily the case.

The UK situation is different from that of the traditionally practising nations – there is stronger governance, and public services are in place across the whole nation in most Western countries. To identify FGM activity, the same resolute focus could be put to work as is applied, say, to the detection of small drugs dealing, another crime that occurs within communities everywhere in close-knit groups. And inducement to alternative behaviours is always possible, where political will to change the situation meaningfully within potentially practising communities is there.

Further, determined efforts to deliver change in illegal behaviours can achieve success almost anywhere if policing, rooting out and prosecution are applied unrelentingly – and especially in matters such as FGM, which is a crime committed knowingly, only after careful preparation.

Cultural change can surely follow from enforcement, as well as the converse. Whatever else is being done, enforcement may need to be one of the earlier strategies, when children's lives and futures are at stake.

Segmenting the 'Message Market'

Market segmentation is a technique used in commerce and business which can also be applied to public health and similar issues. Essentially, the 'segmentation' is a strategy which divides a broad target market population (such as the general public, in this case) into subsets of consumers who have common needs and priorities. Strategies to reach and deliver the message (for example, stop FGM) are then designed for each component subset of the target general population, or 'consumers'.

One challenge for the erasure of FGM is that barely any analysis at the level of segmentation has been undertaken. The discipline is nascent and at the operational level disjointed. In broad terms it might be said that exhortations to adopt a multi-agency approach are interpreted by each agency to mean 'do what professionals/community leaders in my team think best'.

This position is not unique to eradicating FGM – it can be found in many social care and health settings – but it may be more of a challenge in situations such as the one currently under consideration, where the voices of 'survivors' and others (not of all them victims of the crime) with influence of varying sorts within traditionally practising communities are particularly critical in determining outcomes.

What follows is, therefore, an analysis of the nature, interests and influence of some of the 'stop FGM' message subsets. For ethical and privacy reasons the discussion here is largely unreferenced and anonymised. It should be read simply as suggestions for further analysis, rather than as a definitive indication of how FGM messages might in the future be promulgated. The intention is solely to raise awareness of some aspects of this challenge, beginning with individuals directly affected, and progressing outwards, to large-scale political and media perspectives.

Victims, Survivors and Perpetrators

If reported figures on the occurrence of FGM in the UK are a reasonable representation of how many women and girls have experienced it, the number who are willing to mention or discuss FGM in public is proportionately minute. Likewise, the number of family members and friends, especially men, who publicly identify themselves in this context is tiny.

It is difficult, therefore, in the absence of serious research, to know how to approach the subject in these populations; it cannot be assumed that those who speak openly – and sometimes under significant duress – are representative of the community as a whole. The views of community 'leaders', sometimes men from faith organisations, sometimes activists, sometimes 'victims' or 'survivors', are not coherent.

Tussles to establish given vocabularies are not only about individual preferences; they are evident throughout the communities of interest which comprise the fight against FGM, and are fundamentally about extending the influence and territorial dominance of particular protagonists.

Thus, advocates with personal or direct experience of FGM may insist – as is their entitlement – that those who know it at first hand are referred to as 'survivors', and that it is 'disrespectful' (or even exploitative) to illustrate graphically the agony which FGM causes identifiable individuals. This position is completely understandable in contexts where, for instance, explicit and visual references to FGM may cause distress or even trigger flashbacks for a person who has FGM. Adding gratuitously to already massive vulnerability and distress is not acceptable.

To extend the avoidance of graphic impact so that circumvention becomes default may, however, impede progress to stop FGM. Firstly, to debunk the traditional beliefs that FGM is necessary to make a girl whole and marriageable, it is essential in traditionally practising communities to ensure that men, and so-far uninitiated girls, know what the abuse entails.

And it also needs to be made clear that women are women, regardless of their FGM status. The vocabulary of 'survival' can be shared with others who have experienced FGM to demonstrate that it need not define them. In Western societies especially men and women marry each other for reasons other than because they were genitally harmed, or not, in childhood.

Secondly, we simply do not know whether the silent majority of girls and women with FGM think in terms of 'survivors' and/or 'victims' at all. Quite possibly they do not, at least in some communities – in which case the dialogue may not always be helpful. The insistence on specific language is a powerful tool used by many (activists, professionals, the media and others involved) to take control of contexts and understandings. It is the absolute right of women who have experienced FGM to be referred to as they choose, but whether the vocabulary promotes and reflects the perceived realities of everyone thus labelled is uncertain. How this issue can be addressed respectfully in regard to those who describe themselves as survivors (or by any other name) remains currently problematic.

Thirdly – and critically in respect of deterrence and legal enforcement – the focus on FGM as a crime (and not as a naturally occurring illness) may be lost if it is seen as an act which has only 'survivors', not 'victims'. That their parents may at some level believe FGM is an 'act of love' is irrelevant to the real harm it inflicts and to the legal status of the act in the UK.[11] Children who have been violently abused are formally, in the eyes of the law, 'victims' of a crime; they are not yet in a position – assuming they haven't in fact died because of the harm – to choose to become 'survivors'.

The epidemiological patterns and public health aspects of FGM may follow broadly those of other 'social diseases', but there is also a fundamental difference because, in contrast to many medical conditions, it is inflicted knowingly, a sanctioned, premeditated act by adults on helpless children.

People who have had cancer, for instance, may also adopt the name 'survivor', but theirs is not a condition brought about by deliberately planned, intentional (and criminal) action.

Whatever its cultural rationale, FGM is fundamentally a crime and a human catastrophe; and crimes and catastrophes necessarily have 'victims' as well as 'survivors', the humanly-inflicted damage to whom (however they are named or labelled) must be articulated if in the wider community the harm is to be understood, and stopped.

In the case of FGM there may therefore be a divergence between required, necessary respect for the vulnerabilities and sensitivities of people with first-hand experience, the importance of demonstrating to those who have undergone FGM that others with the same experience have not allowed it to define them negatively, and the need to 'get the message out' so that those who commit criminal action are brought to justice, and possible future crimes are deterred.

Thus, personal and clinical care agendas for FGM are not always aligned with law enforcement or media approaches, just as they may not be in other (if not precisely parallel) instances of knowingly inflicted child abuse, famine, civic disturbance or other humanly mediated harm. The necessary balance between these different requirements – respect for those who have been hurt 'versus' justice/future deterrence – has yet to be determined; indeed, the conversation has not even really begun.

In resolving these difficult matters in specific contexts, the first point of reference will be the needs of particular individuals who have experienced the hurt, but the wider contexts are also unavoidable, if, critically, the future risk to others is to be minimised.

The quite frequently expressed requirement by self-identified survivors that others check their privilege (that is, acknowledge one's own inherent privileges and put them aside when considering social justice)[12] is legitimate, as is the advice by others within practising communities that certain modes of language and approach are best; but these cannot be the only criteria by which to determine action,[13] especially when it is to uphold the law and protect children. Further, the silencing of those adjudged to have 'privilege' may also prevent important social justice messages reaching others with influence who need to hear them.

Appropriate ways to meet the specific respect, support and care requirements of those who have experienced FGM must be recognised and delivered, but this may be a separate matter from highlighting demands to prevent it in the first place.

The engagement and advice of women who have undergone (or previously inflicted or been otherwise affected by) FGM is absolutely critical in campaigns to eradicate FGM. But so too is the engagement of others such as the men who have to date largely sidestepped these difficult matters. FGM affects everyone.

It is important to recognise that even within practising communities there may be wide variance in perceptions about the nature of FGM, and that by no means all these understandings will fit easily with the positions and approaches of many nations now which seek to purge the practice of FGM.

Albeit that without them the task of eradication is quite simply impossible, responsibility for how to proceed in these complex circumstances – ultimately the remit of the state – cannot rest alone on the shoulders of those who have found the courage to speak out and define themselves as survivors.

FGM advocacy must not be a burden resting only on those directly affected. It is the responsibility of us all, as citizens, to protect the most vulnerable, and to endorse human rights.

Consensus on who speaks for whom, in what contexts and with what authority, will be hard to achieve. Sometimes, those whose task it is to uphold the law will find that difficult decisions are necessary.

Experts, Advocates and Artists

Similar considerations may apply when it comes to advocates for and experts on the eradication of FGM. Again, segmentation is critical. As we have seen, the voices of specialist professionals must be heard; but so must those of various others who work to eradicate FGM. Context is critical in determining who is best placed to make the arguments, when.

Thus, the public engagement of young women from the relevant communities in this task has grown in recent years, and campaigns to stop the harm increasingly involve them very visibly.[14, 15] These advocates may or may not, and should not unless they actively wish to, disclose their FGM status. All have a part to play in demanding that FGM must stop.

Young people (young men as well as young women, as Leyla Hussein's Channel 4 film *The Cruel Cut* has shown[16]) are critically important when the aim is to alert other children and young adults to FGM as an issue. They can deliver the message in schools and the community in ways not available to the authorities and professionals.

Spreading the message to new audiences, which numbers of young women (supported and helped by their teachers or other mentors) have done very effectively, is not, however, the same as having formal expertise in regard to FGM. The increasing reference in media and campaigning reports to young activists as 'experts' on occasion lies uncomfortably with the concepts of professional knowledge and skills which those normally called experts might be expected to have.

Advocacy is one form of expertise, as is direct personal experience, but sometimes we have here at best a very loose fit with expertise in the conventional sense of the word. Enthusiasm, energy and authenticity, yes; 'expertise'? Probably not.

Nonetheless, young women – though not as yet many young men – do appear regularly on campaigning platforms and in news reports. For most of them (and perhaps also for their mentors) this is a very new experience. The hazards of such exposure are many[17] and there are weighty ethical considerations to be brought to bear when minors or vulnerable adults are placed directly in the public eye.

No single rule fits all situations. Inviting young people, with sustained support, to promote the message that, whatever the beliefs of the past, FGM is cruel, irrelevant to contemporary societies and relationships, and must become history, is a very important campaigning tactic; placing them in situations which require serious professional expertise or complex judgements about strategy or public policy is another.

Enthusiastic advocacy and plausible expertise are very different attributes, often required for different occasions and at different times. Segmentation and phasing of intended audiences (communities) when sending out messages via young people may be critical to credibility and longer-term success.

Other media for spreading the word about FGM are also important. Thus, a number of organisations and one or two individuals have dedicated presses for publishing material on FGM. One of these publishing houses is UnCUT/VOICES,[18] which offers a multimedia platform for dissemination of autobiographies, novels, poetry, plays and other creative work as well as research, legislation and histories of the movement.

Other media are also key in taking out the message/s about FGM. One of the UK leaders in FGM campaigns has been the *Guardian*,[ii, 19] which, under the guidance of their Multimedia Investigations Editor, Maggie O'Kane, has since 2013 produced a large output of films and other reportage, now extending and focusing on the USA, Australia and parts of Africa – especially Kenya, where the *Guardian*'s global media campaign was rolled out in October 2014 with Ban Ki-moon, Secretary General of the United Nations[20, 21] – and The Gambia, as well as the original work on FGM in Britain. Similar work has been undertaken (albeit on a lesser scale) by a number of multimedia organisations in other parts of the world.

But NGOs and other large-scale organisations, whilst they may be the most visible, are not the only activists seeking to combat FGM. Underpinning the publicly observable endeavours are large numbers of professionals (and volunteers bringing to the task professional skills) for whom stopping FGM is part of their day-to-day work.

Some of these people are at the sharp end, working in the public sector for instance as clinicians, school staff, legal personnel, community and social

ii For which FGM programme the current writer has been a writer and consultant.

workers; some approach the issues from another perspective, bringing to bear their directly creative and other skills as artists, musicians, dramatists, authors, scriptwriters and so forth.

The nature of the task varies significantly between such disperse groups of workers. The public servants, often professionals in regulated activity, usually have FGM as part of their role formal responsibilities, often also involving legal obligations; those without statutory obligations may seek to engage the imagination of individuals and groups who choose to participate in or support creative and artistic activities around exploring the realities of FGM and why it must stop. All have important parts to play, whether in practising communities or in the wider society.

So who are all these people?

In truth, they are many more than can be listed, and the roll-call changes constantly, but here are a few of the most visible thought leaders in various sectors within the field:

Leading the way (in 2014–15), at least in the public perception, are those who promote dedicated campaigns in the media to stop FGM in the wider world. Some of them are (in their preferred terms) 'survivors'; almost all are girls and women from practising communities. They represent the human face of the affliction, articulate about the harm it imposes and often understandably impatient to see change. Internationally and historically, this group includes women such as Ayaan Hirsi Ali,[22, 23] Waris Dirie,[24, 25] Khady Koita[26, 27] and Khadija Gbla.[28, 29] British survivor-campaigners include Leyla Hussein[30] and her associates, Valentine Nkoyo, Hawa Sesay[31] and Hibo Wardere.[32] Some of these campaigners also present a pressing case to provide bespoke support for those escaping or having experienced FGM.[33]

Another very significant group of clinician campaigners in the UK comprises individuals who have encountered FGM as a result of their community connections or work, rather than because of direct personal experience. Amongst those in this group is the late Efua Dorkenoo,[34, 35] who came to the UK as a teenager from Ghana, trained as a nurse and devoted much of her professional life to the eradication of FGM; her ambitions for an African-led global network (eventually entitled *The Girl Generation: together to end FGM*[36]) were realised just a week before her death, in October 2014. Others located in London include Phoebe Abe,[37] a GP who set up FGM clinics in her practice, the consultant midwife Comfort Momoh,[38] who was amongst the first to establish FGM clinics in London hospitals, and Sarah Creighton (consultant obstetrician) and Yana Richens (midwife) of the National Clinical Group,[39] founded in 2007, and patron of which was until her death in 2015 the Labour peer and crime-writer Ruth Rendell.[40]

Other non-clinicians working in London include Naana Otoo-Oyortey of FORWARD[41] and, outside London, Sarah McCulloch of the Bedford-based charity Agency for Culture and Change Management (ACCM) and organisations such as End The Fear in Manchester, Integrate Bristol, the Dignity Alert Research Forum (DARF) and the Scottish Refugee Council in Scotland, BAWSO in Wales and the Irish Family Planning Association in Dublin.

Beyond these organisations, as we have seen, are also many more with concerns about FGM, associated with health, education, social care, children and young people, police, legal, faith and other interests and services. All are seriously intent on eradicating FGM and related blights on the lives of girls and women; all work in their own ways.

And this is the point: just as in the UK there are numerous research findings, reports, records of debates, books, multi-agency guidelines and much else, all focused on the eradication of FGM, so the organisations which have embraced this remit are various and disperse.

But more time-limited or modest creative productions are also important in respect of sharing messages about FGM. One such was the BBC television *Casualty* hospital drama serial, which in 2013 carried a two-part drama about British girls at risk of being taken for FGM.[42] Whilst this is not the very first occasion on which the subject has been so covered, in 2013 there was a much wider awareness and interest in both the storyline and the more formal information which was also made available when the drama was broadcast.

There have been creative interventions in spreading the 'NoFGM' message for some years. In 2008 Tobe Levin of FORWARD Germany brought the German Girls' Theater Group to London as guests of FORWARD UK, to present *Respect: A multi-media performance*.[43] Since then this mode of sharing information about FGM has become more frequent.

Other dramatic and artistic efforts since 2013 to engage in the issues around FGM have included live production dramas entitled: *Little Stitches* by Theatre503,[44] an outline production by Queen Mary College, London, undergraduate Yvonne Ossei; *Face Up*, performed in the Channel 4 studios;[45] *Part of Me* by Borderlines at the New Vic Theatre[46] in Newcastle-under-Lyme; and a number of film productions by schoolchildren, various of which are for use in specifically educational contexts.

Sometimes these creative approaches to FGM issues stand alone for anyone to see, sometimes they are a part of formal education and information packages. They may be linked with fundraising events (such as those hosted by Garden Court Chambers[47] and elsewhere) or they may be overtly cathartic. What is significant in all these instances is that the events are likely to engage, speaking to and for people in a way which standardised formal materials cannot.

Reaching out is not simply a matter of devising material and making it available. There is an important market segmentation exercise still to be done concerning how, by whom, and with what materials, various aspects of messages about FGM might best be shared.

These differences are critical to effectively addressing FGM. They are all facets of FGM as a challenge for human rights, public health and wider community well-being, and they address variously elements of the problem which campaigning organisations, politicians and the media must consistently bear in mind.

The potential for synergy between these various professionals and players remains as yet uncertain, given the failure thus far to establish a firm framework and focused central support for action.

The role and duties of those in regulated activity and related contexts has already been considered in this text and is becoming articulated, albeit there remains much still to do. But that work is just a small, though central and essential, part of the whole.

How all these formal roles can connect with the more imaginative and engaging endeavours of the community activists and creatives is yet fully to be explored.

Parallel Campaigns

FGM is not an issue which stands alone. It is legitimately and closely linked both with other violence against women and girls, and with child cruelty and abuse in general.

Particularly significant are the related issues of forced[48] and 'early' or child marriage[49, 50, 51] (in reality, economically driven or culturally permitted paedophilia), beading[52] (also known in some instances as qualified incest[53]), breast ironing,[54] teeth-pulling[55, 56] and similar harmful traditional practices including the emerging evidence of the abuses of leblouh/gavage (force-feeding girls for early marriage)[57] and human (sex) trafficking.[58] All have become the focus of awareness-raising, not least by African women leaders, the World Health Organization and United Nations bodies. Each also has its own eradication lobby, but increasingly these issues are all being perceived as aspects of the same fundamental pattern of underlying oppression.

One development in the UK in 2014 has been the introduction of a collaboration between a range of global players, including the British NGO Options, to drive forward the eradication of FGM world-wide. The UK Government has undertaken ultimately to invest around £35 million (of which £1 million would be for UK research and programmes) via the DfID. Announcements in 2014, at the Girl Summit and on International Day of the Girl,[59] have brought considerable positive focus onto the UK Government's significant global contribution, but less attention to domestic campaigns and how they will continue to operate. Many UK domestic activists remain unsure how much support (if any) they will receive; the contribution in October 2014 in total of another £330,000 – in government spending terms, a triflingly small sum – for British work on forced marriage, FGM, research, engagement of faith leaders and related matters has for instance done little to alleviate these concerns.

Thus, Plan UK, one of the organisations collaborating in 2014 with the British then-Coalition Government to address FGM globally, also has that remit for forced and early marriage[60] (sanctioned paedophilia), along with other forms of harmful traditional practice. This double responsibility makes sense, especially in the light of shocking reports in the UK in recent years of other sorts of child abuse as well as FGM. What is less certain, however, is the depth of experience in the UK in FGM or various other aspects of these fields of some of these leading organisations – a suspected deficit which has also provoked concern or resentment amongst a number of long-established UK specialist FGM bodies.

The UK position remains therefore piecemeal. The scandals in recent years around grooming young women[61] are, for instance, another aspect of forced and early marriage, and they are also connected with the culture of so-called honour killing (murdering female family members to 'preserve' parental/male reputations).[62]

Similarly, FGM has aspects in common with the practice (increasingly reported in the UK) of witchcraft,[63] with its related beliefs that some children, boys as well as girls, are impure (or even evil) and, as sometimes in FGM, 'require' cleansing in ways which cause real and lasting harm.

Nonetheless, few UK national bodies address all these specific and culturally diverse issues, though organisations such as Afruca and the Victoria Climbié Foundation go a way towards doing so. But whilst, at least as of autumn 2014, there remains a lack of articulation between the foci and activities of these various organisations, there is generally acceptance that all have a role to play in making children, girls and sometimes also boys, safe. Their 'markets' and campaigning focus, both for messages and for support, quite often overlap.

Even these very modest sums so far allocated to UK-based work (the match-funding £1 million to be augmented, according to an announcement coinciding with the International Day of the Girl 2014,[64] by another £330,000 domestically) might, however, have greater impact were there greater grounded liaison between the many organisations and lobbies involved. With clear direction and accountability from the centre it would probably be possible, even with relatively scarce resources, to reach a very wide range of interests (segments) within the larger overall population, thus increasing both awareness of the risks to which children may be exposed, and the effectiveness of the protection and remedial recourse available.

Leadership: Taking Responsibility for Eradicating FGM in the UK

Such effectiveness and efficiencies are, however, unlikely to be achieved in the present UK context of direct competition for funding between outsourced organisations (NGOs). There is a lack of direct governmental responsibility or substantive, coherent national direction, leadership and overt accountability at top levels of influence to bolster whatever formal regulation of professional practice comes about.

One illustration of this 'hands-off' approach by the Government is apparent, for instance, in the review of DfID funding regimes undertaken in 2013 in which the degree of purdah (restricted communication during process) which the department maintains in its operations to select NGOs for collaborations and receipt of financial support[65] was criticised.

As in many other aspects of public health and social care, responsibility in the current political contexts is consistently shifted downwards, so that whatever happens it will not be the national government which is brought to account.

And it is also, one suspects, rare for the criteria that determine whether to fund organisations to include demonstrated capacity to liaise and collaborate with other, competitor NGO and independent bodies.

Big challenges such as FGM require clear overall management and firm policy and indeed political direction and investment from the top.

Nor despite its strengths is public health a viable alternative as top level management/direction, given the absence of coherent political leadership and support. Public health is a field with little potential for direct financial return and not therefore an attractive proposition to many commercial service providers. It provides little incentive for investment (funding) in the expectation of straightforward financial and business returns.

Without predetermined maximum clarity of objectives, a free market of commissioned providers is probably not the best context in which to deliver effective large-scale public health programmes and impacts.

Divides between Patriarchy and Feminism; Intactivism

At least in the instances above there is a measure of general agreement about the direction of travel. No-one in mainstream society would dispute the underlying premise of these organisations and lobbies – that is, that children must be protected from identified risks of harm.

One thing which distinguishes the stop FGM lobby from most others campaigning against child abuse is, however, that it sometimes gives rise to overt hostility and opposition. In part this comprises the claim by certain career 'anthr/apologists'[66, 67] (and some radical feminists[68] and African nationalists[69] who challenge mainstream perceptions of FGM) – a small but vocal and identifiable group – that trying to prevent FGM can be construed as an act of racism or cultural/white imperialism.

This position can be countered by the obvious fact that FGM is illegal in most countries, and in any case usually an assault on children too young to give informed consent. It is a proscribed act, regardless of any claimed defence of 'cutting'. Freedom of speech may well, ethical issues aside, extend to campaigning against current legislation; but it does not extend to knowingly flouting the law, or inciting others to do so.

More difficult are the issues around intactivism. Challenges most commonly arise when those – this writer amongst them – who also oppose male 'circumcision', more properly called male genital mutilation (MGM), are attacked online by unidentified 'intactivist' trolls. Frequently, their position is that 'feminists' care only about girls, or even that those who oppose FGM are content that boys continue to suffer genital mutilation. Often these *ad hominem (ad feminam)* attacks are posted anonymously by commentators in the United States where MGM remains a lucrative source of income for medical practitioners who have little apparent regard to the generally established levels of jeopardy which apply 'even' for the genital mutilation of boys.

The hostility of some intactivists to feminism and thus in some (not all) cases to gendered FGM campaigns is usually based on arguments around human rights and the entitlement to an intact body, at least until maturity and informed choice is possible – this is self-evidently a valid position.

The relative risks of FGM and MGM are, however, very context specific. Whilst absolutely no unnecessary risk to the health of a child can be acceptable, both MGM and some FGM campaigners often seem unaware of the real hazards of the other. This can result in a failure to understand why different styles and focus in campaigning are appropriate at different times and in different locations.

Private enquiries suggest that those in the USA who comment on FGM 'versus' MGM anonymously, as trolls – perhaps men who were traumatically circumcised themselves – may actually be afraid to reveal their identities for fear of being socially ostracised or even of endangering their employment and incomes. Similar attacks are observable on many media discussion threads about FGM in the UK, sometimes also from people in the USA and sometimes from people nearer home who wish to divert the conversation to their own MGM preoccupations. (Hence the abrupt interjection, 'Wot about the Menz?', which may be posted in an attempt to curtail this extraneous line of discussion.)

The point in any of these instances – whether nationalist or radical feminist, anthr/apologist or intactivist – is that they divert the consideration of child abuse to considerations of the (de)merits of feminism in one form or another. They variously may or may not also comprise attempts to challenge or embed notions of patriarchy, but they clearly deflect from the intended mainstream FGM agenda of the original writer, that is, the protection and care of girls and young women vulnerable to, or victims of, this particular form of harm.

To that extent FGM – and by implication related forms of harmful traditional practice – are unusual, in that there are few other types of child abuse *prevention* which come under mainstream attack, or precipitate major perceptual schisms, in Western nations.

But whilst it is easy to understand (albeit difficult to accept) that there will be people from traditional cultures, living in the West, who struggle to perceive FGM as the serious abuse it is, the fundamental disagreements between those well acquainted with the Western world are more difficult to address. For a minority of agitators who seek to disrupt online dialogue about FGM this is the point where pro- or anti- (ironically, either) feminist ideology seems to take precedence over the law and legislative structures in their thinking.

MGM defenders and objectors even apart, the necessary legal positions are well embedded (even if often not enacted), but there remains in various corners of the modern world a notion that the law may be put aside when FGM or other so-called 'sexual' violations and/or abuse – actually, criminal bodily harm – such as grooming and forced/early marriage, are under consideration.

Until that often unarticulated underlying belief, that the law need not necessarily be enforced, is firmly challenged by those who form and lead opinion on combatting FGM, it is likely that this state of affairs will continue.

But who will lead, and how? Again, a segmented approach may offer ways forward, this time examining the sources of influence which are focused on eradicating FGM. It is likely that formal deterrence (the legal system) is best placed to have the most immediate and publicly visible impact, simply because it is organisationally the most straightforward ('easy') to direct top-down towards action. That alone, however, will not be enough to secure a real shift in behaviour and fundamental cultural perceptions.

Politics and the Media

The eradication of FGM is unlikely to be achieved unless politicians (or other formal, powerful influencers) at the highest levels commit to ensuring it happens. This applies at all levels, local, national and international.

Politics is, however, a mercurial pursuit. Ideas and trends come and go, and are rarely focused squarely on the longer term – as is evidenced, amongst many other possible examples, by the difficulties so well documented of coping adequately with climate change.[70]

The first and absolute tenet of politics is that without power there is nothing. It is then imperative for all politicians that they show results in a timescale favourable to their continuing to hold this power, that is, before they need to be re-elected.

Cultural change does not fit easily into such a timescale. This is another reason why 'quick hits' such as an enquiry, reports, prosecutions, or even new laws (all with visible outcomes in a relatively short period) are easier for campaigners to achieve, and tend to be more popular with politicians, than manoeuvres to adjust big socio-economic and administrative infrastructures so that things may be better in a decade or two.

The lack of emphasis on embedded long-term change can be a problem for public health issues, of which FGM is one. The work is sometimes painstakingly slow and, unlike, say, acute medicine and pharmaceutical research, it does not hold out the prospect of return on investment and considerable financial reward for those who undertake it.

Further, if infrastructural change is in fact implemented, it may well be accompanied by serious moves on the part of the politicians around initial positioning and/or management of expectations, in the hope that any non- or negative outcomes will be minimal for those who brought about the changes, or perhaps occur well into the future. Politicians tend to be cautious about alienating voters in the short term, however worthy the longer-term cause. This is not always helpful, but such positioning is, quite simply, how politics in a democracy works; it is the nature of the game.

This is well illustrated by reference to legislation in the UK. Earlier legislation such as the 1985 Prohibition of Female Circumcision Act was first thought to be a resolution of what was then considered a matter of minority concern; the lobby to do something had been successful in that the 1985 Act was introduced, and soon the problem would disappear. There was little public interest in (or awareness of) the matter – as was still the case when the Female Genital Mutilation Acts (2003, in England, Wales and Northern Ireland; 2005 in Scotland) were introduced to remedy identified loopholes in the initial legislation.

In the UK at the start of the first decade of the twenty-first century, there was no real sense of urgency, probably because only from that point onwards did the truth begin to emerge into mainstream Western thinking: FGM occurs on industrial scales across many parts of the globe, which increasingly, because of the diaspora, include locations in the first world.

This grim truth was brought very pointedly to the attention of global leaders via the declaration, in a report by the Inter-African Committee on

Traditional Practices Affecting the Health of Women and Children[71] on 6 February 2003, of an International Day of Zero Tolerance to Female Genital Mutilation.[72] (Paragraph 244 of the IAC 2003 report tells us it 'would make great sense' to have a symbol for zero tolerance to FGM, because that would 'greatly touch the lives of others who otherwise would have had no information about it'.)

Now firmly established in the global annual calendar and reported every year by the media, this event has ensured that the realities of FGM are recognised in the West much more widely than ever before; and at the same time the immediacy of the problem has also quite literally been brought home to Western nations by, particularly, the African diaspora.

The synergy between the media and politics is well illustrated by this development. Politicians are generally keen to respond to issues which the media headline or highlight; and the media are almost always interested in what politicians do. When the subject under consideration offers opportunities for reporting strange (to Westerners) practices combined both with potential to confirm or challenge popular perceptions and the prospect, for instance, of pictures of teenage 'girl campaigners', it is inevitable that the story will take off.

And so it has, for the issue of female genital mutilation in politics and in the media.

The decade or more since the IAC's 2003 Declaration has seen massively more news about FGM, both directly as a result of this and subsequent work, and because rapidly expanding technologies have enabled the capacity to share news from around the world with an immediacy never before imagined. News of an arrest for suspected FGM in an African country reaches the public in Britain, Australia and the USA in a few hours, just as the responses of Western governments to the challenge of FGM reach some people in traditionally practising countries equally immediately.

The consequences and ramifications of such dramatic changes, globally and locally, on the politics and perceptions of FGM, are only just beginning to be understood.

Thus, the UK has seen vigorous campaigning both by some print media (*The Times*, *Guardian*, *Evening Standard* and others) and by broadcast media such as Channel 4, almost always featuring young women who may or may not have direct experience of FGM. Often, these campaigns have comprised a challenge to politicians to take action.

One such example is the 2014 *Guardian* campaigns,[iii] working with change.org and both headed up by young women from affected communities, one to persuade the then UK Secretary of State for Education, Michael Gove, to 'Tell schools to teach risks of female genital mutilation before the summer'[73]

---

iii   In which the current writer was involved.

and the other, led by Jaha Dukureh,[74] to the President of the United States of America to 'End Female Genital Mutilation in the US – Commission a prevalence report on women impacted and girls at risk'.[75]

Both campaigns employed a mix of reporting (stories about the lead figures and related FGM-focused events, information about FGM, background material, and so on) and active use of social media such as Twitter and Facebook. Hundreds of thousands of signatories were secured for each e-petition. Within a few months both achieved hugely increased public awareness as well as, to a degree, moving closer to their declared political ambitions.

Thus, in October 2014 Fahma Mohamed was, to her great credit, made *Good Housekeeping*'s outstanding young campaigner of the year, as a result of the *Guardian* UK campaign[76] – an achievement made possible via the active initial engagement of her school and the senior management of the relevant organisations, both newspaper and campaign lobbies. Success on this scale can generally be achieved only when, firstly, some work has already been undertaken to prepare the way, and, secondly, a decision is made at the critical point to commit (relatively) large-scale resources to the task.

A similar example, which did not fully achieve its end, but had serious immediate impact, was the campaign led by her friend Anj Handa to prevent the deportation to Nigeria of a Leeds-based FGM survivor, Afusat Saliu, and her two small children, one of whom was born in the UK.[77] In this instance a flash campaign to ask Virgin Atlantic[iv] not to transport them[78] triggered intense media interest[79] and helped to launch an appeal to provide for the family when they were eventually flown to Nigeria, and for the legal costs of their appeal against the decision to deport of the Secretary of State.[80] Campaigns such as these, some of them carefully planned, and some requiring almost instantaneous response, are all part of the toolkit for those working to abolish FGM and its associated human rights issues.

The results of the large e-petitions demanding action have altered the territory in the UK, the USA and beyond, whilst the Saliu case immediately exposed other recent and pending cases of peremptory deportation of FGM survivors – which in turn provided an opportunity to highlight the findings of the 2014 visit to the UK (on a four-yearly cycle) of Professor Rashida Manjoo, UN Special Rapporteur,[81, 82] when she found considerable evidence that the human rights of women are in some cases overlooked in the UK, as well as elsewhere.[83] It was also the Saliu deportation which brought to light the revelation that the Home Office keeps no record of how many women who say they are in fear of FGM are refused asylum[84] – despite the concerns of the UN Refugee Agency[85] and the European Union.[86]

---

iv   The initial contact with Virgin Atlantic arose from a suggestion by this writer.

There is vast potential to address privation and other human needs in the synergy between public demands for social change, eye-catching media crusades, the skills of the lobbyist, and political positioning and influence. (One of the most dramatic and disruptive examples of campaigning was the demonstration against FGM by Femen members, outside the Houses of Parliament in London, in 2014.[87] Whether this event achieved its claimed objectives is another matter.) Self-evidently, this potential has been increased almost infinitely by the technologies which have come to the fore in the past quarter century.

Where we previously knew almost nothing we can now discover a great deal. People with influence, or whom we must persuade, are now easily located via the World Wide Web, as are people of like mind with whom alliance must be made if global cruelties such as FGM are to be eradicated – whether these allies are located in the next town or on another continent. Common cause to eradicate FGM and similar grievous harmful practices is in this sense more easily achieved now than ever before.

Limitations and Hazards

The same forces which lead to success in media campaigns can, however, lead to other, unintended, consequences. Public interest may be sustained only at the cost of negative as well as positive impressions.

In the case of FGM and related harmful practices, the most obvious of these possible consequences is the risk of racist backlash. A minority of the wider public will use these concerns about children's safety and well-being to inflame racism, focus on stereotypes or promote rhetoric around 'immigration'.

This situation places people from the communities in question at risk of racist behaviour, harm and threats from elsewhere, and it may also make for difficulties within the practising communities themselves, in that some members will be reluctant to speak out against harmful traditions for fear of increasing hostile perceptions and inter-community strife.

Another, sometimes very serious, risk is that publicity involving named survivors is in itself hazardous. There are several accounts of young women in the UK who have been threatened with personal harm, or even death, by their own parents and other family members, for bringing 'shame' on their relatives or wider communities.

Death and comparable threats are also not uncommonly sent to others who publicise or work against FGM[v] in the UK, as well as elsewhere.

---

v   The current writer amongst them.

To date there is little evidence to suggest that the police know how to address such hazards and intimidation.

Less dramatically, but also importantly, where young people are below the age of 18 (in the UK) there is a particular formal requirement (as well as a moral/ethical one, regardless of age) to ensure the well-being of the person concerned. It is interesting in this context to note, for instance, the concerns of the *Guardian* Readers' Editor around the safety of unidentified children discussed in a column in that publication, where he notes that the legal issues are different for journalists than for professionals in regulated activity.[88] To a degree these matters are addressed in the BBC policy on the safeguarding of children and vulnerable adults.[89] Given their increasing prominence in the media, further consideration of these matters by broadcasting, print and online organisations would be helpful.

Beyond the issues of personal peril, and sometimes community shame, there are also, however, broader matters to be considered when the profile of FGM is promoted in the public consciousness.

One potential difficulty arises when FGM enmeshes in the public consciousness with the identities of the young women who agree to be figureheads for campaigns around awareness-raising and efforts to erase the practice. It has already been noted that such young people are unlikely to be 'experts' in their own rights on, say, policy development – much more likely, they will share perspectives and ideas they have gleaned from elsewhere.

Perhaps more important, though, than young people's expertise or otherwise is the possibility that campaigns around the younger generation may become perceived as more about critical but soft issues,[90] around the immediate (and very important) 'needs' of vulnerable girls, rather than equally on the fundamental generic issues of law enforcement, and less palatable aspects such as severe lifelong disablement and even death. For this reason it may be important that campaign leaders ensure a continuing public focus on the specific demands of their lobbies and petitions.

It is important, too, to recognise the ways in which FGM is played in the political arena. The issues around racism and similarly opportunist populism have already been explored, but other aspects of the politics and FGM interface are also relevant.

For some politicians the eradication of FGM is a matter of personal conviction and commitment – they are the ones who have pursued the matter from when they first realised what FGM entails.

A review of the legislation (Chapter 6) demonstrates that at the national level these initiators, people who were concerned from the start, have been from every mainstream political party.

For other politicians, the journey has reflected more closely developments in the news and the media.

To begin with there was considerable reluctance by some UK politicians to be involved (and in one or two cases, when the opportunity initially arose, as in 2011, funding was actually withdrawn from programmes to tackle issues such as FGM). But things have changed; the current position is that announcements about developments and support for programmes continue to be forthcoming – albeit much larger sums of money are at present available on the global stage than for the various small and scattered packages which contribute to UK programmes.

Whether further variations in political support will arise, if celebrity endorsement moves elsewhere, remains to be seen.

The 2014 Girl Summit,[91] where a further £25 million global investment by the UK[92] in CEFM and FGM-related programmes was formally announced,[93] was attended by many and various international figures. It was the fourth in a series of annual high-level events hosted by the prime minister to draw attention to a specific international development issue, and arguably drew the most global media attention of any such event yet.

The convention was in reality a media-intense version of an international development DfID event which occurs annually; but that level of public interest and acclaim is not possible year on year.

It is difficult to discern clearly where and how the interface of the media, politicians and the public will meet to best effect for preventing FGM; there is a lot as yet to be discussed and learned.

Nonetheless, one encouraging aspect of campaigns to stop FGM in the UK is that almost all formal reporting right across the media spectrum, if not all the ad hoc reader commentary, has been considered, respectful and supportive of this cause.

Discuss this chapter at http://nofgmukbook.com/2015/01/29/chapter-11-politics-and-the-media/.

Endnotes

All weblinks accessed on 1 March 2015.

1   REPLACE2 (2015) A New Approach to End Female Genital Mutilation (FGM) in the EU. Available at: http://www.replacefgm2.eu/about/.

2   Global Alliance against Female Genital Mutilation (2013) Press Release. *Geneva Foundation for Medical Education and Research*, 23 May. Available at: http://www.gfmer.ch/Presentations_En/Pdf/CP-GA-FGM-GFMER-UNFPA-23-may-2013.pdf.

3   Global Alliance (2013) *University Chair on FGM and Harmful Traditions*. Available at: http://www.global-alliance-fgm.org/en-gb/projects/universitychair.aspx.

4   Global Alliance (2013) *Annual Report 2012*. Available at: http://www.global-alliance-fgm.org/Portals/0/Documents/Annual%20Report%202012_web.pdf.

5   GIZ (2015) *About GIZ*. Available at: http://www.giz.de/en/html/about_giz.html.

6   International Centre for Reproductive Health (2009) *REPLACE a 12 month Daphne III funded project*. Available at: http://icrh.org/project/replace-12-month-daphne-iii-funded-project.

7   REPLACE (2015) *About the REPLACE Partners*. Available at: http://www.replacefgm.eu/about-the-replace-partners/.

8   Barron, T. (2014) We Must End FGM Everywhere, Not Just in the UK. *Guardian*, 3 July. Available at: http://www.theguardian.com/society/2014/jul/03/we-must-end-fgm-everywhere.

9   Sanghani, R. (2014) FGM Campaigners Call on Nicky Morgan to Educate Children. *Telegraph*, 10 October. Available at: http://www.telegraph.co.uk/women/womens-politics/11152418/FGM-campaigners-call-on-Nicky-Morgan-to-educate-children.html.

10 Stop FGM Middle East (2014) Elimination of FGM in One Generation Possible – After 9 years campaigning 70% oppose practice in Iraqi Kurdistan. *Stop FGM Middle East blog*, 15 September. Available at: http://www.stopfgmmideast.org/elimination-of-fgm-in-one-generation-possible-after-9-years-campaigning-70-oppose-practice-in-iraqi-kurdistan/.

11 Imkaan & Equality Now (2011) Submission to CEDAW-CRC call for papers on Harmful Practices. *OHCHR*, 31 August. Available at: http://www.ohchr.org/Documents/HRBodies/CEDAW/HarmfulPractices/ImkaanandEqualityNow.pdf.

12 KnowYourMeme (2015) Check Your Privilege. *Knowyourmeme.com*. Available at: http://knowyourmeme.com/memes/check-your-privilege.

13 Freeman, H. (2013) Check Your Privilege! Whatever that means. *Guardian*, 5 June. Available at: http://www.theguardian.com/society/2013/jun/05/check-your-privilege-means.

14 Values vs Violence (2015) *FGM*. Available at: http://vvvuk.com/fgm/.

15 Integrate Bristol, Zed Productions et al. (2013) *Silent Scream*. Available at: http://integratebristol.org.uk/2012/01/14/silent-scream/.

16 Hussein, L. et al. (2013) The Cruel Cut. *Channel4.com*. Available at: www.channel4.com/programmes/the-cruel-cut/episode-guide.

17 Schurgin O'Keeffe, G., Clarke-Pearson, K. (2011) The Impact of Social Media on Children, Adolescents, and Families. *Pediatrics*, 127(4 April): 800–804. Available at: http://pediatrics.aappublications.org/content/127/4/800.full.

18 UnCut/VOICES (2012) *UnCut/Voices Press is a publisher dedicated to ending Female Genital Mutilation (FGM)*. Available at: http://uncutvoices.com/about/.

19 Guardian (2015) *Hilary Burrage*. Available at: http://www.theguardian.com/profile/hilary-burrage.

20 Topping, A. (2014) FGM: Ban Ki-moon backs *Guardian*'s global media campaign. *Guardian*, 31 October. Available at: http://www.theguardian.com/society/2014/oct/30/fgm-ban-ki-moon-guardian-media-campaign-un-kenya.

21 Topping, A., Gogenini, R., Carson, M. (2014) UN Secretary General Boosts *Guardian* Campaign against FGM in Kenya – video. *Guardian*, 30 October. Available at: http://www.theguardian.com/world/video/2014/oct/30/female-genital-mutilation-ban-ki-moon.

22 AHA Foundation (2015) *About*. ahafoundation.org. Available at: http://theahafoundation.org/about/.

23 Hirsi Ali, A. (2011) *Nomad*. London: Simon & Schuster.

24 Desert Flower Foundation (2015) Waris Dirie. Available at: http://www.desertflowerfoundation.org/en/waris-dirie/.

25 Dirie, W. (2001) *Desert Flower*. London: Virago.

26 EuroNET FGM (2015) *Stop FGM NOW – Activists around Europe against FGM*. Available at: http://euronetfgm.eu/4.html.

27 Khady with Cuny, M-T. (2010) *Blood Stains: A child of Africa reclaims her human rights*. Frankfurt am Main: UnCut/Voices Press.

28 nofgmoz (2014) *Shame, Stigma and Silence Allows FGM to Continue: Activist Khadija Gbla*. Available at: http://nofgmoz.com/2014/09/13/shame-stigma-and-silence-allows-fgm-to-continue-activist-khadija-gbla/.

29 Jabour, B. (2015) I Don't Like Being the Face of FGM, says Australian Survivor, but I Must Break the Silence. *Guardian*, 1 January. Available at: http://www.theguardian.com/society/2015/jan/02/i-dont-like-being-the-face-of-fgm-says-australian-survivor-but-i-must-break-the-silence.

30 Daughters of Eve (2015) *Leyla Hussein*. Available at: http://www.dofeve.org/leyla-hussein.html.

31 HawaTrust (2014) *Founder*. Available at: http://hawatrust.org.uk/about/founders.

32 Glanvill, N. (2014) Somali-born Hibo Wardere is Calling on Secondary Schools to Explain FGM to Girls in order to Raise Awareness. *Waltham Forest Guardian*, 26 May. Available at: http://www.guardian-series.co.uk/news/wfnews/11236513.Speaking_Out__Hibo_Wardere_on_educating_schools_about_FGM/.

33 Maya Centre (2013) *The Dahlia Project*. Available at: http://www.mayacentre.org.uk/dahlia-project-survivors-fgm/.

34 Burrage, H. (2014) Appreciation: Efua Dorkenoo OBE. *Hilary Burrage blog*, 23 October. Available at: http://hilaryburrage.com/2014/10/23/appreciation-efua-dorkenoo-obe/.

35 Dorkenoo, E. (1996) *Cutting the Rose*. Austin: Harry Ransom Humanities Research Center.

36 The Girl Generation (2015) *The Africa-Led Movement to End FGM*. Available at: http://www.thegirlgeneration.org/.

37 Dr Abe Foundation (2013) *About Dr Abe*. Available at: http://www.drabefoundation.com/drabe.php.

38 Momoh, C. (2005) *Female Genital Mutilation*. London: Radcliffe Publishing.
39 FGM National Clinical Group (2015) *About Us*. Available at: http://www. fgmnationalgroup.org/about_us.htm.
40 Lambert, V. (2008) Ruth Rendell Speaks out against Female Genital Mutilation. *Telegraph*, 7 July. Available at: http://www.telegraph.co.uk/ women/womens-health/3355495/Ruth-Rendell-speaks-out-against-female-genital-mutilation.html.
41 FORWARD: Our team Available at: http://www.forwarduk.org.uk/about/ team/.
42 Boseley, S., Craigie, E. (2013) Casualty Turns Spotlight on Female Genital Mutilation. *Guardian*, 12 April. Available at: http://www. theguardian.com/society/2013/apr/12/casualty-spotlight-female-genital-mutilation?guni=Article:in%20body%20link.
43 FORWARD, Levin, T. (2010) FORWARD-Germany STOPPT FGM Dr. Tobe Levin. *YouTube*, 14 February. Available at: http://www.youtube.com/ watch?v=uvSAq8XX4X8.
44 Finch, A. (2014) Little Stitches at Theatre503. *The Upcoming*, 23 August. Available at: http://www.theupcoming.co.uk/2014/08/23/little-stitches-at-theatre503-theatre-review/.
45 Ossei, Y. (2013) 'Face Up' – Female Genital Mutilation Play Debuts at Channel 4. *Huffington Post*, 9 September. Available at: http://www.huffingtonpost.co.uk/ yvonne-ossei/female-genital-mutilation_b_3881511.html.
46 New Vic Theatre (2015) *Borderlines Performance is Central to Conference Success*. Available at: http://www.newvictheatre.org.uk/77-new-vic/485-borderlines-performance-is-central-to-conference-success.
47 Burrage, H. (2014) Sing and Shout against FGM: Where the arts, human rights, the 'old days' and a big UN announcement all came together. *Hilary Burrage blog*, 30 October. Available at: http://hilaryburrage.com/2014/10/30/ sing-and-shout-against-fgm-where-the-arts-human-rights-the-old-days-and-a-big-un-announcement-all-came-together/.
48 GOV.UK (2015) *Forced Marriage*. Available at: https://www.gov.uk/stop-forced-marriage.
49 Rathbone, E. (1934) *Child Marriage: The Indian Minotaur: An object-lesson from the past to the future*. Reading: George Allen & Unwin.
50 ICRW (2015) *Child Marriage*. Available at: http://www.icrw.org/what-we-do/ adolescents/child-marriage.
51 Sinclair, S. (2008) The Bride Price: Child marriage in India. *Alexia Foundation*. Available at: http://www.alexiafoundation.org/stories/StephanieSinclair?gclid =Cj0KEQjwquOhBRCupYiu4an13scBEiQAss2XkquAuAOZ_9oM0qmSU9qNO xA91p67sgof-EekCTaDhxUaAvt78P8HAQ.
52 Minority Voices Newsroom (2012) *Kenya: Beading young Samburu girls into sexual bondage*. Available at: http://www.minorityvoices.org/news.php/ en/1284/kenya-beading-young-samburu-girls-into-sexual-bondage.

53 Meriwas, J. (2013) Samburu Girl-Child Beading – A Silent Sacrifice. *IWGIA*. Available at: http://www.iwgia.org/publications/search-pubs?publication_id=612.

54 Lynch, C. (2014) Campaigners Warn of 'Breast Ironing' in the UK. *Channel 4 News*, 18 April. Available at: http://www.channel4.com/news/breast-ironing-fgm-victim-girls-chest-cameroon-uk.

55 Borrell, B. (2013) Magic or Medicine? *Aeon*, 1 July. Available at: http://aeon.co/magazine/philosophy/african-healers-and-western-medicine/.

56 Kabiru, A. (2009) The Practice of Tooth Extraction. *Kenya Past and Present 2009*. Available at: https://www.academia.edu/2464192/The_Practice_of_Tooth_Extraction.

57 Abba, A. (2014) Big is so Beautiful in Mauritania that They're Force-feeding Girls as Young as Five. *Thaqafa Magazine*, 21 July. Available at: http://thaqafamagazine.com/2014/07/21/mauritania-force-feeding/.

58 Lines, J. (2014) 'Protect Me from the Beasts' – People trafficking and modern-day slavery. *UN Women*, 10 October. Available at: http://www.unwomenuk.org/%E2%80%9Cprotect-me-from-the-beasts%E2%80%9D-%E2%80%93-people-trafficking-and-modern-day-slavery-3/.

59 Cameron, D. (2014) Girl Summit 2014: David Cameron's speech. *GOV.UK*, 22 July. Available at: https://www.gov.uk/government/speeches/girl-summit-2014-david-camerons-speech.

60 Home Office, May, T. (2014) New Measures to Tackle Female Genital Mutilation and Forced Marriage Announced at Today's Girl Summit. *GOV.UK*, 22 July. Available at: https://www.gov.uk/government/news/new-measures-to-tackle-female-genital-mutilation-and-forced-marriage-announced-at-todays-girl-summit.

61 Bindel, J. (2010) Gangs, Girls and Grooming: The truth. *Standpoint*, December. Available at: http://standpointmag.co.uk/features-december-10-gangs-girls-and-grooming-the-truth-julie-bindel-asian-gangs-pimps-rotherham.

62 Chesler, P. (2010) Worldwide Trends in Honor Killings. *Middle East Quarterly*. 17(2): 3–11. Available at: http://www.meforum.org/2646/worldwide-trends-in-honor-killings.

63 McVeigh, K. (2014) Child Witchcraft Claims Increasing as 'Hidden Crime' is Investigated. *Guardian*, 8 October. Available at: http://www.theguardian.com/uk-news/2014/oct/08/child-witchcraft-claims-hidden-crime-met-police-under-reported.

64 Department for Communities and Local Government et al. (2014) Funding to Prevent Female Genital Mutilation and Forced Marriage. *GOV.UK*, 11 October. Available at: https://www.gov.uk/government/news/new-funding-for-female-genital-mutilation-and-forced-marriage-prevention.

65 ICAI (2013) *DFID's Use of Contractors to Deliver Aid Programmes*. Available at: http://icai.independent.gov.uk/wp-content/uploads/2010/11/ICAI-REPORT-DFIDs-Use-of-Contractors-to-Deliver-Aid-Programmes.pdf.

66 Antropologi.info (2010) *Yes to Female Circumcision?* Available at: http://www.antropologi.info/blog/anthropology/2010/female-circumcision.

67 Levin, T. (2007) *'Highly Valued by Both Sexes': Activists, Anthr/apologists and FGM.* Available at: http://www.accmuk.com/fgm_factsheet_1.pdf.

68 Gruenbaum, E. (2005) Feminist Activism for the Abolition of FGC in Sudan. *Journal of Middle East Women's Studies.* 1(2): 89–111. Available at: http://muse.jhu.edu/login?auth=0&type=summary&url=/journals/journal_of_middle_east_womens_studies/v001/1.2.gruenbaum.html.

69 Patton, A. (2014) 'Nothing can Stop' Fight against Female Genital Mutilation – advocacy group. *Devex.com*, 2 April. Available at: https://www.devex.com/news/nothing-can-stop-fight-against-female-genital-mutilation-advocacy-group-83200.

70 Intergovernmental Panel on Climate Change (2015) *Fifth Assessment Report.* Available at: http://www.ipcc.ch/.

71 IAC (2003) *Report of the International Conference on "Zero Tolerance to FGM", 4–6 February 2003, Addis Ababa, Ethiopia.* Available at: http://www.african-women.org/documents/Zero_Tolerance.pdf.

72 Timeanddate.com (2015) *International Day of Zero Tolerance to Female Genital Mutilation.* Available at: http://www.timeanddate.com/holidays/un/zero-tolerance-day-female-genital-mutilation.

73 Mohamed, F. (2014) Tell Schools to Teach Risks of Female Genital Mutilation before the Summer. *Change.org*, February. Available at: http://www.change.org/p/educationgovuk-tell-schools-to-teach-risks-of-female-genital-mutilation-before-the-summer-endfgm.

74 Guardian (2015) *End FGM US.* Available at: http://www.theguardian.com/end-fgm-us.

75 Dukureh, J. (2014) End Female Genital Mutilation in the US – Commission a prevalence report on women impacted and girls at risk. *Change.org*, February. Available at: http://www.change.org/p/end-fgm-now-protect-girls-from-getting-cut-and-support-victims-of-female-genital-mutilation-in-the-usa.

76 Topping, A. (2014) Anti-FGM Activist Fahma Mohamed Wins Young Campaigner Award. *Guardian*, 13 October. Available at: http://www.theguardian.com/society/2014/oct/13/fahma-mohamed-anti-fgm-wins-good-housekeeping-award.

77 Burrage, H. (2014) How Can Britain Deport a Child at Risk of FGM? Theresa May must think again. *Guardian*, 25 April. Available at: http://www.theguardian.com/commentisfree/2014/apr/25/britain-deport-child-at-risk-fgm-theresa-may-nigeria.

78 Handa, A. (2014) Please Review the Fresh Evidence Submitted for Afusat Saliu's Asylum Case Properly. *Change.org*, April. Available at: http://www.change.org/p/home-office-please-review-the-fresh-evidence-submitted-for-afusat-saliu-s-asylum-case-properly.

79 BBC News (2014) Mother Afusat Saliu 'gets Nigeria Deportation Reprieve'. *bbc.co.uk*, 29 May. Available at: http://www.bbc.co.uk/news/uk-england-27630769.

80 Handa, A. (2014) In Aid of Afusat Saliu. *Mydonate.bt.com*, 12 June. Available at: https://mydonate.bt.com/events/afusatsaliu.

81 Manjoo, R. (2014) Special Rapporteur on Violence against Women Finalizes Country Mission to the United Kingdom and Northern Ireland and Calls for Urgent Action to Address the Accountability Deficit and also the Adverse Impacts of Changes in Funding and Services. *Ohchr.org*, 15 April. Available at: http://www.ohchr.org/EN/NewsEvents/Pages/DisplayNews. aspx?NewsID=14514&LangID=E.

82 Burrage, H. (2014) UN Rapporteur Rashida Manjoo Visits UK – My briefing note on violence against women and girls. *Hilary Burrage blog*, 15 April. Available at: http://hilaryburrage.com/2014/04/15/un-rapporteur-rashida-manjoo-visits-uk-my-briefing-note-on-violence-against-women-and-girls/.

83 UN News Centre (2014) UN Rights Expert Urges United Kingdom to Step up Response to Violence against Women. *un.org*, 16 April. Available at: http://www.un.org/apps/news/story.asp?NewsID=47592#.VDqje_ldWQw.

84 Burrage, H. (2014) The UK Home Office (says it) has no Data on FGM Asylum Claims. *Hilary Burrage blog*, 19 May. Available at: http://hilaryburrage.com/2014/05/19/uk-home-office-has-no-data-on-fgm-asylum-claims/.

85 UNHCR (2015) *Female Genital Mutilation – Committed to ending the pain.* Available at: http://www.unhcr.org/pages/5315def56.html.

86 UNHCR (2013) *Too Much Pain: Female genital mutilation & asylum in the European Union – a statistical overview*, February. Available at: http://www.refworld.org/docid/512c72ec2.html.

87 Ewens, H. (2014) FEMEN Protested against FGM at the Tour de France in London Yesterday. *Vice.com*, 8 July. Available at: http://www.vice.com/en_uk/read/femen-tour-de-france-456.

88 Elliott, C. (2014) The *Guardian* Readers' Editor on Journalism's Code of Confidentiality. *Guardian*, 5 October. Available at: http://www.theguardian.com/commentisfree/2014/oct/05/guardian-readers-editor-journalism-code-confidentiality.

89 BBC (2012) *BBC Child Protection Policy.* Available at: http://downloads.bbc.co.uk/guidelines/editorialguidelines/pdfs/BBC_Child_Protection_Policy.pdf.

90 Ridley, L. (2014) Teenage FGM Campaigner Fahma Mohamed Reveals the Moment that Changed Her Life (Video). *The Huffington Post*, 20 October. Available at: http://www.huffingtonpost.co.uk/2014/10/20/fahma-mohamed-fgm-campaigner_n_6014424.html.

91 Department for International Development (2014) Girl Summit 2014: Outcomes and commitments. *GOV.UK*, 29 August. Available at: https://www.gov.uk/government/news/girl-summit-2014-outcomes-and-commitments.

92 Department for International Development, Greening, J. (2014) New Funding to Protect Millions of Girls from Child Marriage. *GOV.UK*, 22 July. Available at: https://www.gov.uk/government/news/new-funding-to-protect-millions-

of-girls-from-child-marriage http://www.noodls.com/view/51C2B5039421952
D8F86E769A907005035288755?9098xxx1406053859.

93 Department for International Development (2014) Prime Minister to Host Event
to Tackle Female Genital Mutilation and Early and Forced Marriage for Girls.
GOV.UK, 8 March. Available at: https://www.gov.uk/government/news/prime-
minister-to-host-event-to-tackle-female-genital-mutilation-and-early-and-
forced-marriage-for-girls.

12 Will FGM in the UK be Eradicated in a Decade?

How many more girls and young women in the UK (or the USA, or Australia, or in other Western states) will have their health, even lives, put at risk because of FGM?

How long will it be before Western political leaders recognise they must put their own house properly in order, as well as formulating FGM and those who practise it as 'the other'?

And how long must we wait, with children at risk every day, before campaigners in communities and law enforcement authorities find ways to work together much more effectively? How are we to reach the crucial consensus, in traditionally practising communities and elsewhere, that FGM is everyone's business, simply another grimly appalling act of cruelty permitting, of itself, no more 'cultural sensitivity' or special pleading by anyone involved than any other abuse of girls and women?

These are stark questions, but they must be asked. Children in the UK remain at serious risk; lives continue to be ruined in Britain, across the Western world and around the globe.

The short answer to whether FGM can, or rather will, be eradicated in the UK, or the USA or Australia or mainland Europe, within a decade – that is, before the end of the first quarter of the twenty-first century – is, if the truth be told, this:

Very probably, with all the right elements in place. Yes, FGM can be eradicated quite quickly in the UK, regardless of what is happening elsewhere.

Whilst the exact parallels can be a matter of debate, a single generation was all it took to eradicate foot-binding in China.[1, 2] Once the authorities had decided it had to stop, they ensured that it did. Methodologies for enforcing eradication may change, but outcomes need not.

But the longer answer, at the level of prosaic reality in Britain at least, is maybe, No. Unless a considerable number of factors in the UK are adjusted, the likelihood of FGM cessation in one generation, let alone a single decade, remains modest. Is the will to eradicate FGM in Britain strong enough to actually deliver eradication?

More than anything else, it is the political climate (with both a capital P and a small one) that needs to change if substantial progress on FGM is to be made.

Denials, Resistance and Reality

The first step towards eradication in the UK was acknowledgement of the realities of FGM. An understanding was slowly established, thanks to an extent to the introduction in 2004 of the International Day of Zero Tolerance for Female Genital Mutilation (6 February),[3] that FGM comprises a sometimes lethal and overwhelmingly traumatic and dangerous practice which blights, or ends, the lives of millions of girls and women. Then came the tortuously slow acknowledgement also that thousands of these affected people live in Britain.

The long-held denial of the facts may of themselves be understandable. Firstly, the epidemiological evidence base in the UK is at best still partial; and was originally almost non-existent; and secondly it is genuinely unthinkable to most people in normal mainstream society that anyone would knowingly harm a child to the extent that FGM does.

Stories have occasionally circulated in parts of Britain for many years of small girls who have been taken abroad and subjected to some sort of 'cutting', but it is likely that teachers and others who heard these tales interpreted the accounts as an act of circumcision similar to the one still practised in some religions (now, in the UK at least, less frequently – and in the perception of some less acceptably) on baby boys. These teachers were deeply mistaken, but they almost certainly and genuinely believed the consequences of the 'cutting' required simply reassurance of the girl, not an immediate referral to children's services and a doctor.

The consequences of any such misunderstanding for the child (and others) will have been very serious; but the woeful neglect was in all probability unintended – and made worse by the euphemistic naming of FGM as 'cutting' or 'circumcision'. And of such mismatches of interpretation there are doubtless many.

From where we stand now, this sorry tale illustrates the gulf between the world views of traditional communities which continue to observe 'culturally' obliged harmful practices, and those in the modern world where such things are, or maybe were, simply not perceived or thought to be possible, and so were put aside. There are lessons here for everyone involved in the prevention of child abuse; this failure to grasp the significance of a child's story does not 'only' happen in respect of FGM.

Yet there are aspects which traditional and modern communities to an extent do hold in common: in both, the power of patriarchy still holds sway, albeit to varying degrees, and in both there is a significant reluctance – or downright refusal – to discuss matters of sexual health[4] (if such matters are recognised at all; in Nigeria, for instance, only 7 per cent of couples are thought to have conversations of this sort).[5] Traditionalists are much more likely than those who see a more open or progressive future not to discuss these issues, in conversations between the sexes.

Patriarchy and a refusal to acknowledge the realities of human sexuality and physiology, especially women's, together comprise an extraordinarily powerful mode of female oppression (see for instance pre-Roe vs. Wade).[6]

It is no accident of history that, whilst women were (or are) perceived, especially by men, as fragile or feeble beings, whores or workhorses – anything except human beings much like male ones – the fundamentals of how their bodies actually work remain in public discourse largely a mystery.

And this is a characteristic of societies old and new, across the globe. Even now, gender wars continue to rage in modern Western autocracies and democracies where (mostly male) right-wing traditionalists still demand control of women's bodies in ways which incense more liberated (men and) women. Politicians' gravely pronounced claims that pregnancies will self-abort if 'legitimate' (that is, 'genuine') rape has occurred (in the USA[7]), or that women should not drive cars because their ovaries could be damaged (in Saudi Arabia[8]), may well induce intense female fury, but they have less than zero value as contributions to women's physiological health and well-being.

These are of course extreme examples in the context of technologically advanced nations, but the boundaries between technological advancement and traditional ways of life are in any case becoming more blurred. There are technically advanced states and locations throughout the world, in Africa, the Middle East and elsewhere which also have significant populations holding ultra-conservative cultural or religious beliefs – many of them in places where women who defy or resist may find themselves in serious personal peril.

Almost anywhere in the world, such illiberal and ill-informed views may be frequently and zealously promulgated by those with a direct interest in fostering them; but scientific facts as a basis for public dialogue are rarely promoted with such enthusiasm.

World views based on myth and tenets created by the powerful (usually men) have a head-start of several millennia over the empirically testable declarations of modern science. To hold sway the former require only an underlying culture which enforces and sustains them; the latter require literacy and classrooms with qualified teachers.

It is context which defines the legitimacy of belief; and in many contexts around the world, even those where technologies are advanced, the socio-economic context makes it normal (for men and women alike) to perceive women and girls as adjuncts to men, not as equal human beings.

These observations may seem distant from contemporary Western issues such as the entitlement (or not) of children to personal, social, health and relationship education; or even of women's access to family planning, let alone equality in employment.

But is the distance really so great? Whilst in the UK girls are still told that they must avoid dressing in ways which might 'provoke' unwanted advances (and boys are told nothing), whilst the risk continues that those in authority will dismiss children's claims of abuse, and whilst mothers with young daughters protest to no avail against deportation to countries where FGM remains common, perhaps not.

It is not so very long ago, even in the UK, that women did not have the vote; and only in the past half century has family planning become unexceptional (despite the continuing strictures of some traditional cultures and faiths).[9, 10, 11] Still in schools the long shadow of Section 28 (about avoiding discussion of homosexuality in lessons) lurks despite its removal decades ago,[12] still sex and relationship education within the school curriculum is not a core requirement,[13, 14] still 'page 3' publications (see, for example, the *Sun* newspaper, which for years has carried daily photographs of unclothed young women) are thought to be acceptable, even amusing, by significant sections of the population,[15] and still women, especially with families, find themselves severely disadvantaged in the workplace.[16]

The list could go on ... and at the same time in Britain we see overt hostility to 'foreigners'[17] and an increase in support for politicians who oppose immigration.[18]

Unsurprising then that concerns about FGM (oft perceived erroneously as a solely and widespread Muslim practice which happens elsewhere) have been a low priority in the UK.

In a hazy way the stop FGM lobby has been until recently sidelined as a matter only for earnest international development campaigners of a feminist bent. It surely wasn't something which happened in Britain, and it was about issues best left to those who understood other 'cultures' much better than most Britons do.

From one perspective, this extraordinarily relaxed position could at least be regarded as uninformed or benign neglect. There is, however, a conceivable prospect that with more real information and a greater understanding of the scale of FGM as a human rights abuse, there will also come about a racist backlash, especially given the possibly growing trend in the UK (and many other Western nations) as austerity impinges on the person in the street, towards looking inward and backward, to what is familiar and, with rose-tinted hindsight, a more secure and comforting past.

If previous experience of public health issues – all different, yet in some ways all alike – is any guide, this fear may – unless it is carefully addressed – be well founded.

When half a century ago Dr Jonas Salk created a vaccine for polio (then a frequent cause of child death and disablement), he wanted it distributed to children in the USA via schools, as a mass inoculation programme. The American Medical Association opposed this strategy, demanding that the vaccine be administered by (paid) doctors, in their offices; to do otherwise, claimed President Eisenhower's Secretary for Health, Education and Welfare, would be to permit 'socialism by the back door'.[19] The poorest children, no doubt many black ones amongst them, were to be the least protected.

Similarly, when HIV and AIDS were first matters of public concern, there was a tendency in some parts of the Western world (especially the USA) to see it more as a condition involving sexuality and marked as coming from 'Africa' (that is, 'foreign'), than as one which is a serious concern because it makes people ill[20] – many of the more conservative Republicans in particular perceived it in hostile, racist terms – and the same might be observed of the more current public health threat of the Ebola virus. As the *Guardian* columnist Gary Younge observed, Ebola can be seen as a metaphor for everything American conservatives loathe, coming, as it does from 'abroad' (especially, Africa) and requiring concerted public health measures across communities to prevent widespread infection.[21]

And the point for FGM of these observations about polio, HIV and Ebola? When the public becomes aware of a serious extraterritorial public health issue, some members of the wider community are sufficiently uninformed and become horrified or frightened enough to attribute blame, rather than addressing the issues in a responsible and humanitarian manner. Perhaps this tendency is greatest in the USA, but there is also a danger it may occur in Europe and elsewhere, especially in times of perceived austerity and social stress.

The risk is that FGM, as it rises in public consciousness in the West, could become another opportunity for racism and sometimes valid accusations of the neglect of some sections of the wider community. This risk needs to be carefully handled.

Epidemiology and community medicine continue in some respects to speak across each other;[22] and preventative medicine continues to be a Cinderella science lacking the glamour and reward of acute clinical challenges. What would comprise the most effective strategies to halt FGM in places like Britain is not easily determined. Nonetheless, public health measures can make a considerable contribution to the resolution of this very serious problem.

Political and cultural leadership is required to ensure that work to prevent FGM is not overshadowed by racist rhetoric – which is not only unacceptable however it is presented, but would also be a serious obstacle in itself to the eradication of the practice.

Community Change

Another factor in considering the prospects in the UK for FGM eradication within a decade is how ready communities are for change.

It has been claimed by the anthropologist Gerry Mackie[23] and others such as Ann-Marie Wilson[24] that FGM can be eradicated in a single generation in the same way as foot-binding in China.

Both foot-binding and FGM are noted for the way they reinforce patriarchy and both were/are the cause of serious ill-health, being close to universally accepted in the traditionally practising communities where they occurred. In both cases, it is suggested, the influx into these communities of women who have not had FGM, and the discovery by men that the mutilation is not necessary, provide the circumstances to bring about eradication.

Whether or not this analysis holds, in either traditional locations for FGM or in diaspora communities, remains to be seen. What is certain, however, is that the process towards eradication is not uniform in different communities, and that different states of readiness to abandon FGM are likely to be found in different places.

Considerable research has now been undertaken on this issue in a number of European countries, in particular by the REPLACE2 project, funded under the Daphne 111 European Commission programme. The major focus of the programme is research on the 'readiness' of various practising communities to stop FGM.

This research is not a replacement for enforcing the law – all the nations involved have very clear legislation to prevent FGM, and already some prosecutions have been taken – but it seeks to understand how and in what ways the message that FGM is forbidden is received.

What is already clear is that different diasporas perceive things differently. The language and terms they use are different, their understandings or rationales are different, and the ages and modes of implementation vary. A one-size-fits-all approach to stopping FGM is therefore unlikely to succeed.

Much more information is required about British FGM-practising communities before the findings of REPLACE2 in Europe can be applied meaningfully across the UK, where many different communities reside; but the potential for greater precision and focus exists.

How quickly the application of the concept of community preparedness can be taken forward depends on many factors, including resources, but more knowledge of the incidence of FGM in various parts of Britain is a first requirement. The newly required hospital reporting figures – currently some 15 new cases are identified (many will be missed) every day in participating acute hospitals in England alone – may be a guide here.

Differentiated (to refer back to the previous chapter, 'segregated') messages, to whatever extent, are probably essential to preventative work in different communities; but this approach also presents some challenges of its own. One of these is the coordination of such work, and another may be resistance to such an emphasis, if some others working in the field perceive it as contrary, for instance, to fundamental requirements to enforce the law.

Nonetheless, the position of Nazir Afzal, in 2014 the UK Crown Prosecution Service lead on child sexual abuse and grooming,[25] indicates that progress in that direction will be encouraged. Evidence suggests that grooming is a crime particularly (but certainly not solely) associated with Pakistani men.[26, 27] Mr Afzal has made it clear he expects Asian and Pakistani men (of whom he is one) to report any suspected child sexual abuse or exploitation, urging them not to 'walk on by'.[28] A similar position has been taken by the Muslim Women's Network[29] and the Professional Muslims Institute,[30] despite some resistance to being specifically identified on the part of various thus-labelled faith communities.[31]

But specificity may be essential to address particular criminal activities. Messages need to be tailored for maximum impact on those known to be most likely to commit the crime at any given time. 'Readiness' to abandon FGM is a complex concept to apply, but it has considerable potential if adequate information, and consensus on the ways forward, can be achieved.

Nonetheless, in the best possible scenario, it would not be necessary to consider which approach will maximise impact in identified communities. Ideally – if only it could be so – the current emphasis on (inter-)national multimedia communications will soon reach those places where to date the message has not been received and the message to stop FGM will be received everywhere.

Creating a Paradigm

A critical consideration in moving forward is how in real terms to envisage the issues and produce a model for the UK which delivers the eradication of FGM.

Some might suggest that an overall view is not required, but public health considerations and even just marketing experience suggest that this is so, especially if resources are limited. Currently, however, there is little in the way of a paradigm – a generally agreed framework of understandings and operational approaches[32] – within which to place work around the eradication of FGM.

This is contested ground; and until a consensus can be constructed – or at least a positive truce between contestants called – it is likely that the true losers will continue to be the girls and young women who urgently require protection and, if that's too late, support.

In the meantime, there is an emphasis on practical multi-agency[33] work to bring together professionals from across different services,[34] but less concern to create holistic inter-disciplinary models or understandings of the issues and how to address them.

There may be multi-agency guidelines on combatting FGM sufficient to fill a library, and agency representatives enough to comprise a large convocation when invited to gather for 'discussions'; but there is scant evidence of any genuine inter-disciplinary meeting of minds adequate to produce consensus about the way to establish sturdy frameworks for progress.

Many organisations and interests in the UK compete for the same strikingly modest funding and support. They quite literally cannot afford to share too much information; the matter is in their terms commercially sensitive. Often therefore these bodies appear to move forward in an approximately parallel direction, rather than in consensual accord.

Inter-disciplinarity in the full, academic research sense might well produce a freer flow of ideas and constructs in all directions, but few who have charge of an externally funded agency would currently find that level of open exchange attractive.

There are those who would dispute this analysis, and for whom the flexible sharing of ideas and resources is central to their commitment and way of approaching the issues; but they are probably in a minority. Nonetheless, the absence of an agreed and articulated model shared between disciplines as a basis from which to take forward action by agencies and others is a severe limitation on work around FGM.

So if there is to be a model or paradigm, in what shape should (or could) it shaped?

Again, whilst some disagree, the obvious model is public health. Whether the threat (ill-health/medical condition) is directly contagious, a result of socio-economic contexts, or habitually endemic in any given community, the aspect shared by all these conditions is that behaviour change will influence incidence.

There are numerous and diverse representations of how a model public health programme might be operationalised, but certain considerations, touched on above, are held in common in almost every case.

Among the most important (from the present perspective) of these is that public health is definitively not about 'medicalisation'[35] – the process whereby aspects of life become defined in medical terms, usually as disorders or illnesses. Deviant behaviour or phenomena may in such a process become placed under the jurisdiction of clinicians.

The focus in public health, however, is (at least ideally) wellness – the potential to be fit and live positively – not disease or disability. Public health professionals seek to establish conditions in which people thrive, rather than requiring clinical treatment. It is far better, for instance, not to experience cholera, HIV, car accidents or mercury poisoning – all complaints which arise from specific contexts or (whether knowingly or not) from particular behaviours – than to be in need of medical attention for these conditions.

In other words, public health focuses on removing the socio-economic causes of ill-health,[36] rather than on treating conditions once they have occurred. Public health is aligned with epidemiology and social medicine[37] more than with clinical practice as such. At its best it is also associated with many other factors (social groupings, beliefs, influence) which can support remediation of whatever is the issue in question.

This at-one-remove positioning requires excellent understanding of the socio-economic factors which underpin the condition. John Snow, generally regarded as the physician who formulated epidemiology as a field of study,[38] had to perceive the connection between the London water pump and the spread of cholera,[39] before in 1854 he was able to prevent further deaths.

Further, as Blas and Kurup emphasise,[40] achieving various specific global and health targets without ensuring equitable distribution within populations is of limited value. The specifics of the situation must be addressed if real long-lasting impact is to be delivered.

Similarly, with the social interactions which comprise the complexities of FGM, it is necessary to understand which socio-economic or other influences give rise to the perceived rationales or beliefs which account for its continuation. The art of good practice in public health is to find supportive or persuasive ways to alter or vary things so people's behaviour or susceptibilities change positively.

This can sometimes require a different approach from, though it may overlap standard methods for treating a clinical condition (such as the consequences of FGM) or running a medically-led vaccinations programme, or a campaign to explain why it should not occur in the first place.

So, to translate the public health approach to FGM, ideally for the UK – a nation with advanced formal structures and public services, and the money to fund them – there would be people to find out why the phenomenon still occurs (in diaspora communities), people to organise public information and educational programmes about the harm it does and why it must be stopped (with tailored approaches to accommodate the specifics of beliefs in various locations), people to ensure more direct connection with those at high risk of undergoing (or administering) FGM, and people to provide specialist medical and psychiatric/social care for those who have already experienced it.

And there would also be people responsible for protecting potential victims, and for delivering justice when nonetheless the crime of FGM had been committed – as well as others whose responsibility is to ensure that the legislation is fit for purpose with adequate resources (of all kinds) to ensure it is upheld.

Thus it becomes very clear that, as in many other public health scenarios, a wide variety of social and professional skills are required to secure the objective of stopping FGM. Some of these skills are medical or health-related. Many are not. Yet still as things stand the duty of FGM prevention is frequently – though certainly not always – handed to (or assumed by) some combination of clinicians and survivors.

The burden of overall responsibility is rarely otherwise put so squarely, in matters of public health, on the shoulders of those who must attend to the medical needs of, or even who have experienced directly, the issue to hand. FGM can be in some respects be perceived as a similar public health challenge to, say, road casualties, certain socially transmitted infectious diseases, ill-health (especially in children) brought about by malnutrition, smoking and some wider categories of infant mortality.

Yes, there are differences between all these examples; but in every case the damage could or can be avoided by better-informed and more positive social behaviours. We do not in other instances, however, expect the 'victims', albeit their counsel may be critical, to determine and lead the way in preventing further occurrences.

But there remains currently a sense in which women with direct experience, along with those professionals from mainstream society who attend them – being the people who have the most immediate understanding of the damage which FGM inflicts – are still expected to spearhead prevention as well as 'cure' (treatment).

The unique input of survivors would still be invaluable, but of a different (and less onerous) sort, if there were a developed and structured policy position or paradigm, where everyone concerned, from within given communities, from a range of professional disciplines, and from the front line of senior policy-making, had coordinated input to support implementation of a programme to stop FGM.

Resolving the question of who leads and who otherwise has input will not, however, be easy. As it becomes more recognised in places such as Britain, FGM (and perhaps child and gender abuse in general) has become to an extent a matter of contested boundaries.

For professionals involved, as previously discussed, there is evidence of what might be termed turf wars. Despite formal dialogue, each discipline still operates according to its own understandings and procedures, to some degree isolated from other approaches. As the Vaz Inquiry noted, the RCGP, for instance, were not even party to the initial Multi-Agency Guidelines.

Likewise, in wider contexts some people – by no means a majority in either case – who have found themselves marginalised from the mainstream have taken opposing and strongly voiced positions. For numbers of white, mostly working-class citizens, matters such as FGM are adopted as a rationale for racism. For some others, also British citizens or residents and more closely associated with the issue, who may be located in isolated and disadvantaged diaspora communities, FGM has become a symbol of resistance: not a matter of child and gender abuse which must be prevented, so much as a matter which can only be resolved, in private, by those directly affected.

These positions are not helpful; all of them to a degree have put aside the reality that FGM is a violent crime which hurts children (girls who are mutilated; babies of both sexes at birth and beyond) and women, a form of damage which inflicts severe and long-lasting trauma on many who experience it and on their families.

An effective and mature paradigm for preventing FGM, at least in a wealthy nation such as the UK, would be led by those best placed to take a wider view. Some of the personnel in senior leadership roles might well be medical; some would have different backgrounds and expertise. Others with a community base would have significant input. The locus of responsibility for the programme as a whole would be clearly identified and understood, with overt and publicly accountable leadership.

Such a locus would give important impetus to the development of a functional paradigm for eradicating FGM in the UK.

Politics and Paradigms

In such a scenario, those with ultimate responsibility for delivering the prevention (and remedial) programmes would articulate and address clearly the fundamental challenges of such provision. For that to happen, the people accepting the responsibility must, inevitably, be senior national politicians. Only they can bring all the elements together.

Here is the agenda I want to see adopted by UK national politicians, both in Westminster and the devolved administrations, and (appropriately) at the levels of regional and local governance.

Politicians must:

- be clear that they understand and acknowledge their public accountability for the national programme to eradicate FGM;
- accept that it is not a prerequisite of success in the UK that FGM be eradicated globally – such claims constitute an evasion of responsibility, given the much greater wealth, and development of public health, education and legal networks in the UK, compared with many traditionally practising countries;

- insist on, and (whilst continuing current best-effort piece-meal approaches) ensure genuinely adequate funding for, research to enable delivery of evidence-based good practice;
- provide transparent, accessible formal and informal avenues for communication and the exchange of ideas between all partners in the enterprise;
- fix all the current (2014) and any further identified legal loopholes speedily;
- acknowledge and arbitrate between the many ethical and political choices which must in any situation of this sort be negotiated,[41] given that resources cannot, even for something as critical as FGM, be infinite;
- embed proper and transparent evaluation measures into the work, and ensure they are regularly reviewed;
- introduce immediate mandatory reporting via one properly thought-out national channel to register concerns about possible child abuse, for people in regulated activities – and provide adequate training (initial and in-service), a one-route strategy and full support for these professionals to cope with this requirement well;
- offer genuine leadership on the still vexed question of FGM terminology, accepting that the United Nations and Inter-African Committee on Traditional Practices (IAC) is clear that in all *formal* dialogue the act is 'mutilation', not 'cutting' or any other euphemism;[42]
- insist that the bottom line – FGM is never excusable for any reason, ever – is fully and visibly enforced; making it absolutely clear that all types of harm to children, including FGM, will be viewed exactly for what they are, that is, child abuse (similarly for other, adult domestic violence) – there is no mitigation to be had via any excuses, 'cultural' or otherwise;
- attend to the haphazard nature of current child protection provision, so that Local Safeguarding Children Boards become integral to, mandatory and statutorily funded, parts of that service, including and supporting schools fully;
- facilitate and fully support the work of the various community-led programmes, avoiding any suspicion[43] that different interests will be left to compete amongst themselves for scarce resources;
- ensure that those working to eradicate FGM are assigned tasks appropriate to their experience and training;
- ensure that people who need to escape child and other 'domestic' abuse know about and have safe places to go;
- engage the general public constructively in wider issues of child care and abuse, to secure heightened awareness and a greater understanding of what constitutes responsible child protection, nurturing and parenting.

But such grounded, integrated and focused delivery in the context of a coherent paradigm remains a long way off.

The current government (early 2015) is not as hostile to public health as a discipline as the right-wing Republicans discussed above, but it is nonetheless opposed to central control or to itself accepting responsibility for social action. In reality – and despite serious intent on the part of some ministers – governments to the right are unsympathetic to the processes and resource commitment required if focused public health strategies are to succeed.

Whether FGM in the UK can and will be eradicated within a decade may become easier to fathom in later 2015. It remains to be seen whether the new government in 2015, whatever its political colour is better disposed to central management and the development of an adequately funded, cogent and accountable programme for the eradication of FGM in the UK.

Compassion Fatigue

There is, however much it matters, a limit to how much angst the general public can take on issues such as child abuse; and politicians and the media are closely attuned to public sentiment.

The risks that FGM may again become an invisible issue are several.

Firstly, compassion fatigue may be a serious threat to continuity of action. The term has been applied both to practitioners and to the general public, and requires some unpacking to appreciate its relevance.

In respect of the general public, compassion fatigue perhaps comprises the tendency to shift attention, rather than being a judgement by society as a whole. It has been argued[44] that citizens do not lose their capacity to care as such, but over time they do shift the emphases of their concerns.

The likelihood is that, in their constant search for news, most of the media will move on from FGM to other matters, and so then will the politicians. This fluid synergy clearly puts centrally led and resourced endeavours to eradicate FGM at risk.

One proactive response to this risk may be to strengthen understandings that ignoring FGM would have both personal and wider costs; that a one-off investment adequate to achieve FGM eradication will secure substantial human and cost benefits. Delivering such a message is, of course, not easy.

Another aspect of compassion fatigue relates to those who work to address it.[45] There are some people for whom stopping FGM becomes a permanent preoccupation (and for whom therefore the challenge is to maintain a balanced perspective), but this level of dedicated single-mindedness is not for everyone. For others compassion fatigue – a feeling that the realities of the condition are too much to cope with compassionately over the longer term – may set in.

FGM is a deeply disturbing form of child abuse, yet to date there is almost no support for individuals who have undergone it, let alone for those who seek to stop it and to help survivors. There are possible models for such support for professionals, both in terms of professional frameworks[46] and in respect of emotional intelligence and competence.[47] There is a considerable literature concerning 'stress resilience' in social work[48] and also about the ways in which the media sometimes exacerbates already stressful situations (such as the tragic death of Baby P[49]) for social workers.

This attention to the health and welfare of social workers is not a deflection from the core concern about FGM. Rather, it is an acknowledgement that social workers, like others such as teachers and nurses, are also human beings, and they cannot do their jobs properly if they are subjected to overbearing stressors, with inadequate support.[50]

Burnout may be different in some respects from compassion fatigue – more attention needs to be given to these issues if we are to understand them adequately – but there is good reason to suppose that both have an adverse effect not only on the person concerned, but also on their professional performance and commitment. Professional supervision, in the sense of help to maintain equilibrium, is not, however, available for many of those across the range of disciplines and communities involved who work to eradicate (or ameliorate the impacts on survivors of) FGM. Somehow, this basic requirement for support will need to be addressed as the cause moves forward.

This need is particularly important in the case of campaigners who themselves experienced or lived close-by FGM. The noted survivor and campaigner Leyla Hussein, herself a psychotherapist, has reported her own experience of burnout and depression[51] in this context, and she acknowledges that therapy does not remove the pain; it is lifelong.

Here is yet another reason that survivors alone, however passionate, must not be expected to carry the burden of advocating for FGM to be eradicated. Survivors who provide testimony and campaign are a unique and invaluable resource; and they are also a special case when it comes to recognising that support for campaigners and lobbyists to eradicate FGM is essential.

Any perception that those who advocate the eradication of FGM are themselves exhausted will also be unhelpful to the campaign, but beyond even that difficulty there is also another, wider scenario in which energy to drive this crusade may dissipate.

As we begin to understand the grim reality of FGM, so too are we beginning to see that FGM is 'only' one of a range of serious, sometimes lethal, human rights abuses which are inflicted on girls and young women. The catalogue of harmful traditional practices continues to grow, as more types of abuse come to light; and whilst it is essential that these cruelties are all brought into focus, there may be a limit to the concern which those beyond the inner circle of activists are willing to show.

Further, there is emerging evidence of widespread abuse and exploitation of both girls and boys (Jimmy Savile,[52] public schools,[53] Rochdale,[54] the churches,[55] the debacle of the Child Sexual Abuse enquiry[56] and now the jihad[57] ... all very important matters in their own right). Despite developments with The Girl Generation,[58] Ban Ki-moon and the *Guardian* global media campaign,[59] these other matters have the potential to divert attention away from FGM as a specific issue.

Handled carefully, this could be a positive development. That, however, depends on FGM having first been established in the public perception as quite simply a repellent form of child abuse, like the other crimes against children now coming to light.

If such a perception of FGM as criminal child abuse does, as it should, become the norm, it is more likely that currently practising communities in Britain will abandon the tradition. These communities' growing interfaces with mainstream society will help to inculcate the idea that such child abuse crimes may not be performed – and that concerns must be reported if there is any risk they may occur.

Such a transition, from the idea that FGM is a (claimed) 'act of love' – in reality, perhaps an act of economic 'necessity' in some traditional settings – to the conviction that it is a base crime, will not occur unless that latter idea is carefully nurtured and inculcated, in practising communities, in the media and, critically, amongst all those who seek to make it history.

There may have been a case earlier on (albeit an increasingly feeble one, in defiance post-2005 of the Inter-African Committee, the Bamako Declaration[60] and much else) for approaching FGM differently in some parts of the world, but that time has passed. FGM is a cruel crime and the way it is discussed and reported must consistently reflect that.

In Western nations such as Britain the required formal mechanisms have long been established to ensure that programmes to eradicate FGM are deliverable, cogent and convincing. Legislation, reporting mechanisms, health care provision, media messages and public perceptions can and must be coordinated and unerring.

When, beyond that, everyone understands that FGM and other related practices (whether visited on girls or on boys) all comprise shameful child abuse which may not be inflicted, and would result in severe repercussions for any perpetrators, the duty to keep children safe will be more easily discharged.

And people in every community in Britain must understand too that the best interests of all children reside in having a nurturing family in which to grow up, good health, excellent education and autonomy to approach adulthood confident, as individuals in their own right, of the future. The law, and our respect for human rights, demands that nobody may be owned by anyone else. Nothing less will be tolerated.

These observations are not trite. They are fundamental to the safety and well-being of children and, thereby, to the future of us all.

Challenges to Resolve

It seems, however, that, despite declared good intentions and the current positioning by the British government, the deeper meanings which underpin such ideas about eradication are not fully appreciated.

These are some of the underlying issues which militate against a climate conducive to eradicating FGM and other violence against women and children:

- In 2014 the United Nations Rapporteur on Violence Against Women and Girls made serious criticisms when she visited the UK.[61, 62]
- Child poverty in Britain is increasing.[63]
- Sure Start centres are closing across the country.[64]
- Few safe houses remain for victims of domestic violence as usually understood,[65] let alone for girls fleeing FGM.
- Hostility to 'immigrants' is growing.[66, 67]
- Despite public outcries, the Home Office keeps no record of the numbers of women fearing FGM for themselves or their daughters.[68]
- Funding to address FGM in Britain itself (if not globally) remains derisory.[69]

Instead, the Government has openly advised their view that 'action to achieve strong communities is usually most effective when it is led by the people it most concerns', although 'in a few cases [it] also provides funding and support for activities to demonstrate ways to promote community integration'.[70] As evidence to make this point very clearly, in autumn 2014 community organisations were invited to apply for support from a pot worth a maximum, for early and forced marriage together, of less than half a million pounds,[71] which is, in the context of government, tokenistic at best.

At least the Labour Shadow Minister, Seema Mulhotra, was honest in admitting she could not as yet confirm what the budget for FGM action might be in a future Labour government.[72]

These circumstances do not augur well for the speedy eradication of FGM in the UK. The knowledge of what is required, the political will and the operational mechanisms are not yet in place:

- A unit to address forced marriage was set up by the Labour Government in 2005,[73] but a national coordinator post to address FGM, initiated in 2010, was closed by the Coalition Government in 2011.[74]
- In December 2014 a new FGM unit was instituted, but still there are only flimsy connections between attempts to stop CEFM (community-sanctioned paedophilia) and FGM, let alone to connect that with witchcraft abuse or other harmful traditional practices visited on children. There is no clear top-down integration to bring together work to stop all types of child abuse and exploitation.
- Legislation on mandatory reporting is not yet finally secured, and even in the most favourable of conditions reasonably complete FGM statistics in the UK will not be available for a while to come.
- No prosecutions for FGM have (as of early 2015) been secured. Nor is there generally available training, beyond a password-protected Government e-learning course, on how to handle FGM and related child abuse risks in nurseries, schools or clinics.

In these circumstances it is difficult to see how FGM will become history in the UK within a decade, despite the declared intentions of the Coalition Government.[75]

The fundamental underpinnings of FGM eradication in the UK must surely rest on grounded, effective systems for protection, clear determination (and evidence) that perpetrators will be brought to account, and the prospect for all children in Britain, whatever their family or cultural heritage, of bright futures as independent and autonomous adults.

But these conditions do not appertain to the UK as things stand; and whatever the politicians claim, however wilful or otherwise their failure to deliver the required changes to see FGM eradicated, such circumstances are unlikely to be secured in the immediate future. We must continue to press for optimal conditions, but it is improbable that we will see them soon.

There are, however, other routes to travel and avenues to explore.

Where government has failed to take a lead, others must do so.

Over the past few years activism in resisting FGM has become increasingly foundation-funded and professionally based. Some of these bodies have very considerable financial backing and large-scale management structures. If these very valuable resources are not to be squandered, there must now be public, wider political and sponsor pressure to consolidate working more closely together, to agree a publicly articulated and viable model for understandings and action. Much of this can be achieved to some extent whether government as such moves forward as it should, or continues largely to stand aside from its responsibilities:

- Evidence and data now flow more easily; how it is then used requires interrogation and analysis on the basis of agreed understandings, indicators and methodologies. There is essential work to be done to develop a fundamental paradigm from which (critically, shared) strategies and operational models can flow.

- Research agendas must be developed together by the major players, investigating identified areas of uncertainty, and 'common sense' claims about what will and may not work in eradicating FGM – will prosecutions actually drive the practice (further) 'underground', or put even younger girls and infants at risk? How can these risks, if they exist, be mitigated? What segmentation strategies might work best to deliver FGM messages? How can work around FGM be blended to optimal effect with that to prevent child 'marriage' and other abuse?

- Currently available evidence and knowledge from other first-world countries must be accessed and shared. Several European countries have extensive relevant experience of combatting FGM (some of it already shared via the REPLACE2 programme) and slowly the United States and Australia, amongst others, are catching up. In the meantime, the UK must turn to fellow Europeans for further insights and understandings.

- Drawing on the evidence to hand, the respective roles for greatest impact of the various sorts of people involved in fighting FGM need to be clarified between the many active interests concerned. This cannot be achieved until shared understandings have been developed and widely articulated.

- Terminology must be resolved, and in particular resolved in ways which acknowledge the concerns of those women leaders in traditionally practising countries who way back in 2005 produced the Bamako Declaration.[76] The time for euphemism and misguided 'respect' for FGM or its perpetrators, if such was ever appropriate, is well past.

- And most critically of all, ways have to be found of valuing and drawing to some extent on the strength of survivors and others who have been combatting FGM for the duration. The challenge now is to enhance their work through the additional resources of big organisations, not to put it aside as greater guns take up positions.

Veracity and commitment are at the heart of everything to do with eradicating FGM. Those coming fresh to the fray from other struggles, albeit they may bring with them mightier forces, must always remember – as sometimes at present they apparently do not – to respect in word and deed the steadfastness of those from many quarters who came before.

Which takes us to those extraordinary, brave, enduring warriors, relatively few in number but immense in stature, the cadre of committed combatants who have brought us to this turning point in history.

We owe it to them, and they owe it to themselves, to stay angry and calm, both together. Anger from the heart is what fuels the urge to halt the cruelty of FGM – how dare this be inflicted on the bodies and lives of small children? – but cool heads are what converts enraged nascent social movements into mainstream realities.

So, can the corner be turned? Is it possible that this will be the last decade when girls and young women are abandoned to endure FGM, in the United Kingdom at least?

Despite the many and substantial obstacles, despite the opportunism, basic incomprehension or ineptitude of some mainstream political leaders, despite the inevitable infighting between campaigning groups fighting for scraps beneath the table, despite the resistance of others who should know much better in the worlds of academe and radical politics, despite the flightiness of public opinion and sections of the media, and despite the traditionally shrouded world of practising communities, perhaps ... the answer is still:

Yes. It can, and must, be done.

The United Kingdom is as well placed as anywhere on earth to rid itself of FGM and other child abuse. We are one of the richest nations in the world – which means we can if we so choose, and regardless of possible claims to the contrary, deliver whatever action and resources are needed. We have mature and effective legal, education and health services, and border controls, which are directed strategically from the centre and are intended to serve every person in the country. We know how critical it is that every child, girls and boys both, emerges into adulthood independent, healthy, strong and ready to make their own autonomous contribution to our society.

In other words, the UK context is optimal to show the world that FGM can, and will as a matter of immediacy, be eradicated. There are currently tensions – amounting perhaps to inadvertent turf wars[77] – between, for instance, the medical and legal professions, the politicians and the processes, but nonetheless we know the obstacles and are equipped to overcome them.

We in Britain need wait for no-one to rid the blight of FGM. It is the absolute and primary duty of any decent, democratic nation to protect those who are most vulnerable and defenceless; what could be more important? And none can be more vulnerable than children at risk of hideous harm.

When children's lives and futures are at stake there are always crusaders who will persist, pushing with all their might, no matter what. We must unite with them to ensure without delay that, along with other grim child abuse, FGM becomes history.

Female genital mutilation brings about the destruction of lives and futures, and the torture and abuse of defenceless children and vulnerable women. It must, finally and immediately, just stop.

Discuss this chapter at http://nofgmukbook.com/2015/01/29/chapter-12-will-fgm-be-eradicated-in-the-uk-in-a-decade/.

Endnotes

All weblinks accessed on 2 March 2015.

1   Mackie, G. (1998) Ending Footbinding and Infibulation: A convention account. *American Sociological Review.* 61(6): 999–1017. Available at: http://www.jstor.org/discover/10.2307/2096305?sid=21105740081693&uid=2&uid=4&uid=3739256.

2   Wilson, A-M. (2013) How the Methods Used to Eliminate Foot Binding in China can be Employed to Eradicate Female Genital Mutilation. *Journal of Gender Studies.* 22(1): 17–37. Available at: http://www.tandfonline.com/doi/full/10.1080/09589236.2012.681182#tabModule.

3   United Nations (2015) *International Day of Zero Tolerance for Female Genital Mutilation – 6 February.* Available at: http://www.un.org/en/events/femalegenitalmutilationday/.

4   US Agency for International Development (2013) *Facts for Family Planning.* Washington, DC: USAID. Available at: https://www.fphandbook.org/.

5   Joseph, S. (2013) Contraceptive Use in Muslim-Majority Countries. *University of California, Davis,* 30 May. Available at: http://sjoseph.ucdavis.edu/ewic-public-outreach-resources/ewic-outreach-resources/contraceptive-use-muslim-majority.

6   Kaplan, L. (1997) *The Story of Jane: The Legendary Underground Feminist Abortion Service.* Chicago: University of Chicago Press.

7   Eligon, J., Schwirtz, M. (2012) Senate Candidate Provokes Ire with 'Legitimate Rape' Comment. *New York Times,* 19 August. Available at: http://www.nytimes.com/2012/08/20/us/politics/todd-akin-provokes-ire-with-legitimate-rape-comment.html?_r=0.

8   Jamjoom, M. (2013) Saudi Cleric Warns Driving could Damage Women's Ovaries. *CNN,* 30 September. Available at: http://edition.cnn.com/2013/09/29/world/meast/saudi-arabia-women-driving-cleric/.

9   Bates, S. (2010) Condoms and the Catholic Church: A short history. *Guardian,* 21 November. Available at: http://www.theguardian.com/world/2010/nov/21/condoms-birth-control-catholic-church-short-history.

10 Dearden, L. (2014) Iran to Ban Permanent Contraception after Islamic Cleric's Edict to Increase Population. *Independent,* 11 August. Available at: http://www.independent.co.uk/news/world/middle-east/iran-to-ban-permanent-contraception-after-islamic-clerics-edict-to-increase-population-9662349.html.

11 Okeowo, A. (2011) Africa's Abortion Wars. *Latitude Blogs,* 15 December. Available at: http://latitude.blogs.nytimes.com/2011/12/15/africas-abortion-wars/?_php=true&_type=blogs&_r=0.

12 Morris, N. (2013) The Return of Section 28: Schools and academies practising homophobic policy that was outlawed under Tony Blair. *Independent*, 20 August. Available at: http://www.independent.co.uk/news/uk/politics/the-return-of-section-28-schools-and-academies-practising-homophobic-policy-that-was-outlawed-under-tony-blair-8775249.html.

13 Burns, J. (2014) Sex Education 'not Taught Properly by Schools'. *BBC News*, 6 June. Available at: http://www.bbc.co.uk/news/education-27733256.

14 Dinwoodie, R. (2013) MSPs: Give sex education in nurseries and the Pill to 13-year-olds. *Herald Scotland*, 18 June. Available at: http://www.heraldscotland.com/politics/political-news/sex-education-in-nurseries-and-the-pill-for-13-year-olds.21377177.

15 No More Page 3 (2015) *Boobs Aren't News*. Available at: http://nomorepage3.org/.

16 Woodroffe, J., Higham, E. (2009) Alliance against Pregnancy Discrimination in the Workplace. *Fawcett Society*. Available at: http://www.fawcettsociety.org.uk/wp-content/uploads/2013/02/PRENANCY-DISCRIMINATION-2.pdf.

17 Asthana, A. (2014) Immigration: Once 'Pakis' were abused. Now it's Europeans who cause alarm – and I'm a 'good' immigrant. *Observer*, 18 October. Available at: http://www.theguardian.com/uk-news/2014/oct/19/immigration-anushka-asthana-1980s-northern-england.

18 Portes, J. (2014) Immigration: Could we – should we – stop migrants coming to Britain? *Observer*, 18 October. Available at: http://www.theguardian.com/uk-news/2014/oct/19/immigration-policy-ukip-restrictions-european-union.

19 Gander, K. (2014) Jonas Salk 100th Birthday: Polio vaccine developer's extraordinary achievement celebrated with a Doodle. *Independent*, 27 October. Available at: http://www.independent.co.uk/life-style/gadgets-and-tech/news/jonas-salks-100th-birthday-google-doodle-celebrates-the-anniversary-of-scientist-who-developed-police-vaccine-9822226.html.

20 Waller, J. (2015) History Online Courses: History 425 American and European Health Care Since 1800. *Sin, Sex and Science: The HIV/AIDS Crisis*. Michigan State University. Available at: http://history.msu.edu/hst425/resources/online-essays/sin-sex-and-science-the-hivaids-crisis/.

21 Younge, G. (2014) Ebola has Exposed America's Fear, and Barack Obama's Vulnerability. *Guardian*, 19 October. Available at: http://www.theguardian.com/commentisfree/2014/oct/19/ebola-america-fear-barack-obama-virus.

22 Burrage, H. (1987) Epidemiology and Community Health: A strained connection? *Social Science & Medicine*. 25(8): 896–903. Available at: http://www.sciencedirect.com/science/article/pii/0277953687902590.

23 Mackie, G. (1998) Ending Footbinding and Infibulation: A convention account. *American Sociological Review*. 61(6): 999–1017. Available at: http://www.jstor.org/discover/10.2307/2096305?sid=21105740081693&uid=2&uid=4&uid=3739256.

24 Wilson, A-M. (2013) How the Methods Used to Eliminate Foot Binding in China can be Employed to Eradicate Female Genital Mutilation. *Journal of Gender Studies*. 22(1): 17–37. Available at: http://www.tandfonline.com/doi/full/10.1080/09589236.2012.681182#tabModule.

25 Kazi, T. (2014) Facing up to Bitter Truths: Rotherham child sex exploitation cases. *50.50 Inclusive Democracy*, 28 August. Available at: https://www. opendemocracy.net/5050/tehmina-kazi/facing-up-to-bitter-truths-rotherham-child-sex-exploitation-cases.

26 Jay, A. (2013) Independent Inquiry into Child Sexual Exploitation in Rotherham (1997–2013). *Rotherham Borough Council*, September. Available at: http://www. rotherham.gov.uk/info/200109/council_news/884/independent_inquiry_into_ child_sexual_exploitation_in_rotherham_1997_%E2%80%93_2013.

27 Hundal, S. (2014) Why Pakistanis Should Be as Angry as Anyone Else about What Happened in Rotherham. *Muslim Institute Blogs*. Available at: http:// www.musliminstitute.org/blogs/grooming/why-pakistanis-should-be-angry-anyone-else-about-what-happened-rotherham-sunny-hundal.

28 Pidd, H. (2014) Muslim Community Must Address Issue of Street Grooming, says Nazir Afzal. *Guardian*, 31 October. Available at: http:// www.theguardian.com/uk-news/2014/oct/31/muslim-community-street-grooming-nazir-afzal.

29 Muslim Women's Network UK (2013) Unheard Voices – The sexual exploitation of Asian girls and young women. Available at: http://www. mwnuk.co.uk/resourcesDetail.php?id=97.

30 Professional Muslim Institute (2014) *Child Sexual Exploitation – The Muslim Community's Response*. Available at: http://www.eventbrite.co.uk/e/child-sexual-exploitation-the-muslim-communitys-response-tickets-13397647725.

31 Norfolk, A., Azam, I. (2014) Don't Ignore Sex Crimes, Urge Muslim Professionals. *The Times*, 3 November. Available at: http://www.thetimes.co.uk/ tto/news/uk/crime/article4255825.ece.

32 Burrell, G., Morgan, G. (1985) *Sociological Paradigms and Organisational Analysis*. London: Ashgate.

33 Safe Network (2015) *What is Multi-agency Working and Why is it so Important?* Available at: http://www.safenetwork.org.uk/training_and_awareness/Pages/ multi-agency-working.aspx.

34 Safe Network (2015) *Effective Ways of Supporting Children and Families with Additional Needs*. Available at: http://www.safenetwork.org.uk/training_and_ awareness/Pages/different-models-multi-agency-working.aspx.

35 Wikipedia (2015) *Medicalization*. Available at: http://en.wikipedia.org/wiki/ Medicalization.

36 Blas, E., Sommerfeld, J., Sivasankara Kurup, A. (2011) *Social Determinants Approaches to Public Health: From concept to practice*. Geneva: WHO. Available at: http://www.who.int/social_determinants/tools/SD_Publichealth_eng.pdf.

37 Burrage, H. (1987) Epidemiology and Community Health: A strained connection? *Social Science & Medicine*. 25(8): 896–903. Available at: http://www. sciencedirect.com/science/article/pii/0277953687902590.

38 Wikipedia (2015) *John Snow (physician)*. Available at: http://en.wikipedia.org/ wiki/John_Snow_(physician).

39   Tuthill, K. (2003) John Snow and the Broad Street Pump – on the trail of an epidemic. *Cricket*. 31(3): 23–31. Available at: http://www.ph.ucla.edu/epi/snow/snowcricketarticle.html.

40   Blas, E., Sivasankara Kurup, A. (2010) *Equity, Social Determinants and Public Health Programmes*. Geneva: WHO. Available at: http://apps.who.int/iris/handle/10665/44289.

41   Furnham, A. (2014) On Your Head: Lost in a moral maze of business ethics. *Sunday Times*, 19 October. Available at: http://www.thesundaytimes.co.uk/sto/public/Appointments/article1472382.ece.

42   IAC (2009) *Inter-African Committee on Traditional Practices*. Available at: http://www.iac-ciaf.net/index.php?option=com_content&view=article&id=10&Itemid=3.

43   Chakrabortty, A. (2014) I'm Bengali and I'm Black – in the same way that my parents were. *Guardian*, 30 October. Available at: http://www.theguardian.com/commentisfree/2014/oct/30/bengali-black-ethnic-minorities-racism.

44   Campbell, D. (2012) The Myth of Compassion Fatigue. *David Campbell blog*, 29 February. Available at: http://www.david-campbell.org/2012/02/29/the-myth-of-compassion-fatigue/.

45   Abendroth, M. (2011) Overview and Summary: Compassion fatigue: caregivers at risk. *OJIN: The Online Journal of Issues in Nursing*. 16(1): Overview and Summary. Available at: http://www.nursingworld.org/MainMenuCategories/ANAMarketplace/ANAPeriodicals/OJIN/TableofContents/Vol-16-2011/No1-Jan-2011/Overview-and-Summary-Compassion-Fatigue.html.

46   Research in Practice (2014) *Professional Capabilities Framework for Social Workers*. Available at: https://www.rip.org.uk/~rip_user/professional_capabilities_framework/files/assets/common/downloads/professional_capabilities_framework.pdf.

47   Morrison, T. (2006) Emotional Intelligence, Emotion and Social Work: Context, characteristics, complications and contribution. *British Journal of Social Work*. 37(2): 245–63. Available at: http://bjsw.oxfordjournals.org/content/37/2/245.short.

48   Kinman, G., Grant, L. (2010) Exploring Stress Resilience in Trainee Social Workers: The role of emotional and social competencies. *British Journal of Social Work*. 41(2): 261–75. Available at: http://bjsw.oxfordjournals.org/content/41/2/261.abstract.

49   Warner, J. (2013) 'Heads Must Roll'? Emotional politics, the press and the death of Baby P. *British Journal of Social Work*. 44(6): 1637–53. Available at: http://bjsw.oxfordjournals.org/content/44/6/1637.abstract.

50   Webber, M. (2012) Stress in Mental Health Social Work: Research review. *Community Care*, 27 February. Available at: http://www.communitycare.co.uk/2012/02/27/stress-in-mental-health-social-work-research-review/.

51   Hussein, L. (2014) Living with Depression: How I learned to cope with my 'guilty secret'. *Cosmopolitan*, 5 September. Available at: http://www.cosmopolitan.co.uk/reports/a29411/coping-with-depression/.

52 BBC News (2015) Jimmy Savile Scandal. *BBC News*. Available at: http://www.bbc.co.uk/news/uk-20026910.

53 Barker, I. (2014) Schools 'No Safer' Today than They Were 50 Years Ago, says Caldicott sex abuse victim. *The TES*,6 February. Available at: http://news.tes.co.uk/b/news/2014/02/05/schools-quot-no-safer-quot-than-they-were-50-years-ago-caldicott-preparatory-school-abuse-victim-says.aspx.

54 Deith, J. (2014) Double Child Abuse Agony for Rochdale Family. *BBC News*, 16 September. Available at: http://www.bbc.co.uk/news/uk-29159427.

55 Davies, L. (2014) Pope Francis Lambasts Catholic Bishops who Helped Cover up Child Abuse. *Guardian*, 7 July. Available at: http://www.theguardian.com/world/2014/jul/07/pope-francis-catholic-bishops-child-paedophile-abuse-priest-condemn.

56 BBC (2015) The Historical Child Abuse Inquiries and What Happens Next. *BBC News*, 4 February. Available at: http://www.bbc.com/news/uk-politics-28189858.

57 Lakhani, S (2014) What makes young British Muslims want to go to Syria? *The Guardian*, 24 June. Available at: http://www.theguardian.com/commentisfree/2014/jun/24/isis-british-muslims-reality-war-fight-extremism.

58 The Girl Generation (2015) *The Africa-Led Movement to End FGM*. Available at: http://www.thegirlgeneration.org/.

59 Topping, A. (2014) FGM: Ban Ki-moon backs *Guardian*'s global media campaign. *Guardian*, 31 October. Available at: http://www.theguardian.com/society/2014/oct/30/fgm-ban-ki-moon-guardian-media-campaign-un-kenya.

60 IAC (2005) *DECLARATION: on the Terminology FGM; 6th IAC General Assembly, 4–7 April, Bamako*. Available at: http://www.taskforcefgm.de/wp-content/uploads/2011/05/Bamako-Declaration.pdf.

61 Burrage, H. (2014) UN Rapporteur Rashida Manjoo Visits UK – My briefing note on violence against women and girls. *Hilary Burrage blog*, 15 April. Available at: http://hilaryburrage.com/2014/04/15/un-rapporteur-rashida-manjoo-visits-uk-my-briefing-note-on-violence-against-women-and-girls/.

62 Office for the High Commissioner for Human Rights (2014) UK: UN rights expert calls for improved actions to fight violence against women and girls. *OHCHR*, 16 April. Available at: http://www.ohchr.org/EN/NewsEvents/Pages/DisplayNews.aspx?NewsID=14519&LangID=E.

63 Child Poverty Action Group (2015) *Child Poverty Facts and Figures*. Available at: http://www.cpag.org.uk/child-poverty-facts-and-figures.

64 Butler, P. (2013) Hundreds of Sure Start Centres have Closed since Election, says Labour. *Guardian*, 28 January. Available at: http://www.theguardian.com/society/2013/jan/28/sure-start-centres-closed-labour.

65 Laville, S. (2014) Domestic Violence Refuge Provision at Crisis Point, Warn Charities. *Guardian*, 3 August. Available at: http://www.theguardian.com/society/2014/aug/03/domestic-violence-refuge-crisis-women-closure-safe-houses.

66 Grove-White, R. (2014) The Increasingly Hostile Environment to Immigration is Unjust and Short-sighted. *London School of Economics*. Available at: http://blogs.lse.ac.uk/politicsandpolicy/immigration/.

67 Taylor, M., Muir, H. (2014) Racism on the Rise in Britain. *Guardian*, 27 May. Available at: http://www.theguardian.com/uk-news/2014/may/27/-sp-racism-on-rise-in-britain.

68 Burrage, H. (2014) The UK Home Office (Says It) Has No Data on FGM Asylum Claims. *Hilary Burrage blog*, 19 May. Available at: http://hilaryburrage.com/2014/05/19/uk-home-office-has-no-data-on-fgm-asylum-claims/.

69 Department for Communities and Local Government et al. (2014) Funding to Prevent Female Genital Mutilation and Forced Marriage. *GOV.UK*, 11 October. Available at: https://www.gov.uk/government/news/new-funding-for-female-genital-mutilation-and-forced-marriage-prevention.

70 Department for Communities and Local Government, Pickles, E., Williams, S. (2012) Bringing People Together in Strong, United Communities. *GOV.UK*, 13 January. Available at: https://www.gov.uk/government/policies/bringing-people-together-in-strong-united-communities.

71 Department for Communities and Local Government, Government Equalities Office (2014) Community Projects to Tackle Female Genital Mutilation and Forced Marriage. *GOV.UK*, 11 October. Available at: https://www.gov.uk/government/publications/community-projects-to-tackle-female-genital-mutilation-and-forced-marriage.

72 Pidd, H. (2014) UK FGM Funds 'at Risk'. *Guardian*, 23 September. Available at: http://www.theguardian.com/society/2014/sep/23/uk-fgm-funds-at-risk.

73 Foreign & Commonwealth Office, Home Office (2013) Forced Marriage. *GOV.UK*, 4 February. Available at: https://www.gov.uk/forced-marriage.

74 Williams, R. (2011) Female Circumcision Prevention Post Abolished by Government. *Guardian*, 30 March. Available at: http://www.theguardian.com/society/2011/mar/30/female-circumcision-prevention-post-abolished.

75 Ford, L. (2013) UK Funds Aim to End Female Genital Mutilation 'in a Generation'. *Guardian*, 6 March. Available at: http://www.theguardian.com/global-development/2013/mar/06/uk-funds-female-genital-mutilation-generation.

76 IAC (2005) *DECLARATION: on the Terminology FGM; 6th IAC General Assembly, 4–7 April, Bamako*. Available at: http://www.taskforcefgm.de/wp-content/uploads/2011/05/Bamako-Declaration.pdf.

77 Burrage, H. (7 March 2015) *Preventing FGM: Beware a turf war between medicine and law*. Paper presented at the University of Oxford Symposium *Contestations around FGM: Activism and the Academy*. *Available at:* http://hilaryburrage.com/2015/03/07/preventing-fgm-beware-a-turf-war-between-medicine-and-law/.

Further Reading

Abe, P. (2015) *FGM: Female Genital Mutilation an A–Z Guide*. London: Dr Abe Foundation.

Abusharraf, R. (2007) *Female Circumcision: Multicultural Perspectives*. Philadelphia: University of Pennsylvania Press.

Ahmady, K. (2015) *A Comprehensive Research Study on Female Genital Mutilation / Cutting in Iran*. Available at: www.kameelahmady.com/wp-content/uploads/kameel%20-%en%final.pdf.

Ali, N. (2010) *I Am Nujood, Age 10 and Divorced*. New York: Three Rivers Press.

Asaah, A., Levin, T. (2009) *Empathy and Rage: Female Genital Mutilation in African Literature*. Banbury: Ayebia Publishers.

Bradley, T. (2011) *Women, Violence and Tradition*. London: Zed Books.

Bradley, T., Longman, C. (2015) *Interrogating Harmful Cultural Practices*. London: Ashgate.

Brooks, G. (2007) *Nine Parts of Desire: The Hidden World of Islamic Women*. London: Penguin.

Burrage, H. (forthcoming, 2016) *Female Mutilation*. London: New Holland Publishers.

Buzzard, A. (2014) *Consciência*. Leipzig: Amazon Distribution.

Cole, F.A. (2010) *Distant Sunrise. The Strength in her Pain to Forgive* (revised 2012) Marston Gate: Amazon.co.uk.

Corby, B., Shemmings, D., Wilkins, D. (2012) *Child Abuse*. 4th edition. Maidenhead: Open University Press.

Daniels, C., Jackson, J. (2014) *Impolite Conversation*. New York: Atria Books.

Dawes, J. (2013) *Evil Men*. London: Harvard University Press.

De Beauvoir, S. (1949) *The Second Sex*. London: Vintage.

Dirie, W. (2001) *Desert Flower*. London: Virago.

Dirie, W. (2004) *Desert Dawn*. London: Virago.

Dirie, W., trans Martin, W. (2015) *Saving Safa: Rescuing a Little Girl from FGM*. London: Virago.

Dorkenoo, E. (1996) *Cutting the Rose*. Austin: Harry Ransom Humanities Research Center.

Douglas, M. (2002) *Purity and Danger: An Analysis of Concepts of Pollution and Taboo*. London: Routledge Classics.

Dyhouse, C. (2014) *Girl Trouble*. London: Zed Books.

Ehrenreich, B., English, D. (1973) *Witches, Midwives, and Nurses: A History of Women Healers*. New York: The Feminist Press.

El Saadwi, N. (2007) *The Hidden Face of Eve: Women in the Arab World*. London: Zed Books.

Epprecht, M. (2013) *Sexuality and Social Justice in Africa*. London: Zed Books.

Gerry, F., Harris, L., Sjolin, C. (2014) *Sexual Offences Handbook: Law Practice and Procedure*. London: Wildy, Simmonds and Hill Publishing.

Hadikwa Mwaluko, N. (2013) *Waafrika*. Frankfurt am Main: UnCut/Voices.

Hirsi Ali, A. (2007) *The Caged Virgin: A Muslim Woman's Cry for Reason*. London: Pocket Books.

Hirsi Ali, A. (2008) *Infidel*. London: Pocket Books.

Hirsi Ali, A. (2011) *Nomad*. London: Simon & Schuster.

Hodgson, D. (2013) *Gender and Culture at the Limits of Rights*. Philadelphia: University of Pennsylvania Press.

Holmes, R., Jones, N. (2013) *Gender and Social Protection in the Developing World*. London: Zed Books.

Jacobs Brumberg, J. (1998) *The Body Project: An Intimate History of American Girls*. London: Vintage.

Jallow, B. (2013) *The Graveyard Cannot Pray*. Leicester: Global Hands Publishing.

Kaplan, L. (1997) *The Story of Jane: The Legendary Underground Feminist Abortion Service*. Chicago: University of Chicago Press,

Kassindja, F. (1999) *Do They Hear You When You Cry*. New York: Delta.

Khady with Cuny, M-T. (2010) *Blood Stains: A Child of Africa Reclaims Her Human Rights*. Frankfurt am Main: UnCut/Voices Press.

Kostenzer, J. (2013) *Female Genital Mutilation and Cutting in Europe*. Saarbrücken: AV Akademikerverlag.

Kristof, N., WuDunn, S. (2010) *Half the Sky: How to Change the World*. London: Virago.

Laming, L. (2003) *The Victoria Climbié Enquiry Summary and Recommendations*. London: The Stationery Office.

Lee Barnes, V. (1995) *Aman: The Story of a Somali Girl*. London: Bloomsbury.

Leeson, J., Gray, J. (1978) *Women and Medicine*. London: Tavistock Publications.

Lewis, J. (1969) *Anthropology Made Simple*. London: William Heinemann.

Lightfoot-Klein, H. (1989) *Prisoners of Ritual*. London: Routledge.

Lockhat, H. (2004) *Female Genital Mutilation: Treating the Tears*. Faringdon: Libri Publishing.

MacKinnon, C. A. (2007) *Women's Lives, Men's Laws*. Cambridge, MA: Harvard University Press.

Mmaka, V. (2015) *The Cut: Global Voices for Change: Breaking Silence on Female Genital Mutilation*. Edizioni dell'Arco.

Momoh, C. (2005) *Female Genital Mutilation*. London: Radcliffe Publishing.

Mottin-Sylla, M-H., Palmieri, J. (2011) *Confronting Female Genital Mutilation*. Oxford: Pambazuka Press.

Ngozi Adichie, C. (2014) *We Should All Be Feminists*. London: Fourth Estate.

Powell, C. (2011) *Safeguarding and Child Protection for Nurses, Midwives and Health Visitors: A Practical Guide*. Maidenhead: Open University Press.

Prolongeau, H. (2011) *Undoing FGM: Pierre Foldes, The Surgeon Who Restores the Clitoris*. Frankfurt am Main: UnCut/Voices.

Rahman, A., Toubia, N. (2000) *Female Genital Mutilation: A Guide to Law and Policies Worldwide*. London: Zed Books.

Rathbone, E. (1934) *Child Marriage: The Indian Minotaur: An Object-Lesson from the Past to the Future*. Reading: George Allen & Unwin.

Sanderson, L. P. (1981) *Against the Mutilation of Women: The Struggle Against Unnecessary Suffering*. London: Ithaca Press.

Smith, J. (2013) *The Public Woman*. London: Westbourne Press.

Traughber, R. (2012) *Driving the Birds*. Shadwell Publishing.

Tuan, Y-F. (1979) *Landscapes of Fear*. Minneapolis: University of Minnesota Press.

Twongyere, H. (2012) *I Dare To Say: African Women Share Their Stories of Hope and Survival*. Chicago: Lawrence Hill Books.

Valenti, J. (2010) *The Purity Myth*. Berkeley: Seal Press.

Vogelstein, R. (2013) *Ending Child Marriage: How Elevating the Status of Girls Advances U.S. Foreign Policy Objectives*. New York: Council on Foreign Relations Press.

Walker, A. (1993) *Possessing the Secret of Joy*. London: Vintage.

Wolf, N. (2013) *Vagina: A New Biography*. London: Virago.

Wollstonecraft, M., Rowbotham, S. (2010) *A Vindication of the Rights of Woman (Revolutions)*. London: Verso.

What books would you also suggest?...

Discuss this chapter at http://nofgmukbook.com/2015/01/29/further-reading-some-suggestions/.

Multimedia Resources

Online Resources

Home Office (2014) *Female Genital Mutilation: Recognising and Preventing FGM*. Available at: http://www.safeguardingchildrenea.co.uk/resources/female-genital-mutilation-recognising-preventing-fgm-free-online-training/.

NoFGM (2015) *#NoFGM Daily News*. Available at: http://paper.li/NoFGM1/1347915392.

NoFGM (2015) NoFGM website [Sharing ideas and networks to STOP FGM] nofgm.org.

NoFGM_USA (2015) *NoFGM_USA*. Available at: http://paper.li/NoFGM_USA/1400341179.

NSPCC (2015) *Female Genital Mutilation (FGM)*. Available at: www.nspcc.org.uk/preventing-abuse/child-abuse-and-neglect/female-genital-mutilation-fgm.

The Guardian (2015) *End FGM Guardian Global Media Campaign*. Available at: www.theguardian.com/end-fgm.

The Guardian (2015) *Female Genital Mutilation (FGM)*. Available at: www.theguardian.com/society/female-genital-mutilation.

Films/Videos

Ahmed, N., Kardozi, K. (2007) *A Handful of Ash*. Available at: www.imdb.com/title/tt4011398.

Forward (2010) *Think Again*. Available at: www.youtube.com/watch?v=kzBNTtR7toE.

Goswami, P. (2013) *A Pinch of Skin*. Available at: www.imdb.com/title/tt2715480.

Guardian (2011) *I Will Never Be Cut*. Available at: www.theguardian.com/global-development/video/2011/apr/18/female-genital-mutilation-video.

Home Office (2014) *Ending Female Genital Mutilation*. Available at: www.youtube.com/watch?v=HkDuzLA8T9w.

ICOD Action Network (2014) *Chasing the Cut*. Available at: www.chasingthecut.org.

Integrate Bristol (2012) *Silent Scream*. Available at: www.integratebristol.org.uk/2012/01/14/silent-scream/.

Justice for Victims of FGM in the UK (2014) *FGM in the UK: Failure to Act*. Available at: www.justiceforfgmvictims.co.uk/the-film.

NHS (2014) *FGM of Young Girls is Child Abuse*. Available at: www.nhs.usk/video/pages/female-genital-mutilation.aspx.

SafeHands for Mothers, FIGO (2012) *The Cutting Tradition*. Available at: www.youtube.com/watch?v=pUpToERm0q0.

SafeHands for Mothers (2013) *True Story*. Available at: www.youtube.com/watch?v=r8lV1z4zy7g.

St Peter's Lifeline (2011) *FGM and the 'Alternative Rites of Passage'*. Available at: www.stpeterslifeline.org.uk/community/fgm.

What other multimedia resources would you recommend?

Discuss this chapter at http://nofgmukbook.com/2015/01/29/multi-media-resources/.

Organisations

28 Too Many: 28toomany.org; @28TooMany.

Action for Women and Child Concern (AWCC) (USA and Somalia): www.facebook.com/actionforwomenandchildconcern.

Advance Family Planning: Bill and Melinda Gates Institute for Population and Reproductive Health, Johns Hopkins Bloomberg School of Public Health, 615 N. Wolfe Street, Room W4503, Baltimore, MD 21205 USA; +1 410 502 8715; www.advancefamilyplanning.org.

African Women Organisation: Schwarzspanier Strasse 15/1/2, A-1090 Vienna, Austria; +43 1925 15 76.

AFRUCA Africans Unite Against Child Abuse: Phoenix Mill, 20 Piercy Street, Ancoats, Manchester M4 7HY; 0161 205 9274; www.afruca.org; info@afruca.org.

Agency for Culture and Change Management (ACCMUK): 1st Floor, 3A Woburn Road, Bedford MK40 1EG; 07712 482568; www.accmuk.com; info@accmuk.org.

AHA Foundation (Ayaan Hirsi Ali) (USA): 130 7th Avenue, Suite 236, New York, NY 10011, USA; info@theahafoundation.org; theahafoundation.org.

American Nurses Association (ANA) (USA): 8515 Georgia Avenue, Suite 400, Silver Spring, MD 20910-3492, USA; +1 800 923 7709; www.nursingworld.org.

Amnesty International UK: Human Rights Action Centre, 17–25 New Inn Yard, London EC2A 3EA; 020 7033 1500; www.amnesty.org.uk; @amnestyuk.

Amref Health Africa (global): Lower Ground Floor, 15–18 White Lion Street, London N1 9PD; 020 7269 5520; www.amref.org.

Asylum Aid: Club Union House, 253–254 Upper Street, London N1 1RY; 020 7354 9631 (office); www.asylumaid.org.uk.

Bar Human Rights Committee: Doughty Street Chambers, 53–54 Doughty Street, London WC1N 2LS; www.barhumanrights.org.uk.

BAWSO: 9 Cathedral Road, Cardiff CF11 9HA; 02920 644 633; www.bawso.org.uk; info@bawso.org.uk.

Black Women's Health and Family Organisation: 1st Floor, 82 Russia Lane, London E2 9LU; 020 8980 3503; www.bwhafs.com; bwhafs@btconnect.com.

British Arab Federation: 4th Floor, Queens Gate, 121 Suffolk Street, Birmingham B1 1LX; 0121 643 7503; www.britisharabfederation.org; enquiry@britisharabfederation.org.

British Pregnancy Advisory Service (BPAS): 20 Timothys Bridge Road, Stratford Enterprise Park, Stratford-upon-Avon, Warwickshire, CV37 9BF; 03457 30 40 30; www.bpas.org.

Campaign Against Female Genital Mutilation (CAGeM): www.facebook.com/ End.FGM.

Children and Families Across Borders (CFAB): Canterbury Court, Unit 1.03, 1–3 Brixton Road, London SW9 6DE; 020 7735 8941; cfab.org.uk; info@cfab.org.uk.

Churches' Child Protection Advisory Service: PO Box 133, Swanley, Kent BR8 7UQ; 0845 120 45 50; www.ccpas.co.uk; info@ccpas.co.uk.

Clitoraid (USA): 4012 S. Rainbow Blvd, Suite K-401, Las Vegas, NV 89103, USA; +1 858 717 3458; www.clitoraid.org; @clitoraid.

Coexist Kenya: 3rd Floor, Suite #53, Milele Center Off Namanga Rd, Milele Center- Kitengela P.O. Box 281-00515, Nairobi, Kenya; +254 20 2099 201; www.coexistkenya.com.

Cultural Survival: 2067 Massachusetts Avenue, Cambridge, MA 02140, USA; +1 617 441 5400; www.culturalsurvival.org; @CSORG.

The Dahlia Project (Support for FGM survivors): The Maya Centre, Unit 8, 9–15 Elthorne Road, London N19 4AJ; 0207 272 0995; http://www.mayacentre.org.uk/dahlia-project-survivors-fgm/.

Daughters of Eve: 07983 030488; www.dofeve.org; @DaughtersofEve.

Desert Flower Foundation (Waris Dirie): Ungargasse, 241030 Vienna, Austria; +43 1 4027916; www.desertflowerfoundation.org/en; office@ desertflowerfoundation.org.

Dignity Research Alert Forum (DARF): UN House, 4 Hunter Square, Edinburgh EH1 1QW; 07583 434602; www.darf.org.uk; dignityalert@ hotmail.co.uk.

Doctors Opposing Circumcision: Suite 42, 2442 NW Market Street, Seattle, WA 98107-4137 USA; www.doctorsopposingcircumcision.org.

Dr Abe Foundation: PO Box 4618, Iver, Buckinghamshire SL1 0XJ; 07582 179138; www.drabefoundation.com; contact.info.drabe@gmail.com.

END FGM European Campaign: End FGM European Network, Mundo B, Rue d'Edimbourg 26, B-1050 Ixelles, Belgium; +32 2 548 2776; www.endfgm.eu; @ENDFGM_Amnesty.

Equality Now (UK, USA and Kenya): 1 Birdcage Walk, London SW1H 9JJ; 020 7304 6902; www.equalitynow.org; @equalitynow.

Euronet: Stoppt FGM Now: euronetfgm.eu/1.html.

Family Planning Association: 50 Featherstone Street, London EC1Y 8QU; 020 7608 5240; www.fpa.org.uk.

Fawcett Society: 11–12 The Oval, London E2 9DT; 020 3137 0809; www.fawcettsociety.org.uk.

FGM National Clinical Group: 07791 462415; www.fgmnationalgroup.org; info@fgmnationalgroup.org.

FIGO: FIGO Secretariat, FIGO House, Suite 3 – Waterloo Court, 10 Theed Street, London SE1 8ST; 020 7928 1166; www.figo.org.

FORWARD: Suite 2.1, Chandelier Building, 8 Scrubs Lane, London, NW10 6RB; 020 8960 4000; www.forwarduk.org.uk; @forwarduk.

GAMS (USA): 340 Pine Street Suite 302, San Francisco, CA 94104 USA; +1 415 837 1113; @womensfoundca.

Global Alliance Against Female Genital Mutilation (GAFGM): 150 Route de Ferney, 1211 Geneva, Switzerland; +41 (0)22 788 45 48; +33 (0)64 890 81 81; and 693 Rue de Geneve, 01210 Ornex, France; +33 (0)45 28 85 64; +33 (0) 64 890 81 81; www.global-alliance-fgm.org.

Global Sisters Report (USA): Global Sisters Report, National Catholic Reporter Publishing Co., 115 E. Armour Blvd., Kansas City, MO 64111-1203, USA; +1 800 444 8910; globalsistersreport.org; info@globalsistersreport.org.

Guttmacher Institute: 125 Maiden Lane, 7th Floor, New York, NY 10038; 212-248-1111; and 1301 Connecticut Avenue N.W., Suite 700, Washington, D.C. 2003; 202-296-4012; http://www.guttmacher.org/.

Hawatrust: Homerton Road, Hackney, London E9 5QF; 020 3441 4688; hawatrust.org.uk; @HawaTrust.

Healthy Tomorrow / Sini Sanuman (USA and Mali): www.stopexcision.net.

IAC Inter-African Committee: ECA Africa Hall, Menelik Avenue, PO Box 3001, Addis Ababa, Ethiopia; +251 11 551 57 93; www.iac-ciaf.net; iac-htps@uneca.org; @IAC_CIAF.

ICC Services: 020 7724 3363; www.iccservices.org.uk; dr_teinaz@tiscali.co.uk .

Ifrah Ahmed (Ireland and Somalia): www.facebook.com/UnitedYouthofIreland.

Integrate Bristol: integratebristol.org.uk; info@integratebristol.org.uk; @FGMsilentscream.

International Confederation of Midwives: Laan van Meerdervoort, 702517 AN The Hague, The Netherlands; +31 70 3060520; www.internationalmidwives.org; @World_Midwives.

Iranian and Kurdish Women's Rights Organisation (IKWRO): PO Box 65840, London EC2P 2FS; 020 7920 6460; ikwro.org.uk; @IKWRO.

Justice for FGM Victims UK: 55 Tufton Street, London SW1P 3QL; 020 7340 6019; www.justiceforfgmvictims.co.uk.

Lucy Mashua Voice of the Voiceless: mashuavoiceforthevoiceless.blogspot.com; www.facebook.com/MashuaAgainstFGM; @Mashua.

MakeEveryWomanCount: www.makeeverywomancount.org; info@makeeverywomancount.org; @MakeWomenCount.

Mandate Now: mandatenow.org.uk; @mandatenow.

Manor Gardens: 020 7281 9478; www.manorgardenscentre.org.

Maya Centre: 020 7281 8970; www.mayacentre.org.uk; admin@mayacentre.org.uk; @mayacentre.

McKay Foundation (USA): PO Box 3549, Conroe, Texas 77305, USA; +1 936 537 8025; www.protectingchildren.org.

Mental Health Foundation: Colechurch House, 1 London Bridge Walk, London SE1 2SX; 020 7803 1100; www.mentalhealth.org.uk; @MHF_tweets.

Minority Voices (global): 020 7422 4205; www.minorityvoices.org.

Ms Rose Blossom: www.msroseblossom.org.

Muslim Institute: 49–51 East Road, London N1 6AH; www.musliminstitute.org; @MuslimInst.

Muslim Women Network UK: The Warehouse, 54–57 Allison Street, Digbeth, Birmingham B5 5TH; 0121 236 9000; @MuslimWomenUK; www.mwnuk.co.uk.

Muslim Women's League: 3010 Wilshire Blvd, Suite 519, Los Angeles, CA 90010, USA; +1 323 258 6722; mwlusa.org; mwl@mwlusa.org.

National Children's Bureau: 8 Wakley Street, London EC1V 7QE; 020 7843 6000; www.ncb.org.uk; enquiries@ncb.org.uk.

National Secular Society: 25 Red Lion Square, London WC1R 4RL; 020 7404 3126; www.secularism.org.uk; @NatSecSoc.

No More Page 3: nomorepage3.org; facebook.com/nomorepage3; @nomorepage3.

NoFGM Australia: +61 448 621 270; www.nofgmoz.com; paula@nofgmoz.com; @NoFGM_Oz.

NSPCC: Weston House, 42 Curtain Road, London EC2A 3NH; 0808 800 5000; www.nspcc.org.uk; @NSPCC.

One True Voice: Corker Walk, London N7 7RJ; 020 7998 5746; onetruevoice. org.gridhosted.co.uk; one-truevoice@live.co.uk.

Options: Devon House, 58 St Katharine's Way, London E1W 1LB; 020 7430 1900; options.co.uk; info@options.co.uk.

Orchid Project: The Foundry, 17–19 Oval Way, London SE11 5RR; 0203 752 5505; http://orchidproject.org/.

Pastoral Child Foundation: 51 Clark Street, Glen Ridge, New Jersey 07028 USA; +1 973 980 7860; www.facebook.com/PastoralistChildFoundation.

PATH: PO Box 900922, Seattle, WA 98109 USA; +1 206 285 3500; www.path.org.

Plan: Finsgate, 5–7 Cranwood Street, London EC1V 9LH; 0300 777 9777; www.plan-uk.org; mail@plan-uk.org.

PSHE Association: CAN Mezzanine, 32–36 Loman Street, London SE1 0EH; 020 7922 7950; www.pshe-association.org.uk; info@pshe-association.org.uk; @PSHEassociation.

RAINBO Research Action and Information Network for the Bodily Integrity of Women: Suite 5A, Queens Studios, London NW6 6RG; 020 7625 3400; www.rainbo.org; info@rainbo.org.

REPLACE 2: Coventry University, Priory Street, Coventry CV1 5FB; 02476 888 452; replacefgm2.eu; info@replacefgm2.eu; @replacefgm2.

Rosa – The UK Fund for Women and Girls: United House, 4th Floor, North Road, London N7 9DP; 020 7697 3466; www.rosauk.org.

Roshni: Baltic Chambers, Suite 339, 50 Wellington Street, Glasgow G2 6HJ; 0141 218 4010; www.roshni.org.uk; @roshniscotland.

Royal College of Midwives (RCM): 15 Mansfield Street, London W1G 9NH; 0300 303 0444; www.rcm.org.uk.

Royal College of Nursing (RCN): 20 Cavendish Square, London W1G 0RN; 020 7409 3333; www.rcn.org.uk.

Royal College of Obstetricians and Gynaecologists (RCOG): 27 Sussex Place, Regent's Park, London NW1 4RG; 020 7772 6200; www.rcog.org.uk.

Safe Hands for Girls (USA): +1 678 306 6717; www.safehandsforgirls.org; @SafeHands4Girls.

Safe Network: NSPCC National Training Centre, 3 Gilmour Close, Beaumont Leys, Leicester LE4 1EZ; 0845 608 5404; www.safenetwork.org.uk; @thesafenetwork.

Safe World for Women: www.asafeworldforwomen.org.

Sanctuary for Families (USA): PO Box 1406, Wall Street Station, New York, NY 10268; +1 212 349 6009; www.sanctuaryforfamilies.org.

Scottish Refugee Council: 5 Cadogan Square, Glasgow G2 7PH; 0141 248 9799 www.scottishrefugeecouncil.org.uk; info@scottishrefugeecouncil.org.uk; @scotrefcouncil.

Sex Education Forum: National Children's Bureau, 8 Wakley St, London EC1V 7QE; 020 7843 6000; www.sexeducationforum.org.uk; sexedforum@ncb.org.uk.

Sister Somalia (USA): PO Box 28427, Portland, OR 97228, USA; www.sistersomalia.org info@sistersomalia.org; @Sister Somalia.

Soroptimist: 1709 Spruce Street, Philadelphia, PA 19103-6103, USA; +1 215 893 9000; www.soroptimist.org; siahq@soroptimist.org.

Soroptimist International of Great Britain and Ireland (SIGBI): Federation Office, 2nd Floor, Beckwith House, 1–3 Wellington Road North, Stockport, SK4 1AF; 0161 480 7686; sigbi.org.

Stop FGM Middle East: Herborner Strasse 62, D-60439 Frankfurt am Main, Germany; +49 69 57002440; www.stopfgmmideast.org; info@wadinet.de.

Stop Violence Against Women (USA): 330 Second Avenue South, Suite 800, Minneapolis, MN 55401 USA; +1 612 341 3302; www.stopvaw.org hrights@advrights.org.

The Girl Generation: www.thegirlgeneration.org; info@thegirlgeneration.org; @TheGirlGen.

Tostan: 5, Cité Aelmas Ouest Foire VDN, en face CICESB.P. 29371, Dakar-Yoff, Senegal; +221 33 820 5589; www.tostan.org; @Tostan.

Trust for London: 6 Middle Street, London EC1A 7PH; 020 7606 6145; www.trustforlondon.org.uk; @trustforlondon.

UN Women: BM BOX 6658, London WC1N 3XX; 020 3282 7599; www. unwomen.org.

UnCUT/VOICES Press: Martin Luther Strasse 35, Frankfurt am Main, D-60389 Germany; uncutvoices.wordpress.com.

UNICEF: UNICEF House, 30a Great Sutton Street, London EC1V 0DU; 020 7490 2388; www.unicef.org; @Unicef_uk.

Unite: Unite House, 128 Theobald's Road, Holborn, London WC1X 8TN; 020 7611 2500; www.unitetheunion.org.

United Nations Human Rights Council: +41 22 917 9220; www.ohchr.org; infodesk@ohchr.org.

United Nations Population Fund: 605 Third Avenue, New York, NY 10158, USA; www.unfpa.org; hq@unfpa.org.

Victoria Climbie Foundation (VCF): VCF Project Office, Dominion Arts Education Centre, 112 The Green, Southall UB2 4BQ; 020 8619 1191; vcf-uk.org; info@vcf-uk.org.

Violence Is Not Our Culture: www.violenceisnotourculture.org.

Womankind: Development House, 2nd Floor, 56–64 Leonard Street, London EC2A 4LT; 020 7549 0360; www.womankind.org.uk; @woman_kind.

Women's Aid: Women's Aid Federation of England, PO Box 3245, Bristol BS2 2EH; 0117 944 44 11; www.womensaid.org.uk; info@womensaid.org. uk; @womensaid.

World Health Organization: Avenue Appia 20, 1211 Geneva 27, Switzerland; +41 22 791 21 11; www.who.int; @WHO.

What other organisations would you recommend for listing here?
Discuss this chapter at http://nofgmukbook.com/2015/01/29/organisations/.

Appendix: Feminist Statement on the Naming and Abolition of Female Genital Mutilation[i]

Patriarchal Oppression is the Bedrock of Female Genital Mutilation (FGM) and Related Harmful Traditional Practices

The aim of this statement is to gather support, from concerned citizens and from people directly working to abolish FGM, for research, dialogue and activism which derives from such an understanding. To that end we insist, for instance, that FGM be correctly named – as specifically 'mutilation' and not, in formal discourse, by any evasive or softening euphemism.

1. Female genital mutilation (FGM) in all its forms is cruelty and abuse. The United Nations has decreed it a fundamental violation of human rights.[1]
2. FGM is practised in many parts of the world. The World Health Organization estimates that some 140 million girls and women now alive have undergone this mutilation, with around 3 million more experiencing it every year.[2] 140 million is, however, a very conservative figure and the total including, for example, Indonesia,[3] the Middle East and diaspora destinations is likely to be much higher.

---

i   A more detailed account of how the Statement arose can be found here: *Fighting Female Genital Mutilation with Our Keyboards: The Feminist Statement on FGM is Launched Today*. http://hilaryburrage.com/2013/08/28/fighting-female-genital-mutilation-with-our-keyboards-the-feminist-statement-on-fgm-is-launched-today/.

3. FGM, like other traditional practices which harm women and girls,[4] is done from fear in many guises, at the instigation behind the scenes of powerful people who stand to benefit from it, for themselves.[5]

4. The proper, and necessary, response to FGM is to treat it, wherever it occurs, as a very serious, sometimes deadly, crime. There is substantive evidence to suggest this approach, allied with appropriate education and support, is the most effective way of stopping FGM.[6]

5. It is essential to acknowledge that African women leaders themselves, in joint statements,[7] have decreed that FGM should in all formal discussion be called 'mutilation', and not by any other euphemistic term. It is deeply disrespectful of those brave women – and also extremely unhelpful – to ignore their judgement and advice.

6. We are concerned simply and solely with the essential protection from FGM, everywhere, of defenceless children, irrespective of whether the intended FGM operators are traditional practitioners or, in the modern contemporary sense, medically trained.[8] (Note: necessarily, our concern further extends, in some communities, to the protection of women subject to involuntary FGM, for example when their marriages are arranged, after childbirth or after criminal abduction.)

7. We believe that all women and girls who have experienced FGM are entitled, as and if or when they wish, to skilled reconstructive or other surgery and/or additional medical and personal support, free of charge, as part of reparation for this crime.

8. There are many people with different skills and insights who can and should contribute to the work of abolishing/eliminating/eradicating FGM; each of us has a part to play. It is, however, fundamentally important to recognise unreservedly, and to hear, the centrally critical contribution of women with direct experience of this harmful traditional practice who are seeking to eliminate FGM.

28 August 2013

Statement Background

Our aim is to gather like-minded citizens of the world, including activists and academics in many places, to assert that patriarchal oppression is the bedrock of female genital mutilation (FGM)[9] and related harmful traditional practices;[10] and to promote research, dialogue and activism which derives from such an understanding. To that end we insist, for instance, that FGM be correctly named – as 'mutilation' and not, in formal discourse, by any evasive or softening euphemism.

We are aware that many established and university-affiliated researchers, unlike ourselves, are not also activists. Criteria for building a career in academia differ from the standards by which we evaluate volunteers, employees of government agencies, or managers of civil society organisations such as non-governmental institutions and community-based groups. Individuals we hope to attract to our issue-based community are, therefore, both academically qualified and experienced in the field; they also frankly oppose FGM and they use language appropriate to raise general awareness that ablation of girls' genitalia is never, under any circumstances whatsoever, acceptable.

We hope that, by publishing our *Feminist Statement on the Naming and Abolition of Female Genital Mutilation*, we shall find common cause with others who, like ourselves, have a serious commitment both to solidly rigorous academic research and to human rights-embedded, evidence-based and value-led activism.

Unlike the known majority of scholars working on the subject, we subscribe to a feminist understanding of FGM itself and tie that viewpoint to the strategies we support to confront it. In other words, we favour honest, action-oriented and end-result targeted research – the result defined as elimination of FGM, full stop. Specifically, our position is value-led and immovably against any form of medicalisation of this harmful traditional practice – as distinct from an orientation towards ethically dubious research on FGM which claims (the fiction of) intellectual neutrality.[11]

To define the term 'ethically dubious' we can apply the concept to research which appears to collude in, reinforce, at best not disallow and at worst facilitate, the amputation of girls' genitalia.

Why is it so important to name this distinction between 'engaged' and 'ethically dubious' or 'insufficiently engaged' research?

The negative influence of 'neutral' research and non-engagement on policy cannot be underestimated. Recent examples of damage include:

1. The declaratory bombshell dropped on activists by the American Academy of Pediatrics,[12] announcing a 'revision' in its acceptable 1998 guidelines to children's physicians, which was clearly inspired by a 'neutrality' approach. Not entitled as female genital mutilation, but rather ennobled as 'surgeries', the intervention was no longer seen as a violation of children's rights to bodily integrity nor as violence. The cultural–relativist thinking led so far as to propose to doctors that they lobby politicians to repeal laws against FGM and thereby enable them to 'reach out' to practising communities to offer a 'ritual nick'. The vast literature that shows how, for traditional practice defenders of FGM, so-called 'nicks' are insufficient was bracketed out, and instead, an unproven if not disproven idea about harm-reduction

via medicalisation came into play.[13] A global outcry[14] led to almost immediate retraction of this document the following month, but the attitude and input that enabled it remain very much alive.

2. The British Government has recently announced that £35 million will be made available to the United Nations and some others to further the cause of eradicating FGM.[15] Already, however, it is consistently demonstrating a position which bolsters now unsubstantiated claims to have reduced the incidence of FGM in some areas[16] via the 'abandonment model' and community declarations through persuasion.[17] But at the same time we see in the UK a failure (as of summer 2013) to secure even one prosecution, despite the several thousand British children who are forced to undergo this horrendous practice every year.[18]

3. The Australian Government states it is taking 'action' to stop FGM, by 'working with states and territories to ensure that police and prosecutors are in the best possible position to detect, investigate, and prosecute FGM whenever and wherever it occurs'.[19] However, in 2013 the Australian Government awarded AUS$1 million to 15 programmes, none of which was aimed at increasing detection of FGM in at-risk children, resources for child protection or enforcement of FGM laws.

In these contexts, where the lives of many, many women and girls are daily at risk through FGM, it becomes clear to us that passivity as we travel in another direction is not enough.

We must insist, resolutely, that FGM is without exception an abhorrent breach of basic human rights and of women and girls' dignity.

We therefore hereby offer our *Statement* as an invitation to researchers and activists who share our understandings, to assert the criticality of a value-led, feminist perspective via which, we believe, fundamental change towards the abolition of FGM will be enabled.

www.statementonfgm.com

The idea of a *Feminist Statement on the Naming and Abolition of Female Genital Mutilation* arose from private email correspondence between some academically oriented activists in June 2013.

Since then we have sought the advice and views of a diverse range of researchers and activists in the field.

This Statement is the initial result of this consultation. Our thanks to all who have helped and supported us along the way.

Statement Authors

Instigators and authors (summer 2013) of this Statement on FGM are:

Tomi Adeaga (Germany and Nigeria): FORWARD-Germany and FORWARDUK; @FORWARDUK.

Hilary Burrage (UK): Sociologist, writing *Eradicating FGM: A UK perspective*; Advisory Board Member (but not here representing) REPLACE 2 European Programme; Consultant on FGM for the *Guardian*; @HilaryBurrage. @NoFGMBookUK [drafting author, and contact for correspondence].

Paula Ferrari (Australia): Founder, No FGM Australia and independent academic and activist @NoFGM_Oz.

Tobe Levin (Germany and USA): CEO, UnCUT/VOICES Press; Associate, W.E.B. Du Bois Institute for African and African American Research, Harvard University; Fellow, Lady Margaret Hall, University of Oxford (2014–16) @UnCUTVOICES.

Lucy Mashua Sharp (USA and Kenya): President, Mashua voice for the voiceless international.inc; refugees advocacy in the USA; expert witness on FGM and women's rights @Mashua.

Linda Weil-Curiel (France): Attorney (Avocate au Barreau de Paris) and President, Commission pour l'abolition des mutilations sexuelles (CAMS) (Commission for the Abolition of Sexual Mutilations).

Discuss this chapter at http://nofgmukbook.com/2015/01/29/appendix-a-feminist-statement-on-female-genital-mutilation/.

Endnotes

All weblinks accessed on 1 March 2015.

1   United Nations (2012) Intensifying Global Efforts for the Elimination of Female Genital Mutilations, 24 September. Available at: http://www.npwj.org/node/5358. United Nations Bans Female Genital Mutilation, 20 December. Available at: http://www.who.int/mediacentre/factsheets/fs241/en/, and sources of international human rights law on female genital mutilation, available at: http://www.endvawnow.org/en/articles/645-sources-of-international-human-rights-law-on-female-genital-mutilation.html.

2   World Health Organization (2013) *Factsheet 241: Female Genital Mutilation and UNICEF*, 23 July. Available at: http://www.who.int/mediacentre/factsheets/fs241/en/. Despite overwhelming opposition, millions of girls at risk of genital mutilation.

3   See for example this research report: *Female Circumcision in Indonesia – Extent, Implications and Possible Interventions to Uphold Women's Health Rights* (2003). Available at: http://pdf.usaid.gov/pdf_docs/PNACU138.pdf.

4   Which must also be abolished, see for example the World Health Organization website page: *Female Genital Mutilation (FGM) and Harmful Practices.* Available at: http://www.who.int/mediacentre/factsheets/fs241/en/.

5   Levin, T. (2009; 2010) *Feminist Europa. Review of Books.* 9(1); 10(1): 69. Available at: http://www.ddv-verlag.de/issn_1570_0038_FE%2009_2010.pdf and Burrage, H. (2013) *To Stop Female Genital Mutilation in the UK, Follow (and Invest) the Money.* Available at: http://hilaryburrage.com/2013/02/28/to-stop-female-genital-mutilation-in-the-uk-follow-and-invest-the-money/.

6   Thomson Reuters Foundation (2013) *Thirty Million Girls at Risk of FGM Despite Decline in Support – UN,* 22 July. Available at: http://www.trust.org/item/20130722113518-kxhfm/?source=search.

7   Regional Conference on Traditional Practices Affecting the Health of Women and Children in Africa organised by the *Inter-African Committee (IAC) on Traditional Practices Affecting the Health of Women and Children,* 19–24 November 1990, Addis Ababa, Ethiopia, and later reaffirmed in Mali in 2005.

8   World Health Organization (2010) *Global Strategy to Stop Health-care Providers from Performing Female Genital Mutilation.* Available at: http://whqlibdoc.who.int/hq/2010/WHO_RHR_10.9_eng.pdf.

9   World Health Organization (WHO) *About FGM.* Available at: http://www.who.int/reproductivehealth/topics/fgm/en/.

10   WHO: *Female genital mutilation and other harmful practices.* Available at: http://www.who.int/reproductivehealth/topics/fgm/prevalence/en/.

11   The first sort of (good) research is exquisitely illustrated by PLAN – Deutschland in Alice Behrendt's 2010 report, *Listening to African Voices: Female Genital Mutilation/Cutting among Immigrants in Hamburg. Knowledge, Attitudes and Practice.* Available at: http://eige.europa.eu/content/listening-to-african-voices-female-genital-mutilationcutting-among-immigrants-in-hamburg-kno. See also a review of the report available at: http://www.ddv-verlag.de/issn_1570_0038_FE%2009_2010.pdf. A counter-example of ethically dubious scholarship is described in the same issue of *Feminist Europa: Review of Books, Special on FGM* (above, note 5) and Levin, T. (2007) *'Highly valued by both sexes': Activists, Anthr/apologists and FGM.* Available at: http://www.accmuk.com/fgm_factsheet_1.pdf. Or simply search 'ANTHR/APOLOGISTS' on the internet.

12   American Academy of Pediatrics (2010) *Policy Statement – Ritual Genital Cutting of Female Minors,* 26 April. Available at: http://pediatrics.aappublications.org/content/early/2010/04/26/peds.2010-0187.short.

13   Hastings Center Report 42, USA: The Public Policy Advisory Network on Female Genital Surgeries in Africa, *Seven Things to Know about Female Genital Surgeries in Africa.* No. 6 (2012): 19–27.

14 WHO (2010) *Regarding the 'Policy Statement – Ritual Genital Cutting of Female Minors' from the American Academy of Pediatrics.* Available at: http://www.who.int/reproductivehealth/topics/fgm/fgm_app_statement.pdf.

15 Department for International Development (DfID, UK) (22 March 2013) *A Time for Change: Ending female genital mutilation* and *Towards Ending Female Genital Mutilation / Cutting in Africa and Beyond: A programme to demonstrate effectiveness, catalyse change, build the evidence base and strengthen a global movement to end female genital mutilation/cutting.*

16 UNFPA (23 July 2013) *Scaling Up Strategies to Encourage Abandonment of FGM/C.* Available at: http://www.unfpa.org/news/scaling-strategies-encourage-abandonment-fgmc.

17 *UNICEF Report on FGM: A change of strategy needed?* Available at: https://www.gov.uk/government/case-studies/a-time-for-change-ending-female-genital-mutilation. (Interview with Alvilda Jablonko, FGM Program Coordinator of No Peace Without Justice, Brussels, 13 August 2013).

18 BBC, UK (13 June 2013) *MPs Urge More Action on Female Genital Mutilation.* Available at: http://www.bbc.co.uk/news/uk-politics-22880152; and Burrage, H. (2012) *The UK Can Learn from France on Female Genital Mutilation Prosecutions.* Available at: http://hilaryburrage.com/2012/11/28/the-uk-can-learn-from-france-on-fgm-prosecutions/.

19 Minister for Health, Australia (21 July 2013) *$1 Million to Help End Female Genital Mutilation in Australia.*

Index

Note: illustrations are indicated by page numbers in **bold**.